W9-BHS-921

BY STEVEN RINELLA

The MeatEater Fish and Game Cookbook

*The Complete Guide to Hunting, Butchering, and Cooking
Wild Game: Volume 1, Big Game*

*The Complete Guide to Hunting, Butchering, and Cooking Wild
Game: Volume 2, Small Game and Fowl*

Meat Eater: Adventures from the Life of an American Hunter

American Buffalo: In Search of a Lost Icon

The Scavenger's Guide to Haute Cuisine

THE
MeatEater Guide
TO Wilderness Skills
AND Survival

THE
MeatEater Guide
TO Wilderness Skills
AND Survival

STEVEN RINELLA

WITH
BRODY HENDERSON AND OTHER MEMBERS
OF THE MEATEATER CREW

ILLUSTRATIONS BY PETER SUCHESKI

RANDOM HOUSE
NEW YORK

This book contains general information relating to wilderness skills and survival. It is not intended to serve as a diagnosis tool, a guide to safely identifying wild edibles, or to replace the advice and care of a doctor or other professional. The author and publisher expressly disclaim responsibility for any adverse effects that may result from the use or application of the information contained in this book.

Copyright © 2020 by MeatEater, Inc.

All rights reserved.

Published in the United States by Random House, an imprint and division of Penguin Random House LLC, New York.

RANDOM HOUSE and the HOUSE colophon are registered trademarks of Penguin Random House LLC.

LIBRARY OF CONGRESS CATALOGING-IN-PUBLICATION DATA
Names: Rinella, Steven, author.
Title: The MeatEater guide to wilderness skills and survival / by Steven Rinella; with Brody Henderson and other members of the MeatEater crew.
Description: New York: Random House, [2020] | Includes index.
Identifiers: LCCN 2020027192 (print) | LCCN 2020027193 (ebook) | ISBN 9780593129692 (hardcover) | ISBN 9780593129708 (ebook)
Subjects: LCSH: Wilderness survival. | Survivalism. | Hunting. | MeatEater (Television program)
Classification: LCC GV200.5 .R56 2020 (print) | LCC GV200.5 (ebook) | DDC 613.6/9—dc23
LC record available at https://lccn.loc.gov/2020027192
LC ebook record available at https://lccn.loc.gov/2020027193

Printed in the United States of America on acid-free paper

randomhousebooks.com

4 6 8 9 7 5 3

Book design by Caroline Cunningham

For the field crew: Jared, Mo, Nick, Doty, Phil, Brian, Ridge Pounder, Korey, Mike, Adam, The Flip Flop Flesher, Loren, Eric, Dom, Mahting, Dirty Myth, Rick, Washlesky, Brody, and The Latvian Eagle. Holy shit, it's been a wild ride.

CONTENTS

⤜⤜⤜✦⤛⤛⤛

INTRODUCTION

➤➤➤》》《《《←←

The Surprising Dangers of S'mores

I DON'T CARE HOW often I fly in bush planes in Alaska—I never go more than fifteen minutes without considering the possibility of a crash. My concerns don't keep me out of the skies, but I do try to be as pragmatic about it as possible. I don't like to fly with pilots who show off by skimming treetops or aggressively banking through narrow canyon passages. And I'm not into "flight-seeing," or flying in single-engine aircraft just for the thrill of getting a bird's-eye view of the land. In the words of my older brother, who's logged hundreds of hours in bush planes as a wildlife biologist in Alaska, "You get up, you get down, no extraneous messing around."

On a recent September flight, while returning to the village of Tok after a caribou hunt in the Yukon–Charley Rivers National Preserve, I made an exception to my own rule. I asked the pilot of our two-seater Super Cub to divert our course for the admittedly ironic purpose of flying over the debris field of an airplane crash. The debris belonged to a B-24 bomber that burrowed into the mountainside in December 1943. Four of the five crew members on board were killed in the crash. One man, a pilot named Leon Crane, survived by ejecting through the aircraft's bomb bay and parachuting down into the snow-covered wilderness. All he had on him, besides the parachute, were the clothes on his back, a Boy Scout knife, and two packs of matches. He wasn't wearing gloves or mittens. It was −4°F.

Crane made his way downslope to the Charley River. There he wrapped himself in his silk parachute and huddled beneath a spruce tree for a week while waiting for rescuers. None came. He was able to get a fire going but unable to secure food. He chewed vegetation to give himself the sensation of eating but spit it out. He tried killing pine squirrels with a makeshift spear, bow and arrow, and slingshot, but found it impossible. Fearing he would starve to death, Crane started picking his way downstream to the north. Eventually, in a spot we passed along our route to Tok, he found a trapper's shack and an elevated cache of survival rations containing food, mittens, a rifle, and other supplies. Again Crane waited for rescue, this time for over a month. Still none came. In February, worried about dwindling supplies, he left the trapper's cabin and followed the Charley River to the north and east. He walked for another month, killing some ptarmigan with the rifle and repairing his gear with cords salvaged from his parachute. He eventually came across a fresh set of sled tracks. He followed them and arrived at the occupied cabin of a trapper named Albert Ames. The trapper and his family took Crane in and fed him moose meat and pancakes. Days later, they traveled by dogsled to a camp on the Yukon River where Crane was able to be picked up by a small plane. On March 14, after eighty days in the wilderness of the Arctic Circle, Crane reported to his commanding officer in Fairbanks, Alaska.

There's a lot to love about that story, and a lot to learn from it. First and foremost is Crane's mental and physical tenacity. After watching his fellow airmen die, he suffers hunger, cold, and loneliness for weeks on end without giving in to despair or making foolish mistakes. He's calculating in his movements and mindful of when it makes sense to stay put and when it's time to pack up and go. When he travels, he does so with purpose and lets the landscape guide his movements. His ultimate salvation is testament to the fact that he doesn't make big mistakes. Finally, there's the absent trapper and his well-stocked shack, which exemplify the payoff that can come from being supplied and prepared—even in a situation where the beneficiary of one's preparedness is an unexpected guest.

A year after his ordeal, Crane led a team to attempt the recovery of the crash victims' remains. On that expedition, he was photographed with a smile. If only we could all be so resilient. As we continued our flight, I pondered Crane's story. It's wonderful, but also deceptive. Spectacular survival tales about downed pilots and shipwrecked sailors tend to overshadow far more common narratives about people getting into trouble in the outdoors doing normal, humdrum things. A friend of mine used to work for a guiding company that ran extended mountain backpacking trips for high school students. Their leading cause for medical evacuations wasn't snakebites, bear attacks, or even hypothermia. It was cooking accidents, usually burns involving camp stoves, fires, or boiling water. This mirrors the arc of my own childhood experience with injuries and accidents. We had virtually unlimited access to BB guns, .22s, Rambo knives, double-bit axes, and ninja throwing stars. But what usually got us into trouble was fire. In fact, one of the most memorable injuries I witnessed was caused by a flaming marshmallow that landed on my brother's chest rather than inside his s'more.

That anecdotal cooking statistic from my friend's guiding outfit doesn't hold true for the general population of outdoor enthusiasts. In the United States, the most likely injuries to require a medevac are sprains and strains from hiking. But the stat does speak to the truth that the greatest dangers in the wilderness are often our own inattention or clumsiness. I've witnessed two sets of injuries caused by bear spray, though neither involved a bear. One happened when my older brother was unloading his truck and accidentally stepped on the nozzle of his spray canister, breaking the plastic and hosing down everything in the immediate radius—including himself. The other occurrence took place as I was struggling through an alder thicket. One limb managed to release the safety latch on my canister as I passed by, and another managed to pull the trigger. Why wasn't I monitoring such a dangerous apparatus when it happened to be strapped to my waist? Maybe I was preoccupied with worries about bears.

It's not uncommon to see hikers walking along the trail with their noses in their phones as they plot their satellite coordinates or text their friends. I've been guilty of the same, many times. Even more negligent is the urge to document one's outdoor experiences for social media validation. There were 259 confirmed selfie-related deaths between 2011 and 2017 worldwide, but these happened anywhere from highways to the tops of skyscrapers; more relevant to our purposes is data from a National Park Service spokesperson who told me that between 2007 and 2016, the NPS recorded twelve deaths where the person's activity was "associated with photography." That comes out to only about one person per year, but it's worth noting that photos are more lethal than mountain lions. I can't help but think of a favorite photo of mine from a river trip in South America, taken in the jungle literally days away from professional medical care. The photo shows my buddy standing on the edge of the river juggling a pair of machetes. It brings to mind an observation by the journalist Wes Siler: "People have always managed to find stupid ways to die."

And then there are the honest mistakes and slip-ups that come in such a wide variety of forms that it tests one's imagination: an ice fisherman who falls through the ice and is found the next day frozen to death with his elbows still propped up on the edge of the hole he fell through; a pair of campers who die from carbon monoxide poisoning after dozing off while trying to warm their tent with a propane stove; a mountain goat researcher who tried to leap over a section of washed-out trail on a steep slope rather than finding an alternative route; a bowhunter impaled by an arrow that fell from his buddy's quiver and landed in just the right position on the path ahead of him; a man who died of exposure after he got out of his truck to unlock the gate on the road to his remote cabin and then had the truck roll forward to pinch him between the bumper and the still-locked gate. At the risk of alienating doomsday preppers who bought this book in order to fantasize about the zombie apocalypse, the greatest survival challenge you might encounter is the person staring back at you in the mirror.

I once published an essay in *Outside* magazine about all of the unexpected diseases and parasites that I've picked up through a life spent outdoors, including trichinosis, giardiasis, and Lyme disease. In the essay, I recount a lecture and slideshow that I attended in Santa Fe, New Mexico, given by a mountaineer who'd recently attempted an ascent of Mount Everest. During his talk, the climber mentioned a well-known study in which psychologists instructed subjects to watch a video. In the video, a small group of people were playing catch. The subjects were instructed to count how many times the balls passed between the players, who were identified by the color of their T-shirts. For a while the tossing and catching carry on without incident. Then a guy wearing a gorilla suit strolls through the middle of the game, which continues as if nothing had occurred. What's interesting is that half of the study subjects fail to register the gorilla's presence at all. The point of the study was to examine something called inattentional blindness—the failure to notice a fully visible but unexpected object because attention was engaged on another task, event, or object. The mountaineer put a rather fine point on it: people who notice the gorilla are the ones who survive the mountain; those who don't, do not.

I mention the mountaineer's observation often, because it manages to be both spot-on and only half true. Learning to pay constant attention to your surroundings, with an eye to both your immediate environment and landmarks far off in the distance, is one of the greatest outdoor skills that a person can develop. Doing so will help you avoid many bad situations. But it won't altogether prevent them. No matter how alert you are, spend enough time outside and you're virtually guaranteed to find yourself in a tough spot. It could be a situation that threatens to derail your plans, or it could be one that derails your life. Believe me, I have lived through many, from getting lost to hypothermia to grizzly charges. And if you're out in the wilderness, you will, too. It's my hope that if and when you do, the practical skills and knowledge found within this book will enable you to save the day.

Before you get too deep into this book, I'd like to acknowledge a potential problem that might come from reading it. Along with hundreds of tips and tricks that will help you be more confident and competent in the woods, we describe a great many hazards that can be found in nature. I realize that pondering these hazards could result in paranoia about the dangers of the wild. It is not our goal to create those fears, or to reinforce any existing fears that you might have about wild animals or wild places. Instead, our view is that knowledge is power. By learning the actual risks associated with an outdoor lifestyle, we believe that you'll be able to shift your attention away from irrational or unproductive concerns and focus instead on the things that actually matter. When you are educated and prepared for risk, coping with it is easy. At times it can even be enjoyable.

So dig in. Read, study, and memorize. Then head out to practice and make experiences for yourself. And remember, always, that the natural world is sacred and deserves our love and respect. To touch nature is to touch the hand of God. This book is not about running away from the wild. It's about running into her arms, headlong and with an open heart.

THE
MeatEater Guide
TO Wilderness Skills
AND Survival

CHAPTER 1

-->>>)><(((<--

What to Pack and Wear

WHEN I THINK of hard-earned outdoor lessons, I think of the first time that I headed into the Chugach Range of south-central Alaska on a Dall sheep hunt with my brothers, Matt and Danny. We packed like idiots. Not enough clothes. Not enough food. And no first-aid kit, despite the fact that my brother Matt was starting out the trip with an already infected gash on his shin from a failed attempt at doing a box jump onto a stainless-steel lab table. What was supposed to be a fun and exciting trip stalking rams quickly turned into a miserable and hungry sufferfest. And we had sown the seeds for that experience before we'd even left home.

Our lack of preparedness was partly the result of simple naivete. We were inexperienced in terms of mountain travel and didn't know what we were doing. A portion of the blame also lies with a commonplace blunder that is made by even experienced outdoorsmen. The blunder has to do with balancing a desire to be properly equipped in the wild with the equally important desire to not tarnish outdoor experiences with all the luxuries and material bullshit of the indoor world. We go outside in order to enjoy ourselves, sure, but we also go outside to experience life in its stripped-down form. Getting the balance right requires some compromise. On the one hand, you don't want to end up at the KOA, watching satellite TV inside an air-conditioned motor home while heating up marshmallows in the microwave. On the other hand, you don't want to end up like me and my brothers, deep in the mountains and soaked to the bone while trying to cut the last of your throat lozenges into three pieces as part of a daily food ration.

While I'm a big fan of roughing it and a die-hard proponent of maintaining the aesthetic purity of the outdoors, I recognize the importance of keeping your goals and your safety in mind when it comes to packing for an outing—whether that outing is going to last a few weeks or just a few hours. If your goal is simply to see how long you can stay in the mountains without food, clothes, gear, or shelter, then you're gonna have a pretty easy time preparing. Just strip down naked, drop all of your stuff, and head into the hills. Usually, though, goals are more complicated than that. In the case of our ill-fated sheep-hunting trip, our goal was to keep moving at a brisk pace for ten days through a network of mountainous ridgelines and valleys as we scoured the landscape for Dall sheep. There's a tenuous compromise between keeping your pack light to be easily carried for many miles yet still full of the gear necessary to sustain you with food and protection for the duration of your trip. In our case, we grossly overemphasized the importance of traveling light and underemphasized the caloric input that would be required to fuel an extraordinary amount of walking through the wet and cold. In the end, our movements were effectively restricted by the same lightweight backpacks that were supposed to give us freedom.

Going without proper gear can do more than just thwart your plans. One could make the argument that all survival situations are the result of *not* having something: not having water, not having GPS, not having a lighter, not having a functioning boat, not having the necessary medical expertise. In the worst cases, that lack of gear could wind up being deadly. While it's impractical to think that you'll be able to pack enough stuff to prevent any and all forms of trouble, the right gear selections can help you eliminate many of the common problems that lead to canceled ventures and injured bodies. In short, don't think of gear as something that kills the rawness of the wild; instead, think of gear as something that allows you to stick around and experience it to the fullest.

SURVIVAL KITS

Folks who were around in the 1980s probably remember the proliferation of those cheap bootleg "Rambo" knives with the hollow handles that contained what was branded as a "survival kit." If I remember correctly, I bought mine for $7 at the Muskegon Flea Market in western Michigan.

The plastic sheath was outfitted with a coarse sharpening stone for honing the cheap but menacingly large knife blade. The threaded cap housed a bubble compass with a needle that refused to spin unless you shook it like a snow globe. Inside the handle lived a few wooden matches that crumbled like wet ash when you tried to light them. There was a big needle for stitching yourself up, and a stretch of monofilament fishing line that could be used for your sutures or for catching a few fish with the cheap snelled hooks that were also packed into the handle. Of the hundreds of thousands of Rambo knives that were sold in those days, I'm guessing that not a single one was ever actually put to use in a real-life survival situation. But still, I applaud the Rambo knife for having raised awareness around the important topic of survival kits.

By our definition, your kit should contain a lot more than just basic survival equipment. We think of ours more as do-anything, grab-and-go accessory bags that are kept ready and loaded to be stuffed into backpacks, duffel bags, and boat boxes whenever we're headed into or near the outdoors for hikes, hunts, fishing excursions, and even beach vacations. Once you've built your kit, there are two very important things to keep in mind. One, you've got to maintain it and periodically inspect the contents to make sure everything is up to date and in good working order. Alcohol swabs and wet wipes can dry out over time, bandages lose their stickiness, batteries go bad. So be diligent about inspections. Two, no matter where you're going, your kit doesn't do any good if you don't pack it along.

A BASIC SURVIVAL KIT

Survival situations are not limited to wild, remote locations. Plenty of people get injured hunting out of a treestand a quarter mile from their back door. Plenty more get lost on well-traveled trails. So pack your kit, and keep it in a small dry bag or a heavy-duty plastic baggie that is within reach during any outdoor excursion.

- Fire-starting kit—two lighters, a plastic baggie or other sealable container full of cotton balls slathered in Vaseline, and slivers of heartwood
- Water purification system—Steripen and iodine tablets (see page 54 for instructions on their use)
- Single-use 40 percent DEET insect repellent swabs
- SureFire Minimus headlamp and emergency backup light such as the Petzl e+LITE or a simple coin-battery pinch light

- 25-foot length of 3 mm utility cord and 25-foot length of 5 mm utility cord
- Four zip ties
- Compass
- Whistle
- Small, lightweight mirror for signaling, preferably made of unbreakable polycarbonate
- Waxed dental floss dispenser with heavy-duty sewing needle taped to dispenser
- Circle patch kit (Tenacious Tape)
- Uncle Bill's Sliver Gripper precision tweezers
- Fisher Bullet Space Pen (useful for validating hunting tags, leaving notes, writing afterlife wishes and deathbed confessions)
- Single-use tube of all-purpose superglue (to repair gear and treat cut fingers)
- Long-handled titanium camp spoon
- Toothbrush and small tube of toothpaste
- Single-use wet wipes
- 0.5-ounce tin of Dermatone Lips'n Face Protection Creme
- Extra batteries for headlamp, Steripen, GPS unit, etc.
- Work Sharp pocket-size knife sharpener

EXTRA SHIT FOR YOUR BASIC KIT

The items in the previous list are kept in our main survival kits, which we always stash in whatever pack we're using. But many of us also keep a store of additional items in Stanley organizer boxes in our garages. Before every trip, we look through all our extra survival gear and grab anything we feel we might need, depending on the circumstances.

- Emergency thermal space blanket
- Tube of Coghlan's Fire Paste
- Cable saw
- SPF 50 sunscreen
- Mini fishing kit—plastic envelope containing 50 feet of 8-pound fluorocarbon fishing line, four size BB split shot, two size 12 beadhead pheasant tail flies, two size 6 baitholder hooks, two size 8 baitholder hooks
- Two Snare Shop small-game wire snares

- SureFire handheld 1,200-lumen flashlight
- Leatherman bit kit and bit driver extender

THE OFFICIAL OH-SHIT JURY-RIG KIT

Over the years, I've developed this recipe for a do-it-all, go-anywhere repair kit that can get you out of just about any bind you might find yourself in. With this assemblage, which is no bigger than a sneaker and weighs just 3 pounds, you can do basic repairs on tents, rafts, waders, clothes, trucks, snow machines, fishing gear, duffel bags, backpacks, camp stoves, and even aircraft.

- Devcon plastic welder
- Aquaseal
- Tear-Aid Type A patch material
- Seam sealer
- Roll of Tenacious Tape
- Rubber tire patch and adhesive
- Small tubes of two-part epoxy
- Superglue
- J-B Weld
- Duct tape
- Electrical tape
- Alcohol swabs
- Two sets latex gloves, size large
- 5 feet 100-pound stainless-steel hanging wire
- 5 feet stainless-steel lock wire
- 10 feet fine Kevlar thread
- 10 feet 10-pound braided fishing line
- 25 feet 550 paracord
- 25 feet 2.5 mm Dyneema cord
- 1-inch and 2-inch hose clamps
- Assorted zip ties
- WD-40 No-Mess Pen
- Graphite lubricant
- Loctite
- Miscellaneous small screws, nuts, bolts
- Miscellaneous buttons, safety pins, and key rings
- Assorted threaded quick links
- Standard sewing needle and heavy-gauge curved needle

- Small adjustable wrench
- Lighter
- Bit driver and 20-piece bit holder
- Needle-nose pliers
- Small Vise-Grip locking pliers
- Two single-edge razor blades
- Tent pole splice tube

SKILL: TEN USEFUL KNOTS

There are about a million and a half knots out there, but to some degree they're variations on a few basic themes. We think that instead of gaining a passing familiarity with the whole wide world of knots, it's useful to know a few so well you could tie them blindfolded. During our decades in the woods and on the water, we've found that these ten knots will get you through 90 percent of situations—and help you improvise for the other 10 percent.

SQUARE KNOT

This is the most basic knot for joining two ropes of similar width. It's helpful to remember the phrase "right over left and under, left over right and under."

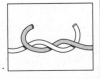

1. Cross the tag ends of the two ropes. Wrap the right-hand rope over and under the left-hand rope, then back around.
2. Take the same tag end (now on the left side), and cross it over, under, around the other tag end again.
3. Pull on the tag ends and running ends to tighten.

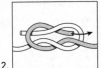

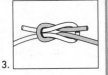

FIGURE-EIGHT STOPPER KNOT

A knot used at the end of a rope to prevent it from sliding loose out of a belay device, cam, pulley, or boat anchor rig.

1. Make a loop. Pass the tag end of the rope behind the running end, then wrap it around the anchor or running end.
2. Pass the tag end back through loop from the back side.
3. Pull to tighten.

FIGURE-EIGHT JOINING KNOT

This is the knot rock climbers use to tie their harnesses securely to a rope in case of a fall. It can also be used to securely tie two ropes together.

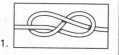

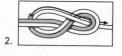

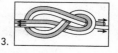

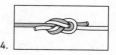

1. Follow the preceding instructions to tie a loose figure-eight knot.
2. Starting from the opposite side, follow the same path in reverse with your second length of rope. Follow the outside of the first rope's path so the knot sits properly.
3. Pull from each side. "Dress" the knot, neatly aligning the form.
4. Pull on individual strands to tighten and secure.

BOWLINE

Don't out yourself as a rube by pronouncing the name of this knot like the two words "bow line"—it's pronounced like "bowlin," and it's one of the strongest and fastest knots out there for making a loop to tie off a boat, hang a bear bag, or even lower a person off a cliff. To commit this knot to memory, use the following device: "The rabbit comes out the hole, around the tree, and back through the hole."

1. Make a loop, with the tag end of the rope in front, then pass the tag end through the loop from behind.
2. Pull the rope through without tightening it, then wrap it around the standing end of rope.
3. Put the tag end back through the loop.
4. Tighten.

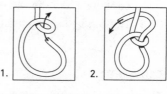

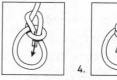

HALF HITCH

This is the most basic knot around, but it's useful to know what to call things. The half hitch is where many other knots begin.

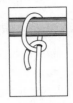

1. Loop the rope around the support, wrap the tag end around the running end, pass it through the loop, and tighten.

TWO HALF HITCHES

Every additional half hitch you put on a knot adds strength and takes up tag end length. This is great when you need to tie off quickly but don't need a rope to bear weight or take on much tension.

1. Follow the instructions for the half hitch, then repeat.

ROLLING HITCH

This is a great knot for securing a rope to a tree branch, raft frame, or other round object, especially if you want the knot to be able to pivot or slide without coming loose. You can also use it to slide one rope up and down another.

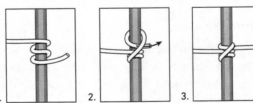

1. Wrap the rope around the support twice.
2. Cross the tag end over the wraps and loop it back around the support. Pass the tag end under the last wrap.
3. Tighten by pulling the tag and standing ends away from each other.

CLOVE HITCH

This is another easy and efficient knot for securing a rope to a pole or tree or cylindrical object.

1. Wrap the tag end of the rope around the support.
2. Cross the tag end over the running end, then wrap it around the support.
3. Pass the tag end between two wraps and pull to tighten.

TRUCKER'S HITCH

As the name implies, this knot is used by truckers to secure heavy loads and big tarps. It's pretty involved but very strong and allows you to cinch the standing line very tight.

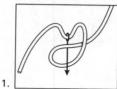
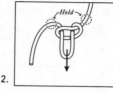
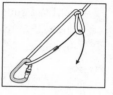
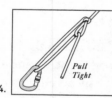
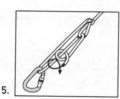
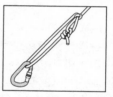

1. Make a loop in the tag end of your rope, leaving a few extra feet. Working from the tag end, pass a second loop through the first.
2. Holding on to both ends of the rope, pull down on the loop to tighten.
3. Pass the tag end through your carabiner or cam, then through the loop created in step 2.
4. Pull against the loop for leverage to tighten your load.
5. Tie a half hitch and cinch it against your tightening loop. Repeat.
6. Pull to tighten.

PRUSIK KNOT

This knot employs a loop of parachute cord wrapped around thicker rope. You can tie that initial loop using a blood knot (commonly used in fishing) or the figure-eight joining knot described in this section.

Climbers use two of these as a system for emergency ascending. With two Prusiks on a climbing rope, you could slide one up, then the other, and move yourself upward. It's also helpful for attaching items to any hanging rope.

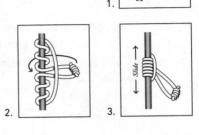

1. Pass a looped cord around a rope and through itself.
2. Repeat twice more.
3. Neaten the wraps, and test out the slide. Do not pull so tight that the knot cannot move.

EMERGENCY CAR KIT

Survival situations aren't limited to folks hiking around in the boonies. Plenty of people get stranded on the side of the road in their vehicles due to simply running out of gas, having mechanical issues, getting stuck in rough terrain, or experiencing extreme weather events. During the severe winter storms associated with a polar vortex in 2019, over a thousand stranded motorists needed to be rescued along Colorado's Front Range. In more remote areas, you could wait for days alongside a dirt road or two-track without having a single motorist come by. And in subzero wind chills and driving snow, getting stranded can be deadly.

Regardless of where you live or travel, you should outfit your vehicle with at least a basic emergency car kit—especially in extremely hot or cold environments. This is particularly true for hunters, anglers, and explorers, who tend to do a lot of driving in areas with limited cellphone coverage and shitty roads.

Adapt this same kit for use in other types of vehicles, including snowmobiles, ATVs, side-by-sides, and boats. If you couple this with your basic kit and our patented Oh-Shit Jury-Rig Kit, you'll be a force to be reckoned with should times get hard. Keep the items stored in a duffel bag or a plastic tote such as a Rubbermaid Action Packer, so that your kit is easy to grab when you need it.

This list will get you through most scenarios, but you may want to add some things if you'll be far from immediate help. We know hunting guides and wildlife biologists who frequently drive around on remote forest service roads. They won't leave home without a chainsaw and a come-along in their rig. If they get stuck or blocked by a downed tree, they're able to handle the situation without having to walk out or call for help.

- Tool kit
- Jumper cables
- Battery-powered car jump starter
- 20-foot tow strap with two ½-inch D-ring shackles
- Tire chains or cables
- Tire repair kit
- Jack
- Fix-a-Flat
- U.S. government-issue E-tool
- Hatchet
- Flares, glowsticks
- Large handheld flashlight and headlamp, with extra batteries for each
- First-aid kit
- Insulated leather gloves
- Insulated coveralls
- Wool hat
- Winter boots
- Wool socks
- Sleeping bag
- Water
- Two days' worth of nonperishable food such as candy bars, energy bars, and MREs
- Candles (for warming car interior)
- Extra gas can for road trips through remote areas or four-wheeling in backcountry

THE BATTERY CONUNDRUM

In real-world survival situations, something as simple as a dead battery could end up being the difference between life and death. Always carry extra batteries for any electronic device you rely on for navigation, illumination, communication, or water purification. However, if your GPS unit runs on AAAs, your Steripen runs on AAs, and your headlamp runs on a CR123, keeping all those different batteries stored and organized can become a hassle. If possible, simplify things by using electronics that take the same batteries. That way, your extra batteries can be used in multiple devices. Next, it's smart to buy and use a decent battery tester to ensure that the batteries you're carrying have a full charge before every trip. You shouldn't expect your extra batteries to work well, or even at all, if they've been sitting in the bottom of your pack for the last couple of years. Instead, it's better to recycle old batteries and replace them with new ones as needed. Finally, for rechargeable devices like cellphones, it's worth packing a portable charger that provides enough energy for multiple charges. Goal Zero, LifeProof, and Dark Energy make durable compact portable chargers designed for use in the outdoors. Also, unless you're using your phone to communicate with the outside world, turn it off or keep it in airplane mode and low-power mode whenever you're not using it to extend battery life. If you follow these practices, your phone won't waste a bunch of energy searching for a signal or wireless connection and it'll go at least a couple days before it needs a charge. For more on how to use your cellphone in the outdoors, see page 272.

HOW MUCH TO BRING

Over the years, we've found there are certain pieces of gear we rely on day in and day out, wherever we go. There are other items we know we can't afford to leave behind even though they rarely get used. Because experience informs our packing decisions, there are also some things we've simply stopped carrying around altogether without ever feeling a sense of loss or vulnerability. Of course, your definition of essential gear can evolve over time as your habits change. Until recently, for instance, some of us regularly hunted in rugged terrain without trekking poles. Now the entire crew rarely leaves our poles behind, because they make hiking in steep terrain with a heavy load of meat easier and safer.

The question of how much to bring comes down in part to how much weight you can carry comfortably and safely in your pack. There are no set rules, but generally speaking, you don't want to pack more than a third of your body weight when hiking for extended periods of time. Physically fit individuals should be able to handle loads approaching half their body weight over shorter stretches. After successful backcountry hunts, we used to regularly pack loads of meat and gear that well exceeded that ratio in order to get everything out in one trip. Toting an overly heavy, unbalanced pack in steep, uneven terrain greatly increases the odds of losing your balance and taking a nasty fall. And over time, packing too much weight can do permanent damage to your body. Now that we're older and wiser, we usually opt to pack lighter loads even if it means making multiple trips.

Whatever the total weight, your gear should be carefully selected based on where you're headed, what you'll be doing, what time of year you'll be going, how you'll be getting there, and how long you plan on being away from civilization. Build your gear list by prioritizing safety. Whenever possible, some sort of reliable communication (see page 270) should be high on your list. Water, food, shelter, and warmth (which we'll be covering in the chapters to come) are also primary considerations. From there, make reasonable choices about what else you'll need to stay alive, what you'll want to keep yourself comfortable, and what you can afford to safely leave behind.

Certain modes of travel may demand special packing requirements. For instance, if you're being flown into a remote area by bush plane, the amount of gear you're able to bring will be determined by a strict weight limit set by your pilot. Likewise, some places and activities require highly specialized and technical gear. Without an ice axe, crampons, and climbing ropes, it's unlikely you'd survive more than a day on a high-altitude expedition in the Himalayas; we're not going to cover that type of equipment in this book, but there are great resources out there, such as *Mountaineering: The Freedom of the Hills*, for anyone who's considering that kind of trip.

While most of us will never summit K2, it's important to consider not only the terrain and weather when choosing what gear to bring into the woods, but also the physical fitness, skill, and experience level of yourself and those in your group. Too many people overestimate their abilities, or their gear, and end up compromising their own safety and the safety of others. By realistically assessing things, it's possible to strike a reasonable balance between safety and comfort without going overboard in either direction.

THE GOING LIGHT VERSUS GOING HEAVY DEBATE

Much of today's gear is way lighter than it used to be, which makes it easier to keep your total pack weight down. But we're somewhat skeptical of the ultralight minimalist craze that's sweeping through every facet of outdoor recreation. Intentionally omitting important gear from your kit clearly elevates the potential for problems. On the other hand, we've seen people loaded down with so much superfluous crap strapped to their pack they could barely hike down the trail. The solution that's going to work best for most people is to find a happy medium between these two schools of thought, but we've presented two takes for your consideration.

THE MINIMALIST

Native tribes managed to thrive for thousands of years without multi-tools, camp stoves, and heavy down sleeping bags. And yet today many of us justify the need to pack an entire gear store inside our packs, "just in case." I used to go that route, too, but over the years my experience has led me to adapt a minimalist mindset when it comes to wilderness travel. What I've found is that letting go of your insecurities about what might happen and focusing on what you truly need to survive can be cathartic.

Going light and fast is both a practical approach in the backcountry and a philosophy that provides mental and physical freedom. One of my favorite ways to push my personal limits and the limits of my gear is to do long-distance wilderness hikes, something we refer to as "death races." On these excursions, the route is usually a mix of on- and off-trail travel through remote mountainous terrain, and the goal is to complete the route in as little time as possible. Weight is paramount, and sleep is optional. It is an uncomfortable test of physical and mental toughness, but I've learned a lot about how to make do with as little gear as possible.

To begin cutting weight from your pack, start by writing down a list of everything you would carry, with the associated weights, and ask if a lighter alternative exists or if you can completely do without it. Do you need ten tent stakes, or will eight work? Do you need a heavy, waterproof, windproof butane lighter, or will a mini Bic lighter suffice? For most people the biggest weight savings will come from the big four: backpack, tent, sleeping bag, and sleeping pad. As an example, my standard shelter is a small floorless tent, which weighs about 15 ounces. My previous "lightweight" tent weighed 3½ pounds.

Walking in the mountains with a light pack is undeniably easier and more enjoyable. A heavy pack weighs you down physically and mentally. It can sap your motivation to go to the next valley or peak and mentally erect barriers for what you perceive as possible. A light pack opens up a world of possibilities and allows you to go farther, with less effort.

—By Brad Brooks, hunter, climber, and co-founder of Argali Outdoors

THE MAXIMALIST

For most of my life, I've spent a couple hundred days a year outside in rough mountain terrain with a heavy pack on my back. One thing I've learned is that going light is nice—but it isn't always practical. Working as a professional hunting guide, there are many things I don't necessarily feel like taking each time I set out on a trip. But I'm willing to pack a few extra pounds if that means staying safe and comfortable. This is critical when I am responsible for others who don't have the skills or abilities that I do. I need to guarantee my clients' safety, success, and, to some extent, comfort, and what I pack reflects that.

In the Southern Alps of New Zealand, the outfitter I worked for would constantly say, "Two is one, one is none." We carried extra headlamps, food, cooking fuel, clothes, batteries, even things like hand warmers, paperback books, or decks of cards. At the beginning of the trip it always seemed like way too much stuff. More often than not, by the end of the trip all those extra items had been used—and many times we would have been screwed without them.

On many trips, it's not logistically possible to go really light. Foul weather conditions and remote long-distance treks may make carrying extra gear mandatory. Maybe you're hiking several miles into the mountains for a weeklong solo elk hunt in late September, when the weather could change from summer to winter without any warning. A sturdy three-season tent is a way better shelter option than a small ultralight tarp, even though the tent is a lot heavier. You'll get by without luxuries like hand warmers, but you're making a big mistake if you start shaving ounces by leaving your backup fire-starting kit behind. Carrying all the basics to survive extreme weather situations or accidents makes for a heavier pack, but that's a trade-off I'm willing to make in order to avoid life-threatening disasters.

Safety is always priority number one, but comfort is also important. The more comfortable you are, the more enjoyable your trip will be and the more success you'll have. If you are venturing out with your kids, maybe someone new to the experience, or someone with very few outdoor skills, it is often wise to carry a few extra items that will make the journey more comfortable for them. That might mean bringing some hot cocoa mix for the kids or packing a heavier sleeping bag for someone who gets cold easily.

In the end, carrying what you need to ensure your safety and comfort is totally worth a little extra weight.

—*By Remi Warren, wilderness hunting guide and host of the podcast* Cutting the Distance

CLOTHING AND ACCESSORIES

Outdoor clothing has come a long way from the cotton thermal underwear, flannel shirts, and cheap army surplus gear we wore as kids. Back then going hunting, fishing, or just being outside meant constantly getting wet, cold, or both. You got used to it and it made you tough—but eventually we began to understand the value of investing in apparel that kept us warm and dry, or, as the case may be, cool and comfortable.

Fortunately, today's technically advanced synthetic and natural materials have made it possible to build a simple, do-it-all clothing system that will keep you reasonably comfortable through 95 percent of the situations you could possibly find yourself in. The top-performing pieces of clothing all come from the skiing, mountaineering, and backcountry hunting industries, so don't waste your time looking elsewhere—beyond the issue of comfort, staying warm (or cool) can mean the difference between life and death. The really good stuff doesn't come cheap, but there are ways to get your hands on technical apparel at steeply discounted prices. Look for off-season or end-of-season sales, dig through the aisles of Goodwill or Salvation Army thrift stores when passing through ski towns, or set up notifications on eBay or Craigslist to watch for select items that might suddenly pop up at bargain prices. We've done all of this, and it works. It might take a bit longer than making a bulk purchase at FirstLite.com, but it can be more fulfilling.

We prefer a combination of modern synthetics and merino wool for almost all of our outdoor activities. These materials are light and insulate well while also breathing and wicking moisture away from your body. They allow us to tackle steep uphill hikes without getting soaked in sweat, but we still stay warm and comfortable during low physical activity in cold temperatures. By tweaking our basic kit depending on when and where we're going, we're able to dress appropriately for the temperature swings and weather patterns we expect to encounter and still be able to account for the inherently unreliable nature of ten-day weather forecasts. Extreme situations, such as a December trip to Kodiak Island, might call for some additional pieces of specialty apparel and gear, but those items would be supplementary to the apparel that we're listing under the must-have section below.

AN ADAPTABLE CLOTHING KIT

Here is an adaptable outdoor clothing kit that'll get you through 95 percent of the weather scenarios North America might throw your way. To save on pack space and weight, the kit consists of lightweight, high-tech layers that you can add and subtract as needed in order to avoid getting too hot or too cold. Notice the use of "too"—it's virtually impossible to go through an outdoor life with uninterrupted comfort, whether that means getting a little chilly or facing up to a blister or two. We actually prefer to start hiking cold rather than bundled up, since we know that we'll begin working up elevated body heat as soon as we hit the trail. So instead of going a half mile and then stopping to pull off an outer layer (and potentially having to hike in sweaty underlayers), save yourself the hassle by starting out chilly. The more time you spend outdoors, the better you'll know the idiosyncrasies of your own body and your own gear. In time, you'll be able to properly layer your clothes without really thinking about it, and you'll avoid many of the chilly and/or sweaty moments that distract you from the task at hand.

LOWER BODY

- Synthetic/merino blend briefs or underwear
- Merino base layer
- Field pants, either quick-dry nylon, merino blend, or premium cotton/synthetic blends
- Lightly insulated soft-shell pants with internal microfleece liner and exterior durable water repellent treatment
- Insulated synthetic puffy pants

- Breathable rain shell pants (big enough to fit over other pants)
- Waterproof ankle gaiters
- Synthetic/merino blend socks
- Flexible nylon belt
- Boots

UPPER BODY

- Merino T-shirt
- Merino midweight long-sleeved base layer
- Fleece or merino hoodie
- Soft-shell jacket
- Down or synthetic down puffy jacket or parka
- Breathable rain jacket, large enough to fit over puffy coat

HANDS AND HEAD

- Merino neck gaiter/buff
- Baseball cap
- Boonie hat for full sun coverage
- Sunglasses
- Wool beanie
- Uninsulated leather work gloves
- Insulated gloves
- Insulated mittens with waterproof choppers (overmitts)

Sunglasses

Some folks might not consider sunglasses to be an essential piece of survival gear. We don't fall into that camp. Somehow we got by without them when we were kids, but these days you can always find a pair on our faces or nestled inside a protective case inside our packs. Over time, UV rays can cause severe damage to your vision, and it doesn't take more than a day of squinting into bright sunlight to get waylaid by eyestrain and the painful headaches it causes. In addition to guarding your eyes against bright light and harmful ultraviolet rays, sunglasses provide some side benefits by protecting your eyes against grit and dust on windy days and preventing you from getting poked in the eye by a wayward branch (see page 389).

Choose a pair of sunglasses with polarized lenses. Fishermen prefer polarized lenses because they eliminate reflected light and glare coming off the water, allowing them to see fish better; those same qualities also help to reduce glare and eyestrain on dry land, especially if there's snow on the ground.

Some folks prefer glass lenses for their greater optical clarity and the fact that they don't scratch as easily as polycarbonate lenses. The drawback of glass lenses is they can shatter, while plastic lenses are more durable. We use both styles but prefer glass lenses for fishing and polycarbonate for hiking. Costa Del Mar makes great sunglasses in both materials, and you can order them with prescription lenses.

MOUNTAINEERING TRICKS FOR SOGGY UNDERTHINGS

The issue of clammy, soggy sports bras seems to be one that modern technology hasn't solved. Although there are some more-breathable merino options on the market, generally the more supportive the garment, the slower it is to dry. That can be a problem when you slow down or when temperatures drop and you're left shivering in a sodden base layer that undermines all the wicking action of the rest of your gear. In lieu of a true fix, several of our female colleagues offered these backcountry workarounds. Carry a second sports bra, and hook your damp bra to the outside of your pack while you hike, for faster drying time. Or wear your sports bra on the outside of your base layer, so that you can easily pull it off and set it out to dry when you get to camp. Not ideal, but better than prolonging discomfort, especially in environments where keeping warm can be a matter of life and death.

FOOTWEAR

As important as it is to get your clothing right, your choice of footwear may be even more consequential. We can't begin to recount how many times we've seen foot problems ruin entire trips. If you're lucky, those problems will be limited to a painful blister on your heel that forces you to limp back to your vehicle, cursing the fact that you didn't bother to take your poorly fitting boots for a test drive before you hit the trail. But the wrong choice in footwear could lead to a much more dangerous outcome. Striding out into the desert for a short hike in your beat-up old Crocs may seem like a cool thing to do, but it's a great way to twist an ankle. And you certainly don't want to become one of those underprepared dipshits who requires yet another newsworthy "flip-flop rescue." Even a poorly fitted boot could wind up causing infected blisters bad enough to hinder mobility, and a boot that's unsuited to the environment can be just as bad. If your feet get soaked or frostbitten, you could end up in a dire situation that you can't walk away from, literally and figuratively.

But before we get into boots, it's important to talk about socks. Even when paired with well-fitted, top-shelf hiking boots, a shitty pair of socks can still wreak havoc. Think of socks the same way you think about the rest of your clothing—they should insulate, breathe, and wick away moisture. The very best socks for active outdoor pursuits are made from a blend of merino wool, nylon, and spandex. They're offered in different weights to match seasonal temperatures, and we've worn them hunting for wild pigs during the summer in south Texas and ice fishing during the winter in interior Alaska. They're durable, too. On backcountry trips, we'll run the same pair of merino blend socks for days on end when we don't have room for a lot of clothes in our pack. Still, it's a good idea to always have at least one pair of extra socks in your pack in case your feet get wet. Few things in this world feel as good as slipping on a clean, dry pair of socks after a long and wet day of hiking.

As for boots, let's get something straight right off the bat. Different makes and models of boots all have their idiosyncrasies when it comes to sizing and fit. If you typically wear a size 10 sneaker, don't blow your money on a pair of size 10 mountain boots and then hike off into the sunset assuming that they'll be comfortable in a day or two. If you're off by even half a size either way, the results could be devastating to your feet. Too big and you'll get a sloppy fit that causes massive blisters that tear the skin off your entire heel, and painful "toe bang" that bruises your toes and removes toenails on downhill descents. Too small and you'll get toe blisters along with cramped, aching feet. Get your boots professionally fitted, making sure they're comfortable and snug, without any slop but with enough room to wiggle your toes a bit. Once you're sure of a good fit, you'll need to put some miles on them to break them in. Some manufacturers will claim their boots don't require a break-in period. That's bullshit. Brand-new boots can cause the same types of problems as poorly fitting boots. They'll also fit and flex differently after several miles of trekking than they do right out of the box. Our buddy Remi Warren, a renowned mountain hunter and guide, doesn't consider a new pair of boots to be comfortably broken in until he's put at least 50 miles on them. At the very least, you should wear them to work and walk around the neighborhood for a month before you set off on a trip that might require a decent amount of foot travel.

And make sure your footwear is up to the task. We hunt and fish all over the place at different times of the year, and we've found it's always a good idea to have something sturdier on your feet than you think you'll need. For instance, the pair of running shoes you wear to the gym will probably get you through a short hike on well-maintained trails just fine, but lightweight hiking boots are far more versatile and open up your possibilities while traveling outdoors. You'll always appreciate the added traction, support, and waterproofing. Keep in mind, too, that there's no one pair of boots that can do it all. We run different boots depending on the demands of whatever environment and weather conditions we'll be encountering.

LIGHT HIKERS

Light hikers or "sneaker boots" are great for warmer weather and mild terrain, but a good pair is also capable of standing up to rougher country, cooler climates, and an unexpected dump of off-season snow. Most light hikers are ankle-high (usually around 7 inches) to provide support, but they're built with plenty of flex for comfortable walking on the trail. To keep them on the light side, they're usually uninsulated and often made out of a combination of synthetic leather and nylon mesh. Full leather models are generally heavier but will last longer. Get a pair with rubber toe and heel rands to prevent your boots from getting torn up by sharp rocks. And make sure they have an internal breathable, waterproof membrane to keep water out while allowing sweat to dissipate away from your feet.

MOUNTAIN HIKERS

A good pair of mountain hikers can run a few hundred bucks or more, but that's an investment we're comfortable making for boots that will last several years and handle everything short of technical expedition climbing. Most mountain hikers are 9 to 11 inches tall and have an internal waterproof membrane. Good mountain hikers also have thick leather uppers, and the best have a thick rubber rand that wraps around the entire lower portion of the leather upper for added durability. They should also have plenty of cushioning and an aggressive tread pattern on a sturdy Vibram rubber sole. The edges of the soles should be sharp and rigid, so that they can dig into the ground on steep sidehills. Whether you buy uninsulated or insulated depends on your particular preferences and needs. At up to 5 pounds per pair, all of these features make mountain hikers stiffer and heavier than light hikers, but they need to be. They're built for support and traction while you're carrying heavy loads in the kind of steep, rocky terrain where you find mountain goats and bighorn sheep and great adventures. Generally, we stay away from anything made solely out of lightweight synthetic materials. Synthetic boots may be a lot lighter than leather boots, but they lack the rigid support and durability you need in the mountains, and they just might fall apart when you need them the most.

Leather boots do require some maintenance if you want them to last and maintain water repellency. Clean away mud and blood after each use and allow them to air-dry. Routinely treat them with waterproofing leather conditioners like Nikwax or Schnee's Leather Conditioner. Failure to do so will ruin an expensive pair of leather boots in short order and can also lead to any number of potentially dangerous foot problems. To get even more out of your mountain hikers, pair them with good knee-high gaiters and you'll be wading streams and plowing through snow without a care in the world.

PAC BOOTS

Mountain hikers will get you through periods of cold, snowy weather and occasional creek crossings, but pac boots are built specifically for extreme wet and wintry conditions. Pac boots have thick rubber lower sections that are completely impervious to water, full leather uppers that are waterproof as long as they're regularly waxed, and thick, insulated wool-blend liners that will keep your feet warm in subzero temperatures. A good tip is to buy an extra pair of liners in case you swamp them in deep water; that way, you can wear a fresh pair while the other pair dries out. Good pac boots will also have a soft air bob sole that grips snow and ice in very cold temperatures. (Vibram soles can become rock hard and dangerously slippery on rock and ice in subfreezing temperatures.)

Pac boots are available in different heights, but the higher the better. We prefer 13-inch models that extend almost to the knee, like the classic Schnee's Pac Boot, which has been a favorite of ice fishermen, mushers, houndsmen, and professional fur trappers for decades.

MAKING THE CASE FOR SILICONE WEDDING RINGS

If you devotedly wear your metal wedding band while hunting and fishing, you could be risking a backwoods emergency and an amputated finger. Should your ring catch on a rock, fence, a piece of equipment, or a broken branch during a jump, trip, or stumble, a finger avulsion, also known as a "degloving," could be the result. In layman's terms, an avulsion results in all of the skin and some of the flesh being rapidly and violently stripped off your finger.

Deglovings often cost people their ring finger or its full use. Even miracle-working microsurgeons can't salvage most finger deglovings, and the injuries can happen anywhere, as the late-night talk show host Jimmy Fallon learned in 2015 when he tripped on a rug and caught his wedding band on a table. Fallon was lucky—a skilled surgeon saved his finger.

Indiana bowhunter Brad Herndon also got lucky after degloving his ring finger on a treestand step in 1989. His ring buried itself beneath the finger's first knuckle as his hand slid off the screw-in step. The doctor sawed through the ring in two places to remove it, and restored the finger with stitches. Ever since, Herndon studies the left hands of passing strangers. "You'd be shocked how many people are missing their ring finger," Herndon said. Among them is a friend's sister, who jumped off a truck's tailgate and lost her finger when her ring snagged on a bolt in the pickup's bed.

Stories like those hit close to home at MeatEater headquarters, where many members of the crew have had close calls. One of us "welded" his metal ring to a boat battery when his screwdriver hit the battery's terminals. On another occasion, the same guy caught his ring between two branches on a tree and gave himself a nice gash. His wife ended up giving him a four-pack of silicone rings for their tenth wedding anniversary, at the whopping cost of $23. It's hard not to question the intelligence of anyone risking a finger to their metal ring. As a side benefit, silicone rings don't clack on your gun or bow when you're trying to be stealthy.

If you don't heed our advice, at least don't be extra stupid by wearing a ring made from tungsten carbide. These can't be cut off by medical equipment; instead, they need to be cracked off with a big pair of pliers. Imagine going through that while your ring finger painfully swells due to a broken bone.

No matter what ring you're wearing, remove it immediately following any injury to the hand or finger. Swelling makes it difficult to remove rings, and rings can restrict blood flow.
—*By Patrick Durkin, award-winning outdoor writer and columnist,*
MeatEater *contributor, and editor-at-large at* Inside Archery

KNEE-HIGH RUBBER AND NEOPRENE BOOTS

Pac boots do a great job of keeping your feet dry, but we also like knee-high rubber or neoprene boots when we know we'll be around water all day long but won't be dealing with excessively long hikes. You'll appreciate the extra height when you're doing things like hopping in and out of boats or slogging through swampy wetlands. XTRATUF boots are popular with commercial fishermen in Alaska, and we've worn them for hundreds of hours while hunting and fishing around southeast Alaska's Prince of Wales Island. Muck and LaCrosse make great products as well, some of which are particularly well suited for subfreezing temperatures. Remember, though, both rubber and neoprene knee-high boots lack the necessary ankle support for serious hiking in steep terrain.

SPECIALTY FOOTWEAR

There are times when you'll need footwear that is designed for very specific purposes and environments. North of the Arctic Circle, daytime highs might top out at −20°F for weeks on end. Even the best pac boots aren't impervious to the cold in those conditions, especially if there's a risk of punching through the ice and soaking your legs and feet. That's why fur trappers who spend the entire winter outside in the Arctic use "Mickey Mouse" boots to keep their feet warm. Developed by the military for use in extremely cold weather in the 1950s, during the Korean War, the boots are recognizable by their oversized white design. With a thick layer of wool insulation and air encased between two thick, impermeable layers of rubber, modern versions of Mickey Mouse boots are built to handle −60°F temperatures. When you get them wet, you can literally dry them out with a towel or shirt and be on your way.

If you're going on a long river journey, it's a good idea to wear some type of water shoe. Wearing wet hiking boots or running shoes for several days in a row is a big mistake, as they don't allow water to drain away from your feet. Feet that aren't allowed to properly dry out could put you at risk of contracting "trench foot," a condition experienced by tens of thousands of soldiers during World War I. Eventually, trench foot can develop into gangrene (see page 368). When it's warm out, it might be tempting to opt for sandals or flip-flops, but they're a poor choice for wading in rocky rivers or any amount of hiking. Instead, wear water shoes with a closed toe, a wrap-around design, and a soft, grippy rubber sole that provides traction; these will protect your feet from getting bludgeoned on slippery river rocks while still allowing for drainage.

Finally, hiking boots are great for scrambling around in the mountains all day, but it's nice to be able to take them off at night while you putz around camp. Some of us carry a set of Crocs in our luggage for camp shoes, as they're light and indestructible. Booties with synthetic or down insulation are a great option for colder weather. They weigh next to nothing, and their soft, packable design allows them to be stuffed into a small space in your pack.

DUDS FOR YOUNGSTERS

If you're bringing young children along on a trip into the outdoors, planning and packing their wardrobe will take some extra doing. Unless you're camping out in a bone-dry desert, kids will inevitably find a way to get wet. They also get cold very easily. While a cold, wet child might not necessarily be a matter of life and death, they can certainly cut your trip short. Worse, your child might have such a bad time outdoors that they'll question your ability to keep them safe and comfortable and eventually come to dread outdoor excursions.

Put as much (or more) attention into your kids' apparel as you put into your own. If you find that waterproof and breathable clothes are comfortable and versatile, so will they. Kids are constantly growing out of things, so check to make sure their boots and mittens are roomy enough to allow for good circulation and the collection of warm air. A pair of boots that keeps your kid warm in November could easily become cramped by February, and it probably won't occur to the child to point this out. When buying new clothes, select items that are a bit oversized so that you can maximize how long your child can use them. And if you have multiple kids, buy the best quality apparel that you can afford so that it's suitable for passing along to the next kid in line. We have a lot of children's cold-weather apparel that's on the fourth or fifth kid to put it to use. Finally, bring extra layers and dry changes of clothes for those "oh shit!" moments when things go bad. Stuffing an extra pair of socks and long underwear into your backpack is a smart move. If you have room, also pack along an insulated poncho from Wiggy's. It can be a trip saver when you're outside with kids in cold weather.

Keeping kids comfortable requires a lot more than just dressing them properly. They lose their hats, get their gloves wet, forget where they left their coats, and wade into the water over the tops of their boots. You need to keep a constant eye on them, especially when conditions are severe enough to be dangerous. On the one hand, you want them to suffer the consequences of their inattention and learn to avoid the mistake next time. On the other hand, you want them to have fun and be excited to return. Strive for a good, reasonable balance between letting them suffer and keeping them safe. When it comes time for them to take care of you, you'll be glad that they learned how to do it in a thoughtful, caring way.

PACKS, BACKPACKS, AND POLES

A good backpack is a foundational piece of gear. You need one, plain and simple. The type you should choose depends on what you'll be doing and how long you'll be doing it. Assuming we're talking about foot-powered endeavors, you'll need a pack that's large enough to hold all your gear and keep it organized and dry. In particularly wet environments, fully waterproof backpacks made from welded thermoplastics are appropriate, but in general it's hard to go wrong with packs made of water-resistant, ripstop Cordura nylon. You'll also want a large main compartment with a few separate smaller compartments, all of which should feature sturdy external zippers. Other features to look for include compression straps that keep heavy loads from shifting and external attachment points such as D-rings where you can strap extra gear to the outside of the pack. It's also a good idea to get a lightweight waterproof cover for your pack, especially if you're carrying clothes or a sleeping bag. And remember, poorly fitting packs loaded down with gear can cause serious neck, shoulder, and back discomfort. Many backpack companies understand people come in all sorts of sizes and shapes and offer suspension systems with different sizes of hip belts and shoulder straps. Just as with boots, you'll want to make sure your pack fits properly and comfortably and test it before you head outdoors for any extended stretch.

DAY PACKS

As the name implies, day packs are backpacks designed for outings where you won't be sleeping in the field but you still need to carry more than a bottle of water and a granola bar. Most day packs max out at about 2,000 cubic inches of storage space. That's a little larger than the size of a kid's school backpack, which is still plenty of room to carry a survival/first-aid kit, food, water, a rain jacket, and a small item or two of specialized gear that's pertinent to whatever you happen to be up to.

MULTI-DAY BACKPACKS

Multi-day backpacks average 3,000–4,000 cubic inches of carrying capacity, so they are large enough to comfortably store enough gear for overnight trips, including sleeping bags and tents. Because they employ a supportive frame system, they also allow people to handle heavy loads, like an elk's hindquarter. It used to be that most multi-day backpacks had rigid external frames made out of metal tubing to which the bag portion of the pack was attached. External frames can bear a lot of weight, and some serious mountaineers and hunting guides still swear by them. However, we prefer internal frame systems designed by companies like Stone Glacier and Mystery Ranch, which utilize materials like carbon fiber and titanium. Modern internal frames are just as strong as the old external ones, but they're much lighter and more streamlined, which makes carrying a fully loaded pack easier to manage.

EXPEDITION BACKPACKS

While multi-day packs will get you through three or four nights out in the woods, for a trip that's going to last a week or longer you'll need a full-on expedition pack. Expedition packs are large—most come in at 6,000–7,000 cubic inches, which is enough space to haul more weight than most people would be comfortable carrying on their backs. If you're planning on living in the backcountry for ten days or more, an expedition pack is the way to go. Some companies make interchangeable backpack systems that allow you to switch from one size pack bag to another on the same frame, so you can customize your setup according to the length of your trip.

WATERPROOF DRY BAGS, BACKPACKS, AND DUFFELS

Wet sleeping bags and clothing can quickly devolve from a mere inconvenience into a miserable and potentially fatal liability. Damp and soggy gear poses a threat to both comfort and survival, so wet climates and trips that involve a lot of water travel demand a higher priority for keeping gear dry. Backpacks outfitted with a rain cover do a pretty good job of this, up to a point, but you'll need to store your sleeping bag and clothes in a lightweight nylon dry bag inside your backpack for some added protection against the elements.

The reality is that even if you're using the best mountaineering pack available, after a few days of hiking through steady downpours or rafting through whitewater rapids, your gear will get soaked. In these situations, it might be necessary to use a different pack system. Whitewater rafting guides have long stored important gear in durable silicone or vinyl-coated dry bags with a roll-up closure system. They're simple and work great at keeping stuff dry, but they're designed to sit in the bottom of a raft, not to be carried around on your back. Completely waterproof backpacks and duffels with submersible zippers and impermeable welded plastic shells are more versatile than roll-up dry bags. When fitted with shoulder straps, hip belts, and other features typically found on mountaineering backpacks, they are an ideal choice for water-based trips that involve portages or long hikes up to campsites on dry ground.

TREKKING POLES

Telescoping trekking poles can be a lifesaver when you're carrying heavy loads over rough or slippery terrain, especially when you're traveling downhill. We'll often keep one or two poles strapped to the outside of our backpacks for use during specific sets of circumstances, such as packing out elk or moose quarters, and then go through an entire trip without ever deploying them. That might seem like unnecessary weight and wasted space, but good telescoping trekking poles are so light and compact that it's a welcome trade-off when you might be saving yourself a blown-out knee. An added advantage of trekking poles is that they can be an invaluable tool for pitching camp. We often use two trekking poles to pitch tarps in a simple A-frame configuration (see page 246); a single pole can be used as an additional center pole support inside freestanding tents in order to beef up the tent's ability to shed wet, heavy snows. As with most outdoor gear, get the best trekking poles that you can afford.

Having junky trekking poles is almost worse than having none at all, since they can fail and collapse as you're putting weight on them. We saw a pair of Black Diamond trekking poles turn a charging grizzly bear when they were swung like a baseball bat against its head. There was zero damage to the poles. If that's not sufficient evidence of a good product, nothing is.

KNIVES, GUNS, AND SHOVELS

Survival knives and guns have been thoroughly fetishized by post-apocalyptic doomsday preppers, and there's a ton of misinformation out there as a result. We're going to do away with discussions about protecting your water supply from zombified neighbors and killing off the hordes of rabid dogs that preppers fantasize about encountering during the End Times. Our idea of a survival gun is, first and foremost, a tool that you'd use to secure small game animals ranging from squirrels to grouse to beavers. Likewise, a good knife is one that you don't know is there until you need it.

KNIVES AND MULTI-TOOLS

Serious hunters and anglers are seldom more than an arm's reach away from a knife or two. We'll have a special knife for filleting fish, another for skinning game, and yet another for butchering quarters of venison down into primal cuts. But for most folks, a simple folding pocketknife—known in some circles as an EDC or "everyday carry" knife—is all that they'll need. Not only can a pocketknife handle camp chores and even some aspects of personal grooming, most of them are more than adequate for cleaning fish and butchering deer as long as you've got some dexterity and patience. Benchmade's Griptillian and Bugout knives are ideal for clipping onto your belt or storing in the lid of your backpack. Pocketknives that feature a combination blade with both standard and serrated edges are especially versatile, as they can handle delicate tasks like gutting rabbits and coarse work such as sawing through a ¾-inch marine-grade anchor line. In order to avoid accidental injuries, always choose a folding knife with a safety locking mechanism. You can go with a fixed-blade knife if your heart's set on it, but it must be sheathed when not in use, and it'll take up extra space. Whatever type of knife you choose, pick one with a blade that's about 3 to 4 inches long. That's plenty long enough to carve a tent stake or break down a big game animal. Longer blades are unwieldy, heavy, and generally impractical.

A good knife can accomplish a lot of jobs, but there are times when you'll need actual tools to build, repair, or modify something out in the field. For decades, the Swiss Army Knife has been billed as the ultimate multi-tool for outdoorsmen. Some models have as many as thirty-three different tools. Some of these are useful in the woods, but you probably won't find yourself using a plastic toothpick or a wine corkscrew in a survival situation. Although they were a standard coming-of-age gift when we were kids, there are plenty of other multi-tools that are far more user-friendly and practical. Leatherman and Gerber reign supreme. The best models are built around a strong pair of pliers. Also look for a knife blade, saw, file, and both Phillips and regular screwdrivers. The nice thing

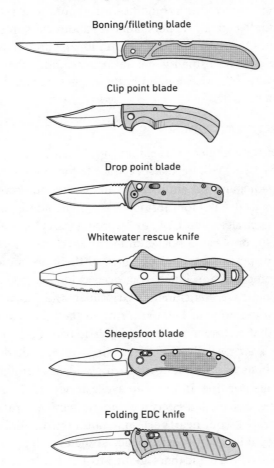

Boning/filleting blade

Clip point blade

Drop point blade

Whitewater rescue knife

Sheepsfoot blade

Folding EDC knife

about multi-tools is that there are enough versions out there to satisfy just about anyone's needs. For instance, we prefer models that are compatible with driver bit kits. This allows us to tighten or loosen screws and other fasteners with a variety of different heads. It's impossible to say how many times our multi-tools were used to turn around potentially trip-ending situations and get everything moving in the right direction. Fixing camp stoves, getting fishhooks out of skin, repairing rifles, making splints, doctoring blisters—we've done it all with multi-tools.

FIVE GEAR TIPS

1. Wrap a few layers of duct tape around your lighter. You'll find all sorts of uses for the duct tape, from reattaching a broken eyelet on a fishing pole to crafting makeshift Band-Aids to patching a ripped tent.
2. Take every opportunity you can get to dry your wet clothes and socks. If it's not raining, you can strap wet clothes to the outside of your backpack and they'll dry out while you're hiking. At night, you can slip a pair of wet socks or underwear into the bottom of your sleeping bag and they'll dry out while you're sleeping. When dealing with wet boots, pull out the insoles at night and place them in or under your sleeping bag. Removing them from your boots allows the moisture inside the boot to evaporate faster.
3. A great way to stay warm at night is to fill your water bottle with hot water and keep it in your sleeping bag with you. Hand warmers work well for this, too.
4. When camping in areas where you need to be extra vigilant—grizz country, stormy weather, etc.—sleep with your headlamp around your wrist like a bracelet. When you get startled awake or your tent collapses under the snow, you won't need to fumble around looking for it.
5. If there's a chance of snow where you're camping, don't leave your cooking gear and other odds and ends lying outside. Stash it under a tarp or in your tent's vestibule. There's nothing worse than kicking around in freshly fallen snow looking for a spoon that got covered under 12 inches of powder.

SURVIVAL GUNS

In a survival situation, you are far more likely to bag small game animals at close range than you are to take down a deer or other large game. However, the small-caliber firearms that we're recommending here can, in the right hands, be used to bring down virtually any animal.

A survival gun needs to be compact and lightweight so you can pack it around for days on end without it becoming an annoying burden. The most obvious choice is the .22 rimfire cartridge. The cartridges are so small that you can stuff a box of fifty of them in your pants pocket, yet they pack a punch. Poachers have been using .22s to kill whitetail deer for decades, so there should be little concern about efficacy. We've even seen domestic hogs and beef cattle dispatched with a single shot from a .22.

For general small-game hunting, shy away from solid-point bullets. On smaller thin-skinned animals, they can zip right through the body without expanding and doing the necessary damage for a quick kill. It's better to use standard 36-grain and 40-grain hollow-point bullets, which will usually kill small game animals even when shots are poorly placed. Unfortunately, these damage-inducing hollow-point bullets are nearly ineffectual on larger animals. To kill a deer or wild hog with a .22, you need to get deep penetration into the brain, heart, or lungs. Hollow-point bullets will break up upon impact with hide, bones, or muscle well before the vital organs are penetrated, and the resulting wounds are typically superficial.

Consider accuracy when choosing a .22. You and your rifle should be good enough to hit a quarter-sized target at 20 yards if you're planning on feeding yourself with small game. You need similar accuracy or better if you want to place lethal shots on larger animals. If you don't have it in you to achieve pinpoint accuracy, consider a small-bore shotgun such as a .410. Rather than a single projectile, shotguns fire a load of small pellets in a wide pattern that makes it much easier to hit small targets at close range. If you're good enough, you can also use a shotgun to hit moving targets like birds in flight and rabbits on the run. A good all-purpose shot size is #6. The downside with shotguns is that lethal distances are greatly reduced and there's little chance of toppling large animals unless you're close enough to damn near place the muzzle against their skull. A good way to increase the efficacy of shotguns for larger game is to buy some shells loaded with slugs or buckshot, but accuracy with these loads through compact-sized survival guns can be disappointing.

We'd be negligent if we didn't mention that you can get a .22 rifle and a .410 shotgun bundled together in a single survival gun from the firearm manufacturer Savage. The Model 42 Takedown can be disassembled in seconds and stuffed into a backpack or strapped to the outside of a pack without snagging on brush and getting in your way. However, the accuracy of this gun leaves a lot to be desired. The gun has a heavy trigger pull and the basic iron sights make precision aiming difficult. But it's a light and compact weapon, and the one-two punch of the rifle-shotgun combo helps overcome that negative.

For more on food acquisition strategies in the wild, see page 88.

AXES, HATCHETS, AND SAWS

Back in the old days, axes were crucial survival tools for professional fur trappers and mountain men. They used them for clearing horse trails, constructing rudimentary log cabins, and even fighting. They're still useful for plenty of work chores and certain labor-intensive pursuits such as beaver trapping and long-distance horse packing, but today axes have greatly reduced relevancy for outdoorsmen. It's simply not practical for most people to tote a heavy, long-handled axe around in the woods, and leave-no-trace ethics have largely evolved us away from needing the support of a full-blown axe. Most of us don't fell trees for firewood, don't stay put long enough to necessitate cabin or lean-to construction, and have never had to build a livestock corral in the mountains. What's more, axes do not lend themselves to casual use by neophytes. If you were born with an axe in your hands, like those fur trappers and mountain men of yore, then you know how to use one without gashing a hole through your shin. If you weren't, then you probably don't. Still, a stout axe can be a handy tool to have around at hunting camp or on canoe trips as long as they're used carefully.

But a smaller tool that's easier and safer to handle might be a better choice. Of the many things that can be done with an axe—breaking down moose carcasses, clearing trails, pitching makeshift tarp camps—most can be accomplished with a small packable hatchet or, even better, a packable saw. A favorite of ours is the Knives of Alaska Bone Saw, which can handle 6-inch-thick trees (see page 263 for instructions on how to safely bring one down) and just about anything else you throw its way. For you bargain hunters, we've got buddies who swear by a carpenter's saw called the Stanley Smoothcut, which will cost you less than a fourth of what the Knives of Alaska saw does.

SHOVELS

If you're car camping and you have the luxury of being able to pack plenty of gear, bring a shovel. Shovels are so damn useful it's impossible to list all the reasons you should bring one along. If your rig gets stuck in the snow or mud, you'll be able to dig yourself out. If there's a pesky rock sitting right in the middle of the one level spot to pitch your tent, you can pry it out of the ground. Other uses run from digging a trench around your tent as a way of keeping water out to extinguishing fires to unearthing worms for fishing bait. Hell, if you catch a fish, you can fry it over a fire on the same shovel blade you used to dig up your bait. Shovels are so damn handy that even on backpacking trips you might find it's worth bringing a small, collapsible version along.

SIX WHIPASS GEAR ITEMS

1. **Contractor trash bags.** These extra-thick, oversized trash bags are incredibly durable. We've used them for everything from emergency rain ponchos to game bags to ground cloths under our tents and sleeping bags. Stash one in the bottom of your backpack.
2. **Camp pillows.** When you're camping in the backcountry, using a rolled-up jacket as a pillow works well enough in a pinch. But if you really want a good night's sleep, get yourself a collapsible, blow-up camp pillow. They weigh next to nothing and pack down to the size of a tennis ball.
3. **Zip ties.** Throw half a dozen 8-inch plastic zip ties in your survival kit. They're small, strong, and have a multitude of attachment and repair uses.
4. **Puffy pants.** We initially started using puffy pants like First Lite's Uncompahgre as a cold-weather outer layer when we were sitting down glassing for animals for long periods of time. We liked them so much we started wearing them around camp, while we were ice fishing, and during any other periods of low physical exertion and cold temperatures.
5. **Insoles.** Not the shitty ones that come with your boots, but the quality aftermarket ones that take footwear to the next level in high-mileage, custom-fit comfort. It's hard to beat Superfeet brand insoles.

6. **Cam straps.** These fastening straps are made out of high-strength nylon or polyester webbing tipped with a locking spring-loaded buckle. Their most popular use is for securely strapping down frames to whitewater rafts, but we've used ones with lengths varying between 1 and 20 feet as makeshift belts for our pants, keeping coolers from shifting around in the back of a pickup, strapping elk quarters to a backpack and hanging them in trees, and as stringers for big fish like salmon.

SPECIALIZED GEAR

Certain environments, weather, and activities require specialized gear. It would be impossible to name every single gadget and doodad that could make life easier and more comfortable in every conceivable outdoor scenario, but the following lists contain the pieces of equipment we've most often used to adapt our own kits. Run through these lists when you're in the planning phases for trips that might involve the following conditions:

Cold weather and snow. Hand, toe, and body warmers for stationary activities; insulated face mask and ski goggles for high winds and blowing snow; insulated coveralls large enough to be worn over puffy pants and coat; two butt pads (one for butt padding, one to stand on); ventilated face mask to prevent icing up your goggles.

Hot weather and sun. Neck gaiter or buff for protecting neck and ears against sun; lightweight synthetic long-sleeved shirt or hoodie; lightweight synthetic convertible pants; Aquaphor; Body Glide; CamelBak bladder; hand-pump mister; bandana for sun protection; polarized sunglasses; umbrella.

Drenching rain. Waterproof boonie hat; Grundens or Helly Hansen rubberized commercial fishing rainwear; Atlas 620 PVC gloves for cool weather; Atlas 460 PVC gloves for cold weather; contractor garbage bag; closed-cell ground pad; zip-lock baggies to protect pocket contents; small sponges for drying gear, soaking up water, and wiping away condensation; umbrella.

In and around water. Hip boots or chest waders with wading belt: breathable nylon for warm weather or neoprene for cold weather;

wading boots; PFDs; float coats; PVC elbow-length gloves, insulated or uninsulated; neoprene whitewater booties; contractor garbage bags; waterproof cellphone case; microfiber towel; wetsuit or drysuit.

On ice. Ice creepers for your boots; ice safety spikes (used to pull yourself out of a hole if you fall in); lightweight spud for checking ice conditions; insulated PVC gloves; knee pads; felted wool boot insoles or closed-cell foam boot insoles.

STEVE'S PATENTED METHOD FOR PACKING AND UNPACKING

I try to make a ritual out of the process of packing before a trip, and the same goes for unpacking. My method takes longer, but in the end it saves you time by preventing you from dealing with the hassles of broken and forgotten gear.

The ritual begins when I start clearing off the large workbench in my garage a few days before my departure; a simple folding table set up in your basement or bedroom will do just as well. Once that's done, I'll begin laying out any items that I'm afraid of forgetting so that I can get them out of my head and move on to other things. Say I walk into my bedroom closet and notice a pair of wool-blend socks that landed in the wrong drawer after the last load of laundry was done. Onto the table they go, along with any new gear items ordered online that have yet to be organized into their proper bins or drawers. If there are items that I can't immediately pack—maybe because they're perishable, or because I need to borrow them, or because I haven't purchased them yet—I'll write them down on a notepad that I keep on the bench. Then, as the items accumulate on the workbench, I'll cross them off my list.

During the next phase, I begin tackling certain categories of gear and placing items in organized piles on the bench as I find the time. If I'm doing sleeping gear, I'll grab my ground cloth, sleeping pad, sleeping bag, bivy tarp, and tent all at once. A key component of my technique is checking the gear as I gather it, looking to make sure the proper stakes and guy lines are all in place. When it's time to tackle cooking gear, I'll gather my camp stove, pot, mug, and fuel, double-checking everything to make sure it's in good working condition. If I'm going big-game hunting and I need optics, I'll place my binoculars, bino harness, tripod, spotting scope, and lens cloth all together on the table. Soon I'll have most of my categories of gear squared away. For whatever reason, I always save my clothes for last, and I pack from outerwear to innerwear. Rain gear first, socks and underwear last. Once I've covered all of my categories, I pull up a master list of gear items that I keep on my computer. This list has many more pieces of gear than I'll ever use on a single adventure, but perusing it reminds me of anything that I might be missing. Once everything is in place, I then move my gear from the table into the appropriate duffels or backpack.

I take unpacking even more seriously than packing. I learned this from my dad, who was fond of two complementary mantras: "Take care of your gear, and your gear will take care of you" and "Take care of your gear before you take care of yourself." When I get home, I put my bags up on the bench and inspect everything as I unpack it. Clothes go into the laundry room, obviously, and everything that's fine goes back where it belongs, into labeled bins and drawers. Everything that needs to be repaired, adjusted, or specially cleaned goes to one end of my workbench, where it'll live until it gets the attention that it deserves. At this point, I also start up a new list of any gear items or accessories that I need to pick up before I head out again. I realize that this might come across as borderline OCD, but I think it's important to embrace that when it comes to outdoor gear. When my friends look at my organizational system and laugh at my obsessiveness, that's when I know that my system must be dialed in.

OTHER IMPORTANT GEAR

Given that a lot of outdoor gear is specific to certain activities, you'll find detailed information on the following items in their appropriate chapters:

First-aid kits: see page 346.
Hygiene essentials: see page 345.
Communication and electronics: see page 270.
Fishing gear: see page 116.
Snowshoes and skis: see page 293.
Canoes, kayaks, and other boats: see page 330.
Tents, tarps, sleeping bags, sleeping pads: see page 232.
Camp stoves and cookware: see page 83.
Water purification systems: see page 54.

CHAPTER 2

→→→≫≮≪←←

Water

I'VE HAD THE misfortune of being afflicted by at least two cases of "beaver fever," a cutesy term for an intestinal illness called giardiasis. It's a common ailment globally, often passed indirectly from human to human through fecally contaminated food. But in outdoor circles it's tightly associated with backcountry travel. You get it from ingesting microscopic parasites called *Giardia lamblia*, which can be transmitted into surface waters such as lakes and streams through the feces of muskrats and beavers. Around 20 percent of the people who contract it show no symptoms. For the rest of us, it's miserable. The bloating makes it feel like something's going to rupture in your gut. You get these unsettling burps that feel like a demon is trying to escape from your insides as a gassy apparition. The diarrhea is even worse. We're all familiar with the usual sense of relief that comes after a spasm of diarrhea, where you at least feel good for an hour or so. With giardiasis, the window of relief hardly lasts as long as it takes to wipe yourself clean of the bizarrely greasy excrement.

If it's so bad, one might ask, how did I allow myself to contract it twice? For the first occurrence, I'll blame nostalgia and stupidity. I was fifteen or so, and my brothers and I were out rabbit hunting a couple of miles from home in the middle of the winter. There's a nearby spot where one marsh drains into another through a small stream, and we used to cross this stream on a pile of logs and branches that someone had thrown across the water as a makeshift bridge. Standing on the bridge, I admired the beauty and clarity of the stream and got to thinking about all the movies I'd seen where cowboys and Indians and frontiersmen had satisfied their thirst by drawing deep gulps from similar looking water. Never in a million years would I have sipped water from the marsh just 100 yards upstream, but something about the fact that this water was *moving* made it seem appetizing. I drank my fill. Symptoms kicked in about twenty-four hours later.

For the second occurrence, I'll blame thirst. I was hiking in Arizona with some co-workers and had slept out overnight, without access to water for refilling our bottles. For dinner we had nothing but energy bars, which are notorious for making you thirstier than hell. By the time we scrambled our way down into a canyon bottom late the next morning, we were completely out of water. I filled my bottle from a stagnant pool and popped in a dose of water purification tablets. The water was cold and the tablets were slow to dissolve. Annoyed, I remember reaching into the quart-sized bottle with my Leatherman in an attempt to crush them up so they'd work faster. After crushing them, I shook the bottle like it was a cocktail mixer. You're supposed to wait thirty minutes for the tablets to do their work, but after ten minutes I decided that I just couldn't wait any longer. I was too damned thirsty and that water looked too damn good, even with the undissolved tablets still sloshing around inside. It took two days for me to get sick. I was in a hospital within a week.

It's fair to say that I had it coming the second time I got sick from giardia, and it's almost fair to say that I had it coming the first. Both incidents were preventable, as is the case in most parts of the developed world. Naturally occurring waterborne pathogens are most likely to afflict outdoor professionals and outdoor enthusiasts who willfully—and sometimes carelessly—expose themselves to the wilderness and all of its attendant risks. We have wonderfully advanced water treatment and sewage processes to thank for the fact that our water tends to be safer at home than it is outside. Such is not the case in the rest of the world, where many people simply do not have access to clean water. The United Nations Children's Fund, or UNICEF, estimates that waterborne pathogens kill 6,000 children every day. Usually it's the associated diarrhea that is fatal. If you include adults in the count, these diseases kill around 3.4 million people every year.

The statistics drive home the fact that you cannot afford to be lackadaisical about water treatment, whether you're camping close to home or traveling overseas. Nor can you be lackadaisical about water consumption. We need it, and lots of it. While Mahatma Gandhi famously went twenty-one days without food during India's freedom movement, just three or four days without water will kill a person. Extreme conditions of heat or physical exertion can reduce the timeline dramatically, so you'd be wise to read this chapter carefully. Knowing how to make a water plan, and what to do when that plan fails, might not be the sexiest survival skill in the world. But it's arguably the most important.

HOW MUCH DO YOU NEED?

The long-standing guideline for water intake is the old rule of eights: drink eight glasses of water per day, at around 8 ounces each. That comes out to a daily total of 64 ounces (a half-gallon). In reality this guideline should be regarded as the bare minimum. For active individuals, current recommendations call for three-quarters of a gallon of water for women and a full gallon for men. The point is that you should be drinking a lot of water, and that measuring your intake is a valuable thing to do. However, there is a high degree of variability when it comes to the amount of water any one individual might need in order to function at peak levels. Some people naturally need more water than others. Variations stem from many things, including our physical attributes and the fact that we sweat at different rates. We also derive different amounts of water from our diets. Fresh fruits and vegetables have a lot of water in them; jerky and Doritos, not so much. Still, when you're out in the woods, shooting for a goal of two 32-ounce Nalgene bottles per day is a great starting point that will help you avoid the nasty ramifications of dehydration. Keep this in mind even when you don't feel thirsty—or *especially* when you don't feel thirsty. Your own sense of thirst is a good indicator for when you need water, but it's not infallible. Sometimes you can deplete your internal fluid levels without actively feeling thirsty. That's especially true in cold weather, when your thirst response will be dimmed and the nearly frozen water in your backpack might not seem appealing. The lack of thirst signal doesn't mean that your body's water needs have somehow vanished. Although you won't be losing as much fluid through sweat evaporation, cold actually causes your metabolism to speed up, which in turn consumes more liquid. Keep drinking regardless of whether you're thirsty or not.

TRICKING YOURSELF INTO DRINKING MORE LIQUIDS

Sometimes, drinking water is a hassle. Maybe the creek you're drawing from has been stained brown by tannic acids from decaying leaves or hemlock trees and it's just not appetizing. Or the water is overloaded with natural sodium and it tastes bad. Or there's a dead deer floating in the lake and no amount of water purification can take your mind off it. Or you're just freezing your ass off and not feeling thirsty. If so, there are tricks for getting you motivated to hydrate. First off, forget the idea that coffee is always a diuretic. Strong coffee is, for sure, but it's been proven that the diuretic effects of weak and mid-strength coffee don't outweigh its hydration potential. In the morning, instant hot chocolate packets can also keep you drinking. Midday, go for Emergen-C packets, instant Gatorade packets, or other sports drink mixes formulated for hydration. Many of these products include electrolytes, vitamin C, and other useful minerals to replace those lost through sweat. These drinks can actually help with your body's liquid uptake, as well. Even just carrying a few lemons or limes in your pack can make a huge difference with off-tasting water. At night, after dinner, herbal or decaf teas will help you pound another cup or two. The Kobuk Coffee Co. in Anchorage, Alaska, makes a decaf version of their phenomenal Samovar tea that is so good it might lead to a shoot-out between you and your friends over who gets the last cup. Whatever route you take, keep this in mind: if it tastes good and makes you want to pound liquids of the nonalcoholic sort, do it.

DOING THE MATH ON YOUR PARTICULAR REQUIREMENTS

When we're calculating water needs for an excursion, we begin with a very rough estimate of 1 gallon per person per day. That's just for physical intake, and does not include water needed to bathe or wash dishes. As noted above, quantities of drinking water can vary quite a bit from person to person, and depending on exertion levels and conditions. If the ambient temperature is going to remain below 60°F or so, you may be able to get by on 64 ounces of drinking water per day, but as the temperatures rise, you'll need more. At 80°F, add an additional 32 ounces, and in extreme heat, you might need to double your normal intake. Next, consider how much you'll be exerting yourself. If your baseline is two 32-ounce Nalgene bottles of drinking water for a leisurely pace through gentle country in cool weather, what about hiking fast through steep, difficult terrain in hot weather? Keep this baseline in mind when making a plan.

There's also the issue of cooking. Mountain House and other freeze-dried or dehydrated meals require the addition of water. A typical freeze-dried meal needs about 16 ounces. When you add in instant oatmeal and coffee in the morning, there's another 12–16 ounces. So for a three-day backpacking trip (assuming you're having the first day's breakfast and the last day's dinner back in civilization) you need roughly 2 gallons of water to get you through. That's a lot of weight and bulk—about 17 pounds, and around a third of the capacity of many common backpacks that might be used for such a trip.

Thankfully, there are very few places where it's necessary to carry all of your water with you. You can usually source it along the way if you take certain precautions and plan properly. We'll cover everything you need to know about procuring safe water in the wild, but first we'll cover some tips and tricks for managing water.

WATER BOTTLES, BLADDERS, DROMEDARIES, AND JUGS

We're fans of the old-school Nalgene bottles for a streamlined water carrying and delivery solution. They're lightweight, reliable, and practically bombproof. They're also compatible with a wide variety of carriers, purification systems, and insulating pouches, and you can easily find new lids to replace any that get lost or cracked. Deciding between wide mouth and narrow mouth comes down to personal preference. Wide-mouth Nalgenes are good for dipping out water from ponds or streams and are more versatile for food prep and other uses. Narrow-mouth Nalgenes are easier to sip from while you're walking or driving without spilling a bunch of water down the front of your shirt. Thirty-two-ounce bottles are standard, but it's nice to have a 48-ounce bottle in your arsenal for when you can't decide between carrying one bottle or two. It might seem like a nitpicky distinction, but there are some folks who'd fight to the death over the superiority of a 48-ounce bottle. All of this isn't to say that the dozens of other bottles out there are useless. Plenty of folks like stainless steel for durability or aesthetics, and that's fine. There are even some purists out there who insist on using recycled soda bottles and brag when they get a year of use out of one. Just get something that doesn't leak and that can handle freezing and you're probably good to go.

THE HIGHLY DIVISIVE SUBJECT OF WATER BLADDERS

There is little consensus among the MeatEater crew about CamelBaks and similar hydration bladders that include a tube for drinking on the go. Some of us couldn't go without them for summer hikes and early season hunts, while others think they're just chintzy pieces of garbage that inevitably end up soaking your gear. Here are some things to consider as you formulate your own opinion.

Pros

- Hydration bladder valves can be rigged to your pack's shoulder strap, making them extremely convenient to drink from as you hike. That's a great way to continuously consume liquids throughout the day whenever you get even slightly thirsty, as opposed to only drinking when you stop and dig out a bottle. There's a creature comfort to keeping your mouth moist in hot, arid weather.
- Your water will stay cooler longer in hot weather inside your backpack than strapped to the side of it. Make sure to blow the water in the tube back into the bladder when you're done drinking so that your next sip isn't solar heated.
- Most bladders carry 100 ounces of water or more, and their efficient design keeps the weight close to your core while allowing pack space for lighter items farther away from your back.

Cons

- Bladders leak. The nylon or plastic bags can tear or pop if you lean against your pack the wrong way. The connection from the hose to the bladder can separate or crack. The threading on the lids makes it easy to accidentally cross-thread, causing the lid to leak. Any of these issues might result in your gear getting soaked, which could put you in real danger if it happened at the wrong time.
- Hoses freeze. Even though many CamelBaks come with a hose insulator, the water in the tube still won't stay liquid very long if the weather is at 32°F or below. Then you're stuck with a bag of inaccessible water and no good way to drink it.
- Lacking shape, bladders are much more challenging to pump water into than a rigid bottle. Even the folks who use them will usually carry a Nalgene as well, as a backup and for filtering/purifying water. They'll fill the bottle, transfer the water to the bladder, then repeat.

- If you don't have a stopper valve at the end of the hose (or don't use it), the pressure on your bladder in your backpack can cause the drinking nipple to leak. We've also seen the scenario where the drinking tube gets smooshed under a backpack in a tent or the back of a car and all of the water drains out and soaks everything around it.

DROMEDARIES

Dromedaries, or "droms," as we typically call them, are heavy-duty collapsible bags used for hauling large amounts of water into places where it will be unavailable, or for ferrying water from local sources to your campsite. One could make the argument that CamelBaks are simply droms with a drinking hose, but there are major distinctions. Good-quality droms are sturdily built, with fabric backings and heavy-duty lids. They lack the weak points of a hose connection, valve, and nipple. We don't use them all the time, but they are an amazing tool to have on backcountry or desert trips. If you're going out for a few days to a spot where you know you won't be able to find water, or if you need to move water from one location to another, droms are the way to go.

CAR CAMPING JUGS

Car camping (sleeping near or in your vehicle) simplifies your water storage situation, but there's still advance planning involved. Big, portable water jugs make life a lot easier. We like the plastic 6-to-8-gallon jugs that come with a spigot for easy pouring. From the standard $20 Aqua-Tainer to fancier metal models, these are a great creature comfort for easily washing hands and dishes off the tailgate, as well as providing the certainty that you'll always have extra water in the rig. Because the spigots are prone to breakage and leakage when tipped, there's an argument to be made for having just one jug with a spigot, and filling it using jugs with heavy-duty screw-on lids. Bear in mind that no water supply is inexhaustible. For a weeklong campout in Baja, for instance, a 7-gallon Aqua-Tainer would barely cut it for one person—and that's not even counting the water needed for dishes or bathing. You might as well overdo it on water when you're car camping, since space and weight are less of an issue. And go ahead and keep a jug of water in your car or truck all through the hot summer months, even when you're not headed out into the wild. There's no downside to being prepared.

CACHING WATER

It's a common practice among desert rats of the Southwest to cache water in their favorite backcountry spots in order to facilitate longer stays. In advance of an extended camping trip or an attempt to bag a dry peak, you might haul in a few backpack loads of collapsible water jugs and then hide them somewhere where only you can find them. If you're going to leave a water cache for more than a week or so, especially if the jugs are baking in the sun, you'll want to treat it so it doesn't go skunky. Products like the ION Alkaline Water Drops both purify water and also increase the pH or alkalinity of water to prevent bacteria and other bad stuff from growing in the container. It would really suck to go to all that effort only to find your stash has gone bad in the interim. It would also suck if you didn't retrieve your jugs and left them to litter up the landscape. If you pack them in, pack them out!

HOW TO KEEP YOUR WATER FROM FREEZING

The coldest weather of the year, and many of the nastiest storms, often seems to coincide with the window for prime hunting conditions. Cold weather shouldn't keep you from going out, and it's a prerequisite for ice fishing. But it does present certain difficulties, not the least of which is keeping your water in liquid form. Vacuum-sealed thermoses do the job for short-term day use, especially if you fill them up with hot water. But they tend to be bulky and heavy, with thick walls that cut down on capacity. A good first step toward keeping your conventional water from freezing is to strategically pack it inside your backpack so that it's insulated by surrounding gear and extra clothes. It'll generally freeze much quicker when strapped to the outside of your pack. A handful of companies make insulated water bottle holders with zippered lids that go a long way toward keeping your water drinkable. On cold nights, it works really well to tuck your water bottles alongside your sleeping bag to keep them from freezing. On *really* cold nights, fill your bottles with hot water and place them inside your sleeping bag, by your feet. You'll reap the dual benefit of toasty toes and drinkable water.

WATERBORNE PATHOGENS

Urban water supplies in the first world aren't immune from incidents of industrial contamination, a susceptibility recently exemplified in Flint, Michigan, during the lead contamination crisis. Despite our advanced water treatment facilities, there have been occurrences of viral and microbial agents contaminating urban water supplies as well. In 1993, a cryptosporidium outbreak in Milwaukee sickened 400,000 people. On occasion, hepatitis A and noroviruses have entered municipal water supplies through stormwater runoff, or they've infected recreational waters through the vector of sick swimmers.

In this chapter, however, we'll be focusing on the parasitic and bacterial contaminants you're likely to contract from natural sources of drinking water such as streams, rivers, ponds, and lakes. In the section that follows, we'll explain how to treat your water to avoid the intestinal fates described below. But first, let's get into it. To put it simply, these pathogens are passed along through shit from wild animals, livestock, or humans. There are only a few of them, but they can cause serious trouble.

Giardiasis. Transmitted through human or animal feces, giardiasis (commonly known as giardia) is the most ubiquitous parasitic intestinal infection on the planet. It's extremely common in natural outdoor water sources, and it can be found in municipal water supplies in the developing world as well. Typically found in lakes, rivers, ponds, streams, and water systems in which human or animal waste has been introduced, the microscopic *Giardia lamblia* parasite (the specific species of *Giardia* that can infect humans) can also be present in uncooked fruits and vegetables that have been washed in contaminated water or grown in contaminated soil. Living part of its life cycle as a spore with a protective shell, the protozoa can survive outside human or animal intestines (on bathroom surfaces, for instance, as well as in water) for long periods of time. As few as ten cysts have been shown to produce infection. Also known as "beaver fever" due to the large rodent's habit of using ponds, rivers, and lakes as both homestead and toilet, the diarrhea-inducing ailment that results from the ingestion of the spores can easily lay waste to a backcountry trip and may result in longer-lasting intestinal damage.

Symptoms of giardiasis usually show up one to two weeks after exposure, but as mentioned earlier, we've seen them show up the next day. The effects include moderate to severe nonbloody diarrhea, bloating, flatulence, greasy stools that float, abdominal cramps, and those crazy burps that seem to come from deep in your guts. The worst symptoms will often work themselves out in two to four weeks, but 30–50 percent of acute cases progress to chronic giardiasis, which can result in several weeks' worth of malnutrition, anemia, and other problems digesting food. Beaver ponds are a notoriously poor choice for drinking water, but lots of other animals can be carriers of giardia, so make sure to look for good places to source water. Always wash or disinfect your hands after relieving yourself and before eating or cooking to reduce human-to-human spread. Use extra caution around hygiene if a member of your group falls ill, but always beware, as many people infected with giardia will never develop symptoms even though they can still pass it along to others.

Although the infection may clear on its own, a course of antibiotics is generally recommended. If you've contracted giardiasis, your outdoor adventure is not going to be fun. The symptoms are going to get worse before they get better, and riding them out in a tent is misery. Get to a hospital or clinic, where they'll likely hit you with a thrice-daily dose of metronidazole for a week or more to help you get better faster.

Chlorine and iodine are effective disinfectants for bacteria, viruses, and most protozoan cysts, but they are not regarded as entirely effective against giardia. Water filters work well, as the protozoa are fairly large and easy to separate; boiling and UV light purifiers are also effective.

Cryptosporidium. Commonly known as "crypto," this microscopic protozoan parasite can live and reproduce in human and animal intestinal tracts. Like giardia, it is passed through fecal matter. Symptoms of crypto usually show up a week after exposure. These include nonbloody diarrhea, stomach cramps, nausea, vomiting, and fever. People with compromised immune systems may develop a more serious and difficult-to-treat iteration of the illness.

If crypto is left untreated, its effects usually pass within two weeks for healthy adults. But that might be the worst two weeks of your life, especially if you're way out in the woods. If you think you've ingested crypto, you're going to want to see a doctor. The antibiotic nitazoxanide will typically remove the infection in five days.

Cryptosporidium can survive on surfaces and be transmitted through the consumption of contaminated raw fruits and vegetables as well as contaminated water. A single bowel movement can contain millions of highly infectious crypto parasites, so hygiene is key. The protozoa's thick outer shell makes them particularly resilient to chemical purification methods such as chlorine and iodine. Filter or boil water to eliminate risk of crypto. Thoroughly cooking any food that might have come into contact with bad water is important, too.

Escherichia coli. The primary cause of "traveler's diarrhea," these bacteria, synonymous with fecal matter, can enter rivers and streams through direct contamination or through stormwater runoff. Many strains are harmless, but a few varieties (particularly those living in the guts of ruminant animals such as cattle, goats, sheep, deer, and elk) produce toxins that can make you very sick.

Symptoms show up one to ten days after exposure, including nonbloody diarrhea, stomach cramps, vomiting, and sometimes fever. In the small percentage of cases that develop into the life-threatening complication hemolytic uremic syndrome (HUS), fatigue and a decreased frequency of urination may signal potential kidney failure. Caused by a specific type of invasive *E. coli*, HUS is usually signaled by bloody diarrhea, fever, and severe dehydration which can result in anemia, blood-clotting problems, and kidney failure.

Most *E. coli* infections clear up on their own. Antibiotic therapy is not usually required, as the illness is self-limited. But you definitely should seek medical care if you are feverish or are passing very little urine or dark urine, if diarrhea lasts longer than ten to fourteen days, or if you're running a fever higher than 102°F. Blood in the stool, excessive vomiting, and inability to keep liquids down are other indicators that you may be seriously sick.

As per always, purify water and practice good hand hygiene, especially before eating. *E. coli* can be eliminated with chlorine and iodine treatment, boiling, and water filters.

TREATING WATER

If you spend any time at all out of doors, methods for treating water are mandatory skills. These are not difficult tasks to learn, but some include a degree of nuance that could mean the difference between killing all the parasites in your water and killing *most* of the parasites in your water. It's valuable to have at least a passing understanding of several means of treatment, so that you have a backup when a fancy treatment device fails.

Many outdoors experts draw a distinction between water filtration and water purification. Filtration involves forcing water through microscopic pores that catch and remove parasitic cysts like giardia and cryptosporidium, bacteria like *E. coli,* mud, muck, bad flavors, and debris. The pores on most filters, however, are not small enough to capture tiny viruses.

Water purification, on the other hand, disrupts the DNA of microorganisms, effectively killing parasitic cysts (giardia, cryptosporidium), bacteria (*E. coli*, salmonella), and viruses like norovirus, hepatitis A, and rotavirus. The process can be accomplished using chemicals, ultraviolet light, or boiling. Though purification renders these potential pathogens inert, it does not remove them, nor does it typically remove any suspended particles in the water or do much to change its flavor. Note that in the unlikely event that natural water sources were to be contaminated by the virus that causes COVID-19, purification would take care of it, too.

Purification is clearly the preferred method, as it destroys most if not all pathogens. But it is worth noting that none of us has ever gotten sick from water that we filtered. While viruses can be found in water anywhere, they are a much less common source of water contamination than giardia or crypto, which can be dealt with through filtering or boiling. It's also worth noting that while filters are functional and safe for wilderness use, they may not be suitable for travel in the developing world, where water may be compromised by human waste or pollution. In a best-case scenario, you can use both methods at once—purification and filtration—in order to kill microorganisms and filter out off-tasting particulates.

WATER FILTERS

There's a mind-boggling array of water filtration products marketed for the outdoors, from pumps to straws, squeeze bags, gravity filters, and more. While the mechanics vary, all filters function by forcing water through the microscopic pores of the filter's internal element, which is usually made of ceramic, activated carbon, or a combination of both.

The process removes particles and bad flavors from water that simple purification will not. This includes mud, silt from glaciers, tannins from trees and leaves, algae, and whatever else might be suspended in your drink. Filtering will make water look and taste better, though it may not take away every hint of foulness. This feature of filters may make them a better choice than purifiers in desert or backcountry situations (away from any chance of human waste) where you are likely to find muddy, goopy, or stagnant water.

Filters will only work for so long, as the gunk that they remove from the water will eventually clog up the pores of their filtration element. This is their major downside, but it can be remedied in part through smart usage of your device. Many filtering apparatuses involve a pre-filter that removes larger particles before they hit the delicate filtering element; the foam ball that is affixed to the intake of some pumping mechanisms is one example of a pre-filter. Make sure to use your pre-filter and clean it between uses. If your filter doesn't include one, there are certain situations in which you might consider adding one of your own. We've had to draw water out of mucky, pissy elk wallows when there was no other option available, and in situations like that you'll want some extra filtration power. Simply wrapping a T-shirt or bandana over the mouth of the bottle you're going to use for dipping water will remove some of the particulates that might clog up the works. When filtering turbid water, it's also a good idea to allow the sediment to settle to the bottom of a container before passing the water through a filter. When filtering water from glacial rivers, it's common practice to let the water settle overnight in a bucket before pumping it.

Upon returning from a trip, follow your filter's instructions for back-flushing, the process of running clean water through the element in the reverse direction to remove clogged particulates. After you back-flush, make sure to allow the filter to drain and dry before packing it away again so bacteria or mold don't grow on it between trips. Water inside a filter can also freeze in cold weather, rendering the filter useless; while it's not in use, keep it in your tent or near your body to ensure that it stays functional.

Pump filters. Of all the water treatment methods, lots of outdoors people will have the greatest familiarity with the pump-style filters that screw onto the top of a Nalgene water bottle. For many of us, the mere sight of one of these pumps brings on vivid memories of sitting on slippery rocks for an uncomfortably long period of time while pumping water from a creek. As long as you replace the filtering element every year or two and keep the hoses clean, pump filters manufactured by companies such as Katadyn or MSR can last a decade or more. Since there are no perishable chemicals or batteries involved, you can tuck one of these into your boat box or bug-out bag and trust that it'll be ready for use when you are. An important thing to keep in mind with pump filters is that they have an input hose and an output hose. Do not mix these hoses up or allow water to pass between them, as you could be introducing unfiltered water into the hose that is supposed to deliver clean water to your bottle. It's a good idea to pump a few ounces of water onto the ground or back into the creek before you start filling your bottle in order to reduce the likelihood of cross contamination.

Straw-style filters. The LifeStraw products and other, similar filters are simple devices that use mouth suction to draw the water through the element. You place one end in the water, the other in your mouth, and you pull. They're small, compact, and simple, and can be a real lifesaver in an emergency. This kind of tool, however, would be no replacement for a bulk water treatment device. Imagine having to bend over a creek and use a considerable amount of mouth suction every time you wanted to take a sip of water. Or being reduced to filling a pouch of freeze-dried food with water that you had to suck up and spit into the bag. Not only is it a pain in the ass, it's decidedly unappetizing. Straw-style filters shouldn't be your primary filtration tool, but they're great as backup or emergency filters.

Squeeze filters. The Sawyer Squeeze filter and others like it were all the rage a few years ago. The appeal is obvious: fill up a bag, screw it onto a filter, then sit on it or squeeze it to pass the filtered water through to your bottle. They're small, compact, and hoseless, and they cost less than half the price of most pump filters. The trouble is that these low-cost filters don't last long. It would be difficult to pre-filter water going into the bag, so any suspended particles in the water you draw go straight into the main filter element, which causes it to clog rather quickly. Also, the strain on the relatively weak vinyl bag from repeated squeezing can lead to failure of the bags. Like the straw filters, these are best reserved for emergencies—not used as your main water procurement apparatus.

Gravity filters. This filtering style usually involves running water from one large receptacle to another, using gravity and a siphoning effect to force the water through an in-line filter between the bags. You can buy a ready-made version, or make your own by placing a straw or squeeze-style filter between two CamelBak or Platypus droms. The method has emerged as a favorite for supplying water for large groups, as it's handy for filtering and dispensing water in bulk. It's very important to always designate one drom for dirty water and one for clean, and to never get them mixed up. Assuming you've got that rule down pat, setup is a cinch: after you've dipped the dirty water bag in a nearby stream, you can simply hang the apparatus in a tree and come back to fill up water bottles as needed.

WATER PURIFIERS

Since filters don't remove every single particle and microorganism from water, many people choose to purify their water instead. Purification will kill pretty much all bacteria, protozoan cysts, viruses, and fungi that can be found in water, but most purification devices and chemicals do not actually "remove" anything from the water. Harmful parasites will be rendered inert, but they're still in the mix. So are the mud, funky flavors, and dead bugs. If you're drawing dirty water from the only place you can find it, it still can be valuable to filter or pre-filter water before purifying it and drinking it.

Ultraviolet light purifiers. We love the Steripen. Unless you've spent hours upon hours bent over a tiny spring pumping water through a clogged filter, it's hard to appreciate how damn nice it is to just quickly zap a bottle full of water with ultraviolet light. These devices certainly were game changers when they appeared in the late nineties, although they're not without their downsides. They function by emitting germicidal short-wave ultraviolet light that disrupts the DNA sequences within microorganisms, thereby rendering them inert and harmless. UV light is very commonly used in commercial water treatment, and the Steripen's manufacturers claim that the devices kill 99.9999 percent of bacteria, 99.99 percent of viruses, and 99.9 percent of parasites.

To use it, you simply insert the batteries in the right direction, remove the light protector, then turn the device on. Usually you'll have to wait a few seconds while it primes. When it's ready, you place the tip into a full water bottle or container to activate the UV. Stir the water gently with the tip of the pen until it automatically turns off, signaling that the water has been treated. Make sure to clean the lip and threads of the bottle too by screwing on the lid, inverting the bottle, and then slightly unscrewing the lid to let a little bit of clean water run through.

Since this purification method depends on the emission of light, the water needs to be clear enough to allow the passage of its rays. If your available water is exceptionally muddy or silty, pre-treat it by straining it through T-shirt fabric or some other basic filter to sieve out some of the particulates. If the water is still murky, treat less of it at once, and double-treat the water if you think it's necessary.

As much as we love them, there are downsides to UV purifiers. Batteries can die or corrode. That usually takes a long time, but the burn rate can be accelerated in cold weather. Also, while you can be very confident in the safety of the water you treat, it will not look or taste any different than when you scooped it up. This could be a problem on trips to places where the only water comes from stagnant and nasty-tasting pools.

Treating with sunlight. The water treatment principle employed by Steripens also applies to the original source of ultraviolet light: the sun. Many communities in the developing world treat their drinking water with sunlight, and to great effect. To follow their lead, all you need is a clear, sealable bottle and a lot of sun. Once the sunlight's UV rays have destroyed bacteria, viruses, and parasites, you should be able to drink straight from the bottle.

Unfortunately, the sunlight treatment isn't the most time-efficient or broadly useful method for purifying water. Even in hot, bright conditions, most guidelines recommend leaving the bottle in direct sunlight for six hours at a minimum, and preferably for a whole day. If the water has any turbidity or there are clouds in the sky, two days' worth of exposure is preferred. Experts also warn that this technique is not effective under 35°F. Keep in mind, too, that it requires a clear water bottle—aluminum won't work. As with many of the backup techniques described throughout this book, this one should be regarded as a plan C rather than a plan A or B.

Iodine, chlorine, and other chemical purification. Chemicals for making water potable have been in use for a very long time. Many survival and first-aid kits still come with a few tablets of Potable Aqua or the like. It's always a good idea to have a few squirreled away for emergencies. These tablets are easy, cheap, packable, lightweight, and effective as a form of backup treatment.

Neither iodine nor chlorine (the chemicals used in most of these tablets) will kill cryptosporidium. Chlorine dioxide (present in some water treatment tablets) has been approved for the parasite, but it takes over four hours to complete the task. That can feel like eons when you're thirsty. Even the much shorter timeline of thirty minutes to an hour recommended for treatment time with iodine or chlorine tablets isn't ideal. An hour may not be a big deal if you're sitting around camp with several bottles and easy access to water, but it could be a pain in the ass if you're really thirsty.

Finally, iodine or chlorine can make your water taste pretty nasty. Some people are okay with this; many are not. Luckily, most modern iodine tablets come with a stabilizing agent that will remove some of that nasty chemical taste. But it never disappears entirely. Some people also report skin irritation from using iodine or chlorine for more than a few days in a row, so it's probably best to save these chemicals for emergency situations.

Boiling. Last but certainly not least, boiling is perhaps the most reliable method for purifying water. Even if all you could scrounge up was a tin can and a match, you could make water safe to drink. We rarely go into the woods for more than a day without a little stove and pot, which are great for making freeze-dried meals and drinks but also serve as an incredibly effective backup purifier. This is always a good thing to remember when your pump filter gums up or your Steripen batteries die.

Most guidelines recommend bringing water to a raging boil for at least a full minute before drinking. If you're at altitude in the mountains, above 7,000 feet elevation or so, that boil time needs to be three minutes or more to kill all possible bacteria, viruses, and parasites.

In the winter, this is sometimes the only purification method we employ. If all the water in an area is frozen or locked up in snow, boiling may be the only way to free water from its solid form. You can put snow or ice chunks straight into your pot to thaw, although dumping in a little water does help facilitate the process. You'll need to continue to pack snow into the pot as it melts, especially with powder snow, as it takes up a lot of space considering the paltry amount of water it actually gives off.

When rehydrating freeze-dried or dehydrated food, boiling makes a lot of sense as a purification strategy since you need to heat the water regardless. There's little sense in purifying the water and then boiling it as well. We'll often dip our cook pot straight into a stream next to camp, boil it well, and pour the water straight into our Mountain House meals rather than using up previously purified or filtered water. However, boiling can be less valuable as a means of making drinking water. Purifying a meaningful volume of water requires a lot of time and fuel, as well as a large cooking pot, then a bit of patience as the water cools to drinkable temperature.

FINDING WATER

The need to plan ahead in order to prevent or circumvent emergencies in the outdoors is a theme we'll be hammering home throughout the pages of this book. And when it comes to hydration, adequate planning is a must. If you're going to spend several days in the outdoors, it's wise to study area maps and satellite imagery beforehand—this will come in handy for a variety of reasons, from knowledge about water sources to the navigation tips we'll be discussing in a few chapters. Even if you're confident that you can carry in or filter all the water you need, take a look at some maps. Bottles and droms break, filters clog, Steripen batteries die. To put it another way: shit happens.

FINDING WATER USING MAPS

Paper USGS quad maps are useful for identifying springs and watercourses, both perennial and seasonal. Use the key below to familiarize yourself with the topographical legends indicating water sources:

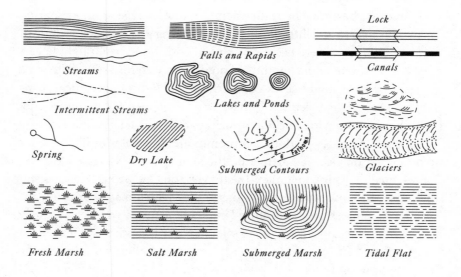

Be cautious, however, about trusting dotted lines that demarcate seasonal or ephemeral streams, which may not be running during the drier months of the year. Also know that there may be water sources that aren't marked on the map; a basic knowledge of topography is helpful for finding them.

In one way or another, water formed most of the land features around us. Even if you don't see a thin blue line on your map coursing down a canyon, that canyon was very likely formed by erosion and may still have water in it. Springs and ponds are surprisingly abundant in the mountainous and temperate areas of North America, so much so that not all of them will appear on the map. Look for the places where the topographic lines form V-shapes pointed uphill. This indicates a crease in the landscape—a gully, valley, fold, hoodoo, coulee, wash, canyon, and so on. If water is present, that's where it might be. To narrow your search even further, look for places where those topo line V-shapes end near the top of a gully or wash. If there's a hidden spring or seep, that's where it is— especially if you can find such a place within a mountain bowl or cirque. Also look for points where the topo lines in gullies space out, which indicate a gentle slope or flat spot. Water may collect here and pool. Any prominent depression or hole, especially in desert coulees, may be a place where you can find water left over after a flash flood. For more on how to read a topo map, see pages 278–281.

Satellite imagery has its own value for locating water, although it shouldn't be regarded as a replacement for topo maps. Major water sources could be hiding beneath a dense canopy of vegetation, rendering them invisible to satellites. Plus satellite imagery is just a snapshot in time. If the images were taken during a historic flood, you might have a grossly inaccurate understanding of how much water is around during a drought cycle. It might seem counterintuitive, but topographical maps give a more accurate picture of what's actually happening on the ground. Still, there's the obvious upside of being able to visually identify water using satellite images, and it's common to identify water or likely places to find water on Google Earth or on the digital app onX maps that aren't represented on your paper map. The tilt view on Google Earth allows you to look at the landscape from various angles, which may help you identify pools, depressions, and other landscape features where water may collect. The onX app allows you to select a water layer that can help identify seeps and springs. Even if you can't see the water, you can use the imagery to identify likely locations. Vegetation is usually concentrated around water. If you can see a line of trees or shrubs in an otherwise barren landscape, there's a good chance there's water in there—or at least there's a good chance it's there sometimes. If you can see more grass or greener grass in one coulee over the rest, that's a good clue. The presence of willows or cottonwoods is very promising.

For more on how to use these tools in a navigation context, see page 270.

FINDING WATER WITHOUT A MAP

When you're trying to find water on foot, the same principles apply. Look for trees and concentrated vegetation. If you're at the head of a drainage and find that it's dry, travel downstream or downhill in search of water. Chances are good that you'll find larger and less ephemeral water sources. If you're at the low end of a drainage and find that it's dried up, don't rule out the possibility of heading upslope or upstream toward the source as you search for exposed water. When looking for water in rocky streambeds, stop to listen for the trickling of underground water beneath the streambed's surface. Oftentimes, water can be easily found simply by flipping some stones out of the way. Inspect likely spots such as shaded rock basins or the crooks in a tree's roots for residual water that didn't drain away or soak into the sand and gravel. Rock basins can range in dimension from the size of a car to the size of a shot glass. No matter the location, north- and east-facing slopes and drainages will likely hang on to their water longer than south-facing basins that get blasted by summer sun.

Also look for seeps—places where water may leak or trickle out of the rock or sand. These can be found at the bases of cliffs, the mouths of caves, the heads of coulees, or deep saddles on mountain ridgelines. The most obvious visual cue to the presence of a seep is bright green algae growing around it or an unusual profusion of grasses or shrubs. Seeps may only leak out mere drops at a time, and may be angled such that you can't get a bottle lip under the flow. In such cases, you can sometimes dig out an area beneath the seep to collect the water by creating a small pool called a settlement bowl. Line the "bowl" with rocks or mud so that the water won't drain out, then let the water pool up as any sediment settles to the bottom. Try to drink off the top without stirring up the bowl.

If all else fails and you can't find standing or flowing water anywhere, locate major bends in dry riverbeds and check the outside edges of the bends. That's where water will be the deepest when the drainage is full, and it's the most likely spot to find subsurface water when the river is dry. If you are able, find soft, substrate-like sand toward the end of areas that look like they would be pools or deep holes when the valley is flooded. Dig down as deep as you can go. If you don't find increased moisture, keep moving. When you do find sand or dirt that feels wet, leave a depression for a few minutes; a small pool of water may form, and you should be able to scoop some out with your hands. If that doesn't work, you may also be able to hold a double handful of wet sand and dirt above a bottle and squeeze out the moisture; if time allows and you have the right materials on hand, you can also construct the solar still described on page 63. We'll make no bones about it: drinking nasty muddy desert water in an emergency situation is not going to be pleasant and might make you sick, but it's better than dying of thirst.

You can also use the presence of animals as an indication of likely water sources. In a dry landscape, cattle, sheep, and horses are rarely too far from a place where they can drink, whether from a spring or from the man-made catchments lovingly known as "guzzlers." Look for prominent livestock trails, especially routes where several trails converge. Deer, elk, pronghorn, bighorn sheep, and other dry-ground ungulates will roam, but they still need to drink water on a daily basis. If you spot some big game, you might be able to track or follow them to see where they go to drink in the evening. These critters move throughout the landscape in a deliberate way, so if you see a well-worn trail descending into a gully, there's probably a pretty good reason.

Smaller animals can be telltale signs of proximity to water as well. Red-wing and yellow-headed blackbirds are rarely far from standing water and cattails. Frogs and toads must hatch and grow in water, so their presence is a dead giveaway. Generally speaking, all life on earth requires water to some degree, so any increased concentration of animals or animal sign should indicate that the life-giving liquid is nearby.

PLACES WHERE YOU CAN RISK DRINKING UNFILTERED WATER

Filtration, purification, or boiling are always smart practices, as there's no way to be certain that any surface water is 100 percent safe. However, some water sources are safer than others. If you're in a situation where you cannot purify water, do your best to get it from one of the following spots:

Springs at the source. Water bubbling up out of the ground is usually coming straight from the aquifer. It is safe to drink it straight in most instances. However, we've encountered situations where we see water that appears to be bubbling clean and clear out of the ground, only to go farther uphill and encounter a series of mucky elk wallows that drain directly into the area of the spring. Just because water is coming out of the ground in one place doesn't mean that's the source. To be completely sure, keep walking uphill until you either reach the top, hit a cliff, or stop finding water.

Glacial high-elevation streams. Many folks in the outdoors community have long believed that drinking meltwater coming straight out of a glacier is a safe practice. Many of us have done it numerous times without consequences. The thinking is that since the glacial ice has been frozen for thousands of years, any bad bacteria would have died off long ago. However, new research indicates that fecal bacteria and other harmful microorganisms can actually be preserved for a very long time in ice. One study found traces of *E. coli* and fecal enterococci in a river flowing out of an Alaskan glacier. Drinking untreated glacial meltwater is only practical if you accept the risks or have no means of purification.

Rainwater. Because precipitation is created by evaporation of water vapor into clouds that later release the moisture, it is generally free of contaminants. Though there are many historical examples of "acid rain" picking up a high pH from industrial pollutants, this is much less of a problem now than it once was. Rain can also pick up atmospheric chemicals like sulfur dioxide from smog, a bigger concern in urban and industrial environs than out in remote areas. The upshot is that if you need water, droplets falling straight from the sky and into your mouth aren't going to hurt you. Neither are they going to quench your thirst, however. Rainwater must be collected somehow to be of much use, and that collection point is the spot where it can be compromised. A concave rock with a pool of rainwater might have had a bird come by and poop in it. Your handmade tarp catchment system is only as clean as the tarp with which you're building it. If you can control such factors, however, you can drink rainwater.

Use whatever materials you have for collection. Tent flies, ground cloths, and even your cooking pots can catch enough water during a downpour to keep you going. Better yet, position rain flies or even rain jackets in such a way that they funnel rainfall into your bottle or pot. It's amazing how much water an 8-foot tarp can catch during a short burst of rain.

Snow. Most of the same considerations and factors apply to snow. It is relatively safe to drink once melted, but you should still carefully consider the snow before you go for it. If you look closely at the top layer of any snow that is more than a day old, you'll notice a good amount of dirt, soot, pollen, insects, and general tree gunk. Dig down a little ways and you'll often find virgin flakes that are perfectly fine to drink or eat. But remember, snow accumulates incrementally, so you'll often find layers a ways down that were once on the surface, collecting particles that you might not want to ingest. When in doubt, filter or purify.

There's a common belief that eating snow will actually dehydrate you because your body expends energy to melt it. Melting snow in your mouth does burn calories, but not enough to make a significant difference in your hydration levels. It wouldn't be a great idea if you're already hypothermic, as it might lower your body temperature. And given that snow is mostly air, you'll need a lot of it to get an appreciable amount of drinking water. All things considered, the most efficient way to hydrate using snow is to melt it into water before taking it in. But under normal circumstances, eating snow can be quite refreshing.

WATER STRATEGIES FOR DESPERATE SITUATIONS

Hopefully, following the strategies we've discussed throughout this chapter will prevent you from winding up in a desperately thirsty situation. But it's better to be safe than sorry, so it's a good idea to familiarize yourself with the following emergency water strategies.

RATIONING WATER

Say you get turned around while hiking through some confusing canyon country. You have a quart of water in your pack but no obvious source for more. It could be two days until you get found or find your way out. What do you do?

It's smart to make a plan around how you'll stretch out and maximize your dwindling supply of liquid. Start by realistically estimating a reasonable timeframe for getting out or getting found. Then divide the number of hours by the approximate number of ounces or sips of water you have left. If you take a half-ounce sip every hour, you could make your water last more than forty-eight hours. Or you could take a 1-ounce sip for every daylight hour. However the math adds up, make a plan and stick to it. But don't try to skip too many drinks. In his seminal memoir *Desert Solitaire*, the naturalist author Edward Abbey writes about rangers in Arches and Canyonlands national parks who would sometimes find lost hikers dead of dehydration, with water still in their bottles. Conserve water in dire situations, but not so enthusiastically that it kills you.

SKILL: MAKE A SOLAR STILL

The concept behind moisture traps or solar stills dates back to pre-Incan days in South America, when villagers would arrange branches and leaves into funnel shapes to collect condensation. The capture of moisture and evaporation is now used on a community-wide scale in parts of the world where clean water is not easy to come by but sunlight is abundant.

The basic, modern survivalist design of a solar still involves digging a shallow pit in the dirt and placing an empty cup or container in the very bottom. If vegetation is available, arranging a pile of branches or leaves around the container in the pit will collect extra moisture as the vegetation dries out. To create a closed environment in which condensation can collect, lay down a plastic sheet, tarp, emergency blanket, or garbage bag to completely cover the hole. Place large rocks around the edges to keep the plastic secure. Finally, set one small rock in the center of the plastic over the hole, denting the plastic to cre-

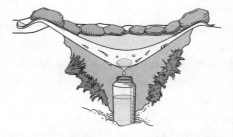

Collect condensation in a shallow covered pit.

ate a 45° downward curve, with the rock resting directly above the container.

As the sun hits the plastic and heats the uncovered dirt and plants beneath it, it will cause any moisture present in the plants and soil to evaporate and rise as water vapor. As the water condenses on the underside of the plastic, it will begin to run down and drip into your cup. That cup isn't going to be overflowing anytime soon, but if you have time to leave it unattended all day or overnight (when cooler temperatures cause even more water condensation), you might collect enough water to slake your thirst for a while. If you have some tubing (the end of a CamelBak hose, for instance), running it down into your cup will allow you to drink out of your still without dismantling it.

You can also supplement water in the soil and vegetation by adding untreated water into your pit. This method can be used to desalinate salt water or even pull potable water from urine. Simply pour untreated water into the pit (either in a separate container or directly onto the soil) before covering it. The sun's rays, intensified as they pass through the plastic, will evaporate the liquid, leaving behind pollutants, bacteria, salts, and minerals while dripping clean, pure water into your catchment.

COLLECT WATER FROM PLANTS

Like most living things, plants are made up mostly of water. Some are over 90 percent water by weight—enabling human beings to regularly take in about a quarter of our hydration requirements without even thinking about it, just by eating our fruits and vegetables. Some mammals rarely drink water at all, acquiring all the hydration they need from their diet of leafy greens. Gorillas are the classic example, but that's true of numerous species. If you can find edible plants (see page 91), you'll be able to simultaneously cover some of your calorie and water needs.

But you can also derive water from inedible plants. Several species of vines can be severed and tapped for water, and some cacti have water reservoirs hidden within the plant. Even in varieties without this reservoir, if you can get past the spines and thick skin, the meat inside will contain a lot of moisture that you can wring and squeeze out into a bottle. The same technique will work with other large, thick desert plants such as agave and aloe.

USING A TRANSPIRATION BAG

In addition to eating or squeezing the water out of plants, you can also take advantage of the plants' transpiration. If you have any sort of plastic bag, find a leafy plant in direct sunlight and place a few of the live, attached branches and leaves inside the bag. Tie the opening tightly around the limb, trying to make the bag as airtight as possi-

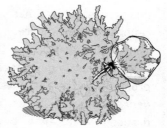

Transpiration bag

ble. As the sun heats the bag, it causes water to evaporate from the leaves (a by-product of photosynthesis). That vapor will condense on the inside of the bag and drip to the bottom. This may take several hours but can produce a surprising amount of water. If necessary, you can even use this process with just-cut branches of living plants, or even roots. The root technique can be especially useful in areas like the dry desert sage expanses of the western United States, where most of the plant structure is underground.

BULLSHIT ALERT: PISS OFF

Popular survival stories often focus on the shocking and extreme measures people take to stave off death, and drinking urine to avoid dying of thirst is a popular entrant in the genre. Reality television star Bear Grylls has repeatedly filmed himself drinking piss. Aron Ralston, the climber who famously amputated his own arm after being pinned beneath a boulder during a canyoneering accident in 2003, also drank his own urine after running out of food and water. Other survivors have drunk their own urine when trapped under piles of earthquake rubble, in wrecked cars, and on marooned boats.

Although it's an understandable response to extreme thirst, tapping your own faucet is a bad idea. Urine is 95 percent water and 5 percent sodium, chloride, potassium, urea, and other waste products. Although that sounds like a promising ratio, consider that seawater is 96.5 percent water and 3.5 percent sodium and chloride. Just like drinking seawater, drinking urine will only dehydrate you further. And in consuming urine, you'll also be taking in all the undesirable stuff that your kidneys just filtered out of your body. Repeat this process a few times over, and your urine will be so highly concentrated with dangerous toxins that it could cause kidney failure. That means death.

As for the claims that circulate among some homeopathy circles promoting urine's curative powers, there is no scientific medical evidence supporting the use of your own bodily waste products for hydration or medication. It won't quench your thirst, cure cancer, or provide relief from jellyfish stings, sunburns, allergies, calluses, or any other ailment you might suffer from. The bottom line is that a human can go about three days without water, and drinking urine won't extend that timeline.

CHAPTER 3

————≫≫≫✦≪≪≪————

Food

WHEN MY BUDDIES and I are sitting around having a few laughs, a popular subject of discussion is weird things that we've been forced to eat on backcountry trips. The stories can be either heroic or absurd, depending on the details. I'll often recount one of my favorite meals ever, when we ran out of rations in the middle of a hunt in Alaska and I wound up eating several meals of black bear meat deep-fried in oil that we'd rendered on the spot from the bear's own fat. On the opposite end of the flavor spectrum is a series of meals that we ate after some stove gas leaked into our food bin on a canoeing trip. The taste of the fuel going down wasn't nearly as bad as the memorable gas-flavored belches that would follow. Another notable misadventure involved spooning powdered hot chocolate mix directly into my mouth in the absence of any liquid and then trying to get it down without choking on it. And then there was a meal of boiled turtle eggs in the jungles of South America. I was startled to learn that the whites of turtle eggs do not harden when cooked. Instead, you need to sip them out like you're drinking a shot from an eggshell.

As fun and funny as such experiences might be when looking back on them, it's important to recognize that food is nothing to joke about when it comes to wilderness travel and survival. Most immediately, the quantity and quality of food that you're eating are intrinsically linked to both your physical performance and your mental well-being. This becomes painfully real when times are bad, but it's even true when things are going well. You can hike longer, climb higher, swim farther, paddle longer, and think better when you're eating a wide variety of nutritious and energy-packed foods. In this chapter we'll lay out the theory and practice of wilderness food planning so that you can quickly and cost-effectively stock up on the appropriate provisions before any outing, be it a solo day hike or a multi-week family canoe trip. If your food planning is handled properly, you'll enjoy greater success in the outdoors, along with a much lower chance of getting yourself into a survival-type situation.

Of course, there's no way to rule out the possibility that things might go horribly wrong, or at least wrong enough that you find yourself looking around at various plants and insects and wondering whether it'd hurt you to eat them. I recently bore witness to an experience that illustrates how easily that can happen. I was tagging along with my brother during an elk hunt way up in the mountains; I was only going to be there for a few days, but he was planning on staying for two weeks. His plans changed unexpectedly when he killed an elk on the first day of the season. He decided to cache his two weeks' worth of food up in a tree so that he and I could pack the elk meat down out of the mountains. In a few days, he'd return with a buddy to retrieve the cached food and they'd hunt together while using up the supplies. That was the plan, anyway, until a black bear climbed up into the tree and ransacked all the food. When the guys arrived at their cache, the entire supply was gone. They had a pretty damned hungry excursion, but stretched it out as long as they could on a diet of raspberries, twinberries, and thimbleberries.

In a situation like that, you've still got the option of walking out. But such is not always the case. Imagine that you and a buddy are flying into the Brooks Range of Alaska for a packraft trip, with plans to get picked up 100 miles away at the mouth of the river in five days. Then your buddy dislocates his shoulder, you rip the bottom out of your packraft, and the dry bag containing your food gets washed away down the canyon. That's when you'll get intensely interested in what sorts of things you can eat in the wild, and how to find them. Generally speaking, sustaining yourself on wild food is much, much harder than most folks imagine. It's true that indigenous people once thrived on diets of self-procured wild food, but they were operating with collections of inherited multigenerational information that was put to use in the local landscape on a daily basis. At times they still starved. Today, individuals who are equipped with the actual skill sets necessary to live off the land are invariably die-hard hunters, anglers, trappers, and foragers who have devoted their lives to these disciplines. Taking a few minutes to read about collecting wild food is a great start, but it'll hardly do any good if you don't study this information and practice these skills whenever possible. If you wait until it actually matters, it'll already be too late.

WHAT FOOD TO BRING, AND HOW MUCH

There are thousands of food items on the market specifically made for hiking, hunting, and backcountry travel. There are a thousand more ways to make similar stuff yourself. Regardless of whether you want to buy store-bought grub or go with homemade, you need to be realistic and pragmatic when planning your diet for outdoor excursions. While a typical day at home or work may burn only 2,000 or 3,000 calories, a long day of hard hiking through rough terrain could cost upward of 6,000 or 8,000 calories. Add in precipitation or cold temperatures and your body burns even more calories as you struggle to keep warm. Your meals in the woods need to replace those lost calories if you want to maintain stamina and have a good time out there. Next to palatability (after all, you have to be willing to eat the stuff), weight and bulk are two of the most critical considerations when packing for multiple days outside.

ESTIMATING YOUR DAILY CALORIC NEEDS

A big, lifted Ford F350 burns more gas than a subcompact Hyundai. Likewise, larger humans burn more calories than smaller ones. This isn't fat-shaming; it's just biology. If you're made up of more cells than the next person, then you've got to keep them fed or they will start to disappear.

The U.S. government suggests an average requirement of 2,000 calories per day, a number that's listed on the nutrition label of any food you buy. But, as with most averages, there are many folks who fall well outside the mean. According to the Institute of Medicine, the 2,000-calorie diet is essentially a baseline, and caloric requirements rise or fall by age, gender, weight, and activity level. According to their equation, an active child four to eight years of age requires 1,400–1,800 calories for girls and 1,600–2,000 calories for boys in order to maintain weight. For kids fourteen to eighteen years old, active girls need more like 2,400 calories, while boys require anywhere from 2,800 to 3,200. That curve levels off in the early to mid-twenties until about the fifties, when it starts to slope downward. Most active adult women will require about 2,400 calories, with men requiring closer to 3,000. Older adults need a little less.

In times of stress, high exertion, low temperatures, and the other extenuating factors that may crop up outside, those caloric needs can double. Usually, no matter how much you eat, under these types of conditions your body will quickly begin to consume its fat reserves. When it's done with those, it'll start going after muscle. It's natural to lose some weight when you're out on an adventure (and often appreciated), but you're going to have a bad time if you're letting your body eat itself. Stomach pangs, diminished mental capacity, and low energy are just the beginning of what you can expect if you're not getting enough to eat. Starvation is a famously awful way to die, so make sure to always plan ahead when it comes to food.

THE IMPORTANCE OF CALORIC DENSITY

Some simple math can be helpful for informing decisions about what foods to pack. Take a look at the nutritional information on your food packaging and divide the number of calories per serving by the serving size. Any ratio more than about 120 calories per ounce (or around 120 calories per 28 grams) is good. If it's much less than that, it's not an efficient food item to be toting around.

Fats are especially calorie dense, and nuts, butter, nut butters, olive oil, chocolate, cheese, bacon, sausages, and other fatty foods are ideal for wilderness travel. They're efficient to pack around, are enjoyable to eat, and provide a lot of fuel for your body's fire. What's more, they tend to be durable. You don't want to pack around food that is too easy to smoosh or crunch. Items such as crackers and bread are not calorically dense, and they don't do well with compression straps, bush plane fuselages, tossed luggage, and rough boat rides.

BREAKFAST

It's a cliché to acclaim breakfast as the most important meal of the day, and we're not even sure that statement is clinically verifiable. But we do know that you need to put fuel in the tank if you want the vehicle to run, and we can vouch from personal experience that a hearty, filling breakfast allows you to hunt, hike, and fish harder. If you're planning on a long trek that's going to burn a lot of calories, then you'd better take in a lot of calories in the morning.

We've tried a number of freeze-dried breakfast options and have been mostly underwhelmed. The eggs always come out kind of runny and un-appetizing and the hash browns are mushy. It seems like they just haven't perfected that preservation method when it comes to breakfast food. We have a lot better luck with dehydrated just-add-water packages, or with cooking our own.

Instant oatmeal has become the de facto camping breakfast due to the ease of preparation, the product's compact shape and weight, the diges-tive benefits, and the universal acceptance of the food type. Plus, there's the little-known fact that you can pour boiling water directly into your paper oatmeal packet and eat the contents with a spoon. No need for a bowl, and the packaging can be burned on a fire. But even with some of the high-tech oat packages on the market now, you'd have to eat more oatmeal than you might comfortably be able to in order to get enough calories for a serious day of walking around in the mountains. Oatmeal is great if it works for you, but we suggest approaching camp breakfast a little more seriously if you want to take your game up a notch.

Sometimes we'll crack a dozen eggs into a water bottle or thermos to bring out into the woods. That way we've got the makings of a hearty, homestyle breakfast without the worry of broken eggs in our backpacks. We use this trick mostly in cold-weather situations, as eggs shouldn't be left out in warm temperatures for long.

There are lots of other good workarounds that'll enable you to get all the calories and comfort food you want while working around space, weight, and durability constraints. Bring flatbread, tortillas, or pita in-stead of normal, smashable bread. Dough or biscuit products that come in a tube are even better. Bacon and sausage links don't pack well, but loose-ground breakfast sausage for patties can get smooshed up no prob-lem. Blocks of cheese are also very durable. Packing real food takes extra planning, effort, and cleanup, but the caloric reward and ease of diges-tion sure can make it worthwhile.

LUNCH

There's something very pleasant about taking some time to lounge under a tree, take a break from hunting or fishing or hiking, and eat a good lunch. Some super-hardo guys choose to just have bars on the go, or even skip lunch altogether and avoid the "food coma" lethargy it can some-times create. But we tend to treat this meal as a good time to fuel up and take a short mental break from the task at hand. If you're spending a few days outside, it's important to stay on top of your food intake and make sure not to burn yourself out.

There's nothing wrong with wolfing down a few bars for lunch, and we've done it lots of times when the elk are bugling or the trout are rising and you just don't want to pull away from the action. And there certainly is truth to the notion that eating a big lunch out on a sunny mountainside will make you sleepy. Sometimes we even plan a twenty-minute post-sandwich power nap into our daily schedule.

Still, this meal, more so than others when outside, shouldn't be overdone. Forcing your stomach to process a big load of food at any time will make you lethargic, and the effects are most notable in the middle of the day. It's good to top off the tank but not overfill it.

A modest sandwich around noon seems to hit the sweet spot for our crew. Flatbread, pita, and bagels are great options for your bread brackets, and we usually carry a small block of hard cheese and some preserved meat for the interior. Salami, summer sausage, prosciutto, and other charcuterie will make your sandwich feel all the fancier, but there have been plenty of outings fueled by packages of cheap, indestructible Buddig sandwich meat. There are so many preservatives in that stuff that it basically couldn't go bad, even after sitting in the bottom of a backpack in hot weather for a week. That certainly has some advantages, but it's not going to make it any more appetizing. So shelf-stable meats are important if you're going to be dipping into them for more than a day or two in above-freezing weather, but which way you go depends on your tastes and budgets. Regardless, any sandwich will be assisted by convenience-store mayo or mustard packets, a thin slice off an onion, or any other condiments that make it feel more like home.

Some folks in our crew and circle of friends have recently adopted ramen noodles as their go-to hunting lunch. There are endless options and brands among these dehydrated soups, especially in the Asian food aisle of the grocery. You need to haul your Jetboil along with you, which a lot of folks do anyway in order to make a mid-morning cup of coffee. Packages of ramen can get all crunched up without affecting the final product, and all you need to do is boil a little water or snow and then dump it into your noodles and spice pack or bouillon. It's a great move, especially on cold days ice fishing or glassing for mule deer. The hot noodles and broth can raise your internal temperature, restore feeling to your fingers, and bring some positivity back to the pursuit.

DINNER

You can't talk about dinner in the outdoors without talking about freeze-dried food. The best way to reduce the weight and bulk of food is through the elimination of water, which is why dried or smoked meat, fish, and fruits (often relied upon as snacks) have long been staples of wilderness travel. Then there are dehydrated foods that can be brought back to life with the addition of water from sources such as creeks, seeps, ponds, and snow melt. But freeze-dried foods are often an even better option, as they more readily accept the reintroduction of water and are easier to digest.

While the concept of dehydrated food is easy to understand—the water is simply dried out—the freeze-drying process is a bit more complicated and warrants some explanation in order to clear up confusion about a food item that might seem somehow synthetic or phony. The best freeze-dried foods are produced by companies such as Peak Refuel or Mountain House, which start the process by producing fully cooked, ready-to-eat dishes that are simple and hearty. Think beef stew, lasagna, mac 'n' cheese, and so on. The cooked dishes are then spread out on large sheet trays and frozen at precise temperatures. Once frozen, the meals go into sublimation chambers, where the air pressure is lowered to about $\frac{1}{10,000}$th of the typical air pressure at sea level. The temperature drops to −50°F. Then, slowly, the racks holding the trays begin to warm up. Rather than turning from a solid to a liquid as it warms, the water inside the food sublimates into a gas and dissipates, a function of decreased air pressure in the environment. At the end of the process, the food is nutritionally unharmed and left looking remarkably similar to its original, unfrozen form. Packed into laminated bags made of nylon, aluminum, and polyester, it has a shelf life that can be measured in decades. It's easy to make fun of the mushy textures and heavy-duty packaging that freeze-dried meals yield, but the fact remains that we bring these handy bags of grub on nearly every multiday backcountry excursion. They provide a quick, clean, reliable, and efficient way to get fed at the end of the day. It's hard to get simpler and more lightweight than tearing open a package, boiling some water, stirring it in, then chowing down. No dishes, no cleanup, just a little trash that conveniently folds up to be packed out. And whatever you don't eat can be saved for the next trip—or the next generation.

If you've got a limited budget or excess time (or an aversion to packaged food and preservatives), some of the more dedicated and health-conscious hunters and hikers among us elect to freeze-dry and prepare their own backcountry meals. By individually freeze-drying such items as rice, peas, potato cubes, and meat strips, then vacuum sealing them together into individual meals, you can fine-tune the flavors to your individual palate and avoid the preservatives required for retail shelf stability. This, of course, requires more than a quick trip to the outdoors store right before your trip. But, working in bulk with a day to prep, you can easily stock up and dry enough foods for the next few months.

If weight is less of a consideration, as on a float trip, for instance, you can also skip the drying step and just make, vac seal, and freeze a hearty meal like spaghetti and meat sauce. Then you can simply boil a pot of water with the vac bag inside and eat straight from the bag.

TEN WAYS TO MASTER THE FREEZE-DRIED EXPERIENCE

1. We have a friend who's been described as tougher than woodpecker lips. He can't be bothered with packing around a stove to boil water for his freeze-dried food. Instead, he adds cold water around midday and says that it usually rehydrates by nightfall.

2. Sophisticated users of freeze-dried food know that normal-length spoons are pretty much worthless. If you want to get to the bottom corners of your freeze-dried food pouch without soiling your knuckles with food, invest in a long-handled Lexan or titanium spoon.

3. If you don't have a long-handled camp spoon, take your knife or multi-tool scissors and cut off the top few inches of your bag so that you have an easier time getting in there.

4. Experiment with more or less water than is recommended on the packaging. A soupier mix is often easier to get down.

5. Bring along individual serving-size packets of coconut oil or olive oil, or sticks of butter during cold weather, and dump these into your freeze-dried food pouch. It improves the caloric load and flavor.

6. Hot sauce can go a long way toward improving the freeze-dried experience. The 0.125-ounce bottles of Tabasco are handy for this.

7. A few days' worth of freeze-dried food can impact the consistency of your bowel movements pretty significantly. They tend to go mushy, with the color of cardboard. Don't worry—it's normal

and all part of the fun. If you want to combat this phenomenon, bring along some fruit and roughage to help out.

8. From the ubiquitous Mountain House to high-end boutique meals, there are a lot of flavors and price points to choose from. Try a few to find out what you like. It's easy to get sick of one particular flavor, so bring lots of options on multi-day trips.

9. As convenient as freeze-dried foods are, don't overdo it. They make a great dinner, but plan on something different for breakfast and lunch so that you don't get totally burned out on them.

10. Keep your freeze-dried meals in mind when planning your water requirements. Many entrée-sized freeze-dried meals require about 16 ounces to rehydrate—in hiker-speak, that's half a Nalgene. If you're not going to camp near water, stash the appropriate amount away during the day. Remember, if you're taking water straight out of a lake or stream, boil it for at least a minute or two to make sure you've eliminated any nasty diseases or parasites.

THE COFFEE CONUNDRUM

We covered the importance of hydration in Chapter 2. Now it's time to talk about a subject that, in our experience, has given rise to more arguments than any other category of outdoor food: camp coffee. There are generally two schools of thought on it. You've got the folks who want to replicate the fine coffee experiences that they can get at home or downtown, and then you've got the folks who just want to get the whole backcountry coffee thing over with as quickly as possible. For members of the former group, there's been an explosion of products in recent years that make it possible to fetishize coffee in the woods. A lot of these contraptions are too finicky or cumbersome to mess with. A couple of years ago, we got all excited about some pour-over coffee filters made for outdoor use. We tested them out on a winter day. By the time the coffee had finished dripping through the filter and into the cup, it was as cold as creek water. Here are three reasonable ways to deal with camp coffee, from the semi-ambitious to the downright pragmatic.

Cowboy coffee. Fill a coffeepot with a quart of water and a few heaping tablespoons of coffee. Let it come to a low simmer on the fire or camp stove, then move it aside to begin cooling. Once the water has calmed down, splash a little cold water over the open pot. This will help settle any coffee grounds that are swirling about on the surface of your brew. Gently pour your mugs of coffee, being mindful not to stir up the settled grounds. Once you get near the bottom of the pot, you can pitch the remainder or filter it through a piece of clothing or a sock and into your mug. The results make for a tasty, albeit somewhat gritty, cup of coffee.

French press. Same as home, but you can get them made out of unbreakable Lexan or titanium with insulated sleeves. The contraption requires an annoying bit of cleanup (a trip to the creek to wash the used grounds away), but the brew is solid.

Instant coffee. This is by far the easiest, most efficient way to get your coffee fix. Black Rifle Coffee Company, a house favorite, makes single-serving packets that are perfect for camping and taste better than pretty much any other instant coffee on the market. They also make a coffee "tea" bag that can simply be steeped in hot water. If you like cream and/or sugar, mix up a combination of instant coffee, powdered creamer, and sugar in a wide-mouth Nalgene jar. (You can get Nalgenes in various sizes: 2 ounces, 4 ounces, 6 ounces, and so on.) Just shake a bit into your camp mug, pour in some hot water, and chug it down.

SNACKS AND TRAIL FOOD

You definitely don't need to stop and lay out the picnic blanket every time you want to down some calories. It's helpful to stuff some jerky, energy bars, or a small bag of trail mix into the pockets on your backpack waist belt or in another handy spot. Often a quick nibble will be enough to get your stomach off your mind. Here are some of our favorite choices from the snack aisle:

Jerky and smokies. Jerky is the original trail food, likely predating civilization itself. Hunter-gatherers dried meat in the sun or over fires (once they learned how to make them) in order to preserve it for overland journeys. Maybe that's why the toughness and the tearing, gnawing sensation seems to scratch a primal itch. Whether it's meat you personally hunted and dried in your own dehydrator, oven, or smoker, or the shrink-wrapped Oberto packs you purchased for $6.99 from the gas station, it just feels good to chew hard on dried meat while feasting your eyes upon a lovely landscape.

Jerky is very easy to make at home using meat you harvested yourself or purchased at the store. Get it slightly frozen and slice it approximately ³/₁₆ inch thick. You can use store-bought jerky mixes, which contain curing agents and spices, or find a staggering array of build-your-own jerky spice blends online. Better yet, check out our favorite jerky recipes in *The MeatEater Fish and Game Cookbook.* The drying process can take place in a dehydrator, your kitchen oven, or even outside if you live in the right climate. Vacuum-seal or zip-lock the results in trip-sized packages, and store them in the freezer until you're ready for action.

Meat sticks, or "smokies," can be even more satisfying than jerky because they typically come with a bit of moisture and fat in addition to the protein. That means you get all the joy of jerky, but none of the tough chewing. A testament to their tastiness and appeal is that you'll rarely if ever see smokies come home from a trip uneaten, while energy bars have an uncanny ability to survive outings without getting opened. There are dozens of varieties available in your average gas station, though you can make a much better product at home with a little know-how and some specialized equipment. You'll need a small-gauge sausage stuffer attachment for your meat grinder, some thin but heavy collagen casings, some pork fat, and some cure/spice mix—you can make the latter, buy it online, or find it at your local sporting goods store.

Bars. Compressed food bars have become almost synonymous with eating outdoors. It's hard to deny their convenience. Many of the commercial offerings are durable, packable, healthy, nutritious, shelf-stable, and tasty. The extra garbage created by the packaging is annoying, but that doesn't stop us from throwing a couple bars in our packs pretty much every time we go out.

There's a staggering array of food bars marketed toward outdoor recreation these days. You've got Clif Bars, ProBars, Kind, Chewy, Pemmican, Lärabars, Kashi, Nature Valley, and dozens more. Some have just a few simple, natural ingredients proudly listed on the front, while others contain a bunch of high-fructose corn syrup or straight-up sugar. Take a look at the ingredients and nutritional info on the back to make sure you're getting what you think you are. And remember, calories, fats, salt, and protein are your friends when you're spending time in the woods. Most bars start from 150 calories on the low end of the spectrum and go to 400 on the high end. Flavor ranges from that of compressed sawdust to pure candy. With so much variability, it's both fun and practical to experiment. We know from experience that if you bring nothing but your single favorite bar out in the woods for a few days, you will hate it by the time you get home. Diversity is the spice of life, so give yourself some options. You may end up eating your least favorite last, but when you're hungry enough, who cares what something tastes like? You'll also get a better idea of what brands and flavors you prefer in order to continue dialing in your selections every time.

Trail mix. Before bars claimed the throne as the standard trail food, a bagful of peanuts and M&Ms reigned supreme. Trail mix still provides advantages over other types of trail food. It's the best thing for when you just want a few bites; it can be a nearly zero-waste choice if you put it in a heavy-duty zip-closure silicone bag; and it can be tailored for allergies and other dietary restrictions. There are countless store-bought varieties out there, or you can make your own blends by visiting your local fancy grocery or any other spot that sells bulk health foods such as granola, seeds, and dried fruit. Get a pound or two each of granola, oats, raisins, dried cranberries, sunflower seeds, pumpkin seeds, chocolate chips, dried apples, dried bananas, almonds, or whatever else strikes your fancy. Bring it all home, mix it up in a tub, pack it in quart or gallon bags, and you're set. Here's a version we've grown to love:

  1 pound small pretzels
  1 pound granola (flavored or plain)
  1 pound dried cranberries
  8 ounces chocolate chips
  8 ounces halved roasted almonds
  10 ounces dried apple chips
  10 ounces dried banana chips
  6 ounces sunflower seeds
  6 ounces pumpkin seeds

A FEW MORE TIPS FOR BACKCOUNTRY EATING

1. When you're fully nourished at home, it's sometimes hard to imagine what you'll feel like when you're calorie starved. To make shopping easier, start a list of your hankerings and cravings when you've been out camping for a few days so that you can do a better job of packing your food the next time.

2. Bring along some chicken and beef bouillon cubes. They're light-weight, taste good, encourage liquid consumption, and put some salt in your system. They can also be a good start to a wild mushroom soup.

3. There's a lot to be said for going totally Spartan in the field, but now and then it's nice to enjoy life a little. One of the nicer trail snacks is a block of Dubliner cheese, some herb-crusted hard sa-lami, and some good hearty crackers like dill-flavored Triscuits. As a bonus, this stuff will keep well without refrigeration for days.

4. Pouches (not cans) of tuna are not as light as dehydrated or freeze-dried backpacking foods, but they're still a good alterna-tive. They add protein to a meal or can suffice as a calorie-dense snack. Many folks find that they're easier on the gut as well.

5. A few backcountry godsends: single-serving packets of almond butter, chocolate-covered espresso beans, and instant miso soup packets.

6. Organize your food by placing each day's ration into its own gallon-sized bag. It's a great way to manage a few days' worth of food, and the bags usually come in handy.

SHOULD YOU BE BUYING ALL THOSE SUPPLEMENTS?

There's a certain segment of the hunting and outdoor sports industry that would have you believe that you couldn't possibly spend time in the mountains without specially formulated protein- and vitamin-enriched drink mixes. Well . . . you can.

Yes, these outdoor pursuits we undertake are strenuous and can be depleting. There are many products on the market to help you replace vitamin C, electrolytes, potassium, protein, calories, iron, magnesium, and any other nutrients you might want to stock up on. There are also plenty of regular old foods that provide the same minerals, though per-haps in smaller doses.

That said, we've found benefit and enjoyment from Airborne, Emergen-C, Zipfizz, and other drink mixes meant to deliver important vitamins and jazz up your water a bit. Again, anything that gets you re-placing fluids is a good thing, and those fruity, fizzy mixes sure can make chugging down a whole Nalgene sound more appealing. We also know folks who swear by the rehydrate-and-recover powders, though they're often singing praises in regard to hangovers cured. Extra potassium and magnesium can help with the leg cramps that often accompany post-holing through deep snow. For extreme high elevation, specific supplements have an important role in assuaging altitude sickness.

By and large, you should get to know your own dietary needs by talking to your doctor and experimenting with products you're interested in. Not everyone needs 500 grams of protein in the morning, just as not everyone has a diagnosed iron deficiency. Figure out what works for you to survive and thrive outside.

FOOD BUFFERS AND SAMPLE PACKING LISTS

First off, don't ever bring less food than you think you'll need or want. The wilderness is no place to try out a weight-loss plan. Even if you intend to supplement your diet with wild fish and game, make sure to have a contingency plan. Fishing and hunting are unpredictable activities, and conditions and game populations change wildly from year to year. Just because you caught enough walleye for several dinners in the Boundary Waters last fall doesn't mean you will do the same again this fall. Lakes freeze, fish migrate, hot action turns cold, or you can lose your gear. You should always have more non-perishable food with you than you expect to need. When going out for a day hike, pack enough food to keep you going strong for twenty-four hours (see the sample packing lists, opposite). It's easy to miss that split in the trail and wind up with a few extra miles back to the trailhead, or worse. When backpacking for seven days, pack food for at least eight. That weeklong high-mountain fishing hike can easily go an extra day or two due to a surprisingly gnarly pass or exceptionally good angling.

This safety buffer shouldn't be too hard to account for. I always leave a handful of extra bars in a bag in the bottom of my day pack, separate from the food I'm actually planning to eat that day. On multi-day trips, I never leave the truck without at least one extra freeze-dried dinner and an extra day or two of bars or trail mix. On a ten-day fly-in caribou hunt in the Yukon, I'd want to have at least three days' worth of extra food in case weather prevented the pilot from picking me up on time. Stash extra food in a location you are likely to return to, such as a base camp or airstrip, so you don't have to carry it the whole time. Likewise, you should bring more fuel for your cooking stove than you plan on using (more on that in a bit). Food buffers are practical not only for survival but also because in the backcountry you often exert yourself more and burn twice as many calories as you would in your everyday life. Climbing up and down mountains can really take it out of you, and an extra snack is sometimes the ticket to keep on keeping on. Take a look at the sample lists below to get a sense of what our crew brings along for outings of various lengths:

Sample Day Hike Packing List

2 energy/granola bars
8 ounces trail mix
8 ounces summer sausage or salami
6 ounces hard cheese
Small pack of crackers

Sample Overnight Packing List

2 instant oatmeal packets
2 instant coffee packets
1 lunch
6 energy/granola bars
1 freeze-dried dinner
1 fast-food packet of hot sauce
2 tea bags/hot cocoa packets

Sample Five-Day Packing List

First-Day Food
Salami stick, small block of cheese, apple, baguette
Breakfasts
1 big bag of granola or 6 packs instant oatmeal
Dehydrated milk in zip-lock bags
6 coffee packets
Powdered creamer in zip-lock bags
Lunch and Snacks
10 energy/granola bars
10 Snickers bars
1 pound jerky
1 pound trail mix with dried fruit
Nuun electrolyte tablets or powdered drink supplement
Chicken bouillon cubes
Dinners
6 high-calorie freeze-dried dinners
1 stick salted butter (for cooking meat acquired while hunting or to
    mix into freeze-dried food)

Hot sauce
6 tea bags/hot cocoa packets

STEVE'S SNACKS FOR CHILDREN STRATEGY

When I'm packing to go outdoors with my kids, snacks and drinks might be the single most important consideration. A well-timed Jolly Rancher puts an end to whining better than anything else I've found. A good way to stock up on materials that can be used to bribe your kids is to implement the Switch Witch Strategy. Here's how it works. After the Halloween festivities are over, give your kids the option to leave their candy out at the front door for the Switch Witch. The Switch Witch is a magical creature who swaps candy for cool toys like puzzles, art supplies, and Nerf gun darts. Then you, the parent, take all of that candy and cache it away for later use. Somehow, kids are slow to put it together that the candy you produce on a fishing trip looks remarkably similar to what they'd placed near the front door a couple of months earlier. Of course, you've got to round out the kids' backcountry diet with nutritional snacks and drinks as well. But it's wise to lean in their direction when it comes to snack selection. Get them the things they like, to encourage plenty of eating and drinking. You can argue with them about liver and onions when you get back home.

BEAR BAGS AND TRASH BAGS

If you're sleeping overnight in bear country, a category that covers many campsites and wild spaces within the United States, you'll need to take food storage precautions. Hang your supplies at least 10 feet off the ground, and preferably higher (see page 216 for a diagram), in a sturdy trash bag or nylon dry bag; in many national parks, you can get a citation for failing to hang or properly store your food. Don't forget to pack up potentially alluring items like toothpaste, and lock your car if it contains any snacks or even any crumbs left over by snacking children—bears are surprisingly good at breaking into vehicles and have been known to go after empty cans of soda.

Speaking of snacking children and adults: if you want to enjoy yourself in a clean and healthy environment, you're ethically (and legally) obliged to adhere to a leave-no-trace policy in the outdoors—even if that means hauling garbage around in your pack for a week. We've all come across trash miles from the trailhead left by some lazy slob with no respect for Mother Nature. Burning your trash, especially plastics, isn't a great alternative to carrying it out, either—just take a look in any campground fire pit if you want to know why. Most are lined with a solid layer of partially burned, melted garbage. Packing out your trash is not as big a hassle as it might seem. First off, you shouldn't be producing all that much of it in the first place. Even on a backpacking trip lasting several days, your total trash haul shouldn't consist of more than a couple plastic food wrappers and wet wipes per day. If some of that food is made up of freeze-dried meals, their resealable packaging makes for a sturdy little garbage bag after you're done eating. You can stuff a lot of energy bar wrappers inside one, and we've found that a couple freeze-dried meal bags can hold a week's worth of garbage for one person. If you're not eating freeze-dried, carry a couple gallon-sized zip-lock bags—they're also handy for keeping electronics or paper maps dry and for storing a couple gutted trout or a bunch of fresh-picked wild blueberries. Lastly, before you leave your campsite, remember to scour the area for what we call "micro-trash." Take the time to pick up tiny, easily overlooked stuff that tends to fall out of pockets or get missed at night, like small pieces of candy wrappers or discarded Band-Aids.

COOKING

The evolution of modern backpacking food seems to be on a trajectory to do away with the need to ever cook in the woods. Even now, for many people, the full extent of outdoor food preparation consists of opening wrappers and boiling water.

Sure, it's great to be fast and efficient and mess-free when you've got more important matters to deal with—like a mountain to summit or a buck to chase—and there are important tricks and tools to know for maximizing your precious time out there. But when you have the time (or the need), the ability to cook over fire or a small stove is a rewarding and valuable skill.

STOVES AND COOKWARE

If you're keeping things simple, with hot meals limited to items like instant oatmeal, coffee, and freeze-dried food, a camp stove with the primary function of quickly boiling water is an essential tool. There are plenty of models on the market, but the modern, integrated Jetboil stove systems are hard to beat for speed and user-friendliness. They run off fuel canisters containing a mixture of propane and isobutane, with the fuel canister attaching directly to the burner, and the burner attaching directly to the pot. With built-in baffles that supercharge the heat transfer, they work incredibly well in most conditions, though performance suffers in extremely low temperatures and at higher elevations. Widely adopted in the outdoor world, they're typically integrated with a pot that fits all the pieces inside when you're done, and some can be used with skillets and other cookware. However, the insulated pots that come with many of these type of stoves can't be used directly on a fire (in the event that you run out of fuel or just feel like doing some more primitive cooking) without parts melting—a major downside for some people. In addition to the canisters being single use, the inability to know exactly how much fuel remains in the canister often leads to packing additional and sometimes unnecessary fuel.

There are several other styles of backpacking stoves that may have fallen out of fashion but still have some merits. At the top of the list would be the precursor to the Jetboil, what we call the "pocket rocket" style. These stoves also screw onto the top of an iso-pro canister, but they have flanges around the heat element to support a small pot or skillet. They often fold down very small and weigh only a couple of ounces. They're very versatile, but they're much less fuel efficient than Jetboils, typically lacking windscreens and baffles. It's also a lot easier to accidentally knock a pot off the top. But on the plus side, the standard-issue pot you pair them with could also be deployed for boiling water next to a fire in a pinch, something we've certainly done when the fuel runs out after a week in the mountains.

Another kind of stove that many of us grew up using and still turn to in certain conditions is the type that runs on liquid fuel. Often also called white gas stoves, liquid fuel stoves typically employ a heating element that sits on the ground and is attached by a hose to a refillable fuel tank; some allow you to use gasoline, kerosene, diesel, or jet fuel as well as white gas. These stoves require priming the fuel bottle with a pump and can be a little more finicky than canister-style stoves, but nonetheless still hold their place. Some bush pilots won't let you bring pressurized iso-pro canisters on their planes, making liquid fuel stoves almost mandatory; white gas also functions better than other fuels in extreme cold or high altitudes.

My brother Matt loves his alcohol-burning stove. He says that's because it's so quiet he can hear elk bugles over it, but I think he just likes the nostalgia and simplicity. These might be the original camp stoves, and they're so simple that you can make one by cutting an empty beer can in half, pouring denatured alcohol into the bottom, and lighting it on fire. They're extremely lightweight and pretty darn cool, but man, do they take forever to boil water. Alcohol isn't highly combustible and doesn't burn hot, which means the DIY route is fairly safe if not terribly efficient.

Each of these stoves has its devotees and its particular benefits, but one thing they all have in common is that they run on a gas or liquid that can spill, explode, get lost, or just plain run out. Not to mention that heating elements can break, get wet, or otherwise fail. As with all gear in the outdoors, it's smart to have a backup option in the form of a metal cooking pot that can be stuck directly on top of a fire if need be. Small, packable skillets are another great option because you can cook up fish, birds, or whatever other meat you may have procured.

Another option is to turn to a new generation of camp stoves that has returned to the original fuel source: wood. Sure, big, heavy, cast-iron woodstoves inside wall tents never went out of style, but good luck getting the 50-pound potbelly on your back, onto a raft, or into a bush plane. Today's space-age titanium woodstoves (like the "hot tent"–style rigs from Seek Outside) pack down to only a pound or two. Made of light but sturdy sheet metal and Erector-set-like hardware, some break down to lie as flat and small as a laptop case. You can find wood-burning camp stoves that are just a few inches long, for boiling water, but there are also models that take up several feet and come complete with roll-up chimneys integrated into matching floorless teepees with stovepipes. It's a pretty nifty trick for both cooking food and keeping warm in your shelter during cold-weather backcountry trips.

The downside to cooking with fire by any method is that wood is a highly variable and inconsistent fuel source. As we discuss on page 259, wood can be very difficult to light in certain conditions and regions. Even when dry wood is in good supply, you have to constantly feed small sticks into a small stove to keep the temperature up. That can be a lot of fun with a good stack of wood when you're snowed into the teepee all day, but it can be tedious just for boiling water.

Going even more primitive, another helpful tool for cooking with fire is a small grill grate. We often pack tiny, lightweight wire racks as small as 4 by 10 inches. For a backpacking trip where fresh grouse or trout might wind up on the menu, a grate is invaluable. Even if you just need to boil a pot of water over a fire, it's nice to be able to make a flat surface above the coals.

There are a few other items that might come in handy. A leather glove is very useful, allowing you to place your pot, position logs, and pluck items from the coals without burning all the hair off your hands and fingers. We sometimes fold up a big piece of aluminum into a small square and use it to cook meat or fish and other foods over coals, as well as for a variety of other tasks such as making a windscreen for the fire or stove. If you're bringing eggs or anything else to cook in a skillet, a small, packable spatula will go a long way. A 2-ounce Nalgene bottle filled with olive oil and a small spice jar full of your favorite all-purpose seasoning mix will make it easier to prepare any fish, mushrooms, or wild game that you're lucky enough to acquire. Nothing is worse than finding a patch of morels without having a little oil and salt on hand. A small combination salt and pepper shaker is another good way to dial in your flavors.

You really only need one utensil for backpacking, and many enthusiasts have embraced the spork. Most freeze-dried meals have a scoopable consistency, and sporks can also be used to spear chunks of meat. We like the models made of titanium or Lexan with extra-long handles. The extra length helps keep your fingers out of the juice in your Mountain House meal packages. But any old, unmatched fork and/or spoon from the back of the utensil drawer at home can get the job done.

CAVEMAN COOKERY

If the above hasn't made it clear, we're of the opinion that any time you're going out into the woods for more than a day, it's a good idea to have some form of stove and pot with you. A stove is pretty much mandatory for eating freeze-dried meals, and it's a good backup plan even if you intend to cook over a campfire. Flames can be exceedingly difficult to come by in coastal areas or anywhere else after a big rainstorm. On the other hand, if shit really goes south and you wind up getting separated from your supplies, cooking by fire—what we call caveman-style cooking— may be your only option. The good news is that we do it all the time, just for fun.

There are three main ways to go about cooking meat or fish directly over a fire: spit, hot rock, and coal burying. Spitting meat over a fire is the most recognizable and obvious caveman method—you're just skewering chunks of meat or whole small animals on a sharpened stick. The biggest worry is your precious meat falling off the stick as it cooks and softens. This is especially important with fish, as we discuss in greater detail on page 129.

Hot-rock style is exactly what it sounds like: using a big, flat stone as your cooking surface. Place the right rock level near the edge of your fire before you begin to cook. Then you can set pieces of meat on it for the direct heat off the stone and the indirect heat of the fire.

Another method is what we call Native American–style small-game prep, taken from the quick and easy method tribes employed for thousands of years. They would simply gut a rabbit, grouse, trout, or any of a myriad of other small animal species and place it right in the coals of their fire. The heat will burn off the hair, feathers, or scales and cook the meat inside. The exterior, covered in burnt hair and ash, isn't likely to be very appetizing, but the meat and fat inside certainly will be.

A variation of the Native American technique is what many outdoorsmen like to call "hobo dinners." If you happen to have or find aluminum foil or another type of leaf or lining metal (perhaps a survival blanket), you can wrap your small game, bird, or fish in this covering and place it in the coals. This will likely provide more edible contents than just sticking the animal straight in the fire.

A traditional field cooking method used by indigenous hunters from as far back as the Pleistocene involves boiling meat in water contained within a large animal's stomach or skin. It works shockingly well. Start by digging a pit and lining it with the stomach or hide, then fill the cauldron with water. Start a fire and use it to heat a small pile of rocks, then place those rocks into the water using a shovel or makeshift tongs to avoid getting burned. Continue until the water boils, at which point you can add your meat or veggies to cook. A downside of this method is the grit and ash that transfers into the water from the rocks. You can avoid this by dip-

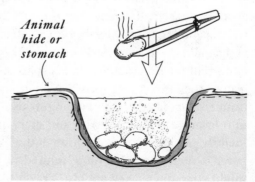

Animal hide or stomach

ping your heated rocks into a separate container of water to rinse them off before plunging them into the cooking pot.

Before cooking small game, you'll usually want to remove the head, guts, and skin (with the exception of birds, which you should just pluck, leaving the skin on). You can get rid of the digestive tract, but keep the musculoskeletal structure intact if you can. Also make sure to hang on to hearts, livers, and kidneys, plus gizzards in birds, because they're delicious and add calories to your meal. The same goes for fish, though we like to leave the head and skin on to provide flavor, texture, and simply more stuff to eat.

We'll discuss cooking methods for each animal and plant class in more depth in the following sections, but the most important rule of thumb is to avoid cooking your food too fast. Don't put meat on a spit directly into the flames or it will quickly char, becoming tough and crunchy as many of its valuable nutrients are burned away. Likewise, hot rocks used for cooking should be set close enough to the fire to receive its heat, but not so close that the flames will touch your meat. To control heat, it is always a good idea to start a fire with a large pile of wood that you can burn down into coals; as you keep this main fire burning at a low level, redistribute coals with a stick to an adjacent cooking area where you can prepare your food at a reasonable temperature.

FINDING FOOD IN THE WILD

If you want to learn the proper approach to surviving on a wild foods diet, watch how a black bear uses the landscape while it's trying to fatten up during the fall. Black bears are opportunistic omnivores, always searching for big hauls of calories while almost never passing up a chance at something small. Even when traveling from point A to point B, bears will zig and zag to investigate any and all food sources. They do just what you should do in a survival situation. They flip rocks to look for insects and small mammals. They smash apart and roll over rotten logs to find grubs. They investigate former human occupancies such as abandoned camps, dilapidated cabins, landing strips, and old mining sites. They peer into briar patches for berries and crab apples. They use their noses to identify carrion. They stalk through the likely habitats of their prey, prepared to pounce on any young, injured, or unsuspecting critters that they might encounter. They are also drawn like a magnet to water sources. Again, water is necessary for sustaining all forms of life, so plants and animals are usually more concentrated in those areas where you can find it. Bears will visit stock ponds, puddles, alpine lakes, ocean beaches, ephemeral streams, and swamps. They roll out streamside rocks in search of crayfish and stonefly nymphs. They roll over beachside rocks in search of crabs. They scour estuary shorelines for shellfish. They work river mouths and waterfalls for migrating fish. In short, black bears are eager, open-minded, and willing to stuff their faces with anything and everything with caloric value. Armed with the right information, you can take a similar approach and find food just about anywhere.

Keep in mind that the killing of pretty much all fish and wildlife other than insects and a handful of nuisance and non-native species is tightly regulated by state and provincial wildlife agencies. You'd be likely to receive leniency from those agencies for catching fish or animals unlawfully if you truly were in a life-or-death survival situation, but don't push it. It's not "survival" if you're just out there practicing. Because of these wildlife regulations, which greatly restrict activities like building pit traps and setting deadfalls for big game, many primitive food acquisition strategies have become largely irrelevant. The only way to develop proficiency with such methods is through intensive practice. And since most people are limited in their ability to rehearse such methods, they shouldn't waste their time trying to figure them out in genuine moments of need. Before experimenting with any of the strategies or foods included in this section, consult your region's fish and game regulations.

The law of calories is another thing to consider when it comes to survival food. You gain calories by eating but lose them through exertion. For most folks, trying to catch and kill big game with primitive tools and limited experience is going to be more calorically costly than it is beneficial. Running headlong after a deer isn't likely to succeed, but it is certain to burn your fuel tank lower. Be cognizant of the fact that you can live for weeks without eating, so you don't need to take unnecessary gambles.

That said, understanding the basic tenets of butchery, sanitation, and preservation, along with a baseline knowledge of which wild foods are safe to eat, could help you stay alert and alive in a real survival situation.

FOOD SAFETY AND FOOD POISONING

The ability to find food in the woods might one day save your life. On the other hand, making the wrong call about what you eat could just as easily threaten your life. From choosing the wrong mushroom to eating contaminated meat to paralytic shellfish poisoning, there are serious dangers to be aware of when selecting something to consume. We will discuss the inherent dangers of specific plants, fungi, molluscs, animals, and fishes within their own sections, but here are some general guidelines and best practices.

Being out in the woods is no excuse to forget the good hygiene and sanitation practices you obey at home. Sure, there isn't always a sink handy on the mountain, but that's no excuse for skipping the hand sanitizer after going to the bathroom. The tiniest fleck of intestinal bacteria could easily find its way from your wipin' hand to your trail mix to your mouth, which could lead you to regret every decision you made that week. Try to rinse off and/or thoroughly cook any plant, fungus, fish, bird, mollusc, or mammal meat in clean water before you eat it. Folks can tend to get a little lazy on cleanliness when they feel like they're "roughing it," but these practices are actually even more important in the woods.

Food poisoning is godawful at home and so, so much worse when you're living in a tent. You'll know it when you get it: stomach cramps, fever, diarrhea, vomiting. Any bloody diarrhea or stabbing pains in the stomach are signs that you should get evacuated pronto. Most food poisoning will usually run its course in a day or two, but it's important to be aware of the effects the symptoms have on your body. First of all, don't try to keep hiking. If at all possible you should try to find or set up a comfortable spot to rest and relax. Second, replace fluids. The runs and the pukes remove a lot of liquid from your body that you will need to replace to get better. This is exacerbated by heat and altitude. Basically you need to keep drinking water.

In an urgent-care facility or emergency room, doctors would administer an oral rehydration solution that includes complex carbs, sodium, potassium, glucose, and other chemicals. You're unlikely to have all those on hand, but you can make an approximation to replace some of your lost minerals. Sports drinks like Gatorade, mixes like Emergen-C, or rehydration-specific mix packets are ideal. But doctors recommend keeping these pretty watery to avoid overdoing your sugar intake. Watered-down fruit juice would also be a good substitute. Lacking such drinks, you could sprinkle some salt in your water to help rehydrate. Even eating some crackers or chips will provide carbs and sodium. Sip your water slowly, only 6 or 7 ounces at a sitting. Drinking too much liquid at once could distend your stomach and induce vomiting again, which defeats the purpose. Continue on this program and mix in light, salty, grain-based snacks, and you should be able to recover from food poisoning in a day or two. The best way to judge your hydration level is to look at urine color. If your pee is really dark, you're dehydrated. Once it returns to a clear, light yellow, you're probably rehydrated.

Poisoning from ingesting toxic mushrooms is often worse than that of bacteria from poor sanitation or sour meat. We'll say it at least three more times in this chapter as we point you toward a few common, identifiable, and edible fungi, but *do not eat a mushroom if you don't know what it is.* There are just as many that will make you deathly ill as will provide a tasty snack. Mushroom poisonings roughly break down into two categories: those that produce symptoms within six hours and those that produce symptoms after six hours. The afflictions that appear within six hours are usually non-lethal and generally include vomiting and diarrhea, and sometimes trouble breathing. Mushroom poisonings that produce symptoms after six hours, however, are cause for serious concern. These might be best characterized by the effects of the death cap mushroom, *Amanita phalloides*, which is responsible for some 90 percent of mushroom poisoning deaths. The symptoms will appear as diarrhea and vomiting about six to twelve hours after ingestion, then go away, making you feel like you're out of the woods. But then the actual shit hits the fan. The poison will cause your liver and kidneys to start to shut down, eventually leading to seizure, coma, and possibly death. In the terrible chance that you or someone in your party eats a mushroom and exhibits symptoms more than six hours later, you must do everything in your power to get yourself or that person professional medical attention immediately.

PLANTS

There are thousands of edible plants and fungi in North America alone, and the pages that follow do not attempt an exhaustive treatment of the subject. Instead, think of them as a reference guide to those species of the greatest relevance to wilderness travelers and foragers. These plants and fungi are fairly easy to identify, so there's a slightly reduced risk of eating the wrong thing by mistake. They are also fairly abundant in their respective habitats, so you have at least a decent chance of finding them during the right time of year once you know what you're looking for.

Depending on your location, there could be an abundance of edible plants around you, but you will need to make rational decisions about which ones are worth spending the time to process, cook, and eat. Obviously, your strategy should be influenced by your circumstances. If you're staying in one place (lost and waiting for rescue, rebooting from calamity, or just looking to supplement your diet with some wild foods), you may have time to deal with effort-intensive but calorie-dense foods like cattails or acorns. If you're hiking long distances toward a destination, your focus will be portable wild foods that are easily gathered and eaten while on the move or handled during short resting periods.

THAYER'S RULES ON WILD FOODS

For most of human history we lived exclusively on foods amassed through hunting and gathering. In my opinion, these are still the two most satisfying (and healthy) outdoor activities around. They can also save your life. I've been gathering most of my diet out in the woods for several decades and have written three books on the subject, as well as teaching foraging classes all over the country. I often go "survival camping" for fun and think every outdoor person would do well to familiarize themselves with some of these plants and practices.

The longer you are in the bush fending for yourself, the more important a balanced and adequate diet becomes—and you can't achieve this with meat alone. The good news is that if you are traveling in the wilds, you will almost certainly encounter some windfall of excellent food in the form of nuts, fruits, roots, mushrooms, or leafy vegetables. But there's a catch: you'll have to be able to recognize these as foods when you see them. You won't have the time to learn this in an emergency, so study plants ahead of time and follow my four basic foraging rules to stay safe:

1. Don't eat a plant or mushroom if you don't know what it is. Don't guess, ever. If you don't know, don't eat it. There are no shortcuts—you either recognize what plant it is, or you don't eat it. Plant poisonings are rarely the result of mistaken identity: most occur when people eat random plants without having made any attempt to identify them.
2. Once you've identified a particular food, don't overeat it. You might be tempted if you are lost, scared, and hungry, but be rational. Wild onions are edible, but eating a pound of raw onions will make you sick. You should be more cautious about overeating acidic fruits than sweet ones. Let your tummy tell you when to stop.

3. Just because it's the right plant or mushroom doesn't make it food. You need the right part, too. Apple pies are not made from apple twigs and seeds. Your subsistence will not benefit from tough leaves or stems, rotten fungi, or unripe fruit.
4. Cook things if you can—you'll digest them better. Always cook mushrooms.

—By Samuel Thayer, author, instructor, and foraging and wild foods expert based in northwestern Wisconsin

FRUITS AND BERRIES

When available, wild fruits and berries are a great source of fructose and vitamin C, which can help balance a diet of pure meat. Many of them are easy to identify. Crab apples look like apples. Choke cherries look like cherries. Wild asparagus looks like asparagus. Wild strawberries look like strawberries. Wild blueberries . . . you can probably guess. Most of these wild or feral forms of domestic plants are widely available, though often for only a month or even a week every year. A good rule of thumb is that most berries that are black or purple are edible. About half of red berries are good to eat, and only about 10 percent of yellow and white berries are safe. Even with that in mind, it's still a good idea to take a little nibble off a berry you don't recognize. If your tongue rejects it, your stomach is likely to do so, too. Play it safe, because certain berries can make you seriously sick, and watch your serving size. Even delicious little morsels like blackberries can wreak havoc on your insides if they are consumed in large amounts on an empty stomach. It can be hard to moderate a starving appetite, but you might suffer the consequences of a berry feast.

Hackberries. The closest thing in the wilds to a hamburger tree, as its fruits are high in calories and contain a mix of protein, oil, and carbs.

Identification: Hackberry trees can grow quite large, reaching heights over 100 feet, though rarely with trunks exceeding more than 4 feet in diameter. The leaves are asymmetrical, toothed, rounded at the bottom, and pointed on the end. The small, purple berries are found tucked away in the leaves.

Hackberry

Region: Most of the forested regions of the United States and southern Canada.

Season: From fall until the fruits are gone (they often last through winter).

Pros: Can be eaten raw. The fruit dries on the tree and does not spoil. Consists of a thin-shelled, tiny nut surrounded by a sweet dry pulp.

Cons: Seed shells may be too hard for some people's teeth to chew up. Fruit can be hard to reach and slow to gather.

Bramble Berries (blackberry, raspberry, salmonberry, thimbleberry, etc.). Beloved by many and perhaps the easiest berries to identify, these sweet or sour aggregate fruits include blackberries, salmonberries, raspberries, thimbleberries, loganberries, and many other subspecies and hybrids.

Identification: Bramble berry plants, as the name suggests, typically form thick, low-lying bushes with intertwining vines that are usually covered in thorns. The leaves are typically wide at the base, tapering to a narrow point, with serration along the edges. The berries are an aggregate fruit, with mul-

Bramble berry

tiple globules of juice forming one berry (picture a blackberry or a raspberry). Ripe berries will usually be black, purple, or red. Unripe berries are still edible, but typically sour.

Region: Common all over North America, except for desert landscapes.

Pros: Delicious and easy to recognize.

Cons: Not a lot of calories. Only available in summer. Thorns may make access difficult.

Gooseberries/currants. These tasty, grape-like members of the *Ribes* genus can be found almost everywhere in North America.

Identification: Small to medium-sized woody shrubs with numerous stems that mostly extend upward. The leaves are small, palmated, and lobed—not unlike a maple

Gooseberry

leaf. Fruits are round and translucent and bear a passing resemblance to grapes. They mature in shades (depending on species) from green to red or purple to black, with a tuft coming out the bottom.

Region: Found throughout North America, except the extreme Southeast.

Pros: Very tasty and easy to collect in bulk.

Cons: Not very calorie-dense and available only in summer.

Serviceberries. Known by many names, especially wild plum, shadbush, and the Cree name Saskatoon, the purple-red berries of this common tree were a favorite of settlers and indigenous tribes.

Identification: Several species of the genus *Amelanchier* are commonly clumped together as serviceberry. These plants range from low shrubs to tall, thin trees, usually with smooth gray bark, waxy oval leaves, and white flowers with five long, thin petals. The fruits look a lot like large blueberries, but with a red hue.

Serviceberry

Region: Found throughout North America, but most common in northern and mountainous areas.

Pros: Higher in calories than most fruits. Easy to harvest in quantity.

Cons: Only available for a short time in summer.

Blueberries. Perhaps the most celebrated and identifiable food on this list. Closely related to the also-delicious huckleberry and cranberry.

Identification: Blueberries grow from low-lying shrubs to tall bushes with small, oval leaves that are pointed at the ends. The fruits look just like the ones in your last muffin or pancake, though often smaller in the wild.

Blueberry

Region: From Alaska's North Slope to the pine forests of New Mexico, blueberries and huckleberries can be found anywhere in the West but are more common in northern and high elevation areas. They prefer poor soil, high moisture, and lots of sun exposure.

Pros: Easy to identify and often found in great quantity.

Cons: Only available for a short time in summer.

Black haw. A less familiar but valuable plant to know for folks living in and exploring the eastern side of the continent. Also known as nannyberry and wild raisin, its fruit comes into season later than most wild berries, often found ripe in September and through October, when few other fruits are available.

Identification: A small tree or shrub with nearly black bark that produces tiny white flowers and clusters of slightly oblong, wrinkly fruits that mature from green to red to purple, blue, or black. The plant's leaves are waxy and oval, with rounded bottoms, pointed tips, and finely toothed edges.

Black haw

Region: Eastern North America.

Pros: High in calories, late and long season for a berry, easy to collect.

Cons: Only found in limited range.

Crowberries. Though a species of the heather family, this plant bears fruits that are nearly identical to blueberries in appearance. They can provide a valuable food source in boreal and tundra regions.

Identification: Crowberry is a dwarf evergreen shrub forming low-lying mats of vegetation. The leaves are small and needle-like, similar to those of pine or fir trees. The berries look just like blueberries, though perhaps slightly darker.

Region: Crowberry is a circumboreal plant, meaning it is found in the northernmost forested areas and up in North America, Europe, and Asia. It grows throughout Canada and Alaska from the boreal forests extending well into the subarctic tundra.

Crowberry

Pros: Tasty, easy to gather in large quantities, and available through several seasons—unpicked berries may persist through the fall and winter, remaining edible into spring. They are less acidic than many wild berries.

Cons: Less juicy, sweet, and nutritious than many other wild berries.

NUTS

A variety of tree nuts can be found in deciduous hardwood forests throughout North America, especially the eastern half of the continent. You are likely already familiar with the key species, as they are commonly cultivated and eaten. They are nutritious, often containing a good deal of calories, protein, fat, fiber, and vitamins. And, due to their protective shells, tree nuts are often available and edible through the winter, when most other types of edible plants have rotted away.

Walnuts. Whether from Christmas nutcracker fodder or atop a fancy salad, most everyone knows what prepared walnuts look like and how good they taste. However, identifying them in the wild can be tricky for someone who's never seen them inside their highly protective husks.

Identification: Large, wide trees with long, oval leaves. The nuts grow all summer inside big green husks that look almost like apples. The husks eventually burst open, revealing a hard, wrinkled shell that falls to the forest floor. The lumpy fruit inside the shell is edible once mature.

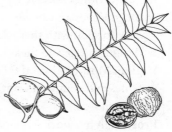
Walnut

Region: Eastern United States, Southwest, California.

Pros: Easy to identify, high in calories.

Cons: Cracking and shelling take time and are easier with tools. Shelling is difficult unless nuts are dry. Smashing the shells with a rock is sometimes the only way to go.

Hickory nuts (including pecans). There are more than a dozen types of hickory trees in North America. Most produce edible nuts, the pecan being the most famous of the lot.

Identification: Hickory trees are a common feature of eastern deciduous forests and can be identified by their ridged or shaggy bark. The nuts can be found inside round, green husks similar to those of walnuts. The husks peel back as the seed matures during the

Hickory nut

fall, revealing the smooth nut shell underneath. Break that open
and remove the meat from each of the chambers inside.

Region: Eastern North America.

Pros: Available in fall and often through the winter. High in calories
and fats.

Cons: Some types are hard to crack and shell.

Acorns. Oak trees may be among the most easily and commonly
identifiable trees on the continent. There are more than 600 species worldwide; all produce acorns for seeds. Any ripe, brown
acorn you find on or below an oak is edible, though they can be
intolerably bitter. Many varieties require soaking in water, sometimes over the course of several days, with repeated flushings, to
remove enough of the tannic acid to make them pleasant to eat.

Identification: Oaks are easy to identify by their
lobed leaves and sturdy trunks. Acorns are
easy to spot, with their classic shell-and-cap
design and halved meat inside.

Region: Most hardwood forests in the United
States and southern Canada, especially the
eastern side.

Pros: High in calories and often available in huge
quantity, easy to harvest, easy to identify.

Acorn

Cons: Must be leached (most commonly boiled
and drained multiple times) before eating in quantity.

ROOT VEGETABLES

Root vegetables comprise a very broad category that refers to all underground plant storage and growth organs, including taproots, tubers,
corms, bulbs, rhizomes, and more. They can be a little bit cryptic to for-
age, as the edible roots aren't immediately visible. You need to know what
the topside of the plant looks like, which is very easy in some instances
but rather tricky in others. Most root vegetables are easier to dig up with
a shovel, but none absolutely require it; a sharpened digging stick is
slower but effective nonetheless. With some exceptions, most root vegetables are difficult to digest when raw.

Cattails. An extremely versatile food plant, almost every part of
which is edible at different points in its maturation. Of particular

interest is the rhizome. This underground (and usually underwater) root is like an elongated tube of flour packed around thread. It's as filling and wholesome as a slice of bread. If baked before eating, which is easy to do on a fire or coals, cattail roots take on a flavor reminiscent of sweet potatoes.

Identification: Whether you call them tulies, reeds, or bulrushes, if you don't know what a cattail is you probably haven't spent much time outside. These tall, cigar-topped plants are ubiquitous throughout the edges of watercourses and wetlands across all corners of the continent. They are visible from great distances and often found in huge quantities.

Cattail

Edible part: The underground rhizome is the tastiest and most nutritious part, and it's edible nearly the whole year. While the main root may become starchy and dry during the summer, its new-growth shoots are quite good at that time. Rhizomes are like bread flour with thread; you chew it up, suck out the starch, and spit out the fiber. You can also boil them or bake in hot coals. Collect rhizomes by pulling and wiggling gently upward on the base of the stalk. Remove the new shoots to eat, and peel the root with a knife.

The core and base of the tall stalk itself is quite good when gathered from spring to early fall. Peel away the dry outer leaves and eat the white base and core raw or cooked. Likewise, the tiptop of the plant, known as the spike, is good when green and growing in early summer.

The distinctive, cigar-shaped tufts near the top of the plant have some utility as well. They produce an edible pollen in midsummer that can be mixed with water and other foods as a thickening agent. They can also be used as fire-starting tinder when dry.

Pros: Very widespread. Certain parts are edible in winter when few other plants are available. Rhizomes are high in calories, easy to harvest, and require no tools or cooking.

Cons: Confined to water, which may be frozen in winter. Can be confused with irises, but iris leaf clusters are flattened.

Thistles. Once you get past the thorns, thistles are a mild vegetable that any hungry person can appreciate.

Identification: Known for their large, bulb-like purple flower and nasty thorns around the edges, these notorious weeds will already be familiar to most.

Thistle

Region: Found throughout North America.

Edible part: The roots are good to eat from fall to spring. The roots of some species are tough, while others are large and tender. New shoots are tender and delicious after peeling, especially when cooked. Even the stalks are edible during the growth time from spring to fall. You have to remove all the leafy parts and thorns, but what's left over is similar to a thin celery stalk.

Pros: Requires no cooking, easy to harvest and recognize.

Cons: Thorny, requires careful peeling.

Prairie turnips. Most root vegetables must be cooked to digest, but prairie turnips (also known as breadroot) can be eaten raw.

Identification: Prairie turnip is a short herb, easy to miss if you don't know what to look for. But under closer inspection, it can be distinguished by the erect hairs that emerge from its aboveground parts, and its small blue or purple flowers. Dig it up and the bulbous root should closely resemble the turnips you're used to.

Region: Throughout the Great Plains of central North America, from Manitoba to Texas, and up into the foothills of the Rocky Mountains.

Prairie turnip

Edible part: Roots, 2 to 4 inches under the surface. You can eat them peeled and raw, dried, or cooked.

Season: Spring to early summer, during and just after blooming.

Pros: Rather high in calories and easy to digest raw.

Cons: Short season, can be hard to recognize and difficult to dig up in some soils.

Wild onions. Pretty much every ecotype in North America has its own wild or feral alliaceous vegetable, whether it be onions, garlic, ramps, leeks, or chives—often in great quantities. There's a good chance you've walked past some of it before, thinking it was grass. All species are edible.

Identification: Scent is the best way to find and identify wild onion species. You may catch a whiff of that onion or garlic scent as you walk through the woods, especially when trampling the plants. If it smells like an onion, it's an onion. They all have long, round, grass-like leaves emerging from a bulb.

Wild onion

Edible part: Fresh shoots are good eating throughout spring. The bulbs remain good even after the leaves die in the summer and into fall.

Region: From high mountains to deserts to coasts, onion species are ubiquitous.

Pros: Found almost everywhere. Easy to recognize (linear leaves and onion/garlic scent). Available much of the year.

Cons: Moderate caloric content, require cooking to be easily digestible.

GREENS

The term "shoot" refers to a tender young stem that is still actively growing. The term "greens" refers to the tender, young, leafy growth of various edible plants. Human stomachs can only handle tender, young greenery; tough greens are a waste of jaw effort and gut space. Even hoofed herbivores focus on tender young growth if they can find it.

Though shoots and greens are low in calories, they shouldn't be ignored in a survival situation. When it comes to vitamins and minerals, they are among the most nutritionally dense of all foods, and they are more digestible when cooked. A few of these veggies mixed with meat or a starchy staple will add nutritional balance to your meal, contribute to your health and energy levels, help you maintain good levels of electrolytes, and reduce cramping and constipation. All of this will become more important with time.

Nettles. Though it might seem counterintuitive to put a plant with such an aggravating sting in your mouth, nettles are actually delicious, nutritious, and a staple for many foragers. Their infamous sting comes from the hairs on the bottom side of the leaves, so you should collect them by pinching down on the surface of the leaves, folding the hairs inside the crease.

Nettle

Identification: A tall weed that grows in large clusters. Wide, serrated leaves with stinging hairs on the underside.

Season: Nettles produce new growths of greens in the spring, but the leaves can be eaten well into the winter.

Region: Throughout North America, except certain high altitude and arid areas.

Edible part: Shoots and greens. They can be eaten raw, but cooking removes all stinging capabilities. The product comes out with a taste and texture somewhere between asparagus and spinach.

Pros: Easy to collect, high in protein and vitamins C and A.

Cons: Low in calories, requires cooking, stings.

Lamb's quarters. Also known as goosefoot, this versatile plant is thought to be among the earliest to be cultivated in North America, thousands of years before the arrival of Europeans.

Lamb's quarters

Identification: Tall, leafy herbs with stems that gather masses of small, consecutive seedpods in late summer. Leaves of one common species are maple-like, while the leaves of the other are more rounded.

Region: All but the coldest regions.

Edible part: Shoots, greens, seeds.

Season: Spring and summer for greens, seeds in fall and early winter.

Pros: Easy to harvest, high in protein.

Cons: Low in calories, seeds are labor-intensive to shell.

Amaranth. A favorite of survivalists and foragers, these tall weeds can be found almost anywhere and provide several uses.

Identification: Tall, narrow weeds with thick stems and thin leaves. They develop thick clusters of seeds later in the growing cycle. Similar in appearance to lamb's quarters.

Amaranth

Edible part: Leaves, shoots, and seeds.

Season: Summer for leaves and shoots, fall and early winter for grain-like seeds.

Region: All but the coldest regions.

Pros: High in protein, easy to harvest in quantity.

Cons: Identification not obvious, leaves require cooking for digestibility, seeds are labor-intensive to use.

Mustard greens (cresses). Mustard plants are found almost everywhere in North America and are easy to identify, especially the black mustard variety. The seeds are easily gathered in bulk in the fall by beating the bush and letting the grains fall into a container.

Identification: Often found as large, branching plants with long, thin stems ending in clusters of small yellow flowers.

Edible part: Greens and seeds.

Region: Throughout North America.

Season: Spring through fall, winter in warmer climates.

Pros: Long season, found everywhere.

Cons: Low in calories, must be cooked to eat in quantity.

Mustard green

MUSHROOMS

A survival instructor from the Air Force's premier survival school once told us that his curriculum completely bypassed wild mushrooms. They were too easy to misidentify, he explained, and the risk of getting poisoned didn't warrant the small caloric boost. There's a bit of truth to that. Without an extremely high degree of familiarity and/or a guidebook, you're just as likely to get the shits (or worse) from a wild mushroom as you are a good meal. That said, in our years wandering around the woods and waters of the United States, we've become familiar with a few favorites that are exceptionally tasty, easy to identify, and widely available. These dozen mushrooms are worth knowing about as a special treat in the best of times, as well as a morale booster and an easy meal in the worst of times. Master them, and you'll have a good foundation in mycology that can grow with further study and experimentation.

Most mushrooms should be cooked, though some can be eaten raw. But the good news is that almost any application of heat will do the trick. Depending on what tools and cookware you have at your disposal, you can sauté in a pan, boil in a pot, or even roast on a sharpened stick over a fire. They make a great addition to anything else you already might be eating and can typically be cooked alongside other items.

There's a classic maxim that there are old mushroom hunters and there are bold mushroom hunters, but there aren't any old, bold mushroom hunters. Remember Thayer's rules about identification on page 92, and never, ever eat a mushroom unless you're certain what it is.

> **Morels.** These may be one of the strangest-looking mushrooms out there, but they're our favorites—and we're not alone. Because they are delicious but extremely difficult to farm, morels are some of the most commercially valuable wild mushrooms. A great starting point in the world of mycology, morels have turned many a turkey hunter into a mushroom hunter.
>
> **Identification:** Commonly described as brain-like with wrinkles and folds, pear-shaped, sometimes growing as large as a soda can but often merely the size of a golf ball. Colors vary between species and environments from yellow or gold to brown or black. Often the color derives from the surrounding environment, making them sometimes tricky to locate at first.
>
>
>
> Morel
>
> **Region:** Most of North America except extremely arid areas. Especially prevalent in cottonwood river bottoms and wildfire burn areas.
>
> **Season:** Spring at low elevations and summer in high elevations. Varies by region.
>
> **Pros:** Very delicious, often found in large quantities, easy to identify.
>
> **Cons:** Short growing season. Their surface collects the substrate around them, so they may be sandy or sooty until cleaned. True morels bear a passing resemblance to false morels, which have a more squashed and lumpy appearance. False morels won't kill you but could make you sick.

Oyster mushrooms. Commonly sold in stores, these familiar mushrooms have some of the cleanest flesh among fungi.

Identification: These white to light tan or gray mushrooms grow in terraced clusters, usually off the side of trees or dead wood, often near water. They have flat tops, rounded edges, and short, slightly funnel-shaped stems with gills.

Region: Found throughout most of the Midwest and eastern United States and Canada.

Oyster mushroom

Season: Spring and fall. They usually appear shortly after rain.

Pros: Very easy to identify, found in obvious places, long growing season, all flesh is edible.

Cons: Somewhat unpredictable in their growth but little else negative.

King boletes. This big, meaty mushroom, also known in its domesticated form as porcini, provides a substantial meal that could be a windfall in a survival situation.

Identification: This is one of the largest mushrooms you're likely to encounter, with the wide, thick, brown or reddish caps sometimes reaching as much as 14 inches across. The stems are also rather thick and sometimes bulbous, usually white or gray. Boletes are often moist to the touch.

King bolete

Region: Widespread in North America, more common at higher elevations, most common under hemlock and oak.

Season: Summer and fall.

Pros: Can be found in high densities, and a single one of these specimens is often large enough to anchor a meal. Easy to identify.

Cons: King boletes often house worms or insects that burrow inside and render the fungus inedible.

Coral mushrooms. As the name suggests, these fungi species look a lot like the coral growing on underwater reefs in the tropics, with numerous individual tubers emerging and branching vertically from a single base.

Identification: Some say corals have an almost cauliflower-like appearance. Avoid brightly colored iterations. The white, beige, or yellow crown-tipped coral mushrooms are the only varieties that are edible.

Region: Most of North America.

Season: Early summer through fall.

Pros: Easy to cook, very noticeable in the woods.

Coral mushroom

Cons: Use caution. There are many similar-looking species that are noxious or poisonous.

Puffballs. These large, round, white mushrooms are about the most obvious fungi you'll encounter. They can range anywhere from baseball to even volleyball size.

Identification: Big and round, usually white but sometimes light tan. Exterior is usually smooth or lightly scaled. When you cut inside, the meat should be pure white flesh throughout. Any yellow-brown or purple flesh is overripe and no good. Some similar-looking, inedible mushrooms look

Puffball mushroom

like puffballs but have stems that run up through the cap to the center, instead of stopping at the edge of the ball.

Region: Everywhere in North America.

Season: Spring and summer

Pros: Easy to find, high in protein, often growing in open areas and visible from a long distance.

Cons: None.

Shaggy manes. One of the most easily identifiable and predictable mushrooms. Many people are familiar with them because they often grow in urban areas.

Identification: Tall, oblong, often bell-shaped fungi with flowery or scaly sides that curl upward. Completely white or slightly tan, and shouldn't be harvested if they appear at all black. Odorless.

Region: Everywhere.

Shaggy mane

Season: Shaggy manes appear after rain events and can be present all year so long as temperatures are above 50°F.

Pros: They grow in obvious places, especially disturbed soils like game trails. Very long growing season, maybe the longest of any wild edible mushroom. Very predictably associated with rain.

Cons: Although they have a long growing season, they have a short shelf life. Shortly after maturing they will start to dissolve and will appear to be melting. Don't eat after this occurs.

Chanterelles. This vibrant, delicious mushroom is a favorite of mycology nerds across the continent.

Identification: Mostly shades of orange but can appear yellow, tan, or red. Trumpet shaped with wavy edges along the cap. Very fruity, apricot-like odor.

Region: Everywhere.

Season: Summer through fall.

Pros: Relatively long growing season, very obvious to spot, all flesh edible.

Chanterelle

Cons: Can be confused with poisonous jack-o'-lantern mushroom. Chanterelles have shallow, false gills that look melted or wrinkled. Jack-o'-lanterns and false chanterelles have true gills and round, uniform caps without waves.

Hen-of-the-woods. These highly prized mushrooms often coincide with hunting seasons, making them popular with mushroom hunters and normal hunters alike.

Identification: Large clumps of brown, tan, or gray soft fans stacked on top of each other, usually on or around stumps or living trees. Most common on hardwoods and in hardwood forests.

Region: Temperate regions of North America.

Season: Late summer into fall.

Pros: Grow in big clusters, providing a big meal. Available later into fall than many mushrooms.

Hen-of-the-woods

Cons: Short shelf life. Hen-of-the-woods can become very hard and inedible as they age.

Honey mushrooms. Many folks consider these to be among the best-tasting wild mushrooms, but their flavor and digestibility don't agree with everyone. Some people experience gastrointestinal distress after eating them.

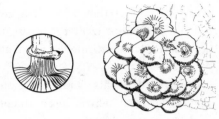

Honey mushroom

Identification: Clusters of long stems with relatively small, rounded caps that are grayish pink to yellow or brown. Densely clustered around living or dead trees.

Region: Everywhere.

Season: Midsummer to late fall.

Pros: Long growing season, considered excellent food quality.

Cons: Some people experience mild poisoning. Should never be eaten raw. Sometimes resemble the poisonous jack-o'-lantern mushrooms described in the "Chanterelles" section.

Fairy ring mushrooms. It's easy to see how this fungus got its name, as it is usually found growing in wide, strange circles as large as 20 feet in diameter that give the appearance of some otherworldly intervention.

Identification: Individual mushrooms growing in small, unattached clumps to large circles. Flattened bell-shaped caps in brown, tan, yellow, or white with distinct gills beneath and slender, tall stems.

Fairy ring mushrooms

Region: Everywhere.

Season: Spring to summer.

Pros: Often growing in open areas, on grassy soil in meadows and shrublands, and thus rather visible.

Cons: They look a lot like several other nondescript hard-to-identify mushrooms. Typically associated with urban areas.

Chicken-of-the-woods. One of the most distinctive and easily identifiable 'shrooms, these get their name because they resemble a rooster's flamboyant colors—but they also actually taste like chicken.

Identification: An exception to the rule that you shouldn't eat vibrantly colored mushrooms, these bright orange or yellow mushrooms taste as good as they look. They always grow on the side of trees in wrinkled fans stacked on top of each other. Often lobed or wavy.

Chicken-of-the-woods

Region: Everywhere that trees grow.

Season: Late spring to early fall.

Pros: Easy to spot, very tasty, grow in big clusters and easy to identify. Nothing else looks quite like them.

Cons: They often house critters that can ruin entire clumps.

Dryad's saddle/pheasant back/hawk's wing mushrooms. Known by many names because of its wide distribution, this fungus is often ignored by even dedicated foragers—but it shouldn't be.

Identification: As the names imply, the tops have a tan, feathery look, not unlike a hen pheasant. Large, thick, brown caps, often fan-shaped and flat, with an under-surface that is white to yellowish. They only appear on trees and are most common on dead elms. Similar habitat to morels.

Dryad's saddle

Region: Throughout the Midwest, Appalachians, and southern Canada to the foothills of the Rockies.

Season: Spring and summer.

Pros: Grow in large clumps, quality taste, easy to identify.

Cons: Short life span. If the mushroom feels like it still has moisture, it's ripe. If it's dry, don't eat it. The stalk is not typically edible.

INSECTS AND INVERTEBRATES

Consuming creepy crawlies has never been popular in modern North America, but if you take a global view, our distaste for these food items is more the exception than the rule. For millennia, insects have been considered ordinary table fare in Asia, Africa, South America, and even Europe. And in a real-world survival situation, insects may be your best food option, since they can often be gathered in bulk with little effort and contain a good mix of carbs, fats, and protein.

As a rule of thumb, it's best to avoid any insect with a furry appearance, such as caterpillars or bees. Bugs bearing bright colorations, strong odors, or an apparent lack of fear in the open should be handled with caution as well, because they are likely noxious if not outright poisonous. Grasshoppers, cicadas, and dragonflies are all okay, and are easiest to catch in the cool temperatures of the morning. Once they get warmed by the sun, they become far more difficult to catch. Most ant species are edible, though sour-tasting. Find ants, termites, and a host of other insects and their larvae by flipping over rocks or logs. While doing so, keep your eyes peeled for cockroaches, moths, and other edibles like grubs. Flip over rocks in the water, too, because you could find edible morsels like stonefly or damselfly nymphs, caddis larvae, leeches, or even tiny scuds and sowbugs. The flying, adult forms of aquatic insects are edible as well. Look for them in the air and on vegetation or stones near waterways. At 3 inches long, a full-grown giant salmonfly is packed with calories. You can also catch (seine) small or tough-to-catch insects by stretching a shirt or bandana between two sticks.

Many insects can be eaten raw or even alive, but it's not for the squeamish. It may provide a more positive culinary experience to boil or roast your bugs first. This will also kill off any bad bacteria or parasites they may be carrying. Remove any spikes, barbs, or thorny legs before tossing a handful of bugs down your gullet. Likewise, many folks prefer to twist the heads off such insects as grasshoppers and cicadas, which also removes the guts.

SHELLFISH

If you've ever seen a small plate of oysters or crabs on special for $40 at a seafood restaurant, you'll likely need no further convincing that shellfish are very good to eat. They are also easy to catch, at least at times. A tremendous variety of shellfish can be found in saltwater and brackish water. While the selection is far less impressive in freshwater, there is still plenty of opportunity there.

CRAYFISH

Crayfish, also often called crawdads or mudbugs, are broadly distributed across the Lower 48 and well into Canada. There are many species, all of which are edible and have the appearance and flavor of small lobsters.

Though it would take a very large specimen to net you more than an ounce of meat, where there's one crayfish, there's often more. Creep slowly along the edges of waterways, keeping an eye out for their distinctive, clawed profile. Turn over rocks and logs at the water's edge that might be hiding crays. To escape, they flip their tails to scoot backward through the water at a surprising speed. But they often don't go far, and you can usually pounce on them like you would a frog. Hand-grabbing them is especially effective at night with the use of an artificial light, as they tend to come out of hiding and are easy to find.

There are several effective ways to catch crayfish in addition to hand-grabbing. Rig up a cane pole with a slender limb and some thread or fishing line and tie a piece of bait—fish guts, frog guts, scraps of virtually any meat—to the end of the line. Lower this to a crayfish and they will latch on with such tenacity that you can usually pull them free of the water and land them in a bucket or in your hand. (Their claws can hurt you, but they won't do any lasting damage. Grip them tightly just behind their claws and there's less of a chance of getting grabbed in return.) Another simple strategy is to pin a fish head or fish guts under a rock in shallow water and then come back periodically to snatch up whatever crayfish have been drawn to the bait.

Any large bucket, barrel, or trash bin can be put to use as a crayfish trap as long as you've got some bait. Drill or bore several 1.5-inch holes through the bucket about 6 to 8 inches up from the bottom. In a creek, lake, pond, or river where crayfish can be found, sink the bucket into the mud or gravel until the bottom of the holes are even with the bottom of the lake. Put your bait in the bucket and secure it beneath the water with a rock or other weight. The crayfish will enter the holes, and once they fall to the bottom of the bucket, they'll have a hard time finding their way out.

The classic and much loved method of cooking crayfish is to boil them whole, shucking the meat out of the tail and sucking the innards out of the head. The largest may even have edible meat in their claws. You can also cook crayfish by setting them on hot rocks adjacent to a fire to let the meat steam and cook inside the exoskeleton. Or simply roll a burning log away from the fire and place the crayfish on the smoldering surface to cook. If you have no means for making fire, however, you can eat the meat raw, although doing so has been linked to a rare parasitic fluke in certain areas.

CRABS

Excluding the furthest southern tropical reaches, there are no freshwater crabs in North America. But there are plenty to be found in any estuarine or inshore waters. From Dungeness crabs in the Northwest to rock crabs in California, from stone crabs in Florida to blue crabs in the Northeast, it's possible to find a tasty crustacean in any coastal area. They're easy to catch and steam nicely in their own shells when placed over a driftwood fire.

Many crab species occupy the intertidal zone, those areas that are either dry or wet depending on the timing of the tide cycle. Crabs will be more accessible during low tides. You can often find very small ones in large quantities in the rocks higher on the beach and tide pools, but these usually won't provide much or any food value. Eater-sized crabs, at least in North America, typically remain in the water, but they can be found in very shallow areas during low tides. You can catch these crustaceans by wading very slowly through eelgrass or kelp beds, keeping your eyes peeled for any hint of red, orange, blue, or shiny black, depending on the species in that area. Crabs can be surprisingly quick in water, so you want to approach with minimal disturbance and strike fast, trying to pin it to the bottom by the top of the shell. Grab the crab by its back two legs, making sure to keep your fingers away from the claws (assuming you want to keep those fingers).

Crabs in North America are typically safe to eat raw so long as toxic algae like red tide are not present. But they're also arguably the simplest animal to cook, so if you have means to make a fire you might as well do so. Once you have a meal's worth of crabs, dispatch them with a sharp blow to the center-forward portion of the shell. Build a fire and place one log nearby but outside of the flames. Set your whole crabs on that log in the indirect heat from the adjacent fire and let the meat steam inside the shell. You can remove the crabs from the log once the shell has changed color and is hot to the touch. Let them cool down, then remove the carapace and separate the two sides by grasping them by the legs (that's four legs per side in each hand) and twisting in opposite directions. Discard the guts, gills, and carapace, then start to pick out the meat. On most crabs, most of the flesh is located inside the main body, where the legs connect. Many crabs have edible amounts of meat inside the legs and claws, too. You can often break the appendages open with your fingers, but smashing them open with a rock may be necessary on larger species like Dungeness.

PARALYTIC SHELLFISH POISONING

Unfortunately, no amount of cooking will eliminate the potential of getting sick or dying from the neurotoxic bacteria that can be present in clams, mussels, oysters, scallops, sea cucumbers, crabs—nearly any type of shellfish. Paralytic shellfish poisoning, or PSP, is produced when naturally occurring marine algae bloom and reproduce. Shellfish consume that algae and can retain dangerous levels of the biotoxin in their flesh.

PSP is often associated with red tide—thick, goopy algal blooms that sometimes appear along coastlines—but the two conditions are not synonymous. It's true that real red tide does produce PSP, but many similar-looking algal blooms are harmless. And PSP may be present even if visible algal blooms are not. Traditional wisdom holds that you should only eat bivalves in months that contain an "R" in their name, as PSP is most common during the warmer summer months of May, June, July, and August. But it can absolutely occur at any time during the year. In many areas, recreational clam diggers are able to consult up-to-date websites or hotlines to ascertain the safety of local shellfish beds. Without that, there's always going to be a calculated risk associated with bivalves. Symptoms of PSP can begin almost immediately with a tingling sensation in your tongue and lips that spreads to your face, neck, fingers, and toes. Symptoms worsen depending on severity of exposure and can lead to respiratory failure in extreme cases. We've seen and heard of various strategies for trying to determine the safety of shellfish without the aid of testing. Before eating untested bivalves, we've known people to rub the meat against their lips in order to see if it induces symptoms. Or to eat just a small sample from a single clam and then wait an hour or so to make sure there are no symptoms before resuming the meal. These are imperfect solutions to a serious problem, and they are not fail-safe. Hopefully in the near future there will be an inexpensive, reliable, and easily transportable PSP test kit. Until then, exercise caution and restraint.

SHRIMP

The jumbo prawns you know from restaurants were either farmed or trapped in deep water. Near-shore shrimp are typically smaller, though many species, such as ghost and sand shrimp, are big enough to warrant the effort of catching them. Their eyes reflect light, so look for them in shallow water at night with a flashlight. They can be scooped up with a bait net, or with a makeshift net made out of a T-shirt stretched over a frame with enough small cuts in the fabric to allow it to pass easily through the water. Shrimp can be eaten raw. The bulk of the meat is in the tail, though smaller shrimp can be roasted on a fire or smoldering log and eaten whole without ill effect.

MOLLUSCS

The world is home to some 85,000 species of molluscs, a phylum that includes gastropods (snails and slugs), cephalopods (octopuses and squids), and bivalves (clams, scallops, oysters, and mussels). These may not be on the top of your mind as survival foods, but they should be. To get a sense of the importance of bivalves as a wild food, consider the enormous size of the shellfish middens found at coastal Native American campsites. Archaeologists study these ancient dumping grounds, where centuries' worth of bivalve shells were discarded, because they can help explain ancient cooking methods, seasonal use, and even village size. There are an estimated 2,000 shellfish middens along the coast of Maine that were large enough to remain recognizable after hundreds of years; some are so large that they were later mined by Europeans, who burned the shells to create lime. That's a lot of clams.

No doubt, the popularity of bivalves with indigenous peoples around the world is testament to their utility. They're easy to locate, simple to cook, and, best of all, they don't run away. They also make great bait for catching fish. Most coastal areas of North America offer some sort of clam, oyster, or mussel. They can be found anywhere from rocks above the water's surface to several feet underground in deep water. Some will be abundantly obvious, but even if you don't actually see them, there are many clues that give away their presence. The first is empty shells, a clear indicator that something else has been enjoying these treats. Spurts of water launching into the air are an even better indicator of hidden clam beds—subsurface clams will often launch little jets of water to rid themselves of sand or defend themselves from predators. Even if you don't see the water squirts, you may be able to locate the source by noticing small dimples on the surface of an otherwise flat sandy beach. And, if all else fails, it can be worth the effort to pick an area of clean-looking sand or small rocks or pebbles below the high tide line and just dig around or kick the substrate. You may be surprised by what you find.

Oysters are much easier to find. They are often concentrated in distinct beds, growing out in the open on top of rocks, mangrove roots, or masses of other oyster shells. If you find some scattered oysters here and there, there's a good chance that a feast's worth of the bivalves is nearby.

Mussels are usually smaller but no less worthy. These oblong black, blue, or purple bivalves attach themselves to whatever they can, including rocks, logs, ropes, and kelp. The largest are quite meaty, but any size will be a good meal if you can gather them in bulk. People who gather mussels for the first time are often surprised by how gritty they are. To get the grit out of mussels, you need to suspend them in clean ocean water inside a mesh sack or perforated bucket so that they can flush out.

Clams, oysters, and mussels are popular cuisine wherever seafood is consumed and they are eaten both raw and cooked, though cooking is generally a good idea. You can pry these morsels open by inserting a knife blade or sharp rock into the shell where it hinges open. If that doesn't work, search the end that opens for anywhere you can find purchase. If you have the means to make a fire, by all means do so. You can set bivalves next to a fire to steam until they pop open, or boil them in a pot of water. This method will likely make them more appetizing, may be easier on your stomach, and will get rid of most (but not all) bacteria and parasites that may be present.

There are several species of freshwater clams and mussels, but they do not hold much meat or food value. If you happen into the motherlode of exceptionally large freshwater clams, it might be worth gathering a few to experimentally cook with, but don't waste too much energy on the project.

Though not related to molluscs, echinoderms like sea cucumbers and urchins occupy many of the same environments as bivalves. Both are very prickly on the outside, but those spines protect the delicious meat inside. If you have a knife or other means of getting inside, make sure not to pass up on these alien-looking animals.

FISH

If you've seen the classic mountain man movie *Jeremiah Johnson,* you'll remember the scene where Robert Redford's character frantically splashes around in a half-frozen creek while chasing a trout. Suddenly he's surprised by the presence of a Native American man on horseback—warm and dry—who's hauling a rope strung with a bunch of trout. It's an iconic moment in American cinema that reinforces a valuable lesson: catching fish can be a hell of a lot harder than you think. It can be hard even when you're armed with space-age fishing tackle, and it can be especially hard when you're not. That might sound discouraging, but don't let it get you down. We've had the fortune of traveling with Amerindians in South America who derive the bulk of their protein from freshwater fish, and they do so without the use of any modern tackle. They hunt fish with homemade bows; they catch fish with hand-woven nets; they employ setlines; they even catch fish by stunning them with toxins derived from plants collected in the jungle. While these tactics have been honed and passed down for thousands of years, they still demonstrate the roles that inventiveness and adaptability can play in the acquisition of fish.

BUILDING A BASIC FISHING KIT

If you were a Navy pilot in World War II, you would have flown around with a white bucktail jig and hand line in your survival kit. This always bothered me. I can't argue against a white bucktail jig lure in terms of its versatility. It will, after all, catch pretty much any fish that swims. I've also seen what one swipe from a barracuda can do to a bucktail. Imagine being the lucky airman who made it to the atoll after bailing out, only to have your best means of thwarting starvation reduced to a hairless jighead after a bite from a single fish. Knowing that a bucktail's durability isn't outstanding, had I been a pilot in World War II, I'd have slipped a few metal spoons into my ditch bag.

No matter where you are in the world, regardless of the water type you're on, if it is populated by fish that eat smaller fish, they'll eat a spoon. Over time, that spoon may become scratched, nicked, chipped, and pitted, but rendering it completely useless is extremely difficult. There is no plastic lip that can break off. It doesn't rely on a soft rubber tail for action. I have some tarnished, if not a touch rusty, metals in my saltwater bag that have been catching stripers since I was in college.

Spoons come in all shapes and sizes, but understanding their two main categories is key. Always carry a few lighter wobbling spoons, such as a Dardevle. Skip those with paint jobs; you want plain silver or gold. In warmer months, reeling in steadily catches fish. As the water cools, slow down and let the lure drop and flutter. When it's colder still, you can finesse a spoon by letting it lie on the river or lake bottom, imparting subtle twitches to make it occasionally hop. If that water is frozen, chop yourself a hole and jig that spoon vertically. Heavier "slab style" spoons, such a Hopkins NO=EQL, are just as versatile and should be part of your kit. They are particularly valuable when distance casting is necessary, or when you're fishing water deeper than roughly 20 feet. In a pinch, you can also use a slab spoon as a sinker to deliver bait.

Unless you'll be surviving near water that only holds 50-pound king salmon or 40-pound snook, a 3500-size-class spinning reel will handle most fish, especially if you know how to properly adjust the drag. Reels that are fully sealed will cost you more money, but they're not a terrible investment considering how little dirt, grit, or gunk it takes to turn a cheap spinning reel into a locked-up pile of junk. Remember that you're fishing to eat, not to set line class records, so spool up with 10-to-12-pound fluorocarbon line, even when smaller trout and panfish are the primary targets. Fluorocarbon is tougher than monofilament and much less visible to fish. Braided line may be stronger, but should your reel fail, you can safely use fluorocarbon to hand-line. With braid, you'd risk slicing your fingers, which could lead to bigger problems than what you'll be eating.

There are plenty of packable four-piece spinning rods on the market in a wide range of prices, many of which include two tip sections—usually one medium- and one heavy-action. The ability to change actions is nifty, but in a potential survival scenario, having two tips in case one snaps is a valuable form of backup.

Carrying a selection of baitholder-style hooks is a smart move in case those spoons aren't producing or more potent fresh bait is available, and while the sizes you'll want will vary by location and species, don't buy the cheapest hooks in the aisle. Budget hooks are usually made from lower-grade stainless steel. They rust easily, they bend easily, and they'll dull if you look at them wrong. Hooks from companies like Gamakatsu and Owner are made of high-carbon steel, they don't bend, and it takes serious abuse to dull their razor-sharp points. Finally, while you could lug around a plethora of sinkers, using them requires lugging extra terminal tackle, too. Make life easy and grab a variety pack of different sizes of lead split shot. You can crimp as few or as many as you need directly on your line above the hook, and if you buy the removable kind (which you should), you won't even need to dig out your multi-tool. Adding and subtracting split shot is one of the many reasons God gave you teeth. Lacking split shot or other commercially produced fishing weights, sink your bait by improvising with whatever you have on hand, including nuts, bolts, or washers.

—By Joe Cermele, senior fishing editor at MeatEater *and former fishing editor at* Field & Stream *and* Outdoor Life

THREE LIVE BAIT SETUPS

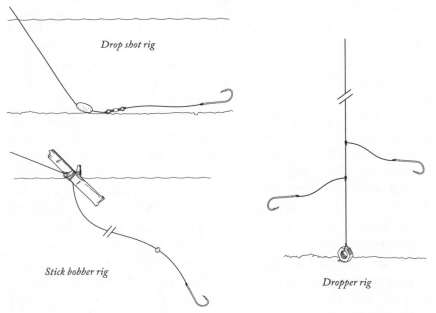

A drop shot rig (top left) allows anglers to fish bait directly on the river or lake floor. Using multiple hooks on a dropper rig (right) increases your odds of catching dinner by presenting multiple baits at different depths. For shallow water or fish eating near the surface, adding a simple stick bobber (bottom left) keeps your bait suspended and makes it much easier to detect strikes.

FINDING FISH

Sometimes fish are readily visible from the banks of a waterway. More often they are not—but that doesn't mean they aren't present. A variety of visual and auditory clues can tip you off to good angling opportunities, if you know what to look for and pay close attention.

Any disturbance of the water is likely a fish or some other edible creature, like a frog or turtle. Many kinds of fish, especially trout and panfish, regularly eat insects and other food on the surface of the water. Sometimes those attacks are violent and loud enough to hear from some distance; sometimes they cause a barely perceptible dimple or swirl just below the surface.

As you creep bear-like along a stream, you may also see sudden wakes, ripples, or plumes of mud—disturbances likely caused by fleeing fish that saw you before you saw them. Don't let this discourage you; take note of the location and its characteristics and try to identify others like it later on. If one patch of habitat is holding fish, similar patches nearby should follow suit.

Below the surface, look for round areas of riverbed gravel or lake bottom mud that appear to have been wiped clean of silt. This usually indicates that fish have spawned in that spot and are likely nearby. Along a shoreline, a smattering of fish bones and guts left by predators is another telltale sign.

In the absence of visual clues indicating fish presence, in many instances it is safe to assume that where there is permanent water, there are permanent residents. Certain areas and waterscape features will regularly aggregate fish more than others. These are best spotted from shore or from shallow waters when wading; boats certainly change the game, but boat anglers will often fish along shorelines anyway. Look for three factors that may indicate fish presence:

- **Depth.** Along a relatively uniform shoreline, the deepest area is likely to hold the most fish. If you can't tell how deep the water is, look at the adjacent land. The angle of the slope of a lakeside hill is likely reflected underwater.
- **Structure.** Trees fallen into rivers or riprap (rocks and boulders) along lake edges are good areas to target. Weed beds, lily pads, docks, or overhanging trees and vegetation also give fish places to hide and/ or ambush prey.

- **Confluence.** Points where two waterways come together are always good places to fish diligently. Whether it's a river outlet into a lake, two creeks coming together, even a cove opening out to a lake, confluences almost always offer better fishing than the areas around them. Fish seek out these places to access colder or cleaner water, to travel up tributaries to spawn, or to create ambush opportunities on a natural bottleneck.

ICE FISHING

Don't rule out fish as a viable source of food during the winter months in places where lakes and ponds are frozen. Since it's difficult to read water depth or locate fish through the ice, start by looking for coves and peninsulas. Once you've settled on a spot to fish, chop a hole through the ice with your hatchet, and use the equipment from your basic survival fishing kit to catch your dinner. Slowly jig a spoon or suspend a bait at various depths, starting at the bottom and working your way up, until you get a bite. Remember, venturing onto the ice does entail some risk; test ice thickness for safety by following the protocols on page 295.

STAY ON THE RIGHT SIDE OF THE LAW

From a legal standpoint, you can't just go killing animals and catching fish willy-nilly. It's important to note that if you're planning on supplementing your food supply with wild fish or game, you must adhere to state and federal hunting regulations surrounding protected species, licensing requirements, season dates, game and fish bag limits, and weapons restrictions and legal fishing methods. These rules can be found on fish and game agency websites and in regulation booklets. Illegal take of fish or game can lead to poaching violations that carry serious punishments including fines and jail time, so it's never a good idea to intentionally violate any of these regulations. Of course, getting ticketed by a game warden during an actual no-shit survival scenario will be the least of your worries. In fact, running into a game warden when you are lost and starving would probably be the best outcome you could hope for.

CATCHING FISH WITHOUT A RIG

Bigger fish are obviously harder to catch—that's why they're the subject of so many metaphors. In a survival scenario, however, instead of fixating on the hefty prize, you'll want to think quantity. Small fish like minnows, shad, herring, bunker, alewife, eulachon, and smelt can at times be caught en masse, providing a meal's worth or more of tasty little fish. Shallow streams and ponds should be focal points. Clear water helps. Again, remember to maintain that opportunistic, ursine mindset. Move sneakily along a watercourse, keep your eyes peeled, and be ready to take advantage of any fish or crustacean you notice before it notices you. When you're ready to pounce, here are two ways to go about it:

Grab fish out of the water. Certain species of smaller fish, dubbed "minnows" by some, can be gently lifted from the water in your cupped hands; it helps to open your fingers just enough to let water run through, so that you're effectively sieving the fish from the water. With larger fish, which are inherently more wary, the primary hurdle is approaching the fish without being noticed. This requires moving very slowly. Fish usually sit facing into the current in a stream, and away from the bank in a lake. You can use this to your advantage by approaching from behind and out of their field of vision. Once you locate your target, get on your belly on the bank, above and slightly behind the fish. Very slowly extend your arm into the water toward the fish. Keep going until you are mere inches away and can accurately gauge your stab. If you move your hand too quickly, the fish will detect the movement of displaced water and bolt. When the moment of truth comes, aim for the back of the fish's head and grip as hard as you possibly can, with your thumb and fingers pinching in on the gill plates. The second-best location to grasp a fish is the junction between the body and the tail, often called the wrist (the biological term is "peduncle"). This strategy only works on fish with a peduncle that is narrower than the tail, as you need to grip the peduncle without letting the tail slip through your hand. With either method of grabbing fish, a glove is extremely helpful in getting a grip on the slimy skin. It's amazing how much a simple rag wool glove will give you command over a large, thrashing fish that would otherwise be impossible to manage. Even just a scrap of cotton T-shirt or beach towel laid in your palm will help. If you do get hold of a fish, don't waste any time in throwing it clear of the water. Just because you're holding it right now doesn't mean it won't slip from your grasp in a few seconds. And take care when handling fish (see sidebar, below)—many have sharp spines embedded in their fins, and some have extremely sharp teeth.

Herd fish into an area where they're easier to catch. If you're starting out in shallow water, where you might find migrating suckers on their spawning run or mullet caught in a receding tide pool, get between the fish and any deeper or open water they could escape to. Flush them, preferably with a partner, into water shallow enough that they can't effectively swim, or into dead-end coves. Expand your presence by using a limb or pole to thrash the water. Some species will flee so fast and recklessly that they'll actually beach themselves. Once you've herded the fish as shallow as you can get them, kick them or sweep them with your arm onto the bank and then pounce before they can flop back into the water. A large rock can also be used to stun the fish in the shallow water. This might sound crazy, but it's legit and we've seen it work many times. Most fish can be easily dispatched with a sharp blow to the top of the head.

Two ways to grab a fish: by the peduncle and by the back of the head

GILL PLATES, SHARP SPINES, AND OTHER FISH-RELATED HAZARDS

There are lots of game fish whose sharp spines can do a lot of damage, even if they lack the venom of the lionfish. Popular freshwater game fish like yellow perch, walleye, bass, catfish, and many sunfish species have needle-like spines embedded in their fins. You'll also see sharp spines in saltwater species such as Pacific rockfish, hardhead catfish, cobia, and others. Some game fish, like snook and northern pike, have very sharp gill plates that will slice through your palm faster than a fillet knife. Finally, watch out for sharp teeth when you're unhooking fish. Bluefish are notorious for biting anglers with their sharp teeth, but even a tasty walleye or speckled trout can mangle a finger if you're not paying attention.

Watch out for sharp teeth, spines, and gill plates when handling your catch.

Use pliers to unhook fish and handle them carefully, whether you're releasing them or filleting them. It's a good idea to wear sturdy cloth or rubber-coated gloves when you're handling and cleaning fish with sharp spines, gill plates, and teeth. If you don't have a pair of those, make sure to carefully fold the fins that house the spines down against the back and body of the fish before grabbing hold of it. Puncture wounds from fish spines get infected easily, so take the appropriate first-aid measures if you get impaled by a fish.

BEYOND ROD AND REEL: SIX MORE WAYS TO CATCH FISH

Even if you aren't planning on turning your excursion into a fishing trip, a few yards of monofilament fishing line and a couple hooks and split-shot sinkers ferreted away in your first-aid or survival kit will give you a major leg up on the food procurement side of staying alive in the woods. With a little bit of searching for a worm, grasshopper, stonefly, smaller fish, or meat scrap for bait, you can apply simple tools (turn back to page 116 for a complete list) to a variety of techniques. Make sure not to put yourself in danger of drowning or hypothermia in the pursuit of catching fish. And don't waste your time attempting the old-school survival technique of lashing your pocketknife into a fishhook. It would be an incredibly ineffective way to catch fish, and an exceptionally effective way to lose a very valuable tool.

Make a cane pole. The most obvious method is to craft up a classic cane pole. Find a long, straight, flexible tree limb, shoot, or bamboo cane. It could be as short as 5 feet or as long as 12 feet. Clear it of branches. Make sure your pole has plenty of flex; this is important to keep your fishing line from busting, as the pole needs to absorb much of the fish's power so that it's not entirely transferred to the line. (That's one of the main reasons fishing rods are bendy.) Securely tie your line to the smaller end. The length of your fishing line should match the length of your pole. Add a hook at the end with whatever bait may be available. A split shot or similar weight is helpful for getting your bait down into the water for quick presentations to fish.

Find an eddy. To use your homemade pole, find high banks over streams or ponds and approach cautiously. Fish will often hold in deeper areas adjacent to the shoreline, especially in eddies where the current is slightly slower and/or there is shade and shelter provided by vegetation, cutbanks, or logs. Extend your pole over the surface and dip the baited hook in the water, allowing it to drift freely on any current that may exist. If you feel any tug or disturbance to the end of your line, lift sharply. Always maintaining pressure, quickly pull up on any fish and swing it up and onto the bank. Dispatch it quickly and remove the guts if possible. Fish intestines make great bait and chum, so catching one fish may help you catch more. But don't go throwing away the heart or liver, because they are quite good to eat.

Try a passive method. Fishing line and hooks can also be used passively. If you aren't doing well with your cane pole but think the area has promise, stick the thick end in the dirt at a 45° angle to the water and let it work as a bank pole while you do other things. Or use a tree. Limb-lining is still a common recreational practice in some areas, and it can be useful if you plan to do some exploring and then return to an area several hours later. First, find a place where branches overhang fishy-looking water. Attach your line to the end of a strong, springy branch, with enough line so that your bait hangs suspended above or just off the bottom. Make sure your bait is well attached to the hook. When a fish grabs, the limb will act to absorb the shock of the bite and the fight. Live bait such as small fish work especially well for limb-lining and bank-poling since it provides its own "action" by swimming around, without the angler needing to infuse it with lifelike qualities by jigging the rod.

Set a trotline. With enough line and hooks, you can set a trotline. To use this potentially high-yield passive method, attach one end of a heavier fishing line to a rock or other unmoving object a ways out in a river or lake. Space your hooks out along the length of the line and add bait. Tie the other end of the line to a secure point on the bank or to another weighted object in the water. Make sure the trotline is pulled very tight, or else it'll get all tangled up when a fish gets caught. Set the line overnight and check it in the morning. Properly set and baited trotlines will often make multiple catches at once.

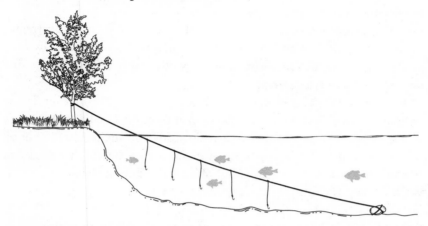

Tying several baited hooks along the length of a trotline might yield multiple catches.

Set a trap. Many indigenous peoples catch fish with a high degree of efficiency using traps, another passive method. If you're lost, you may want to focus more on getting found than playing the long game of building a corral to capture fish. But if you have even a day to wait for help to arrive, with a small amount of effort you could provide yourself with some fish to eat. Improvised nets or traps can be as complex and time-consuming as you want, but simplicity often wins the day for caloric benefit per caloric expenditure.

The simplest and perhaps deadliest fish trap design is that of the funnel and corral, still employed to great effect by many commercial and subsistence fishermen today. Using found materials like rocks, mud, and/or sticks pushed into the mud, create an enclosure of

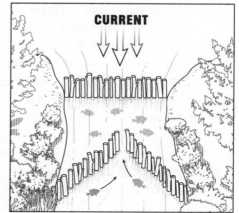

A funnel made out of sticks can be used to catch fish swimming upstream.

water against the bank. On the side from which fish are most likely to approach, use your wall material to build a funnel-shaped entrance into the enclosure with a wide mouth and a narrow neck. Fish may naturally follow the walls inward, but once inside, they will find it difficult to locate the narrow neck in order to get back out. In streams or rivers, build your funnel facing downstream, to intercept fish as they come upstream. Make sets along the bank, or in deeper channels that will naturally funnel fish movements. Once you've successfully trapped fish, use the tips on page 122 to retrieve them.

In water without current, you can bait your trap with whatever fish or animal scraps you come across. Some fish trappers like to lay branches and leaves over the enclosure to provide shade and shelter that might be attractive to fish. In the right situation, you may be able to herd fish toward the funnel of your trap, but oftentimes it's best to just leave it to work while you continue scavenging elsewhere.

Spear a fish. The best fish spears are commercially produced, with sharp, barbed metal tines. It's entirely more difficult to catch a fish using makeshift spears built from native materials or odds and ends you might have on hand, but it is possible. In a pinch, you can create a legitimate spear for capturing or killing fish, frogs, reptiles, and even rodents using a couple of sticks and some cord or string. A fish spear crafted from a pocketknife or sheaf knife might get the necessary penetration but would necessitate pinning the fish to the bottom of the creek or lake and retrieving it by hand; the moment you take off pressure, the fish will be gone. Try the following method instead:

1. Find a strong, straight stick, preferably green and 4 to 6 feet long. With a knife or hatchet, split the last 6 inches of the stick's thinner end. Take a small, thin stick or wood shaving and slide it into the split. This will spread the tip into two prongs.
2. At the base of the cut, lash your shim into place with cord, thread, string, or available materials. As you tighten the cord, angle the prongs slightly inward or outward as materials allow. This will keep your quarry from sliding off the end of your spear; if

the prongs are angled outward, smaller fish and creatures can be caught in the wedge between the prongs.

3. Sharpen the two prongs into fine points.

4. When attempting to spear a fish, frog, or any other edible animal you may see underwater, aim low in order to account for the light refraction created by the water's surface. When looking at a submerged object at an angle (i.e., not straight down), refraction creates an optical illusion wherein the object appears farther away than it actually is. Bowfishermen and frog giggers know this like gospel, but getting the aim right does take a little practice and getting used to.

SKILL: THREE ESSENTIAL FISHING KNOTS

To question another angler's knot choice or execution might be the equivalent of challenging church-going folks' religion and prayerfulness. It's a topic rife with tradition and personal choice, and diving into the fray can be straight taboo. With all that said, we whittled the dizzying list of fishing knots down to three simple, basic knots that will get you through 99 percent of fishing situations you might encounter—especially in the context of survival. Sure, the Bimini Twist is hard as hell and a lot of fun once you've got it down, but don't go telling me you're after marlin while you're turned around in the woods. Argue all you want, but the improved clinch knot, uni knot, and surgeon's join knot are the most direct routes to getting fish on the bank and into your belly.

IMPROVED CLINCH KNOT

This method for tying a fishing line to a fishing hook is so popular and effective that most people simply call it the fisherman's knot. When tied correctly, it is one of the strongest knots, but it only works with monofilament or fluorocarbon line—it does not work with braided line. Once you're comfortable with this knot, you can also tie two of them to connect two lines end-to-end. However, it is most often used to tie line to a hook or swivel.

1. To start the knot, feed 4 or 5 inches of line through the eye of your hook, then pinch the line above the eye of the hook, forming a loop.

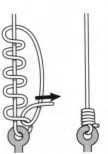

2. With your other hand, begin wrapping the tag end of the line around the standing end of the line above the loop. Three wraps is sufficient for thick, heavy line; you'll need six wraps for thin, light line.

3. Next, pass the tag end back through the loop next to the hook you created by pinching the line above the eye of the hook.

4. Finally, pass the tag end back through the loop you formed above the eye of the hook. Spit on the knot so it seals, then simultaneously pull on the standing end and the tag end to tighten the knot. The base of the knot should settle in a series of stacks right above the hook eye.

UNI KNOT

The uni knot (short for universal knot) is relatively new but has gained wide popularity and appreciation as a strong and versatile knot that can be used with a wide array of line types. It is especially popular for use with thin and slippery braided lines, but it can be used with monofilament and fluorocarbon as well. It is most often employed for tying on terminal tackle, but you can use two (the double uni) to attach two lines end to end.

1. Begin by passing 5 or 6 inches of the tag end through your hook or swivel eye.

2. Lay the tag back along the standing end, then double it back toward the hook to form a loop.

3. Inside the loop, wrap back up around both the standing and tag lines about five times. Lubricate the knot with a little spit. Then pull with more pressure on the tag end and less pressure on the standing end. The knot should settle against the hook eye in a series of stacks, with the tag end emerging from the top of the knot.

SURGEON'S JOIN KNOT

The surgeon's join knot, also known as the double surgeon's, is one of the easiest ways to connect two lines of the same or different diameters. Fly fishermen often use it to attach tippet to leader, and conventional anglers use it to attach leader to mainline. In effect, it is just two lines laid next to each other, then overhand knotted twice. With lighter lines, some folks like to overhand three times for added strength and slip-stopping power—a move known as the triple surgeon's.

1. Start by laying your two lines end to end, then overlap them by 5 or 6 inches.
2. Create a loop with both lines big enough to pass both tag ends through twice. Do an overhand knot by passing both tag ends over the top of the loop and back through, making sure to pull all of the tag through. Repeat this step once, or twice if you're using very thin line.
3. Lubricate the knot, grab the tag ends alongside the standing ends, and pull tight.

COOKING AND CONSUMING FISH

If you kill a fish and are able to remove the guts and clean the body cavity, you should be able to eat the flesh without any issue. Caught, cleaned, and eaten while fresh, fish are safer to consume raw than many mammals or birds.

Gut your fish by making a shallow cut from the anus along the belly, ending just behind the gills. Reach inside and pull out the innards. But if you're actually struggling to survive, don't just cast this offal aside. Much of it can be eaten if you take the time to clean it and cook it carefully. For example, a fish heart or liver skewered on a stick will make a highly nutritious little morsel. The entire head, from nose to cheeks to eyes to tongue, is good to eat if you cook it down a bit. And again, any guts or parts you don't feel like eating can make great bait for a hook or trap.

Fish are an excellent and often accessible source of protein, and one of the best ways to get the most nutrients and nourishment out of any food that needs to be cooked (fish included) is to boil it. That way, you can consume any good fats and proteins that seep out from the food by drinking the remaining water from the pot. Nothing is lost to the fire. But there are plenty of good cooking options in the absence of an appropriate vessel for boiling. To try what we call caveman-style cooking, find a strong, preferably green stick to use as your skewer and spit. Sharpen the business end and remove any branches. After removing the innards

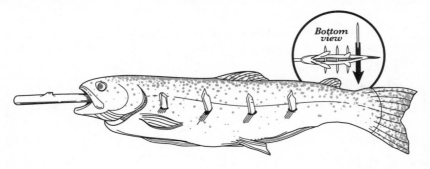

Bottom view

from your fish, insert the stick through its mouth and into its body cavity, driving the point into the flesh near the back of the rib cage. Stabilize the fish by poking smaller sticks through the rib cage perpendicular to your spit stick and bracing against it. This will help keep the fish from spinning on the stick or sliding off entirely. To cook, place or hold the end of your spit stick near coals or flames, but not in them. The slower the cooking the better, so that you don't inadvertently burn the flesh and waste precious calories. Expose all sides of the fish to the heat source and cook for ten minutes or so. Peel back the skin to eat the flesh, but don't forget to eat the tasty, crispy skin as well. The fins, the eyes (with the exception of the lenses), and the meat of the head and skeleton are also great eating.

Beware of bones. Getting a bone stuck in your throat at home is bad enough; doing so without the help of a sympathetic family member armed with a long set of tweezers can be excruciating.

THE RAW AND THE COOKED

Despite what health departments and popular media might tell you, it's not excessively dangerous to eat raw fish and game. It's common practice in many cultures, and we regularly take our chances with both in the name of culinary enjoyment.

When it comes to freshwater fish in North America, there is a ton of misleading information out there about the dangers of eating them raw. The customary reasoning behind such injunctions is the risk of becoming infested with worms. Fish parasites such as tapeworms are fairly common, and there is a chance of transmission due to eating raw fish. But most parasites are incapable of surviving or reproducing inside a human host. Even if you accidentally ingest some worms, it's highly unlikely that you'll suffer any serious damage.

As for meat, humans are hard-wired to detect the smell of rancid flesh, so your best protection is taking a sniff. If you naturally recoil at the odor, best not risk it. Be wary of meat that has a pronounced green, blue, or purple sheen.

Don't assume that just because the outside of a piece of meat is dirty or foul-smelling, the whole thing is worthless. Meat oxidizes when exposed to air. A membrane forms over the flesh and gradually turns into a black rind that slowly penetrates inward. Some of the best chefs and butchers in the world allow their meat to do this on purpose. After dry-aging the meat for weeks or even months, they trim off that black rind—often covered in mold—to access the delicious, aged meat in the center. Keep that in mind if you come across a recent kill or are trying to eat meat over a period of several days. Even if the outside appears to be compromised, cut into the center of the chunk to see if there might still be a salvageable meal inside. If you dig all the way to the bone and things are still smelling sour, crack open the marrow bones and check inside. Often this is the last place to find edible meat on an otherwise compromised carcass.

It is important to note, however, that not all meat can be eaten raw. Omnivores and carnivores such as raccoons, wild pigs, bears, coyotes, mountain lions, and members of the weasel family such as otters and badgers are all capable of carrying various strains of the parasitic worms that cause trichinosis (see page 160). Animals contract this parasite by eating meat infected by the larvae of the worms, which reside in their muscle tissue inside calcified cysts. Digestive enzymes in the new host dissolve the walls of the cysts and liberate the larvae, which develop and reproduce inside the stomach. The legions of newborn larvae then migrate through the host's circulatory system and burrow into the muscle tissue. There they form protective cysts and wait until they are consumed by the next unsuspecting host so that the life cycle can begin again. The insidious thing about trichinosis is that the incubation period is about a month, so it can be hard to trace the point of infection by the time you realize that you've contracted the disease. Symptoms include diarrhea, cramps, muscle pain, and fever. Luckily, there are only around a dozen reported cases of trichinosis each year. In 2014, for instance, there were thirteen cases reported to the Centers for Disease Control and Prevention (CDC). Of those thirteen, six track back to the consumption of black bear meat. Of those six, four were from people who've contributed materials for this book. So don't accuse us of talking the talk without walking the walk!

In addition to carnivorous and omnivorous mammals, thoroughly cook small mammals such as rabbits and squirrels, which may carry diseases such as tularemia (see page 205) that are transmissible to humans. Always cook any meat that might have been compromised by proximity to fecal matter or digestive tract contents, particularly from birds, in order to kill dangerous bacteria such as *E. coli* and salmonella. For information about the risks associated with shellfish, turn back to page 113.

AMPHIBIANS

Frogs, toads, and salamanders are present in some capacity throughout most of North America. Frogs are generally good to eat, but all toads and salamanders should be avoided because of the potent toxins in their skin.

FROGS

Following a watercourse downstream with an opportunistic mindset is a good survival method, broadly speaking—and it's particularly relevant when it comes to amphibians, who are rarely far from water. To seek them out, move slowly, studying the ground and shoreline. Flip over rocks, look under cutbanks, and be ready to pounce. These animals will often flee with a quick burst of speed, then stop and hide in the nearest cover. If you track their path, you can often jump on their hiding spots to grab, pin, spear, or trap them. (In this instance, we're clearly recommending thinking like a raccoon over thinking like a bear.)

Among the three size classes for frogs, there are three primary species: the tiny green tree frog, the midsized leopard frog, and the large bullfrog. Although there are many additional species, the attributes of these three common types can be generalized to others in their size class.

The first class can be pretty much dismissed. Those neon-hued lime green **tree frogs** you'll sometimes see sitting on a branch are rarely more than an inch or so long. It would take a lot of them to make much of a meal, and they're darn hard to find. Best not worry about it too much. Farther into Central and South America, small brightly colored frogs are extremely dangerous to even touch.

Leopard frogs, northern green frogs, and their ilk are a different story. Often stretching past 6 inches from nose to toes, they can provide a good amount of meat. And where you find one, you can often find more. **Green frogs** especially can be located by their banjo twang mating call. Leopards live almost exclusively along the edges of streams, lakes, and ponds once the water warms in the spring and before it freezes in the fall. They can be found from salt marshes on the coast all the way up to alpine lakes over 10,000 feet above sea level in Colorado. Their tadpoles are catchable and edible as well.

You'll often see leopard and green frogs launch off the bank of a stream or lake and dart off into the shallow water. They often won't go far, though, seeking shelter under whatever sticks or grasses they can find. And they think they're better at hiding than they really are. If you can identify where they stopped, it's not terribly difficult to pounce on that location and grab the frog.

Bullfrogs can provide a much more substantial meal. And these hefty amphibians provide audible clues to their whereabouts. During their long breeding season, which lasts through much of the late spring and early summer, males will create and defend a territory while calling to females. These are the loud "ba-ROOM" vocalizations for which bull-frogs are known and get their name. With a little time, patience, and stealth, you can pinpoint the source of this noise and triangulate in on it—hopefully to capture and kill the loudmouth amphibian.

Catching frogs. Frogs can be caught with fishing gear by dangling a small fly, lure, or piece of bait such as an earthworm in front of them. The fishing spear illustrated on page 126 may actually be even better suited to frogs. In fact, gigging is by far the most popular method for recreationally catching frogs. With your spear, try to drive the point downward on the body of the frog or against a hard surface. Though you may be able to lift your catch, it's likely still alive and wiggling and may be able to come free of the prongs. It's safer to hold the frog firmly against a solid bottom and grab it before letting off the pressure. Dispatch with a quick blow to the head.

Cleaning and cooking frogs. Clean your frogs by cutting through the skin just forward of the frog's hips, where a belt might ride. Use your fingers or a multi-tool plier to pull downward on the skin as if you are pulling down its pants. Cut off the feet and skin, then cut through the spine above the hips to remove your leg meat (a delicacy throughout parts of the United States and around the world) from the body. Cook as you would other meats, boiling in a pot or over a fire. Typically only the long, muscular back legs of a bullfrog are eaten, but on a large specimen the meat of the front legs may be worth eating as well. Avoid eating the skin, innards, and head.

TOADS

Toads are more problematic. Though their meat is often edible, many species are outfitted with external glands that excrete poisons. You can tell the difference between frogs and toads by looking at their skin: frogs are smooth, while toads are bumpy. Toads are generally more squat and round, while frogs are longer and more athletic in appearance. Frogs can only hop and walk, while toads can run and jump.

While some cultures consider toad a delicacy, they put a high degree of care into removing the skin first. In a survival situation, it's better to keep looking for another source of food than to try messing with a toad. You would be likely to get toxins on your hands while catching it, and those toxins would be likely to transfer to the meat when you tried to skin it. Treat these lumpy critters as a last resort.

SALAMANDERS

Salamanders and newts, those amphibians that bear a passing resemblance to lizards, are in the same boat as toads. Many common species excrete powerful toxins through their skin, toxins that can cause pain and discomfort when transferred by touch and are deadly poisonous to eat. Don't be tempted to capture, handle, or consume salamanders.

You can tell the difference between salamanders and lizards by looking at their skin. Salamanders have slightly wrinkled, bumpy skin, while lizards have actual scales.

REPTILES

Snakes, lizards, and turtles are ubiquitous throughout most of North America, from swamps and wetlands to deserts and mountains. Most species are catchable and edible, but there are quite a few caveats and exceptions. Reptile eggs are also good to eat and can be treated almost like bird eggs.

SNAKES

Serpentes is the most widely distributed subclass of Reptilia, at least in North America. There are hundreds of species, and they're found everywhere from northern forests to southern swamps. It's thought that a human's natural tendency to recoil from the reptiles is an evolutionary response to perceived danger; our ancestors knew that snakebite could lead to a painful death. Yet some are valuable sources of nutrition.

Rattlesnakes, copperheads, cottonmouths, and coral snakes should be avoided altogether, or at the very least treated with a high degree of caution. Venomous species aside (see page 196 for more information on those), most snakes in North America are relatively harmless, easy to catch, and not too bad to eat. We aren't aware of any species whose flesh is inedible. But that's not to say you can just grab any nonvenomous snake without fear of injury. Many nonvenomous snakes still have sharp teeth that can hurt you and possibly cause bacterial infections. The ubiquitous garter snake excretes a foul-smelling chemical from its anus that is very unpleasant to get on your hands.

Catching snakes. By and large, if you're going to kill a snake, do it quickly and from a safe distance, whether it's a harmless racer or a western diamondback. A sharp blow to the head with a rock or a complete severing of the head with a knife is the best approach. Sometimes, though, you may just need to grab a snake by the tail as it's about to disappear into a burrow or shelter, before quickly stomping the head or whacking it against a rock. We've seen snakes held by the tail and snapped like a whip to send the head flying. But even once the snake is dead, you should be cautious. Many snakes can bite after death, and even a severed head can be dangerous.

Gutting and cooking snakes. Once you've killed your snake and neutralized the threat, cut the skin in a ring behind the head. Place a heel on the head (or just behind if you've decapitated the snake) and pull upward against the skin. With some effort, the skin should peel off like a sock. Remove the intestines as well, then boil the meat or cook it on a spit over a fire. Cook snake meat thoroughly, as many reptiles harbor salmonella bacteria. Nibble the meat away from the bones. Most of the meat is in the backstraps or loins, though some can be found over the rib bones. The mouthfeel may run the gamut from roasted chicken to tire inner tube.

LIZARDS

Like snakes, lizards of different varieties can be found throughout North America, but you'll certainly find more of them the farther south you go. Many species are edible, but very few are large enough to make a meal worth any significant expenditure of energy. They're famously quick and agile, but they can be caught with a few sneaky tricks. Some lizards found in the desert Southwest and Mexico should be avoided, however—namely, the venomous Gila monsters.

Catching lizards. Running headlong after a lizard is a bad idea. You'll never beat one in a footrace. But they are inquisitive, so if you sit still near an area they occupy, they'll often come check you out—especially if you have some means of luring them in. A small scrap of any shiny material—like a candy wrapper dangled from a stick on a piece of string—makes lizards go ballistic. They'll ignore you to attack the fake food with reckless abandon, giving you the opportunity to whack them with a stick or rock. A little bit of fishing tackle can also work well; researchers sometimes collect lizards simply by lassoing them with a long pole and a noose made of fishing line. Reach out slowly with the pole, place the loop over the lizard's head, and jerk tight. Get comfortable with your methods, because it will take a mess of small lizards or geckos to make much of a meal. That said, there are numerous examples of humans surviving for weeks on these animals.

The feral green iguanas that have invaded Florida and other parts of the Southeast are a different story. Just one of these miniature dragons will make a hearty meal. But they are not as easily fooled as their diminutive relatives. Quick work can be made of iguanas with any sort of firearm or bow (see page 402), but bringing one down with primitive means will require a bit more stealth. Iguanas are ambush predators, often hanging out on tree limbs, basking in the sun, and waiting for prey to come along. If you can locate one, approach slowly and attack with a quick burst. Try to knock it unconscious, but don't attempt to grab it.

Iguanas have sharp scales and mean teeth, and they can actually shed their tails as an emergency escape mechanism.

Cleaning and cooking lizards. Lizards are quite edible, but like snakes, many do carry salmonella and other harmful bacteria in their skin and organs. Once you've collected a few, slice them from the anus to the rib cage and remove the guts. Make sure to wash your hands after handling or cleaning lizards. You can then thread them onto a stick and roast them over a fire. Make sure they are very well cooked and crispy to avoid ingesting any nasty bacteria.

TURTLES

Turtles, terrapins, and tortoises make for delicious meals and are enjoyed around the world. But by evolutionary design, it's very hard to get at their meat. Still, these shelled creatures can provide an opportunistic feed for the enterprising outdoorsman. A few dozen species of the order Testudines are found throughout North America south of the tundra regions, from desert tortoises of the arid Southwest to red-eared sliders in the Northwoods to snapping turtles all over the country, and most are edible. One species to avoid is the ubiquitous and unintimidating box turtle. A large portion of its diet is made up of mushrooms, and since a great deal of fungi found throughout the country are toxic to humans, the remnant chemicals in their blood have been credited with numerous poisonings. Big alligator snapping turtles are edible but downright mean. Many an outdoorsman has lost a finger or a toe to these feisty critters, and their shells are as hard as cast iron. Make sure you're ready for a fight before you engage with one, and don't do it unless it's an emergency. Alligator snapping turtles are also protected across their range.

Catching turtles. Though turtles may be difficult to butcher, they make up for it by being easy to catch. Setlines with a hook and a chunk of rope or wire leader are deadly on turtles if you have some fish guts or meat scraps to use as bait. Turtles are famously slow on land, so get between a turtle and the water and you won't have a hard time catching it. Approach from the rear and run toward the turtle. Place your foot on the rear center of the turtle's shell and press down hard to collapse its legs. Species with large tails, such as snapping turtles, can be safely grabbed by the tail. But be careful to hold the turtle well away from your body, as a snapper suspended by its tail can swivel its long neck around and give your leg a nasty bite if you let it get too close. Turtles with small tails, such as painted turtles and map turtles, can be grabbed by the shell. Place a hand on either side of the shell, between the front feet and rear feet, to avoid getting bitten. Flipping a turtle over onto its back will slow it down for a moment, but most have the ability to right themselves. If you find a turtle hanging around on sandy soil in the summer, check around for disturbed soils where the turtle may have dug a hole to lay eggs. Turtle eggs are edible.

Hand-grabbing turtles in the water is much tougher, but still possible. Rush turtles in shallow water and try to grab them before they reach the safety of deeper water. Pin them to the bottom of the lake or river with your foot, or nab them by the tail or shell. If you find turtles that are sunning themselves above the water on logs or rocks, approach them from deep water with just your nostrils sticking above the water's surface. Generally, if you're moving slowly and carefully, you can approach within 40 to 50 feet without spooking them. Then dive down and swim underwater until you're just below the turtle, and pop up as quickly as possible to grab it. Sometimes the turtle will make it back into the water before you can nab it; if so, dive after it. They are fairly easy to catch when you're close. This method is particularly deadly in clear water, when you can see the turtle's sunning location from underwater. It's much more difficult in murky water. Note also that snapping turtles rarely if ever sun themselves, but such an approach on a snapper would be ill-advised, as it would be likely to grab you before you grab it.

Butchering and cooking turtles. It's difficult to properly butcher a turtle, even with a stiff knife and a hatchet. You start by cutting through the joints where the lower shell connects to the upper shell. Then you cut through the hide where it meets the upper shell and wrestle the shell free. Most of the meat is in the legs and neck, though there are backstraps protected within the upper shell. Without cutting tools, you can smash your way through the shell, but that's going to be tough on bigger animals. In South America, we've been served river turtles that were butchered and then boiled in their own shells. Toss the shell on a bed of coals, fill it with some water, and simmer the meat until tender.

CROCODILIANS

The crocodilians include alligators, crocodiles, and caimans. They can be found throughout the Gulf Coast, Mexico, Central America, and South America. All provide excellent meat. However, they do not provide much utility in a survival situation unless you're accustomed to dealing with them and have the necessary firearm, archery, or fishing equipment to catch them. While you could theoretically catch and stab a small gator to death, we don't suggest spending much time on it. They're incredibly fast, surprisingly strong, extremely fierce, and hard to kill. A first-timer is highly likely to get injured in a tussle with a gator.

Catching an alligator. Alligators have a notoriously small kill zone—the size of a quarter is often used for reference. Their brain is protected by a thick bone, so the killing blow with nearly any weapon must be made at the point where the spine attaches to the skull at the back of the head. There is a visible line where the skull ends and the scale-like skin along the back begins. If you do happen to catch or corner a gator, make sure it's good and dead with a sharp blow or shot that detaches the spine from the skull.

Butchering an alligator. You'll want a sharp knife to get at the meat in a gator, but the tough skin actually is easier to cut through than you might think. Start with the animal on its stomach and slice from the back of the head along the two rows of raised spines, called scutes, that follow along the sides of the back. Then pull the skin off the back and continue skinning down along the flanks, tail, and legs. Gators yield a lot of meat, and the best and biggest cuts come from the top and bottom loins along the tail, the shoulders and hams, the "jelly roll" under the belly, and muscle behind the jaws. It is good almost any way you cook it.

HUNTING: THE BASICS

Thus far, we've talked a lot about thinking like a bear in order to find food. Now it's time to talk about the hunt itself. Being omnivorous, the *Ursus* clan is probably our closest allegory in the animal kingdom. Bears may not be the most masterful hunters, when compared against say cougars or foxes, but they certainly are jacks-of-all-trades. Scientists have documented grizzly bears in the greater Yellowstone ecosystem using at least 266 different food sources, from grass, fungi, and moths to trout and moose.

Bears exhibit hunting tactics that are practical for a multitude of prey species. They move slowly and quietly into the wind, but still cover a significant amount of ground in a day. They are observant and curious. It's not often you watch a bear for very long without seeing it turn over a rock or a log, just to see what's under there. They often keep to cover and shadows when on the prowl. They target their efforts on the crepuscular periods of the day—dawn and dusk—and will go nocturnal when they can or have to. They observe and capitalize on patterns. They're patient. And above all, they're ready for anything.

You don't have the speed, strength, agility, or teeth to hunt like a cougar or a fox, but you do have the mental capacity and the physical dexterity to hunt like a bear. Be sneaky, even when it feels like it doesn't matter. Don't speak loudly or step on sticks that will snap and make a sound. We've been amazed by how close we've gotten to feeding deer, elk, and turkeys by moving really slowly, even if we didn't already know the animal was there. Be observant—maybe it's spring and deer fawns have just dropped, providing vulnerabilities you could take advantage of. Maybe it's fall and lots of ducks are passing by; they might be landing somewhere close where you could sneak up on them. Survival hunting is best performed without preconceived expectations. Keep your mind open to whatever opportunities nature presents, and be ready to strike.

Animals tend to associate with either water or cover, often both. That's not terribly helpful to know in deep woods where everything is cover, but even then, certain areas will always hold more critters. In open country, the briar patches, thickets, and stands of trees will be where most creatures spend their day or escape from danger. Spend extra time observing and exploring these zones. Hunters who wander aimlessly will never outproduce those who focus their efforts on high-quality habitat.

With that ursine mindset, let's dive into our two favorite classes of animals to hunt: birds and mammals.

BIRDS

All birds are edible, and many of them are quite tasty. For obvious reasons, birds that spend most of their time in flight or high in the trees are irrelevant as an emergency food source unless you're armed with hunting equipment. But you might happen into a situation where you're able to catch a crow, seagull, magpie, jay, or robin on the ground or while it's perched in a tree. If so, cook it and eat it. Again, all birds are edible, as are their eggs.

Finding and cooking bird eggs. One might imagine that bird eggs would be readily available in the wild, but the twin factors of seasonality and camouflage make this a less-than-reliable food source. In areas of the Arctic tundra, there are instances where people can and do gorge themselves on the eggs and young of ground-nesting waterfowl. Generally, though, birds hide their eggs very well and the window of opportunity to find the eggs of many bird species is only a few weeks or a month every year. After lifetimes spent outdoors, most of us could count on one or two hands the number of turkey nests, quail nests, or duck nests that we've actually stumbled across. Ground-nesting birds are masters at hiding themselves and their eggs, to the point that you can step on them without knowing it. And while they might be less camouflaged, the eggs of tree-nesting and cliff-nesting birds are often hard to locate, hard to access, and hardly worth the risk. If, however, you're lucky enough to find bird eggs, have at it. You can eat eggs raw, but in doing so you'll run the risk of salmonella. If you have means to make a fire, either place them well away from the coals to cook slowly or boil them in water if possible. Another good trick, which we've done with pigeon eggs, is to bury them a couple of inches deep in the sand or soil beneath a fire and allow them to roast that way. Their texture ends up being similar to hard-boiled eggs.

Finding and cooking chicks and nestlings. Chicks and nestlings are just as edible as mature birds, though most are pretty scrawny. They can be a heckuva lot easier to catch, though.

Cleaning and cooking birds. It's common among contemporary bird hunters to retain only the meat of the breasts and discard the leg meat. It's a wasteful practice, and downright stupid if you're hurting for calories. It's better to pluck all the feathers off a bird, then remove the guts by making an incision into the body cavity behind the sternum. Widen the hole with two fingers until you can reach all the way inside the chest, then pull out all the organs together. Make sure to save the heart, liver, and gizzard. The best way to preserve the most calories is to boil the bird whole, but roasting on a spit near hot coals will suffice without a pot handy. Leaving the skin on will help keep some fats and nutrients from dripping out. But be mindful that the fat that drips from the skin is excellent and calorie rich, so try to capture as much of it as possible.

GROUSE

You'll often hear outdoorsmen refer to grouse as fools' hens. It's a generic term, applied to a handful of different species in different corners of the continent. There's a grouse species for nearly every region of North America north of the tropics and deserts. Ruffed grouse span most of the northern tier of the United States, reaching southward along the Appalachians and Rockies, and as far north into Canada and Alaska as the trees grow—much of which territory they share with spruce grouse. Sooty grouse can be found along the West Coast, similar in appearance to the dusky grouse throughout the Intermountain West (both species used to be lumped together and called blue grouse). Across the Great Plains you'll find sharptail and sage grouse, as well as prairie chickens in certain pockets of habitat. Some combination of the three species of ptarmigan (willow, rock, and white-tailed) can be found virtually everywhere across northern Canada and Alaska. Though each of these members of the grouse family can at times be cagey and wary, they are often so easily approached by humans that any fool could kill one with a stick—hence the name.

Hunting for grouse. Grouse have two primary ways of avoiding predators. They use their own camouflage to stay hidden on the ground, or they flee threats with rapid, short bursts of flight. Sometimes grouse are overconfident in these abilities. They'll hunker down in plain sight on the side of a trail, assuming you'll take them for a rock or shrub and walk by without noticing them. Or they'll erupt in a spasm of feathers and noise, usually to safety but sometimes just to a nearby limb that might be out of reach of a coyote but within throwing distance of a human.

We've used sticks, rocks, canoe paddles, trekking poles, bicycle tires, and even elk bugle tubes to kill fools' hens—basically, anything that can be thrown accurately and that has the necessary amount of weight to pack a significant wallop. For reference's sake, a walnut-sized rock or a drumstick-sized stick are way too small. A baseball bat or a rock the size of your two fists are more like it. The object should be at least as heavy as what you're trying to kill; twice as heavy is even better. If you think you might possibly be in the territory of grouse or other upland birds, it's not a bad idea to keep an eye out for a good throwin' stick and carry it with you. A good all-purpose bird and small-game killer can be crafted by crisscrossing two sticks about 18 inches long and as thick as your wrist. Sharpen the ends, then notch the middles so they fit together like Lincoln Logs and lash them together. Throw this contraption hard; using a sidearm throw, so that it flies horizontally rather than vertically, will greatly increase your chances of scoring a hit on a bird.

Whatever you're throwing, it's unlikely that you're gonna deliver a perfect kill shot. Rather, you'll probably just injure the grouse enough to keep it from flying away. Be ready to haul ass in the direction of the bird in order to grab it before it gets away. Kill it by twisting its neck or grabbing its head and pulling it off.

TURKEY

Wild turkeys had been all but exterminated in the United States by the turn of the twentieth century by unregulated market hunting. Thankfully, due to the efforts of hunter-conservationists, the birds are perhaps more abundant now than they've ever been. Every state except Alaska, as well as five Canadian provinces, has enough wild turkeys to support open hunting seasons. The present-day abundance of turkeys, coupled with the fact that they were once nearly hunted to extinction, lulls people into thinking that they must be exceptionally easy to kill. That's not at all true. Turkeys that face constant threats of predation are hard to kill even with firearms. Without firearms, or at least a good bow and arrows, it can be nearly impossible. They are big, strong, fast birds. Pretty much every other predator in the woods is trying to eat turkeys, so they are exceptionally well aware of their surroundings and possess nearly 360° vision. It's extremely difficult to sneak up on one.

Hunting for turkeys. Except for young polts, you're not going to throw a rock hard enough to keep one from running or flying away. You're probably not going to get close enough to whack one with a stick. And you're not going to beat one in a footrace, as they can run at speeds of over 25 miles per hour—twice as fast as you. With the exception of very young turkeys or injured adults, it would be a waste of energy to try to grab one. If you do get hold of a turkey, be aware of the physical defenses. We've had our eyes cut by flailing turkey wings and our hands and wrists gashed by the sharp spurs on mature male turkeys. Their beaks are also formidable. If you're handling a live wild turkey, try to control the bird by the neck while you pin its wings and legs by straddling it. A sharp blow to the head with a large rock will kill it. When hunting a turkey with a shotgun, aim for the head and upper neck. With a rifle such as a .22, aim for the base of the neck, just above the breast. With an arrow, you want to hit the bird where its wing bone joins its body on broadside shots.

WATERFOWL

The classification of birds known as waterfowl includes a host of ducks and geese together with other species of aquatic game birds such as cranes and swans. Like turkeys, they are generally very hard to capture without the use of firearms or archery equipment. They evade predators by taking flight or moving quickly toward deep water at speeds that far exceed a human's ability to swim. The primary vulnerability of waterfowl is their molting phase, which happens shortly after the spring nesting season. While many bird species will molt their primary flight feathers gradually, replacing just one or two at a time, ducks and geese do a simultaneous molt where they lose all of their feathers at once. This renders them flightless for twenty to forty days. They can still escape to water and swim away, but they are far more susceptible to predation at this time.

Hunting for waterfowl. Get between them and the water and you might nab one. With bow and arrow, aim for center mass on waterfowl. The best spot is where the base of the wing meets the body. Close shots with firearms can be made into the head or breast. With shotguns, close shots on the water or land can be aimed for the head. With birds that are 40 or 50 yards away, though, it's better to flush the birds and then shoot immediately as they take flight. This increases the chances of breaking a wing and slowing the bird down. We've seen dozens of instances where people have peppered grounded waterfowl with shotguns at longer distances only to have the birds jump up and fly away, unscathed.

Never discard the skin of a duck if you're in need of calories. It is usually loaded with fat. Once again, note that there should be no casual experimentation with survival strategies on waterfowl or any other wildlife that is regulated by state or federal agencies. Make sure you've got the proper licenses and permits and that you're adhering to legal seasons, bag limits, method of take, and so on.

QUAIL

Quail will sleep on the ground and are vulnerable at night with the aid of a flashlight; we once saw a guy kill a quail with a trekking pole in the glow of a headlamp. It is common practice in areas of Mexico to catch quail with homemade traps, but this is a time-consuming method that requires pre-baiting in order to acclimate the birds to a trap site. Barring these methods, quail are tough to get.

PIGEONS

Known as rock doves in Europe and Asia, pigeons can at times be captured by hand in their nesting sites. However, these birds are typically found in urban and agricultural landscapes, where you're not likely to find yourself in need of emergency food sources. But if you do locate a pigeon roosting or nesting site, climb up there at night and have at it. They are very reluctant to fly in the dark and are disoriented by lights.

Pigeons are a great resource for survival training as well, since these non-native birds are regarded as deleterious pests and are completely unprotected in most places.

MAMMALS

The fantasyland survival guides that we grew up with included pages and pages of information about setting deadfalls for bears or taking down deer and moose with spears made by lashing a pocketknife to a stick. It's pretty much all bullshit. Outside of a few experts who have devoted their lives to mastering primitive traps and hunting methods, most of us are simply unequipped to catch and kill deer, moose, elk, caribou, bears, wild pigs, wild canines, or any other large critter without the aid of firearms, archery equipment, or modern trapping equipment. All of these creatures can easily run three times faster than you can. If you were to corner and go hand-to-hoof or hand-to-claw with a large animal, you'd find an adversary that is shockingly strong and ferocious. Even female cervids without antlers can kick their hooves hard enough to knock you out cold. Putting fantasy aside, hunting large animals is best left to experienced big-game hunters who have the necessary gear and know-how to deal with them. Instead, this chapter is going to focus more heavily on small game.

BIG GAME

Acknowledging the low likelihood of acquiring big game in a survival situation without the appropriate equipment and prior big-game hunting experience, let's go ahead and get into some basics. Unlikely as it might seem, you could find yourself in a position to kill a deer stuck in the mud, scavenge meat left behind by a predator in a rush, or even chase a sheep off a cliff's edge. None of these instances is outside the realm of possibility, and we've seen several with our own eyes. If the meat isn't discolored and smelly, it's probably fresh enough to eat. What next?

Gutting Big Game

Your first consideration should be cooling the meat off. That means protecting it from heat, whether from the sun or from the animal's own body. Large cervids, such as elk and moose, are extremely well insulated in order to survive severe northern winters. The organs in their body cavity and their muscles will retain that body heat for hours after their deaths, even in cold weather. Heat and stomach contents promote bacterial growth and meat souring, so it's important to get the meat away from the guts or the guts away from the meat. This can be accomplished by gutting, skinning, and/or quartering the animal soon after it dies. First, let's get into gutting the animal.

1. Start by cutting through the skin around the anus, completely freeing the rectum. With your knife pointing upward, make a straight line incision through the skin along the belly, all the way from the anus to the neck. Take care not to pierce the abdominal wall.

2. Make the next cut along the same line, this time cutting through the abdominal wall from the base of the sternum to the pelvis. Keep your knife point up, steering clear of the stomach and intestines. If you have a saw or hatchet, cutting through the pelvis bone will make it easier to pull the lower intestine and rectum free of the carcass. But you can also leave the pelvis intact, and pull the rectum and lower intestine free of the pelvis by tugging them up toward the abdominal cavity. Either way, make sure that the lower end of the digestive tract is freed up long before you try to pull the animal's guts away from the carcass.

3. If you do have a saw or a hatchet, use it to cut up through the rib cage to the throat.

4. If you are using a knife, cut away the diaphragm, reach up into the chest cavity, and sever the windpipe.

5. Holding the windpipe, haul out the contents of the chest and stomach cavities. Make sure to separate and retain the heart, liver, and kidneys to eat, then discard the remainder of the body cavity's contents. Take care to ensure that the contents of the digestive system never come in contact with the meat.

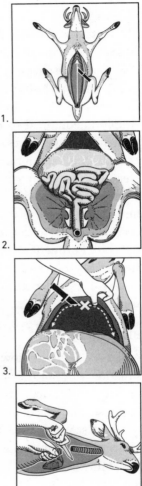

Gutting the animal goes a long way to cooling down the meat, but if the temperature outside is above 40°F, you'll need to do more, and quickly. The first and most obvious solution is to find shade. Air temperatures can vary by as much as 30°F between a patch of sunlit ground and a shaded spot. It's also often helpful to take the skin off the animal and/or the legs and meat off the skeleton, since the hide holds in a lot of heat, too. Removing the legs and meat is often necessary for transport, since elk, bear, or moose can all weigh far more than a grown man.

Skinning and Quartering Big Game

There are multiple ways to skin big game animals prior to quartering them, but let's focus on a common method that begins by using the gutting incision.

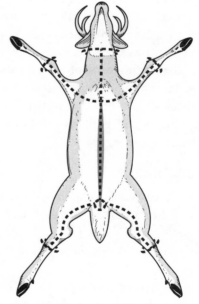

1. Cut through the animal's hide as shown above and remove the legs at the knees. Starting at the gutting incision, skin one side of the carcass. You're simply pulling and slicing the hide away from the muscle beneath. Skin all the way around to the spine on one side of the animal. Then skin the other side around to the spine, so that the hide is completely free and the carcass is lying on the splayed open skin.
2. Remove the upper parts of the legs from the carcass. The rear legs are joined to the hips by a ball joint that needs to be separated by twisting and slicing. The front legs are usually much easier to cut away and do not require severing bony joints. (In some situations, it can make sense to remove legs with the hide still on them in order to protect the meat from dirt, debris, and insects; however, this adds weight and can prevent the meat from cooling properly.) These quarters, as they are known, are easy to transport. Everything besides the bone is edible. (Including the marrow inside the bones.)
3. Not all the good meat is in the legs. There is plenty of meat in the head, including the tongue and jowls, so skin that as well if you're trying to maximize yield. Remove the backstraps, or loins, which are located on either side of the spine. Also the tenderloins, which are found inside the body cavity along the spine of the lower back. Good meat is also found over and between the rib bones, on the neck, and in the brisket. As these pieces of meat come off the carcass, we often drape them over nearby branches, shrubs, or rocks to let them dry out in the shade and allow a light "rind" to form as the

raw meat comes in contact with air. This process will help protect the meat from dirt and insects. But there's no escaping the fact that this meat will not remain edible for very long in ambient temperatures much above 40°F.

4. It is possible to allow very thin strips of meat to dry in direct sunlight with good air circulation in extremely hot, arid conditions. It's also possible to preserve meat by smoking it near a campfire, but this requires a high degree of skill and care. Ideally, you'd have the meat and smoke source enclosed by a blanket or animal hide or some similar covering, and allow it to be immersed in smoke for most of the day. Even still, getting rid of all the moisture from even the thinnest strips of meat without burning them to a crisp is a tall task. But if you happen upon a deer's worth of food on the ground and you're hurting for food, it's worth trying whatever options might be available for preservation.

SMALL GAME

Acquiring small game takes some skill and know-how, but it's hardly impossible with the application of a little effort and some luck. Porcupines, opossums, and armadillos, for instance, can be killed with nothing more than a stick, and these critters have provided many easy meals for lost or hungry travelers. With a little bit of knowledge about track identification and a single strand of wire, it's also possible to set snares for small game, walk away, and come back later to fetch a nice surprise. Don't overlook the less glamorous members of this category, either—in many areas, squirrels and gophers are found in higher concentrations than traditional game animals.

SQUIRRELS

For the sake of discussion, the squirrels of North America can be divided into tree squirrels and ground squirrels. Tree squirrels are typically regarded as a game animal among hunters, and their flesh is excellent. Ground squirrels do not have the same reputation, though they can be eaten.

Catching tree squirrels. The most common tree squirrels are pine squirrels, gray squirrels, fox squirrels, and Abert's squirrels of the Southwest, and in many areas, their ranges will overlap. No matter their size (from a pine squirrel weighing a few ounces to a fox squirrel weighing a couple of pounds), the principles for killing them remain basically the same regardless of type. Any form of weapon—gun, bow, even a slingshot—can be deadly on a squirrel. If you lack such an implement, however, tree squirrels are extremely challenging to kill. They are fast; they are quick to take refuge in the safety of treetops; and they provide only a very small target for airborne rocks or sticks. There are, however, a couple of tricks to keep up your sleeve in case you're lucky enough to chase a squirrel into a hollow log or tree limb. If there are two entrances to the hollow, they can easily be flushed out with smoke by kindling a small fire inside the lower entrance; grab or net them up when they come barreling out of the upper entrance. In a dead-end hollow, with only one entrance, they can be fished out with a chunk of sawbriar vine or a fishhook attached to a long, slender pole. Insert the vine or pole until you make contact with the squirrel, and then twist it in order to snag the squirrel's hide on the hook or a thorn of a briar. You can then pull them out. It might sound crazy, but we've seen it done. For a snaring strategy that can be used on tree squirrels, use the method pictured on page 159. Position a horizontal pole about head high between two trees frequented by squirrels, and it will quickly become a popular travel route for them. Once they get used to the pole, it's a simple matter to affix your snares.

Catching ground squirrels. Ground squirrels, a category that includes prairie dogs, chipmunks, woodchucks, and marmots, might not immediately leap to mind when you're thinking of good eats. But they might represent a windfall in a survival scenario. Often quite gregarious and living in large, easy-to-locate colonies, they're easier to apprehend than their arboreal cousins. The most straightforward method is to use a throwing stick, rock, or club. Ground squirrels will dive back into their holes as any threat nears, but they are very curious. If you sit and wait a bit, they'll pop back up, usually in the same spots. You might be able to pick one off with a well-placed throw or hard whack to the head. If you have a little bit of time and the right tools, though, these holes present a perfect opportunity for the snares described on page 157. Since these burrowing rodents come up to the surface in reliable places, you could set a constricting loop of string, wire, or cable the width of the quarry's head around the opening of that hole. You'd either want to stake the other end of your snare material to the ground or hide nearby to noose the animal as it emerges.

Flooding is an extremely effective method for flushing ground squirrels out from their burrows. This is common practice in the agriculture and ranching worlds, though it's usually accomplished with a hose or irrigation. The ground squirrels usually emerge stumbling and disoriented. They are easy to grab or club.

RABBITS

Rabbits and hares are often more ubiquitous than squirrels; they all provide excellent meat. In northern and mountainous areas you may encounter large, color-changing snowshoe hares. In the deserts and Great Plains you might see jackrabbits. Arctic hares are found in northern coastal environments. And cottontails, which come in many sizes and varieties, are found throughout much of Mexico, the Lower 48, and southern Canada.

Catching rabbits and hares. With the exception of jackrabbits, which are difficult to approach, rabbits and hares can be fairly easy to kill with rudimentary weapons when hunting in areas where they aren't accustomed to human predation. They rely on their camouflage for safety, and will let a human approach quite closely if you don't lock eyes with them or otherwise signify that you're aware of their presence. Walk toward the hare or rabbit at an angle that suggests you'll pass it by without stepping on it, and you might get close enough to cripple it with a thrown rock or stick. Be ready to pounce on it to finish the job. Hunting with modern weapons is a fairly straightforward matter. If by yourself, move slowly and quietly through thickets or other places where you see rabbits or rabbit sign (see page 151) while watching ahead of you for your quarry. The animal might be lying stationary, or moving away from you. With the help of a partner, conduct small-game drives where one of you noisily busts through likely rabbit territory in order to scare the animals in the direction of a waiting hunter who's set up in a likely ambush location. Rabbits and hares can also be taken quite easily in the handmade snares pictured at the end of this section. Most species have a high degree of fidelity to their burrow or warren, and often follow a daily path through their area. In snow, mud, or sand you may be able to identify this travel route through the existence of tracks or a worn pathway. You can force rabbits into your snare by creating a fence of sorts made with a wall of sticks along the trail. Set plenty of snares, as success rates can be low.

OPOSSUMS

Most modern hunters turn up their noses at opossums, the only marsupials native to North America, but anyone in a survival situation would be lucky to encounter one. The phrase "playing possum" is no joke, and though it isn't pleasant to behold, it makes opossums easy to catch. They literally act dead when threatened: going stiff, foaming at the mouth, ex-

Small Game Tracks

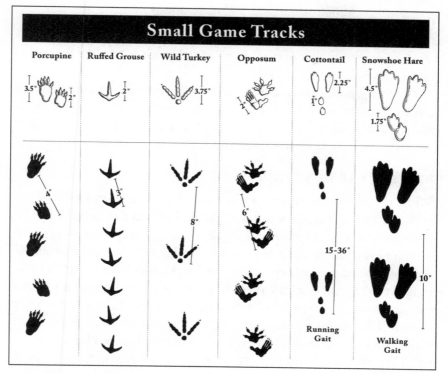

Porcupine	Ruffed Grouse	Wild Turkey	Opposum	Cottontail	Snowshoe Hare

posing their teeth, rolling back their eyes, even excreting a death-like odor from their anal glands. (According to scientists, they don't do this by choice; playing possum is an involuntary response to danger, not un-like fainting.) Even when they don't go catatonic, opossums will usually just stare you down and hiss angrily rather than running away.

Catching opossums. Several of us, on multiple occasions, have stumbled into situations where catching an opossum was as simple as bending over and picking it up. On the other hand, while opossums are quite willing to play dead, they are hard to actually kill. The best way to dispatch an opossum is to lay a stout branch across the back of its neck and place a foot on either side. Then grab the opossum's tail and give a strong, steady tug. Pull strong enough and you'll feel the vertebrae sepa-rate. Pull until you've registered four or five distinct pops. It may sound graphic, but it's the only way to get the job done in a humane fashion.

PORCUPINES

Porcupines can be found in forested areas throughout the United States and Canada from the farthest northern regions down through the West, the Great Plains, the upper Midwest, the Great Lakes, and New England. Like opossums, porcupines are a valuable survival food whose flesh is often compared to that of pigs—notice the French *porc* at the beginning of their name.

Catching porcupine. While these quill-covered critters are heavily armed, they lack speed and agility. You can quickly outrun a porcupine and flip it over on its back with a stick. When encountered in trees, they can be easily dislodged. Kill them with a blow to the head.

BEAVERS AND MUSKRATS

While they're not nearly as easy to catch as opossums and porcupines, muskrats and beavers do warrant attention. Both species are broadly distributed across North America, are almost always in or near water, and leave an abundant amount of easily identifiable sign that makes it simple to tell when and where they are present. Muskrats and beavers both build lodges, or huts, out of sticks, vegetation, and mud, or simply dig burrows into shoreline banks with submerged entrances that allow underwater passage into the subterranean burrow. Muskrat lodges are generally about the size of a bushel basket, while beaver lodges can be as big as a car. They each also build collections of food known as caches—beavers build large underwater feed piles, and muskrats build feed beds and "push-ups" that sit at or above the water's surface. You'll often find tracks, muddy paths, and slides on land adjacent to waters that hold aquatic rodents. Muskrat trails are as wide as your hand; beaver trails are as wide or wider than your thigh.

Catching beavers and muskrats. Beavers and muskrats are usually classified as fur-bearing animals, a category that comes with special regulation. In most states, you need a trapping license instead of a hunting license to pursue them. Of all the fur-bearers, they are two of the easiest to catch with conventional trapping gear, though a learning curve is involved in setting up and using the equipment (see page 156). Body-gripping traps, commonly called conibears, that are set in the entranceways to lodges and bank dens will typically produce within the first day. Snares can be used in the same way. Hunting for these fur-bearers is simple as well. Just wait patiently on shorelines in areas with evidence of beaver and muskrat activity, especially during the first and last half-hours of daylight. Do not shoot the animals unless they are in shallow water, as they're notorious for diving underwater or sinking and becoming forever lost. As soon as you hit them, run out to retrieve them. Head shots are a must.

Catching beavers and muskrats without the use of traps, snares, or firearms is a lot tougher, though still quite possible. On several occasions we've caught them by hand just by getting between them and the water and snatching them up by the tail. While a large muskrat is less than a tenth the size of a large beaver, it is much more likely to stand up and fight when confronted by a predator. Just by rushing after a muskrat, you can trigger its fighting response and get it to stand up to you rather than try to escape. Then you can dispatch it using a sharp smack to the end of the nose with a stick. Beavers are much tougher, but they can be pinned underwater to drown after a substantial blow to the head. Native Americans had a number of ways of catching muskrats and beavers without traps or guns, many of which involved destroying their lodges or dams. Approach a muskrat hut or den in the middle of the day, when they're likely to be inside, and then block the entrance with sticks jabbed into the mud. Then either dig into the bank den from above or simply lift off the top of the lodge. Move fast to grab any fleeing inhabitants when they try to make a break for it. For beavers, Native Americans would breach their dams in order to drain away the water in the beavers' pond. Once the water receded, they'd dig into bank dens or lodges in order to disperse the giant rodents, which could be killed by clubs. It would be laborious, for sure, but we've seen many places where it would be deadly effective. Take note, though, that in many states and Canadian provinces it's illegal to destroy or molest the huts, lodges, and dams of beavers and muskrats without special permits issued for animals that are causing property damage.

RATS, MICE, AND THE LIKE

They might not be the most appealing option, but the smaller members of the order Rodentia are the most widespread members of the class Mammalia. Nearly anywhere you'd care to travel, you could encounter rats, mice, shrews, lemmings, or a host of other tiny, furry creatures. Many of them are relatively catchable and thus should not be dismissed as vermin. And while it might seem clichéd to mention this, we'll add that there are cultures scattered around the world that regard these critters as delicacies.

Catching small rodents. Mice and shrews will often find you. Many seem to be inherently attracted to humans, no doubt drawn to the odors of food scraps. We've had lots of nights in camp where mice were scurrying around and over our sleeping bags within minutes of going to bed. They can be smacked with a stick or rock. Burrows are often penetrable, too. You can dig them out of hollow logs or un-earth them with your hands or rudi-mentary tools. Some species are

A bucket trap set with a rotating dowel, preferably smothered in peanut butter

easily trapped, though doing so usually requires bait and most good mouse baits are edible human foods. You have to consider the return and reward for such small morsels of grub. In some instances, it might be valuable to construct repeating traps that can catch a lot of mice with only limited amounts of bait. There are many variations on repeating bucket traps that can be used to catch scores of small rodents with a single application of bait. An inventive trapper could jury-rig an approx-imation of such a contraption using entirely native materials.

NOTES ON PREPPING AND COOKING SMALL GAME

The principles for cooking small game are generally similar to those of the other classes of animals we've covered. But there are idiosyncrasies to prepping and cooking the various species, as well as some universalities that'll help you make the most of your catch:

- **Small game mammals** lend themselves particularly well to a common style of prep-free cooking employed by many hunter-gatherer cultures around the world. It's unlikely to become your favorite recipe, but it's an easy way to make food when calories are all that count. The instructions are simple: Just toss the ungutted animal onto the coals of a fire and allow the hair to burn away. Keep rolling the animal around on the embers as the skin begins to stiffen and char in the heat. Turn it often. The meat will steam within, and it is usually ready to eat well before the skin has burned away. After removing the hair in this fashion, you can also chunk the animal up and boil the pieces until they become tender.
- Members of the **ground squirrel** family can be prepared and eaten much in the same way as their tree-bound relatives, with the most meat coming from the burly marmot tribe—some of which can reach

beyond 15 pounds. It is worth noting, however, that cases of plague have been found in prairie dog colonies in the western United States. So it's best to observe sanitary cleaning and personal hygiene habits when dealing with rodents of any type, including rats and mice. Keep an eye out for discoloration on the muscles or inside the skin, and avoid the bites of mites or fleas that climb away from the animal's body and onto your skin. Scrub your hands after handling rodents. And cook all rodents well, just to be sure.

- **Rabbit** meat is delicious and easy to prepare, and it is best cooked on the bone. To dress the meat, just strip away the rabbit's hide, then remove the legs at the knee and the head at the neck. The rabbit can be speared on a spit and roasted over a fire, though it might turn out a tad tough. You'll get much more tender results by covering the meat with water and slowly simmering for several hours. Due to the slight risk of contracting the highly infectious bacterial disease tularemia, rabbit meat should be handled with care, using the precautions detailed on page 205.

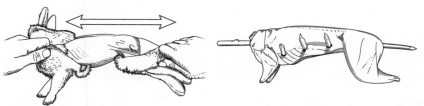

After you tear or cut a slit through the top of the hide at the rabbit's midsection, the skin should be easy to peel away.

Use pins to secure meat when roasting rabbit on a spit.

- **Opossum** meat was popular among many indigenous tribes, early European settlers, and subsistence hunters. Even today, it is enjoyed by some rural southerners as well as tribes in Central and South America. William Strachey, a writer in the company of colonial governor John Smith at the Jamestown settlement in 1607, described opossums as tasting like pork, and Mark Twain wrote about eating them, too. If you kill one, skin it and cook the meat like you would any small game. But do not eat it raw, as opossums could be carriers of trichinosis.
- Cleaning **porcupines** is never fun, but it can be done safely. Open the skin along the unprotected belly, remove the guts, then carefully peel the skin outward while using the hide as a buffer between your fingers and the animal's quills. While they were once an important food source for many native peoples of North America, they are now

treated like pests, without seasons or bag limits, because of the damage they can cause to trees, human housing, and wooden products. While game and fish departments might lock you in jail for practicing your survival skills on a deer without the proper licenses and permits, they're not likely to bat an eye about porcupines.

- **Muskrats** can weigh up to 4 pounds, while **beavers** can weigh over 70 pounds. Meat yield on each is relatively low, as they have enormous digestive tracts, but their flesh is excellent. Most of the meat is found in the legs and backstraps. You can prepare them by skinning and cooking any way you would other small game, with whatever tools you have available. Beavers, however, possess a feature that make them especially valuable to someone trying to survive: the wide paddle tails in which they store excess fat. It tastes like the gristle from a beefsteak, and it's the perfect thing when you're really hungry. We've found that the best way to cook the tails is to impale them on a stick and prop them next to a fire. Let the meat roast until the skin on one side burns and begins to peel away, then turn it to cook the other side. Scrape away the burnt skin to reveal the meat and fat inside.

A NOTE ON TRAPS AND TRAPPING

Judging from the litany of survival guides that have plumbed the topic, you'd think herding an animal into a homemade deadfall was as easy as picking a handful of blueberries. In fact, building a trap from natural materials and luring an animal to its death based on a half-page of instructions and a couple of illustrations would be nearly impossible. Accomplished trappers are, without exception, lifelong practitioners of their art, with impressive problem-solving abilities and vast expertise in wildlife behavior. Mastering their skill requires lifelong devotion, and often, a bunch of gear.

Modern trappers use a variety of specialized equipment, usually employing some combination of foothold traps, body-grippers such as the one shown here, and the snares described below.

A body-gripper, also known as a killer-type or Conibear trap, featuring one or two springs and wire triggers

Body-grippers are probably the most foolproof and user-friendly trap design out there, and a good trapper could easily keep himself alive and fed in virtually any wild landscape using a half dozen of them. But trappers sometimes also use carefully concocted home-made lures derived from animal glands, plant extracts, and various naturally occurring fruits and meats. Whatever the equipment, most of it is difficult to use properly and takes years' worth of trial and error to figure out. Anyone serious about going down this path should consult the books of such famed contemporary trappers as Bob Noonan, Mike Marsyada, and Hal Sullivan.

Trapping is also a tightly regulated activity governed by complex rules and regulations. Be sure to understand your region's trapping laws prior to any experimentation with this ancient lifestyle.

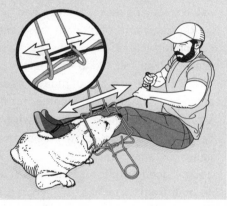

Many dog owners live in fear of their pets encountering traps. Foothold traps and snares are not likely to cause serious damage unless the dog is held in the trap or snare for an extended period of time. Conibears, on the other hand, can quickly kill a dog. Act fast by depressing the springs, either by hand or by using a bootlace for leverage as shown.

SKILL: SNARING

Snares, or cable restraints, belong to a broad category of traps designed to constrict an animal's neck or body as it passes through the loop of the snare. Placed in an animal's line of travel and used in conjunction with a bait or similar enticement, they offer a largely passive means of food acquisition—one that might come in handy in a situation where you need to conserve calories or spend your time scouting the area. Relative to commercially produced steel traps, snaring has a much steeper learning curve for novices. However, the materials are easier to come by.

Historically, snares were made out of animal sinews, roots and vines, and even braided hair, but today's models are commercially produced from galvanized cable and a locking component. A simple handmade version can be fashioned out of a simple piece of braided cable, like the stuff sold in hardware stores as picture hanging wire. It'll be suitable for squirrels and rabbits, but won't work well for catching larger quarry.

A simple snare made from a piece of wire

If you want to get serious about snares, you'll need to work with the equipment favored by modern fur trappers and animal damage control specialists. These contemporary snares are made of commercially produced components including cable, a locking device, and an end fastener.

Reproductions of most of these snares can be fabricated in a pinch. The cable, generally galvanized and often referred to as aircraft cable, is made of many smaller strands of wire twisted together for flex and strength. Many snares are built with 7×7 cable, built from seven strands of smaller cable containing seven strands of wire each; a good all-purpose survival snare can be built from 36 inches of 1⁄16-inch-diameter 7×7 cable.

A snare made from steel cable, a washer lock, and a swiveled end fastener

The lock that holds the loop closed typically consists of washer, cam, and Gregerson and Thompson locks. Washer locks are simple enough to make at home using the commonly available washers found in most any garage or workshop.

The end fastener of a snare is the part that allows you to anchor the snare to a stake, tree, fencepost, or any other object strong enough to hold a captured animal in place. Most end fasteners double as a swivel, to prevent the cable from kinking up while restraining an animal. Swivels are especially important when attempting to restrain an animal without harming it.

To set snares with any chance of making a catch, refer to the small-game tracks on page 151 and to the individual tips on catching small game throughout this chapter as well as to the setups pictured here. While snares are relatively simple to set, putting them in the wrong place is an exercise in futility.

SETTING RABBIT, BEAVER, COON, AND SQUIRREL SNARES

Identify routes to rabbits' burrows or warrens, then set up guide sticks to force them into your snares; use a 5" loop set 5" off the ground.

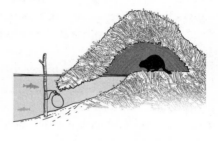

Set beaver snares in the underwater entrance to their lodges, using a 10" loop set 2" off the ground.

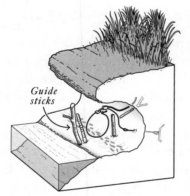

Place coon snares along well-traveled paths, using a 6"-to-8" loop set 4" off the ground.

Set multiple snares for squirrels along a simple roadway made from a branch; use a 3" loop set 1" to 2" above the pole.

Note: Don't go experimenting with snares without consulting all applicable regulations. Some states entirely prohibit snares, while others restrict their use through mandatory modifications such as breakaway devices that allow deer and livestock to pull free from snares, relaxing locks that do not close tightly enough to strangle captured animals, and stops that prevent snares from closing tightly enough to snare the legs of livestock and big game animals.

PREDATORS

Yes, you can eat bears, wild cats (cougars, bobcats, lynx), wild canines (wolves, coyotes, foxes), and mustelids (badgers, otters, fishers, martens, minks, wolverines, skunks). But these cunning animals are among the least likely prey to present themselves for a kill and are obviously problematic to tangle with.

If you do happen to have a weapon, and happen to use it to kill something like a coyote, brace yourself. While bears and mountain lions are quite good, the flesh of many predators can smell rancid even when fresh. It is all edible, but you would need to be really, really hungry to want to eat much. No matter what, make sure to cook predator flesh well, at least to 160°F, or well-done, because any meat-eating animal is capable of carrying trichinosis. We can tell you from personal experience—if you haven't had trichinosis, you don't want it.

AND LASTLY, A FEW THOUGHTS ON CANNIBALISM

The historical record is chock-full of grisly cannibalism tales involving the willful and ritualistic consumption of human flesh by indigenous cultures as well as the taboo consumption of human flesh by people forced to choose between social disgrace and starvation. Quite often we engage in this macabre discussion ourselves: would you do it, or not? Over the years we haven't encountered a single serious outdoorsman who was willing to categorically rule out the possibility of cannibalism. The outdoor lifestyle trains people to understand life and death, it beats the squeamishness out of you, and it enforces a practical and adaptive mindset. No wonder that our friends and associates would be open to the idea, if it came to that. It's worth pointing out, too, that it's not just a one-way street. If we were dead and our buddies had a chance of surviving by eating our flesh, we'd serve it up to them on a plate if we were able. After all, what better legacy to leave behind than friends who survived? If it does happen to you, we hope that you won't hesitate. The best, most easily extracted meat will be in the buttocks. But before you take that first bite, consider the lifestyle of whoever you're having for dinner. A few of us happen to be trichinosis positive, for instance. Cook to 160°F, then enjoy.

CHAPTER 4

―――⋙⋘―――

Things That Bite, Maul, Sting, or Make You Sick

I'VE BEEN CHARGED by grizzlies, poisoned by lionfish, shocked by electric eels, stung by bullet ants, and run over by moose, but the only wild animal that's ever truly hurt me is the size of a sesame seed. It happened years ago, during a bluegill fishing trip with my three-year-old boy in New York's Hudson Valley when we were both bitten by deer ticks. After the telltale bull's-eye rashes showed up, we went through months of physical and mental anguish as we endured the dizzyingly varied symptoms of Lyme disease. Facial paralysis, joint pain, nausea—and in my case, a brief and dramatic episode of amnesia. Thankfully, my son healed quickly after a round of oral antibiotics and was better within a month. I wasn't so lucky. A course of oral antibiotics only seemed to worsen my condition, and my symptoms progressed to the point where I couldn't walk down a flight of stairs without holding the handrail. I called my brothers in tears and fretted that my days of adventuring might be over. Eventually an infectious-disease specialist recommended a minor surgery that allowed me to mainline syringes of antibiotics from a port in my arm directly into a vein at the top of my heart. After canceling a summer's worth of fishing trips and a fall's worth of hunting trips, I started to feel better. Six months from the date of infection, I was finally healed.

If I learned anything from that experience, it's to take a comprehensive and realistic approach to dealing with hazardous plants and animals—no matter how small. Too often, we expend our efforts plotting and planning for how we'd handle a grizzly attack or a rattlesnake bite, while completely forgetting less glamorous but far more likely causes of trouble that can sneak up and get you without you even knowing it. Not that you should take this as permission to ignore the risks posed by grizzlies and rattlers. In the popular media, you'll encounter endless statistics about how unlikely you are to get attacked or mauled by various wild critters. They'll tell you that you're more likely to get killed by a domestic dog or cow than a bear. Or that you're more likely to get struck by lightning twice than bitten by a shark. The problem with these statistics is that they refer to the human population at large rather than to specific user groups who engage in high-risk activities such as spearfishing, wilderness travel, or big-game hunting in Alaska, Canada, or the American West. For these groups, the odds of getting injured or killed by wildlife are much higher. If you spend a decade's worth of Septembers bowhunting for elk in northwest Wyoming, you're practically guaranteed an eventual mixup with a grizzly. If you're a lifelong spearfisherman in Hawaii, you *will* have run-ins with sharks. What happens in those situations will depend largely on how you handle them. How you handle them will depend largely on how well informed you are.

But let's forget about statistics for a moment. Regardless of how likely or unlikely you are to get injured by an animal, there's still a psychological toll that comes from housing the threat in your mind. A fear of spiders or wolves, however unfounded, can prevent you from having fun when you're out in the wild. It can diminish your ability to focus on what you're actually trying to get accomplished. And it can cause you to make poor decisions. Gaining a complete understanding of threats and sorting fact from bullshit is enormously helpful when it comes to keeping a level head in the outdoors. When I was stung on the ankle by a bullet ant in Bolivia, I remember spending an hour writhing on the jungle floor in intense pain. In hindsight, the agony was far more mental than physical. I was uninformed about the threats posed by bullet ants—I knew it was bad to get stung, but I didn't know *how* bad—and I was completely uninformed about how to treat the sting. Things were made worse by my two Amerindian companions, who were trying to use hand gestures to overcome the language barrier between us. One of them kept tracing his finger up the inside of his leg to his crotch. In reality, he was warning me to take precautions so that the ant didn't crawl up the inside of my leg and sting me again. What I thought he was saying was that the ant's poison would travel up my leg via my bloodstream and at some point reach the core of my body. It was harrowing. Obviously, there was no internet access or cell coverage, so I had to lie there in the dark with images of amputated legs and tainted blood coursing through my imagination. Had I known what I know today—you're gonna be fine, just go about your business and the pain will vanish in two hours—I could have avoided a horrible collection of moments as I visualized the worst possible outcomes.

Eventually, when you have gained a little experience and knowledge, the risks associated with an outdoor lifestyle become something that you learn to accept at face value, and even cherish. After all, a little bit of danger is what makes the outdoors so appealing to so many of us. I thought of this a few days ago as I was spearfishing in California just south of an area known as the Red Triangle for its high density of great white sharks. Fittingly, a companion was giving me a rundown on the various shark species. We discussed the pitbull-like qualities of bull sharks, the tenacity of a sixgill shark trying to steal your catch, and the eerie ways in which a tiger shark will disappear and reappear as though it's actually trying to spook you. But on the subject of great white sharks, he had very little to say. "There's nothing you can do. If one hits you, you won't know it until it's too late. So I don't even think about it," he told me. With that, he gave me a smile, adjusted his diving mask, and disappeared beneath the waves.

PLANTS

While they don't get as much press as grizzly bears, plenty of plants and fungi can make you sick or kill you if you eat them. So we're putting them at the top (or rather, bottom) of our taxonomy of living things that might impact your health and safety outdoors. As a general rule, avoid eating plants or fungi that you can't positively identify unless you're in an absolutely dire survival situation and facing starvation. The risk of getting poisoned and incapacitated isn't worth the negligible caloric boost that you might or might not get from eating strange plants. You're better off putting your energy into identifying and avoiding plants that can cause serious discomfort and impaired mobility through physical contact or smoke inhalation.

POISON IVY, POISON OAK, AND POISON SUMAC

Native to North America and spread throughout much of the region, this poisonous triad is the most common itch-inducing vegetation you're likely to encounter in the outdoors. Painful, intensely irritating rashes from poison oak, poison ivy, and poison sumac can last for weeks, making it difficult to sleep, hard to concentrate, and nearly impossible to enjoy yourself. In extreme cases, exposure can lead to a serious infection that could land you in a hospital. What's especially insidious about these infections is that they play out in stages, with new areas of your skin breaking out in rashes over the course of several days, so that it might be a week or more before you know the extent of your troubles.

Poison ivy. There are two distinct varieties of poison ivy, eastern and western, that can be found across much of North America. Virtually the entire eastern half of the United States harbors poison ivy in suitable

habitats such as woods or marshy areas, and the two varieties overlap in northern-tier states ranging from Minnesota to Maine. "Leaves of three, let them be" is an old adage for avoiding poison ivy as well as poison oak, and it's useful although not always foolproof (see below). Generally, a stem of poison ivy has a large central leaf and two smaller leaves pointing out to the sides. The leaves come to a point, and can

Poison ivy

be smooth-edged or toothed. Reddish in the spring, they turn green in the summer and yellowish or orangish in the fall. The plant can produce clusters of greenish flowers and small greenish or off-white berries.

Poison oak. Like poison ivy, poison oak comes in two commonly recognized varieties and can produce clusters of small greenish yellow or white berries. Pacific poison oak occurs along the entire western seaboard of the United States and up into western Canada; it can occur as a shrub or a vine, and grows so thickly in some areas that it becomes the dominant

form of vegetation. The much less common Atlantic poison oak can be found in dry, sandy areas of the southern and southeastern United States, and along the eastern seaboard from northern Florida to New England. Both forms of the plant typically have three leaflets per stem, with a larger leaf in the middle and two smaller leaves jutting out to the sides. The leaves are shaped similarly to oak leaves, but

Poison oak

the leaf count can vary, and the old adage "Leaves of three, let them be" isn't fail-safe advice; some poison oak plants have as many as seven or nine leaves per stem.

Poison sumac. Also known as thunderwood, poison sumac is closely related to poison oak and poison ivy. Growing as a shrub or small tree, the plant can be found around wetland habitats in the Great Lakes states, along the eastern seaboard, and in Gulf Coast states. Poison sumac can be found in the same places as poison ivy, but it is not nearly as abundant or troublesome. The stems of poison sumac are usually red, and the leaves are waxy green. Often, a small leaf grows alongside the last large leaf in each cluster of leaflets.

Poison sumac

All three plants secrete an oil called urushiol through their leaves, and over 85 percent of the population is allergic to the oil. The best way to prevent contact is to wear long sleeves and pants when you're out in the woods. If you come into contact with any of these plants, remove your clothes as soon as it's practical to do so and wash them repeatedly in hot water with a strong detergent—any urushiol that touches your clothing can remain active and cause symptoms later. After exposure to these plants, be very careful not to touch your own bare skin, the skin of others, or any domestic animals in your household until you've taken the proper measures. Household pets are a common source of poison ivy and poison oak infections; people unwittingly expose their skin to urushiol simply by petting or grooming their dogs, who are often protected from symptoms by their fur.

The first symptoms to show will be small, clear, fluid-filled blisters in areas with soft, thin skin like the underside of the wrist, the inside of the elbow, the back of the knees, and between your fingers. Areas of the body with thicker, tougher skin will be slower to break out in blisters.

It's important to act fast once you realize that you've been exposed. Scrub your entire body thoroughly with soap, using hot water to dissolve and remove the oil. Cold compresses and hydrocortisone ointments can reduce symptoms. Severe cases can lead to fever, flu-like symptoms, and a maddening itchiness. Skin contact isn't the only way these plants can cause trouble. Smoke from burning poison ivy, poison oak, and poison sumac can cause serious respiratory problems, so be careful what you're tossing into your campfire. If possible, see a doctor in order to treat severe cases. Steroid creams and oral steroid treatments can take away some of the misery and speed up recovery.

CACTUS

There are hundreds of species of cacti that are native to North America—and though they are generally easy to avoid when you're paying attention, they'll nail you the minute you let down your guard. Most commonly associated with the deserts of the southwestern United States, they can also be found throughout the Rocky Mountains, Great Plains, and southeastern states, where they exist in a dizzying array of shapes and sizes. Like the plants themselves, cactus thorns range wildly in proportion. Some cacti have tiny hair-like needles, called glochids, that are so small you need to use a magnifying glass to pull them out. Others, such as the jumping cholla, have thorns that are big and robust enough to use as toothpicks or sewing needles. No matter the size, all of them have the potential to cause serious discomfort. Kneeling and falling seem to be the most common way to get punctured by cactus thorns, with knees, shins, elbows, and hands being the most vulnerable parts of the body. Redness and swelling are common side effects, with more severe cases leading to infection, nerve damage, and aching joints.

Remove cactus needles from your skin as soon as possible, and check your clothes for other needles that might eventually find their way into your hide. Multi-tool pliers are great for plucking out larger needles, though a small pair of tweezers in your kit is even better. Take your time and get every last needle. Needles that are completely embedded in your skin or that break off while you're trying to pluck them will fester for days or weeks (or even months) before they emerge. Usually they begin to emerge out of your skin at the center of what looks like a pimple. When they do, pop them out. A great trick is to use medical tape or duct tape to remove small, hair-thin cactus needles that can be especially frustrating. Firmly press a piece of tape over the affected area and then rip the tape free. Often it'll drag away any offending thorns. Whatever you do, don't try brushing them off! They'll break, and the remaining portions will be stuck under the skin, where they can cause trouble. After removing thorns, wash the area with soap and water or alcohol wipes and treat with topical antibiotic ointment. If large cactus thorns become deeply embedded in flesh or stuck in or near sensitive areas such as the eyes, ears, or groin, they may need to be surgically removed in the emergency room in order to avoid further damage. Finally, when camping in cactus territory, scour your sleeping area before pitching a tent or placing a sleeping pad. Cactus needles, even those that are dislodged from the plant, can easily poke holes in blow-up sleeping pads.

OTHER THORNY PLANTS

Most of the thorny plants you're likely to encounter out in the woods aren't a serious concern. You might get scratched up picking wild raspberries or busting through sawtooth greenbriar while hunting cottontail rabbits. But all in all, these types of plants are pretty easy to avoid, and the scratches they incur tend to be superficial. However, there are a couple of thorny plants that can turn a day hike or camping trip into a painful nightmare.

Stinging nettle. Widely distributed throughout North America, the leafy, herbaceous plant can reach 6 feet in height and often grows in dense clusters. It seems to have a penchant for growing alongside trails, so a single wayward step can land you in trouble.
The plant's stem and leaves are covered in hollow, stinging hairs, or trichomes, hundreds of which can become attached to exposed skin with just the lightest brush against the plant. The needles release a toxic blend of chemicals that quickly cause an itchy, red, swollen, and bumpy rash with a painful burning sensation. The rashes often form raised lines on the skin in places where contact was made.

Stinging nettle

To treat, avoid rubbing the affected area or scraping the hairs away with a knife, both of which will only spread the reactive chemicals. Instead, remove stinging nettle hairs with duct tape or medical tape. Cover the area with tape, press down firmly, and then peel the tape away. Once the hairs have been removed, wash with soap and treat with cold compresses and hydrocortisone cream; oral antihistamines can also alleviate symptoms. Normally, symptoms disappear within twenty-four hours, but severe allergic reactions can occur and may require medical attention. Hunting dogs can also have severe reactions to stinging nettle.

Devil's club. A shrub-like plant that is usually found in wet, swampy places with dense vegetation, devil's club is common throughout the Northwest, Alaska, and western Canada. Growing up to 20 feet tall, the plant is easily identified by its large, maple-tree shaped leaves and bright red clusters of berries. Native Americans value the plant for its medicinal properties, but the average outdoor recreationist should steer clear. The stalks of the plant are covered with half-inch-long thorns, and the stems have smaller hair-like thorns that break off easily in the skin. A small number of these thorns can be removed with tweezers, but if you're forced to bushwhack through a thick patch of devil's club, you may find your exposed skin covered in hundreds of them. These can cause a painful reaction that can linger for days. For some people, a serious bout with devil's club can lead to mild nausea and chills. In the wet rainforest environments where devil's club is found, there's also a greater risk for infection. Remove and treat as you would stinging nettle; the same treatment also applies to cactus spines.

Devil's club

INSECTS AND ARACHNIDS

Now that we've dealt with some of the perils of the plant kingdom, it's time to move on to the topic that occupies the most space in the popular imagination in terms of potential threats in the outdoors: the creepy, crawly, growly stuff that goes bump in the night. For now, forget all the headlines about people getting mauled or killed by large predators—we'll get to them later. Here, we're talking about the types of living things that are far more likely to cause you serious trouble, despite their small stature. Though the big guys get all the press, throughout the world insects and arachnids actually pose a much greater risk to people than creatures with big teeth and claws. A kayaker paddling around in the swamps of the Everglades is a lot more likely to have his trip ended by hordes of biting insects than to get dragged underwater and torn apart by a gator. And anyone who's contracted a serious viral or bacterial disease from an unseen critter can tell you that an itchy bug bite may just be the beginning of a potentially life-threatening ordeal.

MOSQUITOES

Here's a stark piece of data that should have you quivering in your boots: mosquitoes kill nearly three-quarters of a million people annually worldwide, compared to an average of five fatal grizzly bear attacks per year. Far and away, that makes them the most dangerous creature in the world. The majority of the fatalities they cause are directly related to various forms of the tropical disease malaria. Fortunately, the disease is largely preventable. Anyone planning on traveling to tropical climates in South or Central America, Asia, or Africa should visit their doctor for vaccinations or prophylactic medications against malaria and any other mosquito-borne disease they may encounter. Other potentially fatal mosquito-borne illnesses, some of which occasionally occur in the continental United States, include Zika virus, West Nile virus, and dengue fever.

The bugs are present on every continent except Antarctica, and they plague humans far north of the Arctic Circle. Outside of the tropical climates where the fatal diseases they can carry are a serious concern, mosquitoes are not generally regarded as a mortal threat. They are, however, deeply irritating wherever they are found. At times, their bites can even be debilitating—when traveling on northern rivers or swamps, people without insect repellent can get bitten so severely by mosquitoes that their eyelids swell shut.

Mosquitoes tend to congregate around standing or stagnant water where females can deposit eggs and larvae can develop into winged adults. Those conditions can be met anywhere from the lowcountry of coastal South Carolina to the Canadian high Arctic, where anyone who is going to be hiking, camping, fishing, or hunting is going to have to deal with the pesky buzzers to some degree. In the north country, mosquitoes are active as soon as temperatures rise above freezing in the spring, and they persist until the first hard frosts of fall. In southern swamps, mosquitoes are a year-round pest.

When conditions are right, such as in years of high spring precipitation or flooding, mosquitoes hatch by the billions. Even in years where precipitation is average, low-lying wetland areas typically foster enough mosquitoes for them to be a constant annoyance even though only female mosquitoes bite, feeding on blood to help support the growth of developing eggs.

Some folks are unfazed by mosquito bites, but most of us develop red, itchy bumps as a reaction to the mosquito's saliva, which contains an anticoagulant. Typically, symptoms appear within minutes of the sting and last for about forty-eight hours. The severity of symptoms varies widely among individuals. In cases where a large number of bites occur in a short period of time, or exposure to mosquitoes is prolonged, reactions may be more intense and can include severe itching, fever, fatigue, nausea, and headaches. Bite marks larger than a quarter accompanied by exaggerated swelling and difficulty breathing may be a sign of anaphylactic shock, which can occur during acute allergic reactions to mosquito bites (see page 383).

Protective Gear and Bug Repellent

The best protection against mosquitoes is to cover all exposed skin with layers of clothing that mosquitoes can't bite through. A thin nylon rain jacket, for example, offers much better protection than a light cotton hoodie, which a mosquito can easily poke holes in with its long, piercing stylets. If you know you'll be spending time in a spot where the mosquitoes will be thick, bring lightweight, loose-fitting gloves and a mesh head net that covers your head, face, and neck. In really nasty situations, a mesh mosquito jacket and pants can be a lifesaver. You'll also want to use some form of mosquito repellent.

Hunters and anglers often use portable Thermacell devices, which disperse allethrin, a synthetic relative of the natural mosquito repellent pyrethrum. A Thermacell device requires a butane cartridge and disposable repellent mats, which need to be replaced as they are used up. The devices are very effective, especially during more sedentary activities in light winds when the allethrin is allowed to linger in the air around your body. Permethrin is another effective repellent. The long-lasting insecticide can be applied to clothing and sleeping gear; used properly, one application can last for days.

Burnable mosquito coils and sticks typically work in one of two ways: they contain an insecticide that kills or stuns mosquitoes, or they contain an aromatic substance that repels the insects. The first category, which disperses pyrethrum (an extract from the chrysanthemum plant), pyrethrins (a synthetic version of pyrethrum), or allethrins (another synthetic analog) is very effective at killing mosquitoes if used in a semi-closed space where the breeze doesn't carry the smoke away, but these burnable devices are a serious fire hazard and need to be used with caution. We've seen holes burned into clothing, sleeping bags, and tents due to improperly placed mosquito coils or simply through the inattention of users. In open environments, where the smoke is carried away by the wind, performance is poor.

The most convenient and readily available mosquito repellent is the chemical compound called DEET, which is also effective protection against ticks, biting flies, and other pests (see page 176). Sprays and lotions that contain DEET are available in concentrations ranging from 4 percent to 100 percent. In general, the stronger concentrations are sold in small quantities. While suitable for your ears and the back of your neck in particularly nasty situations, the liquid is viscous and generally difficult to apply evenly over a large area. Lighter concentrations in a spray formula are much better for general use. Off! Deep Woods Insect Repellent V, which contains 25 percent DEET, is an excellent choice that can be applied to clothing and directly to skin.

While you can't argue the efficacy of DEET, its downsides should be considered. It's serious stuff. DEET can remove the finish from fishing rods, warp plastic phone cases, eat holes through tent fabric, make your lips go numb, and give you horrible dandruff. There are rumors that it causes cancer, but the U.S. Environmental Protection Agency stresses that it's safe to use in accordance with product instructions. It's not recommended for use on infants, and should be used only once per day on young children. When deciding if DEET is right for you, you have to weigh the possible potential of unknown, long-term impacts against the very real and immediate impacts of getting mauled by mosquitoes. When traveling in places with deadly mosquito-borne pathogens, the decision is an easy one to make. If you are dead set against DEET, Sawyer Picaridin Insect Repellent Spray is a good alternative.

BITING FLIES

More of an irritant than a potential threat to your health, biting flies of the order Diptera are many and varied, from the nearly microscopic no-see-ums to inch-long horseflies. Unlike mosquitoes, which suck blood through a straw-like proboscis, most female flies are "slash and lap" feeders; they use scissor-like mandibles to slash the skin open and then they lap up the blood. This crude feeding style makes some fly bites very painful at the moment of the bite. Horsefly and deerfly bits, for instance, hurt like hell right from the get-go. The upside of these larger flies is that you can see and hear them coming, and they often appear in manageable numbers.

You can usually swat them away successfully if you're paying attention. Smaller biting flies are more insidious, in that you don't fully register how badly you're getting mauled until it's too late. You might feel some vague tickling or itching around your ankles or behind your ears and not pay it much attention; then, a few hours later, you swell up with dozens of painful welts. This is especially true of no-see-ums or biting midges, which are able to bite through light clothing, and blackflies, which gather in huge swarms during the spring and summer in northern states from Maine to Alaska. If you're not prepared for them, they can ruin trips.

Avoid fly bites by using the same precautions as for mosquitos. Cover exposed skin with thick, loose-fitting garments. Pay particular attention to your ankles, the back of your legs, and, especially when dealing with blackflies, your ears and the back of your neck. Repellents with DEET work very well against biting flies. A key thing to note is that fly bite reactions can be even more painful than their mosquito counterparts. A few years ago, when the MeatEater crew was on an early fall moose hunting trip near the Yukon River in Alaska, the mosquitoes had already died off but there were still swarms of tiny biting flies, called white socks, around. The crappy thing about white socks is that you don't feel it when they're biting you, and you don't show any symptoms until a couple days after you've been bit. In fact, it wasn't until after we got back to town from our moose hunt that the whole crew realized our ears, noses, and fingers were covered in bites that were red, swollen, and intensely painful.

AVOIDING BUGS THE OLD-FASHIONED WAY

If you find yourself in a buggy situation and ill-prepared to deal with it—no Thermacell, no DEET, no bug netting, no tent—don't immediately give up hope. There are a few things you can try.

1. **Get away from the water and brush.** Mosquito and biting fly populations are typically much denser near the water than they are in drier areas. They also tend to show up in heavy vegetation. Try moving away from creeks, marshes, and thick vegetation in order to dodge the worst of the flying hordes.

2. **Be like a caribou.** Caribou live in some of the most insect-infested landscapes imaginable, and they are masters at avoidance. Steal a trick from their playbook and move to exposed ridgelines or hilltops where there's enough breeze to drive away the bugs. When insects are particularly bad, caribou will bed

down on glaciers or remnant snowfields to get a break from biting insects. They will also go to the shoreline of a large body of
water in order to catch onshore breezes that are strong enough
to put down the bugs.

3. **Make a smoky fire.** Usually a clean-burning, smoke-free fire is a
hallmark of a master camper. But in buggy situations, a little bit
of smoke can be a savior. Most campfires will naturally put off
enough smoke to turn bugs away; if your fire isn't doing the
trick, throw on some wet wood, green twigs, or even damp grass
in order to work up enough smoke to give you a break. If the
smoke is harder to tolerate than the bugs, try covering your face
with a wet rag or garment.

BEES, WASPS, HORNETS

Bees, wasps, and hornets (let's call them BWHs for short) differ from
most of the insects and arachnids covered in this section. While many of
these critters bite humans in order to get a meal of blood, BWHs sting
because they are pissed off and want to defend their hives or territory.
Avoiding that territory is tricky, as their nests can be found just about
anywhere: under the eaves of houses, in underground holes, beneath un-
dercut riverbanks, around abandoned structures and farm equipment, in
hollow trees, or just hanging from branches in seemingly random locations. Hunters and anglers are often stung in late summer months by
yellowjackets drawn to fish and game that's being processed in the field.
Whatever the circumstances, the result is the same: the insects deliver a
poisonous venom to their victims, causing a burning pain that is instant,
sharp, and lingering.

Around 5 percent of the U.S. population is allergic to the stings of
BWHs, and about fifty or sixty Americans die every year from serious
immune system complications resulting from bee stings. (An amplified
danger for people with sting allergies is getting stung inside the throat,
perhaps from "sipping" a bee that's found its way to a sugary drink. This
can cause the victim's air passages to swell shut, leading to asphyxiation.)
If you're allergic to bee stings and you don't want to contribute to that
statistic, carry an EpiPen whenever you're outside during bee season,
even if you're only going on a short day hike.

For those who are not allergic, BWHs can still be dangerous. A single
sting might only cause minor pain and swelling that subsides within a

day or two, but multiple stings can result in a toxic reaction that can include nausea, fever, and convulsions. Wasps and hornets can sting repeatedly, which can make them more dangerous than bees. Generally speaking, bees can only sting a single time, but they do leave their stinger and poison sac embedded in the victim's skin, which can continue to deliver poison until it is removed.

The primary threat from BWHs is getting swarmed and stung en masse. This is particularly dangerous in the case of Africanized honeybees, a hybridized species that was introduced into the wild in Brazil and which has since gradually spread northward into the United States. Victims swarmed by Africanized honey bees can get up to ten times more stings than people swarmed by common European honeybees.

Regardless of which BWHs you're dealing with, the key to survival when you're swarmed is to get away as fast as humanly possible. There's an overwhelming urge to flail your arms and swat at the bugs, but that can lead to even more stings unless you quickly put distance between yourself and the swarm. There's also the commonly held belief that the best way to avoid a swarm of bees is to head for the water, but that's only going to save you from getting stung if you happen to have a snorkel. Again, when swarmed by BWHs, you need to run!

When you do get zapped by a BWH, immediately remove the stinger by scraping it off with a knife or credit card (tweezers can put pressure on the venom sac and deliver more venom to the victim). Elevate the affected area if possible and apply a cold compress. Treat with over-the-counter pain medication and hydrocortisone cream to reduce pain, swelling, and itching. If necessary, get medical help for more severe reactions.

FIRE ANTS

Many species of ants will try to bite you if they feel threatened, but fire ants are the only ant species in North America that are cause for concern, having been documented performing feats like killing entire broods of baby quail. Some fire ants spray formic acid as they bite their victims; others double the damage by also delivering a caustic venom through a stinger on their abdomens. When fire ant colonies end up floating in flooded rivers or lakes, the fish that feed on them are sometimes killed from multiple stings to the inside of their stomachs. On human skin, a fire ant's sting immediately causes an intense burning pain, which later gives way to itching, redness, and pus-filled blisters. A couple of bites aren't anything to be worried about. Treat them as you would a bee sting, with cold compresses and hydrocortisone ointment. However, individuals who disturb a fire ant nest are often exposed to dozens of bites that can lead to a toxic reaction with symptoms including nausea, fever, and convulsions. Seek medical attention if symptoms become severe. In the event of severe allergic or anaphylactic symptoms, call 911 or immediately get to an emergency room.

CHIGGERS

Chiggers can be found throughout most of the world, including the Lower 48 of the United States and much of Canada. While relatively rare across much of their range, they are a very common nuisance in the southern United States. The juvenile form of a type of mite, the arachnids are surprisingly temperature sensitive. They typically bother humans when the ground temperature ranges between 77 and 86°F. Temperatures lower than 60°F will shut them down, and temperatures lower than 42°F will kill them. They are also nearly impossible to see with the unaided eye, as they measure only about ⅟₁₅₀th of an inch.

Chiggers

Contrary to popular belief, chiggers do not lay eggs on your skin or burrow into your skin. A related wives' tale maintains that chigger bites reveal the location of an embedded chigger, and that covering the bite with nail polish will suffocate the arachnid. Neither is correct. Chiggers *do* feed by boring into the skin and injecting a caustic saliva that liquefies skin cells into a slurry, and they may stay attached for days on end while they gorge. Bites are often concentrated in great numbers in areas such as the waistline and ankles, where chiggers are able to get around a person's clothes and attach themselves to exposed skin; they result in extremely itchy red rashes and blisters that can last for days and take up to a month to heal. When chiggers have gone to town, you'll look like you've got a bad case of poison ivy.

Chiggers linger in low-lying vegetation where there's ample humidity, so take precautions when traveling through thick grass or weedy fields during the warmest part of the day in summer months. Wear clothing made of tightly woven fabrics, with your shirt tucked in and a tightly cinched belt at your waist. Tuck your pants into your boots or socks in order to keep chiggers and other creatures from crawling up your legs. Button your sleeves to keep them from crawling up your arms. If the chiggers are really bad, seal off your wrists and ankles with duct tape. DEET is an effective preventative as well. Make sure to apply it to the clothing at your ankles, wrists, and waistline. Keep moving when passing through areas known to host chiggers. Don't lie down or linger.

Folks who live in chigger country will suggest dozens of home remedies for healing the bites or killing chiggers that have latched on. Some, such as scrubbing yourself down with gasoline-soaked rags or bathing in bleach, border on the extreme. Instead, thoroughly scrub the affected area with soap and water and apply topical anti-itch ointments like hydrocortisone or calamine lotion to the bites. While chigger bites aren't poisonous, some people are susceptible to more acute symptoms that require prescribed steroid treatments. Males, particularly young boys, are susceptible to something called "summer penile syndrome" when bitten by chiggers in the groin area. Symptoms include painful urination and swelling of the penis.

Some research suggests chiggers may also be possible vectors for alpha-gal syndrome (see Lone Star ticks, page 179).

TICKS

Whether you're fishing the Great Lakes, hunting in the Rockies, or simply picnicking in your local state park, ticks are an environmental X-factor that needs to be taken into account. A potential issue for anyone who spends time outside, they've even been known to cause problems for golfers on manicured country-club greens.

The small and pesky creatures are most active from late spring through summer, but in many places you can run into them even in the coldest months. We've dealt with ticks during the month of January while hunting Coues deer in northern Mexico's Sonoran desert. In the northern tier states, winter ticks have become one of the biggest threats facing moose populations; a single moose can carry tens of thousands of ticks, resulting in the creature's eventual death due to blood loss, anemia, disease, and starvation.

Like mosquitoes and biting flies, ticks bite humans and other animals in order to procure a meal of blood. The trouble with ticks isn't so much the actual bite (although the bites can be itchy and annoying) as the variety of pathogens they carry—pathogens that can have life-altering consequences for the victim. Unfortunately, the number of confirmed cases of tick-borne illnesses in the United States has more than doubled in the last decade or so. There could be a link between the proliferation of these diseases and climate change, as milder winters allow more ticks to survive into the next year, also allowing ticks to spread into areas where the climate was previously unsuitable.

Whatever the cause, arming yourself with a bit of knowledge about the main culprits for tick-borne diseases is key.

Deer ticks. Also known as black-legged ticks and sometimes called bear ticks, the diminutive creatures are common throughout most of the eastern half of the country. Adults reach only about ⅛ inch in length; in their nymphal stage, the ticks are 1/16 inch long, and they're half as long during their larval stage. Immature deer ticks and adult males have dark brown or black legs and a dark, reddish-brown abdomen, while adult females have dark legs and a reddish orange abdomen.

Attaching themselves to a host animal by burying their head in the skin in order to feed (and then remaining attached until their abdomen becomes engorged with blood), deer ticks can carry several different diseases—the most well-known of which is Lyme disease. A bacterial infection named after the town of Lyme, Connecticut, where symptoms were first documented in 1975, the disease had been around long before it was first scientifically identified. Since then it has become the most common tick-borne illness in the United States. Cases are most common in the Northeast, the Mid-Atlantic states, and the upper Midwest, but they've been reported throughout the country.

HOW LYME DISEASE IS TRANSMITTED

Although deer are frequently targeted as a source for Lyme disease, the real culprits are farther down the food chain—ticks, which are commonly implicated, and mice, which are often left out of the picture. While adult deer ticks prefer to feed on whitetail deer, ticks in the tiny larval and nymphal stages feed mostly on white-footed mice. The primary source of Lyme disease infections, the mice play host to the *Borrelia burgdorferi* bacterium; when a tick feeds on a mouse carrying the bacteria, it then passes the disease on to its next host, animal or human.

Transmission of the disease is not immediate. When a deer tick attaches itself to a host, the *Borrelia burgdorferi* bacteria that cause Lyme disease aren't transferred until well after the tick has begun feeding. It's only as the tick's stomach fills with blood that the bacteria are eventually distributed into the host through the tick's saliva, a process that takes thirty-six to forty-eight hours. That's why early detection is key, along with the anti-tick precautions and tick removal instructions described on page 180. Unfortunately, humans are more likely to be infected by tiny nymphal ticks than by the more easily detectable larger adult ticks.

Lyme disease symptoms vary widely and can be particularly hard to identify. Many people may not know they've contracted the illness until years after exposure, and even trained medical professionals can have trouble diagnosing Lyme disease. Early symptoms, such as headache, fatigue, and fever, are often mistaken for the flu or common cold. But if those symptoms are accompanied by a rash, especially a red, expanding, circular "bull's-eye" rash, that's a telltale sign of Lyme disease. If left untreated, the disease can cause chronic and debilitating muscle and joint pain, dizziness, swelling in the spinal cord and brain, memory problems, and other major complications.

Since Lyme disease was initially identified in the United States, the number of cases has skyrocketed. The CDC documents 30,000 confirmed cases of Lyme disease annually but estimates as many as 300,000 people are infected each year. It's important to get a blood test if you suspect you've been exposed to Lyme disease. Often doctors will prescribe patients who are diagnosed early an intensive round of antibiotics that can effectively treat the disease. Some doctors will even prescribe antibiotics based solely on exposure to tick bites in areas where there's a high prevalence of Lyme disease, rather than waiting for the actual symptoms to develop.

Dog ticks. Also known as wood ticks. This term actually encompasses a few different species of ticks common throughout the western and central portions of the country. At about a quarter inch long, they're twice the size of deer ticks, and most are a reddish brown color with some lighter coloration on their thorax.

Dog ticks can be vectors for dangerous pathogens such as tularemia (see page 205), but the most serious disease humans can contract from them is Rocky Mountain spotted fever. Although cases of Rocky Mountain spotted fever are rare compared to Lyme disease, this potentially fatal bacterial infection is considered one of the most deadly tick-related illnesses in the world. Around 5,000 cases of spotted fever occur in the United States annually, and up to 5 percent of these cases are fatal.

The CDC reports that Rocky Mountain spotted fever occurs throughout the United States, but over half of the documented cases come from North Carolina, Oklahoma, Arkansas, Tennessee, and Missouri. Elsewhere, the number of Rocky Mountain spotted fever cases in Arizona has been rising sharply over the past decade.

Belonging to a family of tick-borne spotted fever illness known as rickettsioses, Rocky Mountain spotted fever is a particularly gruesome and fast-moving disease. After an incubation period lasting anywhere from three to twelve days, early warning signs of Rocky Mountain spotted fever include a high fever, swelling around the eyes and hands, nausea, and vomiting. These symptoms last for about four days. Most people infected with Rocky Mountain spotted fever also experience a rash with small pink spots that begins on the arms and legs and spreads to the torso.

Next, the rash changes to large purple and red spots, which is a clear indication that the disease has moved into the severe, potentially deadly stage. If a victim fails to receive antibiotic treatment within five days of the initial symptoms, respiratory problems, coma, and amputation due to necrosis are likely, and eventual death due to organ failure is not uncommon. Seek immediate medical attention at the first sign of Rocky Mountain spotted fever.

Lone Star ticks. Hunters in the know pay careful attention to any news around Lone Star ticks, as the arachnids can transmit a wicked disease known as alpha-gal syndrome. Once the disease is contracted, the victim develops a severe allergy to red meat. For the unlucky sufferers of alpha-gal syndrome, a disease for which there is no known treatment, eating red meat can result in serious anaphylactic symptoms like labored breathing and swelling in the face and throat. To someone with a freezer full of self-harvested venison, this sounds like a fate that's almost worse than death. Several hunters who've contracted alpha-gal syndrome have reported to us that they also developed unexpected allergies to food items such as gummy bears, which include animal gelatin.

Lone Star ticks are found throughout the south-central portion of the country, and their range is expanding. Though they are about the same size and color as dog ticks, they're identifiable by the bright white spot or "star" on their back. Ironically, it's the very same deer we so enjoy eating that are at least partially responsible for the increase in cases of alpha-gal syndrome. Deer help the ticks expand their range by carrying them into new territory, thereby exposing more people to the disease.

Tick Precautions

Anyone who spends any amount of time in the outdoors is going to be exposed to ticks. Even in urban areas, they are impossible to completely avoid, so what you can and should do is try to minimize contact. Ticks prefer to lie in ambush in vegetation ranging in height from ground level up to deer height, making game trails that weave through thick brush ideal tick stomping grounds. For hunters, fishermen, and other outdoor enthusiasts, avoiding such areas is not realistic, so be sure to religiously apply repellent to exposed skin and clothing before heading into the woods. Natural repellent products can be used, but the most effective tick deterrents are those that contain DEET. As an added safety measure, close off entry points where ticks can reach your skin by keeping your shirt and socks tucked tightly into your pants and keeping your belt cinched down. Also consider wearing hooded upper layers to protect your head and the back of your neck.

Be vigilant about regularly checking yourself for ticks during and after any outdoor activity. It's an hourly ritual for the MeatEater crew to do a quick inspection for ticks during spring turkey season, though dark-colored ticks can be tough to spot on camouflage clothing. If you're not trying to conceal yourself from wild turkeys or other game animals, it's a good idea to wear light-colored clothing so that you can see ticks more easily. If you've got kids, it's doubly important to give them regular inspections if they've been outside. Kids don't seem to notice or be bothered as much by ticks crawling around on them. Pay particular attention to areas like hairlines, armpits, and the groin area, where ticks like to burrow in and can be hard to see when they do. Also check your kids' belly button area. Additionally, if your dog or cat spends any time outside, get them treated with tick prevention medications in order to protect not only them but you and your family.

When you get back from an outdoor trip, shake out your clothes and backpacks before bringing them inside your home. It's not a bad idea to let your clothes hang out on the clothesline for a day or two. Otherwise, you may bring ticks into your house who have hitchhiked home with you. When you strip down for a shower, give yourself a thorough examination to make sure your entire body is free of ticks.

Even if you take all the necessary precautions, you may still find a tick attached to you. If so, remove it immediately. Most tick-borne pathogens, including Lyme disease, aren't transmitted to humans until the tick has been attached for a day or two. If the tick is removed early enough, it's less likely that a disease will be passed on to the host.

Removing ticks. There's all kinds of bad information out there about the best way to remove a tick with its head buried under the skin. Some folks recommend burning the tick or covering it in oil or Vaseline in order to suffocate it and get it to pull its head out. However, the simplest and most effective way to get rid of a tick is to grasp it as close to the skin as possible with a pair of tweezers and slowly pull it out, making sure the head is attached. After the tick has been removed, wash the area thoroughly with water and soap or rubbing alcohol. If there's a chance that the tick was attached for a day or more—if the bug's abdomen is engorged with blood, it's likely to have been there a while—you should save it and have it tested by a doctor. Also see a doctor if you develop any kind of fever, pain, swelling, nausea, or rash after you've been bitten by a tick. Follow this precaution even if symptoms don't occur until days or weeks after being bitten.

SPIDERS, TARANTULAS, AND SCORPIONS

While most spiders deliver some venom when they bite their prey, the vast majority still pose little threat to humans. Funnel web spiders, black house spiders, and wolf spiders can produce painful bites, but they're only dangerous to people who experience an allergic reaction to their venom. However, there are a small handful of dangerous and potentially deadly spider species. It's important to consider here that outdoorsy types aren't necessarily at a greater risk for their bites. Most of the time, people are bitten in their own homes—but the culprits are worth mentioning as a necessary precaution.

Black widows. Distributed throughout the United States, Canada, and Central America, black widows prefer dark, protective habitats. In the wild, they favor animal burrows and brush piles, but they're also commonly found in man-made habitats such as outhouses and firewood stacks. About an inch long and recognizable by their dark brown or black color and a bulbous abdomen with a red hourglass

Black widow

marking, black widows can be aggressive, attacking well over 2,000 people every year in the United States. Their venom transmits a strong neurotoxin that causes intense pain, nausea, cramps, and difficulty breathing. These symptoms are particularly dangerous for infants and the elderly, but keep in mind that not a single death has been attributed to black widows in the United States over the past few decades. However, anyone who has been bitten by a black widow should call a poison control center or head straight to the emergency room for immediate treatment.

Brown recluse spiders. Also known as "fiddler spiders" and more common in the southern and central parts of the country, the inch-long arachnids are easily mistaken for common brown house spiders. Brown recluse spiders have a recognizable feature on their back, however, in the form of a dark, violin-shaped mark on their thorax. Like black widows, brown recluse spiders prefer dark,

Brown recluse spider

protected spaces like piles of leaf litter; dusty old deer camps and boathouses are just as attractive. People are often bitten by brown recluse spiders when they step on them, reach into some sort of crevice, or roll onto them while sleeping. Most won't require medical attention, but a minority of bite victims experience necrotic skin ulcers called "volcano lesions." If left untreated, these lesions can become gangrenous. For this reason, it's advisable to see a doctor anytime you've experienced a painful spider bite.

Tarantulas. Although tarantulas can be big and bad enough to kill small rodents and reptiles, they're not particularly aggressive. But they can and do bite people occasionally, so it's best to give them plenty of space. All tarantulas are venomous, but the species found in North America (mostly in the desert of the Southwest and in the southern states) and South America don't deliver life-threatening bites; you can treat the bites the same way you'd treat bee stings (see page 173). If symptoms such as severe swelling, intense pain, or labored breathing develop, call your doctor or go to the closest emergency medical clinic.

It's worth noting that some tarantula species have another line of defense, which can cause problems for anyone who gets too close or stupidly decides to handle one. Tarantulas found in the Western Hemisphere have tiny, barbed, bristly hairs covering their abdomens. When threatened, these species will use their legs to throw hundreds of their "urticating hairs" into the air, causing severe irritation if the hairs are inhaled, ingested, or expelled into your eyes.

Scorpions. North America is also home to dozens of species of scorpions—and they're not just relegated to the Southwest. We've encountered northern scorpions all the way up into Montana while turkey hunting, and you can run into them as far east as North Carolina. All of them are venomous, but

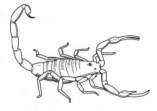

Arizona bark scorpion

most are only capable of delivering a sting that's on par with a wasp's and should be treated as such. The exception is the Arizona bark scorpion, a small tannish yellow scorpion between 1½ and 3 inches long that is found throughout the desert in the Southwest. Deaths from bark scorpion stings are extremely rare due to the availability of an antivenin; not a single known human fatality has occurred in Arizona in the past forty years. However, human fatalities are much more common in rural Mexico, where antivenin treatments are harder to find. Although a bark scorpion sting isn't likely to kill you, it can cause intense burning pain, nausea, vomiting, breathing difficulty, and numbness. Allergic reactions may also escalate into difficulty swallowing. Get to an emergency room immediately if symptoms progress quickly, especially if an infant or elderly companion has been stung.

HOW TO AVOID SPIDER AND SCORPION BITES

It's impossible to completely rule out an encounter with spiders and scorpions, but there are common sense steps that will reduce your chances of being bitten or stung.

1. **Clear away hiding spots.** While traveling with Amerindians in South America, we took note of how they use machetes and rakes made from tree branches to clear away leaf litter and debris at their campsites before stringing hammocks and tarps. By getting rid of hiding places for scorpions, spiders, and snakes, they were making a safer camp spot. You should take extra precautions when pitching tents or sleeping next to rock piles or brushy areas.
2. **Seal yourself off.** When you're inside your tent, keep the zipper

shut at all times if you're in an area with lots of spiders and scorpions. At night, store your boots and backpack in your tent or hang them from a tree branch, and keep your pack zipped up when it's not on your back.

3. **Beware of nocturnal visitors.** If you must store shoes and packs outside on the ground, shake them out in the morning before putting them on. While you're at it, give your sleeping bag and clothes a good shake before climbing into them. At night, also make sure to inspect the inside of your tent in case any spiders or scorpions managed to sneak in through an open zipper or by hitchhiking on your clothes.

4. **Use common sense out on the trail.** Don't stick your hands into holes in logs or cracks between rocks without visually inspecting them first. Always be aware of where you're putting your hands when rolling over logs or rocks or collecting firewood. And remember, walking around barefoot is asking for trouble. Many bites and stings occur when spiders or scorpions get stepped on.

LEECHES

While they do like to snack on human blood, the good news about leeches is that they aren't carriers of dangerous disease. In fact, the aquatic worms have been used throughout history to treat various ailments, with leech therapy currently being incorporated into some post-surgery treatments as a way of draining off excess blood.

Predatory by nature, they can generally be found in ponds, lakes, and slow-moving streams, although some species can live on land. The dark-colored creatures (usually seen in hues of black, brown, or purple) are excellent swimmers, moving through the water with an undulating, serpentine motion.

They also make excellent fishing bait. Untold numbers of walleye and smallmouth bass have been caught on simple rigs using nothing more than a split shot, a hook, and a live leech. But leech bait can quickly turn the table on fishermen or anyone else who might be spending time in the water, with the bait becoming the hunter as the worms slither up to fish or animals (including humans) in search of a liquid meal. For blood-drawing purposes, they're outfitted with twin "suckers" on each end of their body; the oral sucker found at the thin end of the body houses raspy jaws used for feeding, while the posterior sucker helps anchor it to its host. Once they've latched on, leeches saw through the skin and begin feeding on blood, and a natural anticoagulant in their saliva keeps the blood flowing while they gorge.

Removing leeches. There's nothing to gain from letting a leech get a free meal at your expense, so it's wise to remove them as soon as you find them. When we were kids, the go-to removal method was to cover them in salt and then watch them fall away. That works, but it's easier and quicker to just press your fingernail against the skin to the side of the leech's oral sucker (the one at the thinner end of its body) and then scrape the sucker away with your fingernail. Once the oral sucker is removed, grab the leech and detach the posterior sucker by plucking it away from your skin.

In rare cases, leeches can become dangerous if they attach to the inside of a person's throat or nose. As the leech feeds and becomes engorged with blood, airways can become blocked. This form of asphyxiation is known as hirudiniasis. In this situation, the leech needs to be removed immediately. If a portion of the leech is visible, grasp it with your fingers or a pair of pliers and give it a hard tug. Or try pouring hard liquor or salt on the leech to get it to release itself. If neither of these do-it-yourself remedies is a possibility, you'll need professional medical assistance.

FISH AND REPTILES

Snakes, alligators, sharks. . . . For many people they evoke more deeply rooted, visceral fear and loathing than any other members of the animal kingdom. Maybe it's because we can't relate to them the way we can to creatures we're more familiar with. The behavior of bears and wolves, for example, is often remarkably similar to our own. But there's nothing even remotely human about sharks or alligators. Their mindless, alien nature makes them seem all the more frightening. That's because for the most part, big sharks and large crocodilians don't view humans with any kind of fear—nor do they see us as any different from their more typical prey. It might be gruesome, but it shouldn't be all that surprising when a white shark that normally feeds on seals decides to make a meal out of a person diving in murky coastal waters in Northern California. And a Florida gator that makes a habit of dragging wild pigs and deer into the water could easily decide to try to do the same to someone wading in the shallows of some backwater swamp. Even poisonous snakes don't distinguish humans from any other animal that might threaten their safety. If a rattlesnake gets stepped on, whether by a horse or a human, it's going to protect itself by biting.

Whether you're a hunter or a hiker, a surfer or a surfcaster, there's simply no way to completely avoid everything that slithers or swims. So it pays to understand which types of swimmers and scaly slitherers can hurt you, how they can hurt you, where you might encounter them, and how to handle the situation if you do. Rattlers are just one of a handful of species of venomous snakes in North America, for instance. And stingrays are known to pack a painful wallop, but even run-of-the-mill game fish like bluefish can inflict serious injuries. Saltwater environments are home to a host of aquatic organisms capable of causing intense pain, serious injuries, and in rare cases even death.

JELLYFISH

Although many species of jellyfish can deliver painful stings via the stinging cells called cnidocytes or nematocysts, only a select few of the gelatinous invertebrates can kill you. Common to both North American coasts, moon jellyfish have tentacles that cause only mild pain and skin irritation. Sea nettles, numerous on the east coast around Chesapeake Bay, have a sting that is extremely painful but only very rarely life-threatening. Box jellyfish, on the other hand, found off the coast of Australia and the Philippines, are some of the deadliest creatures on the planet.

Tens of thousands of beachgoers and anglers are stung by jellyfish in the United States every year, and members of our team have regularly gotten stung fishing and hauling crab and shrimp pots in southeast Alaska. Strong tidal currents sweep jellyfish into fishing lines and pot ropes, where their sticky tentacles break off and get stuck. If you're not wearing gloves and you grab the line, a burning pain will immediately let you know that you screwed up.

If you do get stung by a jellyfish, remove any pieces of tentacles still attached to your skin with a gloved hand, tweezers, a stick, or any other implement that eliminates further skin contact. Even dead jellyfish or pieces of jellyfish are capable of stinging. You'll hear folks recommend urinating on jellyfish stings, but it's more effective and practical, and less likely to get you arrested for indecent exposure, to simply rinse the area of the sting with seawater. As soon as possible, wash again thoroughly with warm fresh water or vinegar; the acids in the latter will help break down the venom. If necessary, treat jellyfish stings with cold compresses and hydrocortisone cream. See a doctor if symptoms become severe; some victims have dangerous allergic reactions to jellyfish stings.

Box jellyfish (deadly)

Moon jellyfish (harmless)

FISH SPINES AND PUNCTURE WOUNDS

There are lots of fish whose sharp spines can still do a lot of damage, even without the venom of the lionfish. Popular freshwater game fish like yellow perch, walleye, bass, catfish, and many sunfish species have needle-like spines embedded in their fins. You'll also see sharp spines in saltwater species such as Pacific rockfish, hardhead catfish, cobia, and others. Handle them carefully, whether you're releasing them or filleting them. It's a good idea to wear sturdy rubber-coated gloves when you're cleaning fish with sharp spines. If you don't have a pair of those, make sure to carefully fold the fins that house the spines down before grabbing hold of a fish. Puncture wounds from fish spines get infected easily, so take the appropriate first-aid measures if you get impaled by a fish.

Venomous fish spines are bad enough, but sharp teeth can be even worse. Take barracudas, a large, tropical saltwater fish that anglers like to catch and divers love to photograph. Although barracudas aren't venomous, they do pack an impressive set of large, razor-sharp teeth built for lightning-fast attacks on smaller fish. We've had bonefish on the end of our lines sliced in half by big 'cudas before we could even register what was happening. They'll also badly slice open the occasional human being, although it's usually a case of mistaken identity rather than any kind of predatory behavior on the part of the barracuda. Attacks can be triggered when a barracuda mistakes a flashy ring or bracelet for a baitfish. The resulting injuries to the unlucky swimmer or diver can be severe enough to require dozens of stitches. Fishermen need to take care with barracudas as well; many anglers are badly cut when they're unhooking the fish. Always use long pliers or hemostats to remove hooks from barracudas or other toothy fish like northern pike, bluefish, and sharks.

STINGRAYS

Stingrays live in shallow brackish water and saltwater around the world. Several species are common along North America's East Coast, including Atlantic stingrays, southern stingrays, and common stingrays. Round stingrays are found along the Southern California coast, and several other species swim in Hawaiian and Caribbean waters. No matter the species, all stingrays prefer shallow water, where they bury themselves in the sand or mud in order to ambush small fish, shrimp, and crabs. Because most stingrays are drab-colored ambush hunters, they're very difficult to see in their natural environment. And rather than fleeing from danger, they tend to stay put and rely on their camouflage to keep them hidden from large predators like sharks. It's this behavior that gets swimmers and anglers in trouble.

A stingray's primary defense is the sharp, serrated, venomous barb on its tail. If it's unable to get out of the way when threatened, the ray whips the offender with its tail and drives the barb into its victim's flesh. Despite this impressive weaponry, stingrays aren't considered aggressive, as they only attack as a last resort. Steve Irwin, the host of the wildly popular television show *The Crocodile Hunter*, was killed in a freak accident when a stingray he was handling pierced his heart with its barb—but this is far from a common occurrence, and deaths by stingray are extremely rare. Swimmers and wading anglers generally run afoul of stingrays when they step on them and get stung on the lower leg or foot. In the United States, thousands of people are injured by stingrays per year, but the vast majority of these injuries are minor. Stingray venom causes intense pain and inflammation, but it won't kill you. Occasionally the barbed spine breaks off in the flesh and may need to be surgically removed. Serious infections can occur, so deep puncture wounds and lacerations need to be closely monitored and treated with antibiotics. More commonly, people who get hit by a stingray are treated for minor cuts and given over-the-counter pain medication. Several of us have been zapped by stingrays while we were wade-fishing for bonefish in Belize and surfcasting in

Baja. It hurt for a while, but it was nothing we couldn't walk away from.

If you're wading in waters where stingrays are common, keep an eye out for partially buried rays. On sandy or light-colored mud bottoms, any exposed parts of the ray will often be darker than the surrounding bottom. You should also watch for puffs of

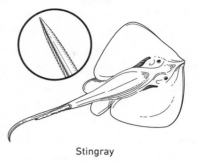

Stingray

mud where a ray has recently disturbed the water and for visible tracks along the bottom of the ocean floor. Sometimes, though, stingrays are tough to see even in crystal clear water. In turbid water, they're all but invisible, so the most surefire way to avoid them is to wade slowly and shuffle your feet, keeping constant contact with the ocean floor or lakebed. Usually any stingrays in your line of travel will sense your approach and swim away. But if not, you're more likely to bump a ray with your foot rather than step on top of it, and the ray is more likely to take off than sting you. If you're fishing, always wear wading boots, no matter how tempted you are to go barefoot. If a stingray drives its barb deep into the sole of your foot, your fishing trip will be over in a hurry.

LIONFISH

Conventional anglers, spearfishermen, and divers also need to watch out for lionfish. They're native to the Indian Ocean, but illegal aquarium releases have created a large invasive population of this beautiful but venomous fish in the warm coastal waters off the southern Atlantic Coast and Gulf of Mexico. Efforts to eradicate lionfish have been largely unsuccessful, and it looks like they're here to stay. In recent years, the fish have become a favorite target of inshore anglers and spearfishermen. But their popularity comes at a cost. Lionfish are armed with poisonous spines in their dorsal, anal, and pectoral fins—spines that are used as a defense mechanism against larger predatory creatures. When the spines puncture flesh, they deliver a neurotoxin that causes searing pain and swelling but isn't lethal. If you're diving or snorkeling, don't get too close to a lionfish. When targeting their tasty flesh for a meal, handle them with extreme care. Most lionfish incidents occur when a fisherman is trying to get a thrashing lionfish off the end of a spear or a hook. Even after the fish is dead, its spines can still deliver venom.

If you're stung on the hand, don't panic—but do remove any rings you might be wearing right away, before your fingers begin to swell. Otherwise, you may be facing an emergency partial amputation of your fingers in the ER in order to prevent further tissue damage. (See sidebar on page 25 for more on why.) Immediate self-administered first aid includes inspecting the sting area to be sure a spine hasn't broken off under your skin. Remove

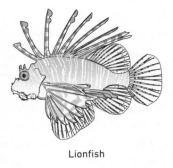

Lionfish

any spines immediately with tweezers or pliers. Next, clean the sting area and then disinfect with hydrogen peroxide, alcohol, or antibiotic ointment. If possible, soak the area of the sting in hot water for half an hour—some experienced spearfishermen always carry a thermos of hot water on their boats in case of a lionfish sting. Lionfish venom is denatured, or rendered harmless, at high temperatures, so it isn't an issue in the cooked fish. Over-the-counter antihistamines and anti-inflammatory medicines can help alleviate pain and swelling. If an allergic reaction occurs, head straight to the hospital.

SHARK ATTACKS

Over 440 species of shark roam the world's oceans. They're found anywhere from the tidal line to depths of over 5,000 feet, and they range in size from 6 inches to over 40 feet. They inhabit all five of the earth's oceans, and even some rivers. Yet within this massive array, only three species are known to have caused double digit human fatalities: great whites, tiger sharks, and bull sharks. In 2019, the global tally of these species' unprovoked attacks landed at sixty-four, with a total fatality count of only two. Provoked shark attacks, in which victims were shark-fishing or engaging the shark by attempting to touch or feed it, came in at around forty. It's worth noting that shark attack data rely heavily on reporting, which can be inconsistent in various parts of the world. But however you slice it, the dread instilled by movies and general shark attack sensationalism is largely unwarranted. Our real fear should be an ocean without its greatest predator.

Shark attacks do have a direct correlation to human population density, tourism included—and, of course, to the type of activity in which victims are engaged. There's a widely touted statistic that says your chances of getting attacked by a shark are one in 3.75 million. But the math isn't really fair if it's putting a swimmer in shark-infested waters in the same risk assessment bucket as a guy sitting on his couch in Idaho. Surface recreationalists (mainly surfers, but also boogie boarders and people floating on inflatable rafts) account for 53 percent of attacks, partly because surfers in particular spend so much time in the water. Swimmers come in at number two, accounting for 30 percent of attacks, and divers account for approximately 6 percent. But even in the higher-risk scenarios, the numbers are quite low. As a spearfisherman, I have put myself on a platter in the middle of some of the world's most remote oceans. So far I've got lots of stories to tell my grandchildren—and although I've had some close calls, I've never been bitten.

The ocean is the world's ultimate "public land." It covers 71 percent of the earth's surface, and a very small percentage of that expanse is off-limits. Don't let a fear of sharks prevent you from exploring it.

THE MISUNDERSTOOD GREAT WHITE

When I was starting out as an abalone diver in Northern California's Red Triangle, the great white was the shark we all feared but rarely talked about. The frigid 50°F water and poor viz took enough mental fortitude to push through. We knew the sharks were around and that at some point we might run into one (or, more likely, that one would run into us). For me that moment came when I least expected it. I never saw the shark, and at no point could I have taken evasive or defensive action. It was a classic attack from below that luckily ended without a bite.

Explosive ambush hunters, great white sharks often silhouette their prey on the surface, but they can also react to movement and vibrations in the water. Seals and sea lions are the main diet of mature great white sharks, and unfortunately abalone divers and spearfishers often mimic pinniped movement. Frequently living in waters with poor visibility, great whites roll their eyes back into their heads when attacking, leading to what are called exploratory bites. These bites account for a majority of white shark attacks, often with the shark never returning.

Also known as the white pointer, the great white has been protected in California waters since 1994, under the California Endangered Species Act. While the species' movements are often misunderstood, recent tracking efforts have revealed that great whites are highly migratory, moving from Northern California to as far away as Hawaii. On the East Coast, great white sightings are becoming more common, with their migratory patterns taking them from the Gulf of Mexico or the southeast region toward New England as the waters warm. Reaching lengths of up to 20 feet and weighing as much as 4,200 pounds, great whites can live as long as seventy years, with females taking up to thirty-three years to reach sexual maturity.

THE OMNIVOROUS TIGER SHARK

While technically second to the great white in fatalities, the tiger shark is number one on my list. Those things remind me of a velociraptor from *Jurassic Park*. Always observing, almost studying you. Sometimes you can't help but feel like you really are being hunted.

The largest tiger I was lucky enough to interact with was swimming through the Gulf of Mexico as I was doing a deep scuba dive to 237 feet off an oil rig named Lena. I was chasing an American red snapper when I spotted a tiger shark swimming right behind my friend. I distinctly remember mumbling, "Holy shit." Like many of the tigers I'd had past experiences with, this one was like a ghost—there one minute, somehow disappearing the next. Observing and evaluating their prey from a distance before an investigative bump and a final attack, tiger sharks have an innate ability to show up where you least expect them, often approaching from behind or from the side. Sometimes it's better to just change locations than play the stalking game with a tiger.

Unlike the great white, which rolls its eyes back during an attack, the tiger shark has what's called a nictitating membrane, a clear eyelid that protects its eyes during attacks. Its diet includes fish; sea snakes; dolphins; and loggerhead, green sea, or leatherback turtles. Nicknamed the "garbage can of the sea," the tiger shark is omnivoracious, with a stomach that has been found to contain everything from terrestrial animals such as goats and dogs to man-made detritus like oil cans, bottles, license plates, and even tires.

Characterized by black stripes and spots that fade as the shark ages, the tiger shark can reach lengths in excess of 18 feet with a weight of over 2,000 pounds. Commonly found in tropical and subtropical waters, in the United States its population is concentrated in the Gulf of Mexico, up the East Coast, and around Hawaii. Hawaii leads the United States in tiger shark incidents as well as being the only state that has reported fatal tiger shark attacks since 2010.

THE BRAZEN BULL SHARK

Some people run with the bulls and some people swim with them—I'd rather be a member of the second group. Also known as Zambezi sharks in Africa, bull sharks derive their names from their short, stocky frames and their often unpredictable and brazen demeanor. If you ever find yourself off the east coast of Florida during the cobia run or off Texas hunting monster wahoo, break out a speargun and prepare yourself for a wild time.

Averaging around 8 feet long and 290 pounds, bulls have been known to reach up to 11 feet and 700 pounds. Distributed in the Gulf of Mexico and up the East Coast, the bull shark is considered by some to pose the largest risk to humans, being responsible for 20 percent of all unprovoked shark attacks in Florida since 1926. Bulls generally prefer water shallower than 100 feet, which places them in bays and close to shore, where most water activities are carried out.

Somewhat uniquely among shark breeds, bulls are diadromous, meaning that they can survive in both fresh and saltwater. While freshwater interactions are rare, bull sharks have been found up the Mississippi as far as Alton, Illinois, around 700 miles from the Gulf of Mexico. Like tiger sharks, they have a very indiscriminate diet, chowing down on anything from bony fish, sea birds, and turtles to dolphins, stingrays, and crustaceans. Bull sharks can be solitary but are also found in schools (aka gams, shivers, or frenzies).

SHARK ATTACK PREVENTION AND PREP

As already mentioned, shark attack rates are heavily linked to population density and recreational activity. Partly because of that, the United States leads the world in unprovoked shark attacks (Florida, Hawaii, California, South Carolina, and North Carolina top the list), with Australia coming in second.

If you spot a shark while you're in the water, remember that a shark moving slowly and calmly is rarely a threat—its swimming should loosely mimic an S or wavelength shape. Sharks get excited by thrashing noises and vibrations, so stay calm, enjoy the experience, and you'll wind up with a story to share.

If the shark starts to swim in an accelerated, jerky, Z-type movement, however, it's a good time to contemplate your exit options. As the shark gets more excited, it will start to hump its back, pushing its pectoral fins down and sometimes raising its snout (complete with gaping mouth). This will rarely happen if you are merely snorkeling or swimming. Many times this display is initiated by an activity such as spearfishing or chumming, in which there is competition for food.

If you are being attacked, what comes next? I can tell you first-hand that punching a shark in the wrong place feels like punching the sidewalk, and it's just as ineffective. There are three areas where you should concentrate your efforts: the nose, eyes, and gills. Shark noses contain a high volume of supersensitive sensory organs, including the ampullae of Lorenzini, a set of electroreceptors the shark uses to navigate electric and magnetic fields in the water, so a hard punch or poke to this area usually is enough to ward off the first approach. If you find yourself in the unfortunate position of being on the shark's flank, concentrate on the eyes or gills. While sharks are predators, they still have a degree of self-preservation.

For those who may want to take a proactive approach, there are many devices out there that can be used as shark deterrents. Shark Shields are the only such device that I have personally tried and have some faith in. The downside is that this thing can shock the piss out of you if you aren't careful, and it needs to be charged. There are some newer devices out there that are based on magnetic technology—I'm just personally not convinced they will work on a charging great white, tiger, or bull.

And now for the real lowdown. If you get bitten by a shark, chances are pretty good that you are not going to see it coming or that the attack happens so fast that there will be few defensive actions you can take. The one thing you can do to save yourself as well as others is have a proper hemorrhage control kit or device. A vast majority of fatal attacks are due to blood loss, not trauma—meaning that most fatalities could have been prevented with a timely application of a tourniquet or compression bandage coupled with timely notification of rescue personnel.

My personal bite kit includes a tourniquet, two Israeli trauma bandages (used in places where a tourniquet cannot be, such as the abdomen), and a Garmin InReach device (see page 285). Make sure you get training on how to use that tourniquet, and practice applying it to yourself and to others. Remove any difficult-to-open packaging (many of these items come in pretty vacuum-sealed packages that can be a liability in the heat of the moment), and have your kit easily accessible.

—*By Greg Fonts, National Spearfishing Team champion, USA World Team diver, Louisiana state champion, and owner of UltimateSpearfishing.com*

SNAKES

Although across the board, snake-related fatalities in the United States are pretty rare, the following snakes present a real concern for outdoorsmen and women.

Rattlesnakes. While rattlesnakes are most common in the arid deserts of Arizona and Texas, they can be found in plains, mountains, forests, and swamps from coast to coast; various species hang around in every state except Rhode Island, Alaska, and Hawaii. Belonging to the class of pit vipers who use heat-sensing "pits" on their heads to detect both predators and prey, rattlesnakes are universally ven-

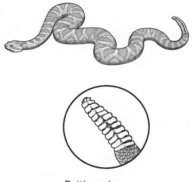

Rattlesnake

omous and capable of causing excruciating pain, lasting damage, and even death. If it seems like rattlesnakes get all the press, there's good reason: rattlers alone bite as many as 8,000 people annually in the United States. Rattlesnakes and other pit vipers vary greatly in size and color, but most species are 2 to 4 feet long with a large triangle-shaped head and a striped or spotted pattern on their backs. All pit vipers inject their venom through long, hollow hypodermic-needle-like fangs that fold into the roof of their mouth when not in use and snap into position when the snake feeds or defends itself.

Cottonmouths and copperheads. Also known as water moccasins, cottonmouth snakes are another species of North American pit viper. The only venomous water snakes in the United

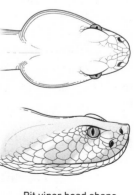

Pit viper head shape

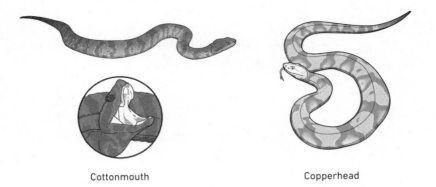

Cottonmouth   Copperhead

States, these large, aggressive snakes are widely distributed throughout the Southeast and Gulf Coast. The smaller copperhead variety of pit viper is common in much of the eastern and central portions of the country.

Coral snakes. These poisonous slitherers come in two subspecies— the eastern coral snake and western coral snake. The eastern subspecies is found in several southeastern states, while western coral snakes live in Arizona and New Mexico. Coral snakes aren't nearly as aggressive as heat-sensing pit vipers, but they are highly venomous. Rather than injecting their venom, these small, brightly striped snakes deliver the poison by chewing on their prey with small, fixed fangs.

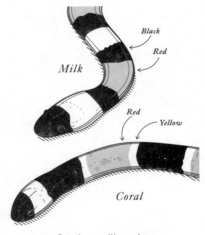

Coral vs. milk snake

Because they share a similar striped pattern with coral snakes, harmless milk and king snakes are often mistaken for the venomous species. Learn the coral snake rhyme to tell these lookalike snakes apart: "Red touches black, you're okay, Jack! Red touches yellow, you're a dead fellow."

Constrictors. While the greatest reptilian risk to adventurers in North America comes from native venomous snakes, there is increasing concern over the growing population of non-native constrictors like Burmese pythons in Florida. Not only are they an ecological disaster for native wildlife, they're also potentially dangerous. Thus far, no humans have been hurt by these invasive snakes in the United States, but pythons and other constrictors have killed people in other parts of the world. In Florida, they're known to prey on human-sized animals like deer and wild hogs.

Avoiding snakebites. Getting bitten by a venomous snake is serious, but actual fatalities are rare. Of the thousands of people bitten by rattlesnakes every year, only an average of five will die. But anyone who's seen gnarly footage of what the aftermath of a bite can look like knows it's something to be avoided at all costs. Regardless of the species, the primary function of a snake's venom is to render prey immobile so it can be easily tracked down and consumed after being bitten. Most rattlesnakes produce venom containing hemotoxins, which kill through the destruction of blood cells; coral snakes and some rattlers deliver venom containing neurotoxins that attack the central nervous system. Neurotoxins are generally faster-acting than hemotoxins, but both are extremely dangerous. People who are bitten by snakes with hemotoxic venom experience excruciating pain, internal bleeding, and tissue damage with the potential to lead to the loss of extremities. Neurotoxic venom can cause vision failure, muscle weakness, and complete respiratory failure. For information on how to treat a snakebite, see page 395.

Snakes generally bite people when they're stepped on accidentally. Contrary to popular belief, rattlers don't always rattle as an early audible warning sign, so the best way to avoid them is to stick to established trails where you can see the ground and avoid areas where visibility is limited, such as thick brush, rock piles, and tall grass. Be careful where you're putting your hands, too. Snakes like to hide under rocks, logs, and junk heaps, and even in old, broken-down domiciles—basically anywhere they can hunt for small rodents.

ALLIGATORS

Classified as an endangered species in the United States until 1987, American alligators have made an amazing recovery. Their population now numbers in the millions, and they've been spotted in eleven southern states. Florida and Louisiana sport the highest numbers, each being home to over one million alligators. They're doing so well that there's an entire industry built around gator meat and hides collected by commercial trappers. They can also be legally hunted in several states. But alligators can and do hunt people on rare occasions. The long-lived crocodilians regularly reach sizes exceeding 10 feet and several hundred pounds, which is plenty big enough to kill a person.

Alligators typically hunt large prey animals by ambushing them at the shoreline and dragging them underwater to drown. Their large jaws are lined with sharp, sturdy teeth, and they have one of the strongest bites in the animal kingdom—exerting over 2,000 pounds of force per square inch, twice as much as a grizzly bear. But as big, strong, and numerous as the gators are, attacks are rare. In the United States, ten people are attacked by gators per year. On average, only one of these attacks results in a fatality.

Still, you shouldn't go looking for trouble in gator country. Swimming in an area where alligator warning signs have been posted is just plain stupid. Watch out for them when you're paddling or fishing, too. They can be attracted by splashing that resembles the sound of fish or animals struggling in the water. And remember that alligators like to eat pet dogs, so keep a close eye on Fido.

MAMMALS

These days, car accidents and cancer are far bigger mortal threats than predators. But for millennia, humans were a regular menu item for a plethora of large mammalian predators. Our ancestors were hard-wired to fear and avoid anything that was capable of killing and eating them, and that innate fear stuck around. We've spent enough time camping in the backcountry to know that those rustling sounds outside the tent are almost always some small, harmless critter going about its nightly business. Still, it's easy to imagine there's only a thin layer of nylon between you and something with big teeth and claws.

The fear of what's creeping around out there in the dark shouldn't be completely ignored. Bear, mountain lion, and even wolf attacks do happen on occasion, so anyone who spends time outside where big predators live needs to take certain precautions. But it's not only big predatory mammals that hunters, anglers, campers, and hikers should be thinking about. Big game animals like moose and bison can be just as dangerous. Just look to places like Yellowstone National Park, where unsuspecting tourists are regularly injured by wild ungulates. It's also a good idea to know the risks associated with smaller, less glamorous critters like rats and raccoons. They may not be able to rip your throat out or stomp you to death, but they are certainly capable of transmitting a wide variety of unpleasant diseases.

RODENTS

When you're sleeping out under the stars, it's not unusual to wake up in the middle of the night due to a deer mouse or a packrat skittering across your sleeping bag. For creatures that weigh a few ounces, small rodents can deliver several pounds' worth of scare. In fact, in our experience, there tends to be a disproportionate relationship between the size of the animal and the amount of fright that it can incite. It's not all that irrational, given our long history of trouble with rodents damaging crops with their insatiable appetites or passing along deadly diseases like the black plague, which was transmitted through the bites of fleas festering within rat and mice populations. Today, thanks to public sanitation and modern medicine, we no longer live with large-scale plague epidemics, and only around ten Americans contract the disease annually. But there are other rodent-borne diseases to be aware of.

Hantavirus is one such example. A class of viruses less familiar to many of us than the plague, yet far more common in the United States and Canada, hantaviruses live in the urine, droppings, and saliva of infected rodents; if the viral particles are disturbed and become airborne, humans who inhale them can become infected. Infections can lead to hantavirus pulmonary syndrome, which is fatal a whopping 38 percent of the time.

There are several varieties of the virus, each endemic to a certain species of rodent. Deer mice of the western and central United States and Canada carry the Sin Nombre hantavirus; white-footed mice of the northeastern United States carry the New York hantavirus; and cotton rats of the southeastern United States carry the Black Creek hantavirus.

Most hantavirus cases are contracted by people who live, work, or play in closed-air environments such as barns, sheds, or outbuildings that are infested with mice. Sweeping mouse shit out of an old barn, for instance, would be a textbook way to contract the disease. However, hikers and campers can be exposed to hantaviruses while camping in backcountry shelters or cabins that are infested with mice, or in natural mice habitats such as cave mouths or rocky overhangs. Initial symptoms include fatigue, fever, and muscle aches in the large muscles of your legs, back, or shoulders. Seek immediate medical attention if these occur.

Although cases of modern plague are rare, they're not unheard of. In

2007, a Grand Canyon National Park wildlife biologist named Eric York responded to a mortality signal emitting from a radio-collared mountain lion. He found the dead lion and packed her out of the canyon on his back, hoping to discover the cause of her death. A few days later, the cause found him—he was discovered dead in his home, having been bitten by a plague-carrying flea that had hitched a ride on the dead lion. Lions aside, danger zones for plague occur after massive rodent die-offs, when hungry fleas leave their deceased host animals to look for fresh sources of blood. The most common epidemics among wild critters occur within prairie dog colonies in the western United States; when infected colonies are discovered, they are eradicated by animal control specialists using toxic gas. But other small rodents like mice and squirrels can also carry fleas capable of transmitting bubonic plague, as can rabbits and hares. If you want to play it ultra safe, avoid coming into contact with rodents as a general rule, especially when you're traveling through areas where there's evidence of a large die-off.

For small-game hunters who handle squirrels and rabbits, the risk factors don't warrant anything beyond careful handling practices. Don't encourage exposure to fleas by overhandling small game or storing dead animals near your bedding, and discard the skins a safe distance away from your campsite. There are cases where humans have contracted plague by handling the flesh or bodily fluids of infected animals, so latex gloves might be a good idea if you have concerns when skinning small game.

Early plague symptoms begin with fever, headache, and swollen, painful lymph nodes. Symptoms then progress to intense abdominal pain, shock, bleeding, and blackened skin. If the disease is left untreated, severe pneumonic symptoms quickly develop, and death due to respiratory failure is likely. If by some freak chance you do contract the plague, immediately seek medical attention. The disease is treatable with modern antibiotics.

BATS

Bats engender a lot of fear. While you don't need to worry about a bat attacking you in order to suck your blood, the creatures are well-known carriers of disease—as we've seen with several viral pandemics, including COVID-19, that were likely traceable to human-bat interactions.

Outside of the risks entailed by prolonged contact with bats, disease transmission via bites can be another source of concern. Over forty species of bats numbering in the tens of millions live in the United States and Canada, and though the vast majority are harmless insectivores, bats *will* bite when threatened or cornered. A bat bite has always been bad news, even before the coronavirus made its way around the globe—bats account for nearly a third of animals infected with rabies, and in the United States, they are responsible for a full 70 percent of human rabies cases. Though the population of bats capable of transmitting rabies amounts to less than one-half of 1 percent, the viral disease is almost always fatal unless a person receives the necessary treatments.

The vast majority of humans who contract rabies are exposed through having been bitten. Simply touching an infected animal isn't enough to transfer the disease, which is typically transferred directly into the human bloodstream via the animal's saliva. Once contracted, the virus has an incubation period averaging anywhere from twenty to sixty days—though there's an off chance that incubation could be as short as five days or as long as six months. Some rabies victims don't reveal symptoms until over a year after their initial exposure. Rabies symptoms can include fever, headache, nausea, vomiting, agitation, anxiety, confusion, hyperactivity, hallucinations, insomnia, and partial paralysis. Victims also typically experience hydrophobia, an extremely irrational fear of water that is often accompanied by difficulty swallowing and excessive salivation. Ultimately, if the disease has progressed to this point, death follows.

Fortunately, if it is caught during the incubation phase, rabies can be treated successfully with post-exposure prophylaxis, or PEP, a fast-acting immune globulin shot that is followed up with a series of four more shots over a two-week period. Because early action is so important, the treatment is administered to anyone who might have been exposed to rabies, with some 30,000 to 60,000 people treated annually as a precaution. As a result, rabies-related human deaths are now extremely rare in the United States. Prior to 1960, the annual mortality rate from rabies was around 100 human deaths per year; in the sixty years since, a total of just 125 fatal human rabies cases have been documented by the CDC. Vaccinations for domestic animals also helped to greatly reduce the number of human rabies cases, and in the United States the majority of rabies cases are tied to wild animals. However, rabies, which is also known as "mad dog disease," still kills around 59,000 people worldwide every year, mostly in less developed countries where treatment is not easily accessible and the risk of being bitten by a rabid dog is much higher.

WHEN WILD ANIMALS BITE

In addition to bats, a whole host of wild mammals have been known to transmit rabies to humans. These include groundhogs, raccoons, skunks, foxes, coyotes—and even wolves, as in the case of James Nall, a member of Daniel Boone's scouting party who was bitten on the forehead by a rabid wolf that attacked him in his sleep in 1775. Nall's wound healed, but later that fall, while hunting for deer at night along the Clinch River, he was stricken by such a bad case of hydrophobia that his hunting partner had to jump out of the canoe to escape the berserk man. Nall was brought home and tied up to prevent him from hurting his friends. He died soon after.

Since most of us are more able to judge potentially strange behavior from four-legged mammals than we are from bats, we can at least know what to avoid. If you see mammals that are aggressive and drooling excessively, steer clear: these are telltale signs of rabies. Many wild animals will also lose their natural fear of humans, and those that are usually nocturnal may be seen wandering during the day.

If a wild animal does bite someone in your party, the ideal scenario is to trap or kill the animal so that a biopsy can determine whether it has rabies or not. (A friend of ours once watched his father get bitten by a raccoon; the group retrieved a .22 rifle and shot the coon down from a tree in order to submit its head for testing.) Unvaccinated domestic animals who bite someone are required to be quarantined and monitored for rabies symptoms for ten days. For safety's sake, if the animal cannot be captured or quarantined, the bite victim must undergo treatment. It is absolutely vital that you see your doctor if there is any possibility that you have been exposed to the rabies virus. Remember, once the infection has taken hold, the disease is almost always fatal.

SKUNK BOMBS AND PORCUPINE QUILLS

At some time or another, human beings have been bitten by just about everything that walks, from muskrats to wolverines. But these rare and typically avoidable occurrences don't really warrant further discussion beyond a reminder to disinfect wounds and apply bandages. When it comes to the generally innocuous fraternity of small and midsized mammals, however, there are a couple things to be wary of besides being bitten.

Though it's neither dangerous nor life-threatening, getting sprayed by a skunk is nasty business. If you don't take steps to counter it, the skunk smell can linger for weeks before it completely dissipates. If you're trying to remove the odor, forget about the old folk remedy of tomato juice, which does nothing but mask the scent. Instead, add a half cup of baking soda and a teaspoon of dish detergent to a quart-sized container of 3 percent hydrogen peroxide, soak a rag in the solution, and start scrubbing. It's not likely to completely remove the odor, but it will greatly speed things along. Trappers will sometimes use gasoline to clean away skunk essence from animal hides, but this isn't recommended for use on live creatures or on people.

Contrary to popular belief, porcupines cannot actually shoot their quills. They can, however, deliver dozens of quills into your skin with a quick flick of their tail if you get too close. There's only a single occasion on which we've personally seen someone get smacked by a live porcupine—it happened during an Alaska Dall sheep hunt, when the party in question accidentally walked under a porcupine perched in an alder tree. The porcupine placed a handful of quills into her skin right where her shoulder met her neck. Generally, we see porcupine-related injuries that occur while skinning porkies or through the secondhand delivery of quills that happened to be embedded in the skin of deer, mountain lions, or hunting dogs.

When trying to remove porcupine quills, ignore the conventional wisdom that cutting off the ends of porcupine quills will make them easier to remove. (It won't.) Do heed warnings that quills can work their way deeper and deeper into your skin the longer you leave them there. Porcupine quills are sharp and barbed, similar to fishing hooks. Even slight pressure will push them into the skin, and their barbs will prevent them from backing out. Quills can also migrate through flesh and emerge inches away from where they entered. To remove them, get a firm grip with a pair of pliers or your teeth, and pull them straight out with one sharp jerk. A deeply embedded quill might drag out a small hunk of flesh with it. Clean the wound, treat it with antibiotic ointment, and don't be surprised if it gets a little infected and begins to pus up in the coming days or weeks.

PORCUPINES AND HUNTING DOGS

The word "porcupine" doesn't strike fear into the hearts of most people. However, for those of us who wander the woods and prairies with our dogs, the quill pig is a very real threat—in part because of the curiosity factor. Dogs just can't help being nosey when they smell the distinct, musky odor (similar to very rank human body odor) of what the French call *porc-épic* or "thorn pig." And although porkies are nocturnal and primarily tree-dwelling, hunters who spend enough time outside will eventually encounter them.

Though porcupines cannot throw their quills, when under pressure the quills will be released into an attacker's skin or hide. Many dogs get a nose full from simply getting too close to the porkie, whose natural musk can be an attractant. When they're feeling defensive, porcupines will chatter their teeth, stomp their feet, and rattle their quills in an effort to intimidate their aggressors. If those moves don't cut it, they may swing around and strike with their tails. These types of porkie-canine encounters usually wind up with the dog getting a few dozen barbed quills in the muzzle.

In cases like these, you could leash up the dog and, using a multi-tool or pliers, carefully grab the quills as close to the dog's muzzle as possible and pull them straight out. Some dogs, however, will continue the battle and attempt to bite or kill the porkie even after getting a snoutful. At this point the situation can become dangerous. I've had one of my dogs return to me with hundreds of quills on his head, and almost as many in his mouth. The North American porcupine has approximately 30,000 quills on its body, so it can inflict plenty of damage.

In these cases, it's time to head to the nearest veterinary clinic for removal of quills under anesthesia. If you are unable to get to a clinic, and if the dog is calm enough and you have trained it for mouth examination, you can place a stick about 1 inch in diameter in the dog's mouth horizontally, all the way back to the last molars; then, using a shoelace or cord, secure each end of the stick to the collar. This keeps the dog's mouth open, much like the tool used during a dental procedure on a human. At this point, using the aforementioned multi-tool or pliers, the quills can be removed from the interior of the dog's mouth. It's a good idea to practice this method of restraint on your dog prior to hunting season. You may be able to salvage your hunting trip and save yourself a costly trip to a clinic.

In the contest of dog versus porkie, a fresh road-killed porcupine may be your best defense of all. For preparation during the off-season, many hunters employ avoidance training to teach their dogs to stay safe. Using an electronic training collar, carefully place the dead porcupine around different training areas. Each time the dog is drawn to the odor (as it inevitably will be), give an appropriate amount of stimulation for the dog to leave it alone. Refrain from using any verbal commands, so that the dog will come to believe that the stinky smell he so badly wants to investigate is itself causing the correction from his collar. In most cases, a dog will need only one or two lessons, and you might never have to worry about the "pincushion of the pines" again.

—By Ronny Boehme, lifelong bird hunter and sporting dog enthusiast, MeatEater contributor, and host of the podcast Hunting Dog

RABBIT FEVER

Something small-game hunters should be aware of if they're not already is the highly infectious disease tularemia, commonly known as "rabbit fever." Most often transmitted to humans by cottontail rabbits but present in snowshoe hares, jackrabbits, and squirrels as well, tularemia is caused by the bacterium *Francisella tularensis*, which can also hitch a ride with fleas and various tick species. Perhaps most unsettling is its capacity for airborne travel, leading to reported cases where victims contracted tularemia after hitting dead rabbits with lawnmowers. Because the bacteria that cause the disease are able to move through air via contaminated dust, the CDC believes tularemia has the potential to be used as an aerosolized bioterrorism weapon. Small-game hunters probably shouldn't spend much time worrying about that possibility, but the risks of handling infected animals should be on their radar.

In addition to flea and tick bites or inhalation, the disease can be contracted through exposure to bodily fluids while gutting and skinning an infected rabbit. The safest bet is to always wear latex or rubberized gloves while cleaning small game animals and to wash your hands with hot, soapy water after the field dressing job is done. Hunters can also identify rabbits that are infected with tularemia by carefully inspecting the animal's liver. Infections are betrayed by small white or yellow spots on a swollen liver that is often a dark bluish red color. Safely discard any rabbits that exhibit these symptoms. When preparing small game animals for a meal, always cook the meat thoroughly as a backup precaution to kill any harmful bacteria. As scary as tularemia might sound, it's important to note that we've been hunting, cleaning, and eating rabbits and squirrels our entire lives and have never gotten sick or come across one we suspected of having the disease. Still, tularemia can be fatal, so it's important to minimize your chances of exposure. Mass die-offs often occur in infected rabbit populations, so it's never a good idea to hunt an area if you're finding a lot of dead cottontails, or any small game animals for that matter.

Dozens of human tularemia cases are recorded annually throughout the United States, with the highest concentrations occurring in the south-central portion of the country. There are several forms of tularemia, including glandular, pneumonic, and typhoidal. Symptoms vary widely depending on the strain of the disease and how it entered a person's system. Signs of tularemia might show up as skin ulcers, eye inflammation, swollen lymph nodes, chest pain, coughing, and respiratory difficulties. Fortunately, antibiotics can be used to effectively treat tularemia, but it can be difficult to diagnose. If you suspect you've contracted tularemia, see a doctor immediately, especially if you've been handling small game animals or were bitten by a tick or fleas. Also keep in mind that dogs and cats can become infected with tularemia and transmit the disease to their owners.

HOOFED MAMMALS

Far and away, the most likely way a person is going to get injured or killed by a hoofed mammal is not by a stampede or by the gnashing of terrible teeth, but by the grinding of gears and the squeal of brakes—in other words, by hitting such an animal with a car. While the initial impact will be the most dangerous part of any collision, make sure to approach vehicle-struck wildlife with great caution. Quite often, "dead" animals are merely stunned. I experienced a harrowing situation with a roadkilled animal as a kid once when my dad ran over a deer in the middle of the night and nonchalantly tossed it into the back of the Jeep with me and my brothers. More meat for the freezer. No sooner did we get rolling down the road then the deer was standing up in the back of the truck, quite alive. You can imagine the ensuing chaos.

Besides dying or getting injured in collisions with heavy hoofed animals, every year dozens of people are gored, stomped, kicked, and run over by deer, elk, moose, bison, and even wild pigs. Usually these incidents aren't random attacks. Most often they're the direct result of humans not giving adequate space to mothers with young offspring or mature males during mating season. Within the city limits of Fairbanks, cow moose are known to guard their calves aggressively by charging any human who approaches too closely—the same tactic they'd use against bears or wolves. There's a widely circulated video of a moose killing an elderly man who'd gotten too close to the animal outside of a store in downtown Anchorage. In Yellowstone National Park, rutty buffalo bulls crazed and enraged by an overload of testosterone and competition for females won't tolerate the constant barrage of tourists snapping selfies nearby. Every summer, a handful of bison get annoyed enough to hook someone with their horns and toss them through the air. In fact, buffalo injure more visitors at Yellowstone National Park than any other creature, including grizzlies. And remember, we're talking about substantial animals here—elk can reach 700 pounds, moose top out over 1,200 pounds, and bison can weigh over a ton. Even an average-sized whitetail buck outweighs most people. Throw in sharp antlers, horns, and hooves and these animals are more than capable of turning a fragile human into a broken, bloody mess.

The National Park Service advises all visitors to remain at least 25 yards away from all animals and at least 100 yards away from bears. Keep in mind, these are critters that are often habituated to the constant presence of humans. In wild places where animals don't often see people, their comfort zone might become compromised at even longer distances. And when these animals feel threatened, they can cover a lot of ground in a hurry. Even a world-class Olympic sprinter isn't going to outrun an angry buffalo or moose for very long. The point is, there's no good reason to get so close to any animal that you might change its behavior enough to make it uncomfortable and aggressive. Wild animals are best observed and photographed from a distance, in their natural state.

Of course, there are times when keeping your distance might not be possible. Once several of us came around a sharp bend in a trail and found ourselves face-to-face with a cow and calf moose. The cow immediately bristled her hackles and laid her ears back behind her head in a protective, aggressive posture. We quickly dove off the trail into the woods and gave her a wide berth, and the pair continued down the trail as if nothing had happened. If you happen to find yourself in a similar situation, back away quickly and quietly in a nonthreatening manner. If possible, try to put barriers like trees or boulders between yourself and the animal. Learning to read the body language of animals can also keep you out of trouble. The males of horned and antlered animals will often sway their weaponry back and forth or lower their head toward a threat to show they mean business. Female ungulates may lay their ears back and raise their hackles as a warning sign that they're becoming agitated.

Despite some beliefs to the contrary, hiking with your dog won't necessarily dissuade big game animals from attacking. In fact, off-leash dogs can actually increase the likelihood of you getting charged by large animals that are accustomed to aggressively fending off advances from coyotes or wolves. Dog messes with moose; moose chases dog; dog runs to owner; owner gets stomped.

When it comes to our relationship with animals like deer and elk, hunters obviously fall into a different category than hikers or campers. After all, the whole point of hunting big game is so that we can eventually get our hands on one and turn it into food. But any hunter who grabs hold of a large felled animal before determining that it has actually expired could be making a very serious mistake. We've received emails from several hunters who relayed the experience of walking up to a deer they assumed to be dead, only to discover that the animal was very much alive when it jumped to its feet. This will certainly scare the hell out of you, but it can also be extremely dangerous. One hunter sent us a disturbing and bloody picture of himself after he had been severely gored in the head by a whitetail buck he believed was dead. Another hunter we know was run over by an injured buck; to make matters worse, in the mayhem the hunter was gashed by the broadhead of his own arrow. You can avoid a similar outcome by observing downed big game for a minute or so before approaching. When you do approach, come from an uphill direction and move toward the animal's rump rather than its head. Watch for breathing or blinking eyes. Stay away from the hooves, head, and antlers until you're sure the animal is dead. To confirm that it's safe for you to get closer, lightly poke the animal in the eye with a stick, arrow, or rifle barrel to make sure there's no flinch. If there's any indication the animal is still alive, you'll need to do what's necessary to keep yourself safe and end any suffering the animal might be experiencing. You can shoot it behind the ear or at the base of the head, or cut its throat.

LARGE PREDATORY MAMMALS

Dating back to the time when we sheltered in caves at night, human beings and our ancestors have shared the landscape with large mammalian predators capable of tearing us to shreds. Today in North America, this suite of animals includes black bears, grizzly bears, wolves, and mountain lions, also known as cougars or pumas.

Despite the risks posed by these predators, the presence of large carnivores on the landscape is indicative of a relatively intact ecosystem. We cherish the privilege to walk among creatures that are far more powerful than we are, and by and large, current state and federal regulations do a good job of ensuring they'll continue thriving where human tolerance and appropriate habitat exist. This level of tolerance wasn't always the norm. In the United States, beginning in the mid-1800s, we devoted the better part of a century to extirpating large predators from much of their historic range in the Lower 48 through poisoning campaigns, bounty systems, and unregulated hunting and trapping. Thankfully, we stopped this madness before it was too late. Wildlife managers implemented regulatory structures to save and, where possible, recover predators. Today, we have thriving populations of all species on suitable habitats, with stable or expanding numbers of mountain lions in roughly twenty-three states and Canadian provinces, black bears in fifty-two states and provinces, grizzlies in ten, and wolves in nineteen. Millions of us live within easy driving distance of large predators, and millions more travel to such locales every year. Whether you live near them or travel near them, you should know what to do when you encounter large predators.

Black bears. The most common large predatory mammal in North America, black bears number over 400,000 in the Lower 48. Some of the corn belt states lack stable populations of the species, but the bears can be found pretty much everywhere else; they're also widely distributed throughout Alaska, Canada, and northern Mexico. Black bears are currently increasing in number, with their range expanding as well. Some of the highest densities in the country are found in New Jersey—a state with one of the highest human population densities in the United States. They also grow very big there, with some of the animals topping out over 600 pounds. Typically, though, most adult black bears weigh somewhere between 150 and 300 pounds. One thing to note is that not all black bears are black. "Color phase" black bears could be blond, cinnamon (reddish brown), or chocolate (dark brown). There are even white black bears in British Columbia and blue or "glacier" black bears in southeast Alaska.

Despite the great abundance of black bears, they can safely be regarded as a nonthreat. Only a small handful of people get injured by black bears every year, and typically, when black bears do attack humans, they are operating on a predatory impulse. While grizzly bears will attack humans in order to neutralize a perceived threat, black bears are generally looking for a meal. You'll often hear that it's wise to "play dead" during a bear attack, but that's a losing strategy when it comes to black bears. If a black bear follows you or approaches you in an aggressive manner, stand tall and make a lot of noise. Do not run, as that will only increase the likelihood that the bear regards you as prey. Wave your arms and present yourself in a menacing fashion. If you're with someone, stand close together in order to amplify your stature. If you're attacked, fight your ass off. Punch the bear's nose, gouge its eyes, stick a knife into its ribs—do anything you can think of to help the bear realize that you're not an easy meal. If you successfully repel a black bear attack, move away from the area while standing tall and making a lot of noise. Do not let your guard down until you've reached safety.

Brown bears (grizzly bears). Before we get into their traits, we'd like to clear up some taxonomic confusion surrounding brown bears. The species, *Ursus arctos*, is found across much of northern Eurasia and North America. In Canada and the United States, the bears are more commonly known as grizzly bears. In Alaskan vernacular, it depends on where you're sitting. The bears that live near the coasts and have a strong reliance on salmon are known as brown bears; in the interior of the state, the same species is recognized as grizzlies. To make matters more confusing, there are indeed some morphological differences between them. Brown bears tend to be more uniform in color than grizzlies, which have a wider array of colorations—including the classic "grizzled" color that gives the bears their name. Brown bears are also bigger, with some going well over 1,000 pounds while most grizzlies max out at half that weight. But these bears all belong to the same species. Taxonomically, a brown bear on Alaska's Kodiak Island is the same thing as a grizzly bear in Yellowstone National Park, and we tend to use the second term to refer to species as a whole.

In the Lower 48, there are about 1,800 grizzlies. Aside from a small handful that flirt with Washington's northern border, these bears are relegated to western Montana, northwestern Wyoming, the Idaho panhandle, and along Idaho's border with Yellowstone National Park. While there are plenty of rumors of grizzlies in Colorado, at present the rumors have not been confirmed. The bears are far more abundant in the north, where some 55,000 of the animals are distributed throughout Alaska and across the western third of Canada.

Grizzlies are far more dangerous than black bears. To get an understanding of their destructive potential, consider that those 1,800 grizzlies living in three states with exceedingly low human population densities manage to maul or kill several people a year. Now compare *that* ratio to the hundreds of thousands of black bears living among tens of millions of people and, most years, killing not a single one.

What makes grizzlies so dangerous is their unpredictability. Like black bears, they will attack humans out of a predatory impulse to kill and eat. But unlike black bears, they will also attack humans to defend themselves, their cubs, and their food resources. If you're heading down a trail and you surprise a black bear that's feeding on berries, the black bear will almost always respond by putting distance between you and itself. Surprise a grizzly and it might respond by swatting you to the ground and biting the back of your skull. In cases like these, most victims survive being mauled by curling into a ball and playing dead; grizzlies often lose interest if a person is no longer perceived as a threat.

Of course, your chances of a dangerous encounter with a grizz are greatly diminished if you always take commonsense safety measures. Before arriving at the trailhead, check in with the nearest fish and game office. Wildlife managers keep track of problem bears and human/bear conflicts. If necessary, they will prohibit access to certain areas where human safety is a legitimate concern. Once you're in grizzly country, the key to staying safe is to maintain constant vigilance. The importance of a heightened sense of spatial awareness can't be overemphasized anytime you're in the outdoors, but when you're sharing the landscape with grizzlies you can't ever let your guard down. For instance, you'll need to focus on more than just the narrow band of trail ahead of you or the incredible views off in the distance. Make a habit of doing things like watching for fresh tracks and scat, checking your backtrail, and keeping an eye on dark, brushy areas. You're much less likely to surprise a bear if you notice them before they notice you.

Keep in mind, we're not suggesting you become so "bearanoid" that it becomes impossible to enjoy a trip into the backcountry. We've spent

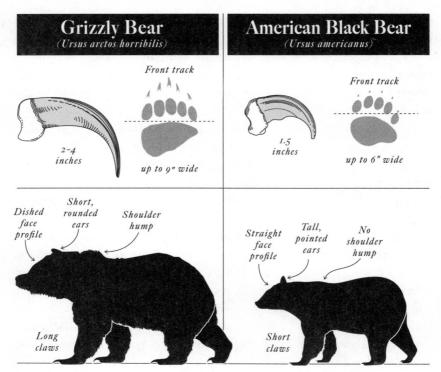

Grizzly Bear *(Ursus arctos horribilis)*	American Black Bear *(Ursus americanus)*

Front track

Front track

2–4 inches

up to 9" wide

1.5 inches

up to 6" wide

Dished face profile — Short, rounded ears — Shoulder hump

Long claws

Straight face profile — Tall, pointed ears — No shoulder hump

Short claws

hundreds of days and nights in grizzly country, and along the way we've had more than a few run-ins with Ol' Grizz. Usually, though, we don't even see any of them. But we know they're out there, accept their presence, and act accordingly.

SAFETY PROTOCOLS FOR CAMPING AND HIKING IN GRIZZLY COUNTRY

Thousands of people hike, fish, camp, and hunt in grizzly country every year without even seeing a bear, let alone having a dangerous encounter with one. Although it's impossible to completely eliminate the chance of an attack, here are some widely accepted practices that will help to keep you safe:

- Heed trailhead signs warning of bear activity in the area.
- Always stay alert.
- Hike in groups.
- Talk loudly.

- Avoid thick brush and low-visibility areas.
- Stay on established trails.
- Camp in open areas with good visibility.
- Keep a clean camp.
- Do all cooking and dishwashing 100 yards from camp.
- Hang all food and garbage high in a tree at least 100 yards from camp.
- Always carry bear spray and know how to use it.
- Consider using portable electric fencing around your camp.
- If you encounter a grizzly from a distance, give it plenty of space and do your best to scare the bear off—group together, shout loudly, wave your arms.
- If you encounter a grizzly at close range, group together, talk calmly, and back away slowly. Leave the area immediately.

BULLSHIT ALERT:

MENSTRUATION AND BEAR ATTACKS

The claim that menstruating women are more likely to get attacked by predators first gained popularity in 1967. In separate incidents on the same night, two 19-year-old women were killed by grizzlies while camping in Glacier National Park. One woman was menstruating and the other had tampons in her backpack (investigators said she was expecting her period soon). Although officials concluded that unprotected food and trash were to blame, the general public speculated that grizzlies were targeting menstruating females.

Soon thereafter, the National Park Service and other agencies began warning women that bears might be attracted to menstrual blood. One ranger district in the Shoshone National Forest went so far as banning employees from the backcountry while they were on their cycle. Was the concern warranted, or the result of a combination of bear mythology and menstrual taboo?

In a 1983 study, four captive polar bears were presented with a series of different odors, including used tampons, non-menstrual blood, food scents, and seal scents. Scientists reported that the bears had a "strong behavioral response" to used tampons and seal scents, but not much else. The team collected similar data on wild polar bears, reporting that the bears easily detected used tampons but ignored non-menstrual human blood and unused tampons. A 1991 study on forty-six wild black bears found different results. Twenty-six bears were presented with used tampons from twenty-six women, and twenty bears were exposed to four menstruating women on different days of their flow. None of the bears, regardless of age or sex, showed interest in the tampons or women.

The majority of the data strongly suggests that no one should be deterred from being in the outdoors while on their period. Proper handling of used menstrual products, however, is key. Dispose of them in a zip-lock bag, stash it in your bear bag (see page 82) overnight, and pack everything out. If using menstrual cups, bury blood 200 feet away from your camp.

HUNTING IN GRIZZLY COUNTRY

Hunting where grizzlies live requires even more caution than hiking. Unlike a hiker, the goal of a hunter is to be silent and stealthy and to avoid spreading his scent toward animals. So walking around in plain sight with the wind at your back and yelling "Hey, bear!" every minute or two isn't really an option. Yet all of this quiet sneaking around naturally puts hunters at much greater risk in grizzly country. Historically, hunters account for the lion's share of grizzly attack victims. Factor in the reality that hunters are often dealing with freshly killed deer and elk at a time of year when grizzlies are most actively searching for food, and the risks become even more obvious.

During the fall months, a grizzly's only concern is to consume as many calories as possible, as fast as it can. During this period of hyperphagia, bears are cruising around all day and night. For this reason, it is not the best idea to do a solo backcountry hunt in grizzly country during the fall, or at any time. Hunting with partners is always much safer, especially in the evenings, as attacks on groups are less likely than on individuals. The MeatEater film crew has safely scared off several grizzlies that wandered into our camp over the years. We wouldn't like to think about what might have happened had we faced these predators alone.

It's no secret that the last hour of daylight is often the most productive time to hunt big game. Regardless, there is a case to be made for heading back to camp before sunset in grizzly country. Tracking an animal shot at last light is difficult enough without having to worry about bears. If there are grizzlies in the area, butchering and packing an animal at night adds an unavoidable element of danger. One option is to build a big fire as a deterrent and suffer through a sleepless night next to your kill. We've done it, and it's a miserable experience. It's also a risky move, since bears tend to be more active at night and detecting their presence isn't possible until they are too close for comfort. The safest bet is to gut your animal, drag the gut pile as far away as possible from the carcass (or vice versa), camp a safe distance away, and return in the morning. The same goes for a wounded animal you didn't manage to recover before dark. Finish the tracking job the following morning unless rain or snow threatens to wipe out the blood trail. In either case, approach the area the next day from an upwind direction with extreme caution and make plenty of noise on your way in.

If you kill an elk or deer, operate under the assumption that a bear is going to take notice once the butchering begins. The bear might not show up right away, but it will find the carcass sooner or later. Bears can pick up the scent of blood and meat from miles away, and many conflicts occur at or near kill sites. This doesn't mean you should operate in a constant state of panic. Just be cognizant of your surroundings and do what's necessary to keep yourself out of harm's way. If you are butchering an animal alone, your head needs to be on a swivel throughout the entire process. Hopefully you're with a partner, so that one of you can be on constant watch for bears while the other works on field butchering (see page 145). Make noise and work carefully and efficiently—but don't rush. If you work too fast and make a mistake, you could cut yourself so badly that a bear attack will be the least of your concerns.

After the butchering is done, get all the meat well away from the carcass. Bears tend to hit rank gut piles first, before going after meat. Whatever meat you are unable to pack out right away should be hung in a tree far from the carcass, as shown. Grizzlies aren't great tree climbers, but if there's meat within reach they'll find a way to get it. If possible, hang your meat stash in an open area you can see clearly from a long distance. Take plenty of time to watch the area around your meat tree before heading in to pick up another load. Ideally, it'll be a spot where the prevailing winds carry your scent toward the spot where the meat is hanging. As you approach, yell loudly every few seconds. Get in and get out quickly every time you come back for a load of meat; don't linger in the area. Under no circumstances should you challenge a bear that claims your kill or meat stash. If it's necessary to store meat at camp for a night or two, use the same precautions. Hang it in a spot that's visible from camp, but at least 100 yards away (the farther the better). If no appropriate hanging trees are available, such as you might find to be the case on the Alaska tundra, use rock outcroppings or any other elevated spot. Cover the meat with small branches, clothing, or a tarp.

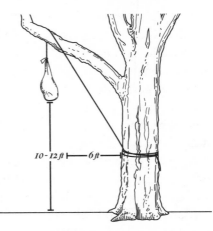

10-12 ft ⊢ 6 ft

Hang food and meat from a sturdy branch at least 10 feet off the ground and 6 feet from the tree's trunk to elude bears.

THE BEAR SPRAY OR SIDEARM DEBATE

When it comes to bear spray versus handguns for personal protection, most people fall firmly into one camp or the other. You'll hear some people claim that carrying a pistol is a dangerous waste of time, while others believe bear spray to be a laughably inadequate line of defense. The truth is, both have their place. Among our hunting crew, we carry sidearms during archery season elk hunts in southwestern Montana. Later in the fall, during rifle season in the same area, we don't usually double down by bringing a sidearm. But on any trip through grizzly country, we keep bear spray holstered on our hips at all times.

The statistics don't lie: bear spray, also known as pepper spray, is an effective deterrent against aggressive grizzlies. When grizzly attacks happen, however, they happen fast. The spray won't do you any good if it's stored in your pack, or if you have no idea how to use it.

Anyone carrying bear spray needs to be trained up on carrying and deploying it safely and quickly. We spoke with a grizzly bear researcher who was severely mauled by a grizzly but managed to spray the bear in the face while it had her pinned to the ground. The grizzly immediately gave up the attack, and the researcher credits bear spray for saving her life. On the other side of the spectrum, a bush pilot related a story to us about a client he dropped off on a remote beach. As the pilot was taking off, he watched the man spray himself down with bear spray just like he was using mosquito repellent. The pilot had to turn around to rescue the man, who had fallen to the ground writhing in agony.

As effective as bear spray is against bears, it can also be harmful to humans. Because the cans can rupture if they overheat or be accidentally triggered when stepped on or jostled, they need to be kept in sealable containers during air travel and car rides. Not only does the spray destroy pretty much everything it comes in contact with, it could blind a driver or pilot and lead to a crash. A classic steel army surplus ammo can is a great option for safely transporting bear spray.

Another drawback is that bear spray requires ideal wind conditions—a tailwind or no wind at all. A strong headwind can blow the spray back into your face, and a stiff crossing breeze may send it off course. We know many Alaskans who don't trust bear spray to save their lives during an attack. These are people who deal with grizzlies on a regular basis, and they wouldn't even consider going into the woods without some serious firepower strapped to their hip or chest. The noise of a gunshot can often be enough to scare off a curious bear, and if a real attack occurs, a sidearm might save your life. In the event that things get ugly, sidearms give you a fighting chance—but only if you can draw, aim, and shoot quickly and accurately. Bear attacks can happen when other people are around, so using a gun safely in that situation requires a cool head and plenty of practice.

In untrained hands, both sidearms and bear spray can become more of a safety hazard than an angry bear. If you can't hit the broad side of a barn with your pistol or you don't know how to operate a canister of bear spray, you may as well leave them behind.

Wolves. Wolves certainly have their detractors. Many big-game hunters dislike them because they can have adverse impacts on populations of big game. Ranchers often have problems with them because they can be hell on sheep. Both perspectives are valid. What doesn't pass muster, however, is the idea that wolves present any kind of legitimate safety concerns to humans. Currently, there are 2,655 wolves in Minnesota, yet the state has never had a confirmed human fatality due to a wolf. Same with

Wisconsin, which has roughly 940 wolves. Even in Alaska, where there are an estimated 7,000–11,000 wolves, only one person has been killed by wolves in the last ten years. The only true risks posed by wolves are bites from animals infected with rabies (see page 202) or attacks by wolves that have been seriously weakened from starvation due to disease, injuries, or dental issues that prevent them from hunting effectively. Such animals can be driven to desperate measures to obtain food, and they have been known to make attempts at killing humans. Obviously, avoid any up-close interaction with a wolf that seems sickly or unafraid of humans.

Mountain lions. Also known as cougars or pumas, mountain lions warrant a small amount of concern. Keep in mind, though, that North America has seen fewer than thirty confirmed human fatalities related to mountain lions in the past century. The number of individuals who have been injured by mountain lions is higher, but even that figure averages out to only around one person per year.

While a mountain lion weighing just 130 pounds can take down a 600-pound bull elk, they tend to focus on smaller prey, and the vast majority of human fatalities from mountain lion attacks are women and children. Attack victims are often alone, and often playing or jogging.

Like black bears, mountain lions attack out of a predatory impulse. Their intention is to kill and eat you. If a mountain lion approaches you, talk loudly, wave your arms, and try to look as big and bad as you can. If a lion pounces on you, fight with everything you've got. Punch its muzzle, jam your thumbs into its eyes, let its teeth lock down on your forearm rather than your throat. If you're accompanied by someone who is attacked by a mountain lion, do not run away. Their life is in your hands.

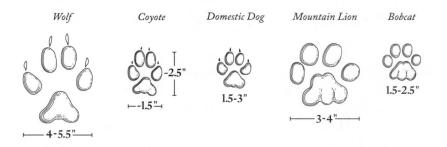

Track identification for coyotes, mountain lions, bobcats, and wolves

Go at the lion with everything you've got and convince it that this won't be an easy meal. Lions kill their prey quickly and do not engage in knock-down drag-out fights. A strong, spirited resistance is your best bet at deterring them. Playing dead is a horrible idea.

THE LATVIAN EAGLE WEIGHS IN ON BEAR DEFENSE ARTILLERY

In certain circles, you'll hear a lot of debate on the subject of the best firearm for bear defense. Since we're talking about close-range encounters, there are really only three choices: semiautomatic pistols, Magnum revolvers, and pump action shotguns. Here's my thinking on how to make the decision.

If I'm traveling through grizzly country but not planning on hunting, I prefer to carry a short-barreled pump-action 12-gauge shotgun loaded with heavy slugs. A shotgun is easier to aim than a pistol, and a 12-gauge shotgun slug can deliver way more lethal energy than the biggest, baddest handgun load. The trade-off is that it won't be as useful during a close-quarters surprise attack. A shotgun also has a lot more weight and bulk than a handgun, so it's not realistic to carry one around all the time, especially on solo trips when I'm planning on hunting with a bow.

In these kinds of situations, some hunters prefer a lightweight, compact semiautomatic pistol, because it can hold a lot of cartridges and delivers a fast shot. It'll definitely allow you to spray a lot of lead around, but most popular pistol cartridges lack grizzly-killing power. Semiautomatic pistols also have a nasty habit of jamming when you need them most. Neither of those factors is acceptable during a bear attack—which is why I carry a revolver during this kind of scenario.

Revolvers are reliable—they don't jam. They're also powerful. On trips into grizzly and brown bear country, I pack a Smith and Wesson Model 329PD AirLite revolver in .44 Magnum loaded with the heaviest solid bullets I can find, usually around 300 grains. My thinking here is to have something with lots of penetration; during a full-on bear attack, you'd need plenty of firepower and a bullet tough enough to bust through heavy hide, muscle, and bone.

More important than the type of firearm is where you carry it. Belt holsters and underarm holsters can be harder to get a gun out of while you're getting mauled by a bear. I use a chest holster made by Razco that sits under my FHF binocular harness. If I was balled up in a fetal position during an attack, my revolver would be within inches of my hands.

No matter what the scenario, I always carry pepper spray—even when I'm packing a gun.

Ironically, during my closest unplanned encounter with a bear, I didn't use either. It took place back in October 2017, when a bunch of us were hunting Roosevelt elk on Afognak Island in Alaska's Kodiak Archipelago while filming an episode of the *MeatEater* TV show. It's a beautiful and remote environment teeming with fish and wildlife. The animals are oversized in that part of the world, and the heavy rainfall feeds an abundance of thick, equally oversized flora. The massive coastal brown bears are so prevalent that hunting permits come with an explicit warning: the animal carcass stands about a 100 percent chance of being claimed within twenty-four hours of the kill by a predator who's a lot bigger and badder than you are. We were fully aware of the risks.

Four or five days into our trip, we managed to kill an elk. We butchered the animal, quartered the carcass, hung half the meat in a tree, and packed the other half on our backs back to camp. After taking a rest day, we set out to fetch the rest of the meat. We were cautious, knowing that there was a high likelihood the hanging meat could have attracted a bear. After spending some time glassing the area from a distance of 300 yards to see if we could spot any suspicious movement, we made lots of noise as we approached the tree. Our bear spray canisters were out, and we had our eyes peeled for scat or tracks on the ground—and once we got closer, we looked for claw marks on the bark of our meat-hanging tree. Up until that point we'd done everything right, but not finding any cause for worry, we let our guard down. We *should* have immediately retrieved the meat out of the tree, thrown it in our packs, and gotten the hell out of there, watching for trouble behind us. Instead, we foolishly decided to plop down in a rough circle at the foot of the tree to have lunch. We even started heating up some water for tea.

A couple of bites into our sandwiches, a member of our crew heard something in the thick alders just up the hill. The rest of us pricked up our ears, but a few seconds later a bear came running full bore straight down the hill at our little group from a distance of less than 20 yards. From this point forward, everything happened very quickly, but with the slow-motion quality and tunnel vision brought on by an emergency. The bear was a giant ball of fur with a face at the center, big yellow teeth, shiny black nose, and eyes that looked impossibly small for an animal of that size—probably 600 pounds at a minimum, but maybe 1,000. Time slowed down enough that I could see minute details about the way the bear was moving, its hide rippling over the muscles driving it forward.

My bear spray was clipped onto my belt. Earlier I had taken my pistol out of the holster and set it next to me on the ground. Both items were thoughtfully placed within inches of my hand. But when the time came, my brain did not settle on the gun or the bear spray. Instead of using the defenses that I had prepped for this exact occurrence, my reflexes snapped back to a more primal instinct. I'm pretty sure that if I'd just gone for the bear spray, I would have had time to pull it out of the holster, undo the safety latch, and spray. Instead, I got to my feet, picked up my Black Diamond carbon-fiber trekking poles, squared off as if I were preparing to hit a fly ball, and, as the bear suddenly barreled into us, swung at its head with all the force I could muster. The blow was enough to spook the bear off its course. It left as quickly as it had come. This all happened so fast that some of the guys, Steve included, didn't even have time to get up off the ground. Some got up but tripped and fell as they tried to jump out of the way. Our videographer, Garrett, somehow fell onto the bear's back for a second and disappeared as the bear made its exit. By the time I followed them over the roll of the hill with my pistol in one hand and my bear spray in the other, thinking that was probably the last I'd see of my friend alive, he was on his way back, completely unharmed.

The possibility of leaving the meat behind was not even discussed. Steve climbed into the tree and lowered the meat to the ground as the rest of us closed rank in an outward-facing circle, ready to fire on the bear if it came back. It never did, and we started hiking for camp, mostly in shock, but with enough presence of mind to realize that, even armed with bear spray and sidearms, our carelessness could have cost any one of us our lives.

—By Janis Putelis, director and executive producer of the MeatEater TV series and co-host of the MeatEater podcast

CHAPTER 5

⇶≫≫⟩⟨⟨⟨⟨⟵

Shelter and Warmth

ONE OF THE MORE harrowing nights I ever experienced was on a mountaintop just above tree line on Alaska's Prince of Wales Island. I was with a film crew of about eight people that included a handful of completely inexperienced campers. We had hiked only about 3 miles and 2,000 vertical feet from the coastline, but we'd done so through a deluge of rain. Over the course of that deluge, our route to the mountaintop had turned into a death trap. In places, you had to scramble up small cliff faces and nearly vertical slopes using handholds. There was only a thin layer of mossy soil over the rocks, and it was so saturated that it just peeled away and turned to slick muck when you touched it or stepped on it. It became clear that there was no way we could safely take the same route back down. Instead, we continued to climb.

As dusk hit, we were stuck on the mountaintop with no possibility of moving off in the dark. We were cliff hung. Every square inch of land was occupied by either a boulder or standing water. The temperature was plummeting, and the wind was gusting enough that you had to lean into it. I hadn't even begun to formulate a plan, and I was already feeling the laziness and lack of clarity that comes with the early stages of hypothermia. One of my companions who was particularly panicky asked about the possibility of calling for help, presumably from the Coast Guard. I looked at the cloud cover, which was touching the ground as a thick fog, and explained that we'd have better luck waiting on a unicorn than hoping for a helicopter to land. At that moment, it occurred to me that we were on the precipice of a survival situation.

There's no denying the extreme importance of food and water when you're in the wilderness. But the nice thing about hunger and thirst is that they don't sneak up on you. You see them coming from a long way off. Cold, on the other hand, has its way of hitting from out of nowhere. You fall through the ice. Your canoe flips. You get soaked in the rain. What's especially nasty about the cold is that it cripples your ability to address it. Hunger might drive you to do bigger and bolder things than you'd normally be willing to do, but cold makes a pathetic mess out of you. Your hands lock up and you can't work the spark wheel of a lighter or even the zippers on your clothes. Your decision-making abilities go to shit. You get into trouble, and it gets worse and worse by the minute.

What ultimately saved us that cold and rainy night on Prince of Wales Island wasn't some heroic act of woodsmanship. Instead, we were saved by technology and preparedness. We had packed for reality rather than some fantasy about "roughing it." We just had to pull ourselves together enough to erect a couple of freestanding tents between the boulders and use extra lengths of paracord to guy them out against the wind. Ground tarps and inflatable sleeping pads provided enough flooring to get us out of the water that seeped through the tent fabric from below. (No "water-proof" tent is waterproof when it's actually sitting in water.) Once we could cram inside the tents and get out of the driving rain, we were able to change into the dry clothing that we'd carefully packed in waterproof bags inside our backpacks. Since we had brought sleeping bags with synthetic insulation rather than down, we didn't have to worry so much about getting them wet. We were able to remove them from their stuff sacks amid all of our soaked gear and clothes long enough to crawl inside and get our core temperatures up. During a lull in the weather, we crawled back outside and prepared our camp for the night, including precautions against severe winds. Jetboils and freeze-dried food made dinner preparations quick and easy. In the morning, we had moved beyond the impending disaster and managed to pull off a comfortable day of work. The following night, we did the nearly impossible and kindled a ripping fire from wet wood in order to dry out all of our gear. Within a day of near disaster, we were back to perfect. (Getting everyone down from the mountain was terrifying, but that's another story.)

If it wasn't for all that gear, could someone have actually died that night? Hypothermia kills hundreds of Americans every year, typically twice as many as hyperthermia, or overheating. In the Lower 48, the leading states for hypothermia are Montana and New Mexico; rates in Alaska are over twice as high. And most of these deaths occur during moderately cold weather rather than extreme cold. So yes, someone could absolutely die in a situation like that. But we would have avoided such a disaster because our group included some seasoned backcountry travelers with the necessary ingenuity and know-how to manage the situation even in the absence of sophisticated gear.

This chapter will detail a winning approach for handling shelter and warmth in the wild—the same approach that we used on Prince of Wales. Before you go, plan and pack carefully to head off trouble. While you're out, manage your gear properly so that it's ready when you need it. Finally, develop the skills necessary to get by without it. You'll never be completely bulletproof, but that'll get you as close as possible.

WEATHER

The weather, both what's happening now and what's forecasted to happen later, will impact every decision you make outdoors, or at least it should. To those of us who had been traveling to Prince of Wales Island for years, the shitty weather we experienced wasn't exactly a surprise, and so we came prepared for the conditions. But even if you're headed to a place you've never been, you should understand the area's general environment, climate, and seasonal weather patterns. That information will allow you to make informed decisions about what type of shelter and other gear you'll need to stay warm, dry, and alive. The ultimate goal is to avoid survival mode and be able to enjoy yourself even while experiencing what most folks consider to be horrible weather conditions.

UNDERSTANDING METEOROLOGY

People often use the terms "weather" and "climate" interchangeably, but an area's climate is an overview of its long-term weather trends, while weather is a report on short-term atmospheric changes. You'd be foolish to go out into the woods or on the water without first understanding the long-term climate trends for the area. Obviously, you also need to know the weather forecast for the period you'll be outside. Whenever possible, you should make a habit of checking your phone or GPS unit for weather updates throughout your trip. If you're headed into the backcountry for a week, ten-day forecasts will give a good idea of what to expect. But be careful about putting too much faith into long-range forecasts. Everything beyond a day or two should be regarded as a rough prediction, not fact. Even short-term forecasts can change on an hourly basis. Something as simple as a slight shift in wind direction can have a huge impact on local weather conditions. When you're factoring the weather into your outdoor plans, it's best to account for a wide range of possible temperatures and conditions. Many survival situations come down to getting caught by surprise without the tools needed to survive inclement weather.

Weather forecasters rely on a vast array of sensors and satellites, radar, wind gauges, thermodynamic algorithms, powerful computers, and even data gathered from airline pilots to predict how the weather is expected to behave in a given region. Within the United States, all of this data is gathered and translated by the National Weather Service and the National Oceanographic and Atmospheric Administration; the information is then made available for use by news channels, websites, smartphone apps, and GPS devices. The field has advanced light-years in recent decades, but even the scientists behind it don't claim to predict anything with absolute certainty. Forecasters are pretty confident about what will happen in the next few hours, based on what's happening right now up-current of your particular location. Forecast certitude begins to crumble quickly after that. There's a reason weather forecasters use percentages when predicting the likelihood for precipitation. Anything above zero doesn't rule out the possibility of foul weather. If you see there's a 10 percent chance of snow, read that to mean that it actually might snow. The same goes with air temperatures that are forecasted to fall within a certain range; prepare for the extremes at either end of the spectrum. Take note of the average highs and lows and record highs and lows for the time of year you're visiting an area to understand how hot or cold it could possibly get. Use weather apps that show real-time radar and thermal maps.

While the National Weather Service operates some 700,000 weather stations around the country, it's important to remember that current and forecasted conditions for any given station are particular only to that exact geographic location. Many weather stations are in towns and airports. The forecast for the little village at the base of the mountains you're hiking into might be reflective of the general weather patterns for the region, but the conditions may be much different in the mountains above town. You can expect that at a minimum the temp will be at least 5°F lower for every thousand feet of elevation you gain, often more. That can mean the difference between a rain squall in the valley and a snowstorm on the mountain. If you really want to understand an area's weather patterns, spend some time observing radar imagery to see how storms tend to travel across particular landscape features. Low-pressure systems often follow relatively predictable paths from one particular direction. It's also completely worthwhile to ask local guides or park rangers in an area what you might be able to expect. Collect as much weather data and insight as you can leading up to a trip, especially in the final few days before your departure. But always keep in mind that the atmosphere exists in a near-constant state of chaos. When it comes to weather, hope for the best and plan for the worst.

READING WEATHER IN THE FIELD

Most of us know innately that black clouds showing up on the horizon spell trouble. That's one thing if you're looking for wild mushrooms at a local park, but it's an entirely different situation if you're way out on the open prairie where dirt roads become impassable after a rain. So it pays to know how different weather conditions may affect your activity in different environments. When you're in the field, keep a constant eye on the horizon. In much of the United States, storms tend to travel from west to east, but prevailing winds, the jet stream, and nearby high- or low-pressure zones can greatly alter that general pattern. Giant storm clouds welling up are clearly a bad sign, but even a slight haze can spell trouble. You can track the speed at which storm clouds are approaching by comparing against fixed foreground features or by noting the ground covered by their shadows. If the shaded areas are expanding rapidly in your direction, it's time to take cover. Other warning signs of inclement weather might not be as obvious. A subtle drop in temperature or a shift in wind direction can indicate bigger changes are headed your way.

In forests or other areas where you can't get a good view of the whole sky, you can often detect an advancing storm by watching the trees. Winds rise in advance of strong weather as low-pressure air floods into an area. You may not be able to detect the increased current on the ground, but high winds rocking the treetops may indicate that precipitation is imminent. Anecdotal and even some scientifically documented reports indicate that numerous animal species can detect major weather events in advance and will behave or relocate accordingly. If you see all the birds headed in one direction or a herd of elk coming into the open to feed much earlier in the day than they normally do, a storm may be coming. Don't read too far into animal behavior—they often do things for reasons we don't understand—but do take note of patterns. Paying attention to the clues offered up by your surroundings might mean the difference between setting up your tent in time to wait out a rainstorm and setting it up *during* a rainstorm.

BAROMETRIC PRESSURE

The atmosphere exerts varying amounts of pressure on the earth, and that pressure fluctuates in measurable ways relative to weather patterns. Generally speaking, clouds and storms generate low pressure, while sunny, clear skies are associated with high pressure. The current pressure as well as upward or downward trends can be tracked with barometers— devices that use water, mercury, aneroid cells, or even microsensors inside smartphones, watches, and GPS devices to measure air pressure. Standard atmospheric, or barometric, pressure is 29.92 inches of mercury or 1,013.25 millibars at sea level. It's possible to predict general weather trends by taking note of whether the atmospheric pressure is rising or falling, and how much it deviates from standard pressure measurements. Dropping pressure indicates that clouds and precipitation are coming; the lowest barometric readings ever recorded took place during hurricanes. Meanwhile, rising pressure suggests clear, sunny skies and stable conditions. Many hunters and anglers pay attention to how changes in barometric pressure affect the behaviors of fish and game. For instance, fish generally bite better as air pressure drops, while turkeys respond to a falling barometer by gobbling less frequently.

LIGHTNING

According to the National Weather Service, a cumulative average of forty-nine Americans die from lightning strikes every year, although over the last decade that number has shrunk to an average of twenty-five per year. NWS estimates that 9 or 10 percent of people who are struck by lightning die from the event, but most survivors still experience nerve damage and other health issues. Eighty percent of people killed by lightning in the United States are men.

Texas, Florida, and the South in general see a large portion of the United States' lightning strike deaths, but deadly strikes can happen anywhere. Two-thirds of the people killed by electrical storms in the last fifteen years were "enjoying outdoor leisure activities" at the time, according to NWS, with fishing topping the list with most deaths per activity. While many people assume it's the graphite rod in your hand that attracts the bolt, it has more to do with the fact that boats out on open water are vulnerable to conduction. We know a fisheries biologist who was struck by lightning after removing fish from a stream using a method called electroshocking. Basically, it comes down to electrocuting fish, with a variable charge that can either stun the fish or kill it. After putting his equipment away, he was walking away from the stream carrying a sack of fish that he intended to analyze. Lightning hit the ground next to him, then the bolt zapped up out of the ground and struck the fish and his hand. We joke that it was some sort of divine retribution.

Most government guidelines tell you to go indoors or get in a hard-top vehicle when a lightning storm shows up. That's all well and good, but our crew has often wound up in situations where that just wasn't possible. There's no perfect answer for what to do when shelter isn't available, but here are a few factors and tips to keep in mind.

Thunder is a shock wave produced by lightning's electrical discharge. You can gauge how far away an electrical storm is by counting the seconds between the lightning flash and the sound of the ensuing thunder. The old rule of thumb is that every five seconds equals 1 mile. Many guidelines suggest that you're in danger anytime you're counting thirty seconds or less between flash and boom, as the storm approaches and as it leaves. Keep in mind that lightning can travel several miles away from a cloud and it doesn't have to be overhead to hit you.

Lightning typically strikes tall and/or isolated objects. The physics of the phenomenon is wildly complex, but suffice it to say that you don't want to be out in the open near tall, isolated objects like trees. The electrical current from a strike will travel down such objects and often outward through the ground, air, water, and anything else that can conduct it. That means that while it might seem smart to shelter from the thunderstorm and rain under the branches of a tall tree, you're actually putting yourself in more danger; sheltering under trees accounts for a good number of the deaths and injuries caused by lightning.

Say you're traveling in the mountains when a thunderhead shows up. First, get out of the open and away from peaks and high, exposed rocks. The safest bet is to head downhill—a lower, more densely for-ested area is less of a draw for lightning strikes than isolated trees, peaks, or rocks. Down South or in the Midwest, where lightning strikes are more common, avoid hilltops and open fields during thunderstorms. Stay clear of telephone poles and particularly tall or isolated trees. In wide-open desert or prairie, seek out whatever lower ground you can find, even if it's just a shallow depression. Lacking that option, get out of the path of the storm as fast as you can. If you're wading or boating when lightning starts heading your way, you don't want to be the lone high point on an otherwise flat surface. Seek shelter on shore or make a run for it to get out of the storm's path.

A few people die almost every year when lightning strikes their tent. Don't set up your tent on open high points if there are better options nearby. If you're forced to put your tent in such a spot and a thunderstorm threatens to pass overhead, exit the tent and head downhill. Of course, this might not be a good idea at night or during heavy rains. All outdoors dangers are situational, so try to under-stand the factors at play to make the best possible decision. Your odds of getting struck by lightning are famously low, but they do in-crease when you're outside—and they're much, much higher if you make stupid decisions.

—By Sam Lungren, MeatEater *fishing editor, former commercial fisherman, and former editor at* Backcountry Journal

SHELTER

Having a place to get out of the elements during a survival situation could mean the difference between living and dying. That's true whether you're talking about an old-school canvas wall tent, an ultralight moun-taineering tent, or a lean-to made out of sticks and bark. The type of shelter you choose will depend a lot on your circumstances. On over-night hiking trips, people generally carry their shelter around in their backpack, but day hikers don't have any reason to be packing a tent around. Still, lots of day hikers get lost and spend unplanned nights in the woods. They're not the only ones. What if you're on a canoeing trip during rainy weather and fail to reach the backcountry cabin you re-served before sunset? You'd be forced to improvise a shelter. In a pinch, huddling up underneath an overturned canoe will keep you relatively dry during short rainstorms, but during an emergency it's hardly the best choice for a couple of people who need to get out of the weather for an entire night. Packing a simple tarp and some rope on a canoeing trip takes up very little space, yet it gives you the means to make a dry and spacious shelter when used in combination with your canoe and paddles. Every outdoorsman should understand how to improvise in this way, and have the ability to set up a warm, dry camp under a wide variety of conditions and circumstances. No matter how remote or intimidating the surroundings, closing out the day by sitting outside your shelter next to a blazing fire with a hot drink in your hands will bring on a sense of security, comfort, and well-being.

UNDERSTANDING THE LINGO: BASE CAMPS AND SPIKE CAMPS

Growing up, for many of us the term "base camp" evoked a cluster of dozens of colorful tents pitched on a flat snowfield at 18,000 feet in the shadow of Mount Everest. That type of base camp does exist, but it's one of the world's more extreme examples. Most of us would consider the trek to an Everest base camp an adventure in itself. It typically takes six days of hiking just to get there, with multiple rest days mixed in for elevation acclimation. You don't start the real climbing until you leave base camp behind and start using spike camps.

In reality, base camps come in many forms. A base camp could be a vehicle parked at a trailhead, a boat anchored in a secluded bay, a remote airstrip, a cabin at the end of a road, or even a buddy's house, as long as it's providing you the jumping-off point for your adventure. As an elk-hunting guide, our buddy Janis spent countless nights in a base camp consisting of six canvas wall tents sitting at 9,000 feet above sea level on the edge of the Flat Tops Wilderness in Colorado. That particular camp is only 2 miles from the nearest road. You can hike there in an hour, even at a casual pace. Although it's very different from the tent-city base camp used by Mount Everest's mountaineers, they both serve similar needs. A base camp is a stopping-off point prior to the major element of a journey, usually one that's going to take place on foot. It is the last place where comfort will be a consideration. The Everest base camp serves to set up climbers to bag the tallest peak in the world; that base camp in Colorado served to get hunters closer to the haunts that elk called home. In both cases, the camp provides a warm, comfortable shelter that is capable of weathering severe storms. A well-stocked base camp should also provide the means to refuel and replenish. Everest climbers need to acclimate to the altitude, as do hunters coming from sea level to hunt at 10,000 feet. Sleeping arrangements at base camps are usually cozy and comfortable considering their surrounding environment—they might even involve cots. The trade-off is that outfitting a base camp with resources requires a lot of time and effort. That elk-hunting base camp in Colorado had no water source, so the guides prepared for the season by filling a 1,000-gallon tank, hauling in 5-gallon water jugs on horseback, one trip after another. Several other trips were made to pack in the tents, cots, woodstoves, and food before hunters arrived in camp. Then the group would set up the tents and cots and cut a couple cords of wood. Listening to a bull elk bugling right outside camp, from a comfortable bed with a belly full of hot food, made all that work worthwhile. Within 200 yards of base camp, you'd be hunting that same elk first thing in the morning.

More adventurous hunters sometimes "spike out" up higher in the mountains. When you set off for a spike camp, everything you need, for however many days you plan to be out, will be on your back. Whether you're summiting a mountain or trying to kill a high-country buck, you don't know where you'll end up at dusk, so you need everything with you. It might seem like a significant energy expense to carry your tent, sleeping bag, stove, fuel, and food with you, especially when your truck or cabin is only a few miles away. But sleeping wherever the end of the day finds you has some major benefits, even if it's not nearly as comfortable as base camp would be. Hiking those extra miles back and forth to only have the same starting point every morning uses much more energy and time than waking up right where you want to be when the sun comes up. Walking 4 extra miles on a flat gravel road is a piece of cake, but the same distance in steep, rough country in the dark could take hours.

You'll avoid all those hassles by spiking out, but you'll sacrifice comforts. The less gear you bring, the faster you'll be able to travel, and clothing is the easiest place to shave a few pounds. There's no need for redundancy. That means one pair of undies or long johns and one pair of socks. Wearing the same clothes for three to four days is not going to kill you; it'll just make you a little stinky. Use your insulated puffy jacket as a pillow at night. Skip the camp shoes. Some folks will even forgo a stove and fuel, which means no hot meals or drinks. In warmer weather, a lightweight tarp can be substituted for a tent, shaving off as much as 4 pounds. In dry weather, you can go with no tent or tarp at all. Any suffering that occurs is made tolerable by the knowledge that you have a nice base camp within a day's walk. When you've had enough, you can head back there to restock food, put on fresh clothes, and get a good night's sleep before heading back out again.

TENTS

You can ride out some pretty horrible weather in a tent as long as you and your gear stay dry. We've spent days cooped up inside our tents in relative comfort while we waited for storms to pass or fog to lift. Compared to the old heavy canvas pup tents and cheap, leaky nylon tents of our youth, we have it good these days. In the last decade or so, tent manufacturers have been making progressively lighter offerings that are easy to set up and virtually weatherproof. As with other outdoor gear, spending more money gets you more features and less weight, but you can get a great tent at a very reasonable price. No matter how much you spend, you'll have to decide what size tent you'll need and what design features make the most sense for your particular style of camping.

Tent Sizing and Shape

Tents are sized according to the number of people that can lie down in them. Sounds simple enough, but different manufacturers use different specifications. Sizing is a matter of perspective, although generally speaking, most tents do fall a little short of their advertised size. Nemo makes fantastic and durable tents, but their two-person tents seem more like 1½-person tents. Same with many other manufacturers of high-quality mountaineering tents. A two-person tent does make for a roomy, comfortable one-person tent, and we often use ours that way. For a tent that you plan to mostly share with another person, you may need to bump up to a three-person size. Before you buy a new tent, it's a good idea to check out a few different models. Don't just consider how much sleeping space they have when they're set up. You also want to think about headroom.

Frankly, trying to get dressed inside a tent when you can't even sit up is a pain in the ass. Look for tents that have a vestibule area outside of the main sleeping area. Vestibules allow you to store your pack, food, cooking kit, and boots under a weatherproof cover without taking up a bunch of space inside the tent. Think of your vestibule as the camping version of an attached garage.

Tents also come in several shapes and configurations, from old-school ridgepole A-frames to domes, tunnels, pyramids, floorless teepees, and hybrid designs. All have their pros and cons. For example, pyramid tents are simple to set up and shed water well, but they don't have much headroom. Other designs are roomier, but can be heavy and take forever to set up. When in doubt, go with a dome tent—you'll gain a little extra headroom without stinting on performance in wet and windy conditions.

Single-Wall or Double-Wall Tents

One of the most important considerations when choosing a tent design is the difference between single-wall and double-wall tents.

The average human releases about a pint of moisture per night through breathing alone. That moisture, along with condensation from humidity, sweat, or soggy gear, could soak your sleeping bag and the inside of your tent, leaving you cold, wet, and miserable. The best way to fight condensation is with a double-wall design that uses a waterproof rain fly over a vented tent body. This design allows the warm, moist air from your body to rise through the inside canopy and condense on the fly. Many tents accomplish this with minimal venting, while others have an inside wall made almost entirely of nylon mesh screening that resembles mosquito netting canopies.

Single-wall tents have one wall of fabric, either breathable waterproof material or non-breathable material with a waterproof coating. They are typically lighter and faster to set up than double-wall tents, but they lack the ventilation that prevents condensation. Still, single-wall tents are preferred by many serious mountain climbers because condensation isn't generally a big problem in high alpine zones where it's cold and dry.

Three-Season Tents

The most versatile tents are double-wall three-season models. They'll get you through most of the weather conditions you're likely to encounter during spring, summer, and fall in northern latitudes or at high elevations. But a freak storm that lays down a foot of heavy wet snow could cause them to collapse. Most three-season tents use dome or hybrid designs that only require a few poles, which keeps the overall weight of the tent down and makes them a good choice for backpacking trips.

Four-Season Tents

Technically, you can use four-season tents all year long, but they're really built for camping in harsh winter conditions. They're favored on high-elevation mountaineering expeditions where winter conditions prevail even during the summer months. Four-season tents are usually designed with sturdy dome frames built to withstand strong winds and heavy snow loads. With extra poles and heavier, more durable material, four-season tents are typically a little larger in order to account for the extra gear necessitated by mountaineering trips.

Groundsheets

For most tents you'll want the waterproof vapor barrier of a groundsheet to place under your tent. Groundsheets also protect the bottom of your tent from pinholes and abrasions caused by thorns, rocks, and general wear and tear. Some tents come with groundsheets, but if not you can buy them separately or make one by cutting a tarp to size. Groundsheets should be sized with a footprint slightly smaller than the footprint of your tent. This prevents rain from falling directly onto the groundsheet or draining off the tent onto the groundsheet and then pooling under the tent floor.

Tarps

For those who are confident in their woodsmanship and want to travel fast and light, a simple tarp is all that is needed for a comfortable shelter. Tarp shelters won't keep out all bugs or precipitation, but when rigged the right way they make for a relatively protected place to sleep. You can use ridgepoles, stakes, and guy lines to turn your tarp into a shelter with a roof and floor, as on page 246. You can also use your tarp to make quick, simple sun and rain shelters for use during the day. Grommets make rigging your tarp

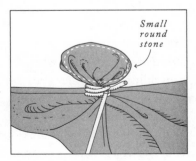

Small round stone

Tie down tarp corners with rocks.

much easier; if your tarp doesn't have any, pick up a grommet kit at the hardware store and do it yourself—it's easy. In the field, you can also rig a tarp by using a stone in place of a grommet. Place a round stone in the corner of your tarp and then fold it into the fabric like loading a pebble into a slingshot. Then wrap cord around the packaged stone and tie it tight.

You can find high-quality ultralight nylon tarps made by Nemo and Black Diamond that pack down to the size of a burrito and weigh less than a pound. An 8-by-8-foot sheet of silnylon also works well and is fairly light and cheap.

Bivy Sacks

These one-person mini shelters are basically waterproof bags that slide over your sleeping bag. Bivy sacks have no poles and don't require any assembly time, so they're light, pack easily, and you can pull them out and throw them on the ground wherever you find yourself at sunset. But overnight condensation inside the bivy sack will often leave your sleeping bag damp. For all their lightweight simplicity and convenience, we're not big fans of bivy sacks—backpacking tents will net you a bunch of advantages while adding only a little extra weight to your load.

Backpacking Tents

These tents are designed to be lightweight and pack small while still providing a weatherproof shelter. Quality models usually have just two or three poles, weigh in between 2 and 4 pounds, and pack into a stuff sack not much bigger than a loaf of bread. They're great tents for any kind of backcountry endeavor; we've used them on big-game hunts from Alaska to Mexico. The interior typically has a pretty small footprint, just big enough for one person to lie down, so we prefer models that incorporate a vestibule area as part of the rain fly.

Family Tents

Family tents are built for spaciousness and convenience rather than easy portability. They're great for car camping and give you plenty of room to stand up, or, as is often the case, for your kids to have pillow fights. Some have large vestibules where you can cook or set up a table for eating dinner. Tents this size have a big profile. If they're not staked down securely, they can collapse or get carried away by strong winds. Check out Nemo's Wagontop series for a good car-camping family tent.

Wall Tents

Many hunters, ourselves included, love hunting elk and mule deer out of a canvas wall tent. Wall tents are sturdy fabric shelters that are supported by either a metal frame or wood poles that are cut on-site. These classic outdoors abodes are often outfitted with chairs, cots, a cooking area, and plenty of space to dry your clothes while you sit by the woodstove shooting the shit with your buddies. Erecting a wall tent takes a significant amount of time, even with a few people working together. They are also heavy and only practical in places you can access in a vehicle or with a string of pack animals. But if you have enough food, water, and firewood, you can live for weeks or months in a wall tent while feeling perfectly at home.

Teepees

Teepee tents are modeled after the traditional bison-hide shelters associated with Native American tribes who lived on the Great Plains. Occasionally you'll see older canvas teepees set up for nostalgia's sake at a roadside attraction or in someone's backyard, but they're heavy, take time to set up, and are impractical for most recreational camping purposes. Modern teepee tents are built using the same lightweight composite poles and nylon materials used with quality three-season tents. They're compact and light enough to pack into the backcountry with a simple design that makes set up fast and easy. Sizes range from two- to eight-person versions. Some teepee tents don't come with a floor, which we haven't found to be a problem since their shape sheds water better than just about any other tent design, plus adding a ground cloth is always an option. Over the past several years, we've become big fans of floorless teepee tents, specifically the models made by Seek Outside that can accommodate a lightweight titanium woodstove. Even when it's set up on snowy ground, the stove is capable of drying the inside space. There are, however, a couple of downsides to teepee tents. They catch a lot of wind, so they're not ideal for extreme environments where wind gusts top 25 or 30 miles per hour. And they require a lot of stakes around the periphery, so rocky or frozen ground can be a serious hassle.

ANCHORING YOUR SHELTER

If you've ever seen a tent get yanked out of the ground and go tumbling down the mountain during heavy wind, you'll understand the importance of proper site selection and anchoring. Whenever possible, find a spot to pitch your tent where topographical features or clusters of trees or rocks provide a good windbreak. You also want ground that can hold a tent stake. Too rocky and you can't drive the stakes in; too soft and they won't hold. Pound stakes into the ground at every grommet around the tent's perimeter. Angle the stakes into the ground so they're tipping slightly away from the tent. In the absence of commercially produced tent stakes, you can get away with sharpened pegs of wood that are about ½ to 1 inch thick. Green wood is easy to sharpen, but a stout, inch-thick stub of dead tree limb will hold very well. If you're going to be leaving your shelter unattended for any amount of time, or camping in high country or other areas prone to unpredict-

able weather, take a little extra time to make sure your tent is fully supported. Where found, rocks are a great starting point. Place a heavy rock on top of each stake. On rocky or frozen ground, where stakes can't be driven in, you can tie several feet of guy line to the tent grommet and then tie the other end to a rock. In extreme cases, pile the entire length of the line with rocks.

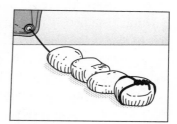

If you can't gain traction with a stake, you can use guy line and rocks to anchor your tent.

Anchor a tent in snow with a dead man's stake.

Some tents come with an extra lip of fabric around the periphery that can be pulled out along the ground and anchored with sand, rocks, or snow. When staking a tent in snow or soft ground such as sand, you can make what's known as a "dead man" by tying your tent off to a rock or heavy stick buried in the ground or snow.

Add guy lines for extra stability. We keep a supply of 3 mm cord on hand for this purpose. Run lengths of cord out from the fabric loops or D-rings on the outside walls of your tent and tie these off to surrounding stakes or brush or rocks. The rolling hitch (see page 10) is very useful for keeping these lines taut.

SLEEPING BAGS, SLEEPING PADS, AND SLEEPING WELL

We've all spent nights freezing our asses off because we didn't have the right sleeping equipment for the situation. It's miserable. Not only does it make the night drag on and on, it impedes your ability to function at your best in the daytime.

Sleeping Bags and Insulation

Sleeping bags always land near the top of our list of things that you should spend as much on as you can afford. The simple truth is good sleeping bags aren't cheap, and cheap sleeping bags aren't good. But money alone isn't enough to ensure you're going to sleep like a baby in the outdoors—you also have to match your bag to the conditions by weighing a few factors.

Insulation. You've got a couple different options for sleeping bag insulation. The first is natural down. From a weight-to-warmth perspective, goose down feathers are the best sleeping bag insulation material. Goose down creates a lot of loft, or air space, which retains heat. It's also light, easy to compress, and long-lasting. For backpackers, the weight of a sleeping bag and the amount of space it takes up in a pack is a big concern. However, goose down insulation has one serious drawback—when the feathers get wet, the filling loses its loft and insulation properties. Get a goose down sleeping bag soaked and it becomes heavy and worthless, making moisture management a constant priority. In rainy weather or humid climates, keep your down sleeping bag stored inside a dry bag whenever it's not being used; if it does get wet, you'll need to let it air out to dry, which can take a long time.

It's best not to use a down sleeping bag if there's a good chance it will get wet. Instead, opt for synthetic insulation, a much safer bet. Unlike down, synthetic insulation will retain heat when wet, meaning you might be uncomfortable but would still be able to stay warm in a wet sleeping bag. Synthetic insulation also breathes and dries out fairly quickly. You can get in the bag with damp clothes or socks on at night, and they'll be dry in the morning. For those reasons, a lot of folks choose a bag with synthetic fill for all-purpose use. It's certainly the smartest choice for damp climates and rough use. The downside of synthetic insulation is that it doesn't have the same warmth-to-weight ratio. You need more of it to get the same effect, so your bag will be heavier and won't compress down as small.

However, a third option for sleeping bag insulation has recently been developed. Hydrophobic down is goose down that's been treated with a chemical coating that prevents the down from absorbing water. Hydrophobic down has all the lightweight packability and insulating properties of down and comes close to synthetic insulation's performance when it gets wet, though synthetic is still a better choice in extremely wet environments. We've used bags with all three types of insulation and do feel that treated down is a decent compromise.

Temperature ratings. No matter the type of insulation, sleeping bags are categorized by their temperature rating. You may see EN (European Norm) ratings on sleeping bags, but ISO (International Organization for Standardization) ratings are more common. These systems assign a variety of ratings to sleeping bags based on the temperature at which the average person will remain comfortable and/or be able to survive inside the bag. Some sleeping bag manufacturers may only provide a comfort temperature or a survival temperature, but it's increasingly common to see both ratings listed separately. In some cases, additional temperature rating information is also provided for men and women, or warm and cold sleepers, since no one reacts to cold temperatures the same way. This all might seem a little confusing, but when in doubt, go for a warmer bag with a temperature rating lower than what you think you might need. We typically go for at least a 10°F buffer, meaning we'd bring along at least a 15°F bag if overnight lows were reaching 25°F. In extreme cold, this buffer should grow. Heading into 0°F weather, we'd probably grab a -20°F bag. Worst-case scenario is you'll have to open the bag up, which is way better than shivering through the night. Of course, few people have the luxury to buy an arsenal of sleeping bags. If we had to pick one bag for three-season use in temperate climates, it would be a bag with a 0°F survival limit rating. Ideally, though, you'd at least have two bags to get you through year-round use. If so, go with a 0°F or -10°F bag for colder weather and a 30°F bag for the summer months. Regardless of the bag's temperature rating, always take your bag out of its stuff sack and give it some time to fluff up before bedtime. And never, ever store your bag compressed in its stuff sack, which will damage the insulation and can be a recipe for mildew. Store the bag in a place where it can rest fully fluffed.

Size and shape. Mummy bags, shaped like a pharaoh's sarcophagus, are more efficient and warmer than rectangular bags because their design leaves less empty, unused space in the bag. Rectangular bags aren't a bad choice for car camping or sleeping in a cabin, but you'll want a mummy bag for backpacking or sleeping in cold weather. Mummy bags are designed to keep in heat with a tapered shape that is wider at the shoulder than the feet and by wrapping around your head with only a small opening for your face. Usually, the tighter the fit, the warmer the bag. However, don't get a bag so tight that it's going to make you feel restricted and uncomfortable. For sizing, most sleeping bags are offered in at least two sizes, regular and tall (or long), but some companies make bags with more specific size specifications.

Sleeping bag liners. You can add a liner to your sleeping bag for extra insulation, or to keep your bag from getting soiled and greasy from contact with oily skin and dirty clothes. (Oils and dirt hamper a sleeping bag's ability to loft and breathe, impacting its insulation properties.) Insulated and zip-up polyester fleece liners do a good job of keeping you warm but are almost as bulky as some sleeping bags. Silk liners are a better choice. They add some warmth, breathe well, and don't take up much space in your pack. Vapor barrier sleeping bag liners are designed to add extra warmth by preventing the evaporative cooling that occurs as moisture transfers from your body to your sleeping bag throughout the night. But we're highly skeptical of vapor barrier systems—unless it's really cold and dry, you'll wake up drenched in sweat. You're much better off just going with a warmer sleeping bag.

Sleeping Pads

Sleeping pads aren't just about comfort. They also play an important role in keeping you warm and dry by preventing precious body heat from seeping away into the cold ground beneath you. The right sleeping pads also create enough elevation to keep your bag off a wet tent floor.

It wasn't all that long ago that we were using thin closed-cell foam sleeping pads. A lot of folks still use them today. Some are just a human-sized piece of 1-inch foam—sometimes covered in a nylon shell—that you roll up for storage. They're bulky and impractical for backpacking. The lighter "egg crate" versions, such as the Z Lite models produced by Therm-a-Rest, are about a half-inch thick and are divided into several hinged sections to allow for easy folding and packing. Foam sleeping pads tend to offer minimal comfort, but they're durable and versatile. No need to worry about them popping or getting burned, so you can pull them out next to the campfire and relax. Unfortunately, they don't provide a high level of insulation despite taking up a lot of space in your backpack. (A lot of folks strap their foam pads to the outside of their packs; that's another area where their durability pays off.) They are also relatively inexpensive. We've taken to buying full-sized Z Lite pads just to cut them up into butt pads that you sit on while hunting turkeys or spending long periods of time behind a set of binoculars; they're especially nice to have when there's snow on the ground.

Higher-quality inflatable sleeping pads aren't cheap, but they're comfy as hell and get you away from the ground. Most are designed with a series of tube or baffle chambers that you inflate by blowing into a one-way valve. To deflate them, you open a release valve and push the air out. Most weigh less than a pound and compress down to the size of a jar of spaghetti sauce. Some companies like Big Agnes and Nemo have started making insulated inflatable sleeping pads that minimize heat loss. They also make sleeping bags with a full-length pocket on the bottom that holds your pad in place while you sleep. But beware of sleeping bags that reduce or remove insulation on the bottom based on the assumption that you're using an insulated sleeping pad and therefore don't need it. Pads pop, and people roll over in their sleep. You want a bag with full insulation. There are also self-inflating sleeping pads that use a combination of foam and air padding. When you open the valve, the foam expands and pulls in air. It's convenient, as blowing up pads can be tedious and you often get a head rush by the time you're done. Still, we prefer the kind you blow up yourself because they're lighter and more packable. Treat any inflatable pad gently. Valves fail. Pads get punctured by sticks, cactus needles, and even the soles of your boots. Most are sold with a small puncture repair kit containing a patch and some glue. This will take care of most problems outside of a leaky valve, so don't lose the kit.

TIPS AND TRICKS FOR STAYING WARM AND COMFY

- The oldest trick in the book for staying warm while you're sleeping is curling up next to another warm body. And by "next to," we mean assuming the spoon position just like any happy couple would. In a survival situation, you'll pretty quickly get over any inhibitions you might have about close bodily contact with someone you don't normally share a bed with.
- You can add extra layers of insulation by sleeping on top of your clothes and piling them on top of you.
- Keep one set of clothing, like a base layer top and bottom, strictly reserved for nothing but sleeping and use them only for that purpose. When you're not wearing them, store them in a small dry bag or plastic garbage bag so they're always dry.
- If you've only got one set of clothes or socks and they've gotten damp in cold, wet weather, don't take them off before you get in your

242 | The MeatEater Guide to Wilderness Skills and Survival

sleeping bag. It might be uncomfortable for a while, but they'll dry inside your bag while you sleep. This only works for damp clothes, not thoroughly soaked ones. If they're sopping wet, sleep naked inside your sleeping bag to make sure that, at the very least, your bag stays dry and you've got a place to warm up and sleep. If you are using your sleeping bag as a clothes dryer, take advantage of any opportunity to air-dry your bag in the sun between uses.

- Pack the stuff sack for your sleeping bag with extra clothes or a puffy jacket for a good custom pillow.
- On cold nights, fill a Nalgene bottle with hot water, shove it in a wool sock, and bring it into your sleeping bag. You won't believe the difference it makes.
- When you leave the tent for the day, open the vents to help moisture escape, but always keep the screens and doors zippered shut to keep out bugs and unexpected precipitation.
- Don't bring wet, dirty boots inside the tent unless you have a woodstove to dry them out. Otherwise, leave them under the vestibule outside the tent at night. However, you can and should break this rule when it's below freezing. There's nothing worse than trying to pull on wet leather boots that have frozen solid overnight.
- Keep important stuff like your headlamp, bear spray, sidearm, knife, phone, GPS and the like in a hat placed right next to your head every night. That way, you'll always have your essentials within easy reach without having to frantically search for things in the dark. In dangerous areas, it's a good idea to wear your headlamp around your wrist like a bracelet.
- When you get home, take the time to unpack your sleeping bag and tent to thoroughly clean and air them out. You'll prevent nasty funk, mildew, and mold from building up, and you can look over your tent, pad, and bag for any repairs that might have to be made.

HOW TO PICK AND PREPARE A CAMPSITE

The more you camp, the pickier you become about where you camp. From the rainforest jungle to the Arctic tundra, we've slept in some very harsh environments and uncomfortable places. Still, in the hopes of getting some rest, we do our best to select the best few square feet of ground available to us in any given environment.

Choosing a site. Making the choice of where to camp starts with where you don't want to be. Don't camp on high rocky peaks or ridgelines, where you are most exposed to wind and lightning. At the same time, you don't want to camp in the lowest spot in a meadow, where all the cold air collects overnight. It's also smart to avoid camping on sandbars, beaches, low-lying islands, or anywhere else below the high-water mark, especially if it's raining. Many a floater or hiker has awakened to a rising tide or river swishing into their tent. Sometimes, however, sand and gravel bars are the only places where you can find flat ground and get out of the muck and brush. If that's the case, be vigilant about monitoring water levels.

Campsites that have everything you need or want are rare. Usually there will be something wrong. In an otherwise wet environment you might find a relatively dry, elevated spot to throw your tent down, but there's a slight slope to it. Or perhaps you manage to locate the only flat, sheltered bench on the side of a mountain, but the nearest water is a mile away. Think about your priorities and put them in order of importance when choosing a campsite. How close is the nearest water source? Is there plenty of firewood around? How about wind protection or dry ground? Is the site full of mosquitoes? Is flat ground available, or will you have to do with pitched? Is there adequate room for everyone to spread out?

Once you've selected your site, take the time to groom it. In country with biting spiders, snakes, or scorpions, clear away any debris or leaf litter that could hide nasty creepy crawlies. Use the heel of your boot or a tool to level out the ground where you'll be sleeping by plucking out or smoothing over any rocks or twigs or dirt mounds that could dig into your back in the middle of the night. If you're camping in snow, you'll want to take extra-special care to level out a flat platform for your tent and compact the snow. Before pitching your tent, actually lie down on the ground for a few seconds right where you think you'll be sleeping to make sure you don't need to adjust the pitch or dig out any annoying roots or rocks. A little bit of effort before throwing your tent down can make a huge difference in how well you sleep, which can make a huge difference in how well you fish, hike, or paddle the next day.

Camping regulations. On much of the country's millions of acres of federal BLM and national forest lands, you're free to engage in dispersed camping pretty much wherever you want. Dispersed camping in these areas generally means camping in a spot that is not supported by any services or facilities (that means no dumpsters, toilets, picnic tables, or fire pits). But depending on where you are, you may not have a choice about where you can camp, or your choice may be limited to very specific spots. Some land management agencies don't allow any overnight camping at all, or allow camping only on a seasonal basis. In some places, camping may be restricted to fee areas and developed campgrounds only. Or you might need a reservation or a permit to camp in certain backcountry areas. Rules may also dictate how far you need to be from trails or waterways. Public lands managers increasingly need to regulate exactly where and when campers should set up their tents in order to protect sensitive environments and to manage crowding. Check land management websites regarding the camping regulations where you're going and pay attention to any signs with camping information in the area.

You should also be respectful of where other groups are camping and try your very best to set up a polite and reasonable distance away. Remember that we all go out in the woods for the peace and quiet, so don't get too close unless you're invited to camp nearby. As a rule of thumb in the backcountry, if you can hear another group talking, you should look for another site.

EMERGENCY SHELTERS

The purpose of an emergency shelter is simple. All they really need to do is keep you out of the elements, particularly wind, rain, and snow. Some emergency shelters can insulate you from cold temperatures as well as from the brunt of the elements, and some can be used to create shade in hot, sunny environments. There are a lot of ways to find or make an emergency shelter when things go bad, especially if you take advantage of natural materials and the terrain's existing features. But keep in mind that shelters constructed out of natural materials often blend in extremely well with the surrounding environment. If you're lost or stranded, place a bright piece of clothing or gear on top of the shelter, high in a nearby tree, or out in a field close to your location so search and rescue teams will have a better chance of spotting you from the ground or air when you're holed up in your shelter.

Survival Blankets and Emergency Bivy Sacks

Emergency bivvies (not to be confused with the sleeping bag covers mentioned above) resemble a thin sleeping bag weighing just a few ounces. The good ones are far more durable and warmer than those cheap foil survival blankets that come folded up in a wallet-sized package inside store-bought first-aid kits. Still, even a cheap survival blanket is better than nothing at all. It'll reflect some heat back to your body, keep you off wet ground, block wind, and stand out as a highly reflective signal for search and rescue teams.

Contractor's Bags

Heavy duty garbage bags, often called contractor trash bags, can be used to make ponchos and very simple, effective, and packable emergency shelters. Get the kind that are at least 3 mils thick, with a 40 to 55 gallon capacity. Cut a slit in the middle of the bottom seam, just big enough to poke your head through, and slip the bag over your head. When you're sitting or curled up with the bag tucked under you, you're protected from rain or snow. The bag will also trap body heat, and can be stuffed with dry leaves or grass for added insulation. We keep a contractor's bag stashed in the bottom of our backpacks at all times. They have saved the day countless times, serving as dry bags, emergency ponchos, ground cloths, water-carrying devices, and liners to protect your pack from the blood of freshly butchered game animals.

Emergency Tarp Shelters

A good tarp is a terrific piece of survival equipment. We nearly always have one on us when we head into the field, whether it's the ground cloth for our tent or a separate tarp we use to get out of the sun or rain. There are countless ways to use a tarp for shelter, and a few of them are pictured on the next page. We know a few hard-core backcountry elk hunters who just get in their sleeping bags and then wrap themselves up in their tarps like sleeping burritos. Even without a sleeping bag, during a bad storm the burrito approach can keep hypothermia at bay and might save your life. With a little more work and some paracord, you can also construct a very effective emergency shelter with a leakproof roof. Or, if you've got more materials and time, tarps can be used to create wind and water barriers on the outside of survival shelters made with natural materials. To facilitate a quick setup for any such uses, a great modification to make to a survival tarp is the addition of 8-inch loops of thin shock cord or bungee cord to the tarp's grommets. These shock cords can be wrapped around brush, rocks, or branches, and the grommets themselves can be used to anchor stakes made out of trekking poles or rowing oars.

The classic tarp shelter lean-to is an effective design that's been used for hundreds of years. To make one, run a length of paracord or pole as a ridgeline between two trees about 4 feet high. Then hang and secure some of the tarp over the front of the line to create an overhanging roof. Next, stake or tie the other end of the tarp to the ground, sloping at a 45° angle. A tarp lean-to keeps water out and heat in when paired with a fire backed by a reflector wall (see page 261). They're pretty comfortable as far as survival shelters go. To maximize overhead coverage, you can also stake the tarp symmetrically into an A-frame shape over a ridge pole or length of cord.

And again, don't forget to use what you've got—a canoe and a set of oars can act as the base for an effective emergency shelter."

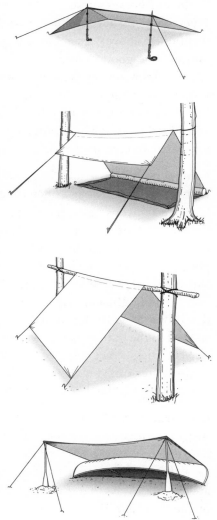

Hole Up Under a Tree or Rock

Many large evergreens such as spruce and pines have a sheltered space near the base of their trunks that can offer respite during a storm. Protected by the tree's thick mats of needles and boughs, you can tuck up against the trunk and under overhanging branches that'll keep most of the elements out and some of the warmth in. It's a great place to huddle up with your garbage bag or tarp wrapped around you. You can insulate the spot even more by piling up some cut boughs in any open, exposed spaces around or above you.

In snowy conditions, you can use the same principles to shelter in the naturally forming well of snow at the base of fir and pine trees. The best tree wells form where deeper snow piles up around the circumference of low-hanging branches. This creates a small, sheltered, insulated area around the tree's trunk. You can dig out the snow in the well and stack it outside to further bolster your shelter. Line the expanded hole with cut boughs and reinforce any thin overhead areas with cut and stacked branches. A word of warning, though: if you start a small fire in your tree well to stay warm, rising heat could melt snow in the branches

Dig out a tree well for shelter in snowy environments.

above, getting you soaked and extinguishing the flames. Place your fire strategically, where it will provide some warmth without melting overhead snow—you may have to knock some snow out of the tree branches or dig a space for your fire far enough away to prevent unwanted melting.

Caves and overhanging rock ledges are another type of ready-made natural shelter. You won't find full-on caves very often, but a small ledge or hollow in a rock wall that's just big enough to curl up under is really all you need. Heat reflects very well off rock, and you can build a big, warm fire near or against rock without needing to worry about the fire damaging your shelter. Before you take shelter in a cave or under a ledge, make sure you won't be sharing that space with rattlesnakes, bats, packrats, or any other unwanted housemates. Finally, give your rock shelter at least a cursory examination for stability before you commit to crawling into it. Sleeping under an unstable sandstone or shale ledge where large chunks have collapsed in the past could get you killed.

Sheltering under a rock ledge

BUILDING SHELTERS WITH NATURAL MATERIALS

In most environments, if you can't find a convenient preexisting shelter, nature will supply all the materials you need to build one. You'll need at least a couple hours of daylight to collect your building materials and create a viable shelter, so get to work. In *The Land of Feast and Famine*, a 1931 memoir of a fur trapper's journeys through the Canadian Arctic, Helge Ingstad describes how he and his travelmates would stop in the early afternoon while winter camping in order to spend several hours preparing to survive the night.

There are a few types of shelters you can build using materials such as wood, leaves, moss, and conifer limbs. The simplest is just a big pile of dry, dead leaves and brush that you burrow into for the night. Unfortunately, you'll rarely encounter the right leaf conditions for this. More importantly, with just a little effort you can make a much better shelter.

Using wood. The easiest option in wooded areas is to build a lean-to.

Find or make a ridgepole that runs 2 or 3 feet longer than your body, and use it to span a similarly sized gap between two trees or other supports. Secure each end of the ridgepole in a tree crook, or tie the ends to the trunks at a height of between 3 and 5 feet off the ground. Next, gather poles to make a roof that angles from the ground to the ridgepole. Cover your roofing poles

A lean-to shelter made of natural materials

Teepee-shaped wood shelter

with pine boughs, leaves, moss or whatever other materials you can gather to trap heat and shed water. That's a very basic lean-to design, but you can also add side walls, line the floor with dry leaves or pine boughs, and secure the shelter with cordage. Lean-tos can be built against the side of large rocks or steep banks, and there are other versions of wood-framed shelters that you can waterproof and insulate with vegetation, including double-wall shelters with a tapered wedge shape and teepee-shaped round lodges and wickiups.

During the winter in northern latitudes, you can add a layer of snow on top of the vegetation for extra insulation.

Using snow. You can also make a shelter using just snow. Many in-

A-frame wood shelter

digenous people and plenty of animals have long employed the insulating power of snow to stay warm. We're not talking about making an igloo, however. Building those structures requires very specific snow conditions, a lot of time, and a lifetime of knowledge and experience. There are much simpler and faster ways to use snow to create a windproof shelter that is warmer than the outside environment.

Provided the snow is deep and stable enough to pack and hold some weight, you can dig a snow cave. Look for a spot where deep snow is piled up against a slope or bank. For a simple shelter, dig a small cave that's just big enough to huddle in, get inside, then push some of the snow from the inside of the cave to plug up the entrance, leaving just a small opening for ventilation. Some of your body heat will be trapped, raising the temperature inside

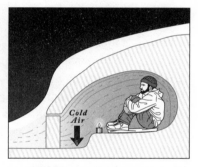

A raised platform helps trap body heat around the sleeper.

the structure. But you can increase the insulating efficiency of a snow cave by making a raised sleeping platform that sits higher than the entryway, as pictured. This allows cold air to sink below you when you're sleeping. When you're building a snow cave, avoid the temptation to completely shut yourself in and don't bury yourself under so much snow that you'll be trapped and suffocated if the cave collapses.

USING YOUR VEHICLE AS A SHELTER

As an elk-hunting guide, I'd drive from Colorado to Arizona every fall. The drive was just long enough that I couldn't safely pull it off in one push, so the backseat of my 2002 Tundra was permanently outfitted with a sleeping bag and a pillow. When I got tired, I'd find a pull-off, crawl into the backseat, and burrow in. Sleeping in the back of my Toyota wasn't comfortable, but it got me enough rest to finish out the drive. Once I got to Arizona, I'd spend weeks scouting the area before my clients showed up. I'd glass all morning, drive to another glassing point midday, then glass all evening. My campsite was wherever I'd parked my truck. Instead of sleeping in the back of my truck, I'd pull out a cot and sleep under the stars—with the option of getting back in the truck if it did start raining. For protection from wind and rain, the bed of a pickup covered with a quality topper is better than any tent.

By stashing a few items in your truck bed or car trunk, you could prevent an unexpected night in the woods from turning into a survival situation. Years ago, a friend and I got stuck at the end of a clay-based two-track in northwest Colorado after a six-hour thunderstorm made the road out impassable. Our tires were packed with wet clay, and every attempt to move was pushing us farther off the road and into the sagebrush. We decided to quit before we got ourselves more stuck. The forecast showed no rain overnight, so we knew the road would dry soon and free us from the temporary inconvenience. Although it was the end of May, it was cold and rainy and we were soaked to the core. The truck's heat felt good, but the truck's fuel gauge was below half, making us reluctant to run the engine too much. I had my down jacket, but Dan hadn't brought his. To pass the time as we waited for the road conditions to improve, I bundled up and snoozed in the passenger seat while Dan lay awake, cold and miserable. It would have been a very different experience if we had bothered to keep the truck properly supplied with some extra clothes, a first-aid kit, water, a small camp stove, and some snack food. All of this could have been packed into a 10-to-14-gallon plastic storage container and tossed into the back of the truck. Trust me, I never made that same mistake again.

When stranded or lost in a vehicle, think long and hard before deciding to abandon the vehicle to search for help on foot. It's much easier for rescuers to find a stationary vehicle on a road or trail than a moving person. Not only that, leaving your vehicle will expose you to the elements. Your car will provide you with shelter from sun, rain, and wind, and you may need to use your vehicle as a heat source. On average, cars will burn $\frac{1}{7}$ to $\frac{1}{5}$ of a gallon of gas an hour while idling.

Most cars hold 12 to 15 gallons of gas. A 3.5-liter Ford Explorer can idle for thirty-three hours on a full tank. If you ran the engine only thirty minutes of every hour, you'd double your idling time. But do be careful sitting in an idling vehicle; carbon monoxide poisoning is a real danger. Make sure the tailpipe isn't clogged by snow or mud, and crack the window for airflow. If you're close to falling asleep, leave the window open, or better yet, just shut off the engine. Never fall asleep in a running vehicle. Plenty of people have done that; many never woke up.

—*By Janis Putelis, director and executive producer of the* MeatEater *TV series and co-host of the* MeatEater *podcast*

FIRE

You don't always need a fire to enjoy a comfortable camp. Many nights in the backcountry, in all kinds of weather, we've camped by the blue glow of a backpacking stove, which provided just enough heat to boil water for simple backcountry cooking. "Cold camps" often have real advantages in terms of simplicity and efficiency—building fires takes time and energy when sometimes all you really want to do is crawl into your sleeping bag. And cold camping may be required due to wildfire risks, land management regulations, ecological impacts, or just because poor conditions make maintaining a fire more trouble than it's worth.

But a rip-roaring fire does make for a far more enjoyable campsite. You can sit around the fire and cook, tell stories, or just quietly listen to the night sounds.

In a survival situation, the ability to start a fire can be the difference between life and death. If you plunge through the ice or fall out of your canoe into frigid water, building a fire is your number one priority after you make it back to dry ground. Or say you get turned around and your day in the woods is going to last until tomorrow morning. A fire will keep you warm and calm, and it just might alert rescuers to your position.

The trouble is, plenty of folks overestimate their ability to reliably start a fire, especially in rainy or windy conditions. Even under ideal circumstances, making a fire using natural fuel sources can be hard work. In order to succeed, you'll need to understand the fundamentals of fire building.

BUILDING BLOCKS OF FIRE

There are five critical ingredients to building a fire: ignition, tinder, kindling, fuel, and oxygen. Screwing up any one of them may doom your attempt to get a fire started or keep it burning.

Ignition

Simply put, the ignition source provides the spark, heat, or flame that starts your fire. There are many ways to achieve ignition, with some being vastly easier than others.

Lighters. Some outdoorsmen prefer windproof electric or butane lighters, and now and then you'll see an old-school Zippo get put to work. But a disposable Bic lighter—or rather, a bunch of them—will do the trick. You should have at least one in your survival kit, and another stashed somewhere on your person. It's also a good idea to have one in your fishing vest, life jacket, camper, glove box, boat bag, or wherever else it could wind up being needed. One caveat: disposable lighters do sometimes have trouble firing in extreme cold. To remedy, simply keep the lighter warm by tucking it into an inner pocket close to your body. Make sure to keep an eye on fluid levels inside your lighter. They'll need to be replaced periodically, or refilled if you're going the non-disposable route. For folks who travel by air, a final consideration is that while the TSA allows classic lighters, the agency will confiscate butane lighters from both your checked and carry-on bags.

Waterproof matches. Don't count on a book of flimsy paper matches to save the day in the event that you are separated from your lighter or run out of lighter fluid. Paper matches get ruined when wet, and drying them out won't help. You want the sturdy waterproof wooden ones that ignite easily even when they're wet, burn hot, and stay lit for a long time. They should be stored in a waterproof match safe or pill bottle.

If you want to go the DIY route, waterproof matches are also easy and cheap to make at home. Just take sturdy wooden matches, preferably the strike-anywhere kind, and wrap a length of cotton yarn around the shaft for extra fuel and burn time. Then, using pliers or forceps, dip the entire match in paraffin wax that you've melted over a double boiler. Let the matches dry on a piece of foil. You may need more than one coat. Store them in an old pill bottle. When you're ready to spark up, scrape the wax off the tip and strike the match.

Sparking tools. Striking flint and steel together to create a spark is an ancient method of ignition that is often touted in survival circles, but that takes hours upon hours of practice to master. Even if you can manage to produce sparks, you'll need to know what to do with those sparks once they appear. Countless hours have been wasted landing feeble sparks on substances that are incapable of fostering a spark into a flame. Back in the days when flint and steel were in common use, people carried supplies of charred cloth, punk wood, and shredded grass to act as early stage tinder for fire starting. Without such deliberately sourced and prepared materials, trying to use flint and steel is a lost cause.

Contemporary strikers made of magnesium and ferrocerium are much, much easier to use. They're windproof and waterproof and have little chance of breaking or malfunctioning. The sparks they throw are hotter and more plentiful and can easily set a piece of toilet paper or newsprint ablaze. Using your knife to scrape shavings from the sparking material into your tinder will make it even easier to get a fire started. Once a spark strikes these shaved bits of magnesium, you get an intense bit of heat that can be effectively managed. Contemporary strikers come in a variety of forms, including magnesium blocks; rods of magnesium tethered to sharp metal strikers; spark wheels similar to the striking mechanism on a standard lighter; and "plunger" firestarters that can be operated with a single finger. Of these, the magnesium rods that come attached to a striker are the best choice. They are effective, durable, and easy to use.

TINDER

Tinder is the material that first accepts a flame or spark; once ignited, it can be used to light your kindling. Selecting proper tinder is the part of fire building that most people screw up. Typically, they try to go too big, too fast, ending up with smoke and little else. Tinder should ignite almost immediately upon contact with a hot coal or small open flame. Lots of stuff both natural and man-made can be used as tinder.

Natural Tinder

If you know where and how to find it, there is plenty of effective material in nearly every ecosystem: dry grasses, mosses and lichens, downy seed heads, shavings of the inner bark of aspen, poplar, and cottonwood trees, and pitch wood dug out of dry pines, to name a few examples. Most of these tinder sources need to be manipulated before they can be used. Shred bark into fine, stringy strips, shave off bits of dry inner wood, splinter the ends of branches by crushing them with a rock. You want to wind up with a fluffy ball of material resembling a nest. If you're having trouble finding dry tinder, poke around under evergreens where the lower layers of branches are shielded from rain and snow by the canopy above. We make a habit of grabbing good bits of natural tinder whenever we pass them by.

Fungus. To spot usable fungus, look for crusty growths at the forks of branches or on damaged areas of trees. Birch tinder fungus is a bulbous black growth that appears on white and yellow birches. Its punky dry inside should be reddish brown, orange, or a dirty yellow. Horse hoof fungus is a gray tree-growing shelf fungus shaped like a horse's hoof and about the size of a fist. It grows on a variety of trees in the Northeast. Cracked cap polypore grows throughout the Southeast, often on dead black locust trees. To use any of these, break open the fungus and shave and grind it into a powder. Carefully capture the dust, and use it to catch sparks and ignite a tinder bundle made with small strips of the outer layer.

Birch bark. Papery, curling strips of birch bark are easy to strip from this common tree. They contain plenty of natural oils and burn extremely well, even when it's damp. Peel off thin strips and shred until you have a loose nest of material. Larger sections of bark make good bases for your tinder pile.

Dry moss and lichens. In the South, dry Spanish moss takes a flame well. Many dry mosses and lichens in other areas will light and burn. Form a loose bundle under small dry sticks and ignite.

Cedar and juniper bark. These common coniferous trees are a great source of tinder. To gather, just peel off a pile of shaggy bark. Shred it and rub it together between your hands until it's very fine. Arrange it into a bundle or nest to catch sparks.

Sagebrush bark. Peel off the dry bark from this common western shrub. Shred it into thin strips and make a pile of tinder topped with thin dead sagebrush branches.

Dry grasses. Any number of dry grasses can be gathered and arranged into a very good tinder bundle. Shred grasses and fluffy seed heads and form into a palm-size nest.

Cattail fluff. This recognizable plant is common around wetlands. You can always find dry, downy, highly flammable cattail fluff on the thick seed head on the top of the stalk. Form it into a fluffy ball.

Pine needles. Dry needles from evergreens and cedars can be used for tinder.

Pine pitch. Look for deposits of sticky pine sap. Roll the pitch into a ball for tinder that's easy to light and burns for a long time.

Dead leaves. Dead dry leaves usually light easily. They often burn quickly, so have enough handy to feed in until the kindling catches.

Inner bark shavings. The inner bark of many species of dead trees, like aspen, poplar, and cottonwood, works as a very good tinder. Use your knife to get at the inner bark, cutting away long strips. You'll need to split, rub, twist, and fray the bark until it's fine and can be formed into a nest of material.

Bird's nests. If you're lucky enough to find an old, dry bird's nest tucked into the crook of a tree, you've found some great tinder.

Tinder You Bring

There are many effective tinder and fire-starting aids that you can either buy from sporting goods stores or make from widely available materials that can be found at hardware or grocery stores if you don't have them lying around at home.

Char cloth. Lots of folks don't know about or use this one, but it's been in use since the 1600s for good reason: there is nothing better at reliably catching sparks and holding an ember. Char cloth is any cloth made with 100 percent plant fibers (cotton is very common) that is allowed to char but not burn. It's remarkably effective with traditional flint and steel. You can make it by cutting some squares from old clothes such as cotton jeans or shirts. Grab a small sealed metal container (such as an Altoid tin) and poke a hole in the top with a nail to let gases escape. Place your fabric squares in the container, close it, and place on the coals of a fire or on the low burner of a camp stove. Wait until smoke stops coming out of the hole (ten to thirty minutes), then remove the container from the flames and allow it to cool. The fabric squares should be colored like charcoal and will turn to powder when torn apart with your fingers. Handle them gently.

Dryer lint. This otherwise useless stuff will ignite well with a magnesium striker, or with a flame. It works even better when mixed with a little lamp oil or paraffin at home and packed along in a plastic bag.

Cotton balls and Vaseline. Smear a few cotton balls in Vaseline and store them in a pill bottle or chew tin. When you're ready to start a fire, pull one out, fluff it up, and pull it apart slightly. It will light readily and hold a good flame for a while. A nice thing about this method is that the Vaseline serves double purpose in your pack. It's a firestarter and a good skin treatment for chapped lips and chafed skin.

Egg-carton fire starter. Fill the cups in a cardboard egg carton with a mix of sawdust, dryer lint, and paraffin. Break the cups apart and store them in a zip-lock bag.

Batteries. You can use the polarity of a live battery to ignite a fire by creating a metal circuit between the terminals. Steel wool or tinfoil gum wrappers work best. If you're working with a gum wrapper and an AA battery, you want to cut the wrapper so that it tapers to a narrow point between two wide ends. Hold the ends, metal side in, to the terminals and a flame should appear at the narrow neck. With a 9-volt or D-cell and steel wool, simply hold the wool to the terminals until it glows red hot. Transfer the wool to your tinder fast, as the effect won't last long. And note that the wrapper, steel wool, or any other metal you use must be dry and rust-free.

Desperate times. Use what you've got on you: candy wrappers, bits of hunting and fishing licenses, pocket lint, a wad of duct tape. If you've got any books around, rip out the pages you've already read. Check your wallet for receipts—even money will burn. Is there any junk lying around that you can scavenge, like cut bits of old rubber tires or stuffing pulled from a cushion? Did you pack any greasy snacks like corn chips? They'll go up if you put a match to them.

Commercial stuff. There are all manner of pastes, cubes, putties, and other highly flammable accelerants that you can pack along for help starting a fire. Coghlan's Fire Paste, Pyro Putty, and UST's WetFire are all excellent. A word of caution for air travelers: TSA agents will pull commercially produced firestarters containing chemical or fuel-based accelerants from your luggage. You could even get a hefty fine for packing them. When traveling by air, stick with homemade paraffin and Vaseline-based firestarting aids.

KINDLING

Good kindling is made up of thin lengths of dry wood that burn hot, providing a flammable base that gets the fire going before you start adding larger pieces of fuel. Most people start with kindling that is too big. Ideally, kindling should be from the size of a toothpick up to about the diameter of your thumb. Small dead twigs and sticks work great. The dry, dead limbs on the lower trunks of coniferous trees are a prime source of kindling because they are shielded from rain and snow by the overhead canopy. Collect an armload of kindling before starting your fire, especially when you're working under challenging circumstances. Running off to find more kindling is a bad idea in those moments when you're struggling to nurture a small flame into life.

Fuzz stick. Also called a feather stick, a fuzz stick is a great tool for starting a fire and getting wet wood to burn. You make one by taking a foot-long length of softwood like pine or spruce and using your knife to carve thin curls of wood out from the stick. You're trying to shave a thin slice that curves away from the stick but remains attached. Do this all around the stick until you have a thick cluster of feathery, curling slices of wood.

Fatwood and dry pine cones. Sometimes when a pine tree has been badly wounded, the pitch will permeate the wood, giving it a varnished, denser look and heavier weight. This is known as fatwood and it burns like crazy. The cones that fall off pine, fir, spruce, and other evergreen trees often contain a lot of pitch and burn very well too once they're brown and dry.

Splits of logs or branches. Look for shattered dead wood on the ground where a tree could have been damaged by wind, fire, or lightning. You may also find standing dry timber that's been killed by beetles or disease. A hatchet will allow you to not only buck up a bunch of larger pieces of fuel but easily knock out smaller split sections that make great kindling. A big fixed-blade knife can work, too. Find a heavy stick to use as a club or mallet, put the blade of your knife against a crack or other likely spot for the log to split, then use the stick to hammer the back of the knife blade, driving it into the log like a wedge to leverage out pieces of kindling. You can also use this technique to cut poles from live trees to build shelters.

FUEL

Fuel sustains a fire for the long haul, giving off enough heat so you don't have to fetch more wood every few minutes. You want firewood that is dead and dry. Once you get your fire ripping, it's okay to add dead wood with a wet surface, but trying to burn rotten, thoroughly saturated wood or live, green wood will smother flames. Aim for pieces of firewood about

Use your body weight and a pivot point to bust up longer pieces of wood.

as thick as an arm or leg. Within that range, you can usually bust longer lengths of wood into manageable pieces without an axe or a saw. Wedging the end of a large piece of wood between two trees and applying pressure to the opposite end as shown is a great way to bust up wood.

Or lean a length of wood on a rock or fallen tree trunk, then stomp the middle with your boot. When you want uniformly sized wood or short pieces that can fit inside a wood stove, a cutting tool will be helpful. A small folding saw with a 10-inch blade is great to have when you're building a stash of wood big enough to keep you warm for the night. Always exercise caution when felling trees for firewood; see page 263 for instructions.

AIR

Air is free for the taking, but your fire needs just the right amount to get started and keep burning. First, pay attention to the wind before you build the fire. A wind blowing at your back will push too much heat away from you, while a wind blowing in your face can drive an unbearable amount of smoke your way. A crossing wind pattern is ideal. Keep this principle in mind when trying to warm a lean-to. A breeze blowing across the opening is preferable to a breeze blowing into the shelter.

A big mistake people make is choking off airflow by piling way too much fuel on the fire before it's had a chance to really get going. Make sure there's enough space between pieces of fuel for the fire to breathe and flame up. Another common mistake is the failure to feed the fire the air it needs. You've got to blow on smoldering tinder to make it flame up hot enough to ignite kindling. Get down low and blow on the base of the fire. A fast and hard fan with a hat or a sleeping pad can cause a dying fire to burst into flame.

SKILL: HOW TO BUILD A FIRE: AN ALMOST FOOLPROOF GUIDE

Practice is the only way to get good at building fires. If every fire you build is juiced with a splash of gasoline, you're probably not going to be prepared to build a fire when you have minimal gear and everything around you is soaking wet. If you want to get proficient, you need to do real-world exercises with naturally sourced materials and minimalist equipment. Here's how to go about it.

STEP 1: GATHER YOUR MATERIALS

At the minimum, gather two handfuls of quality tinder material, two armloads of kindling, and one knee-high heap of larger fuel. Stack the material neatly in three piles within easy reach.

STEP 2: CLEAR THE AREA AND BUILD YOUR FIRE-STARTING STRUCTURE

If it's raining or really windy, find a spot that provides some over-head cover. Clear away vegetation so that you're working on rock, sand, or mineral soil. Dig a pit if it helps you reach dry ground or creates a sheltered space away from the wind. If you're building a fire on snow or wet ground, lay larger dry sticks side by side to con-struct a platform for the fire. Placing a ring of stones around your fire circle can do a handful of helpful things. The stones can help block excessive wind while absorbing and reflecting the fire's heat. They can also help contain the fire and limit the risk of it spreading to the surrounding vegetation and duff. Arranged properly, rocks can also provide a nice framework to support a wire cooking grill or a rack of green limbs.

When you're ready to light the fire, loosely stack your smallest kindling in a teepee shape. Leave an open space at the center of the teepee for your burning tinder bundle. The typical teepee structure allows you to stack small and then slightly larger kindling, still leaving plenty of space for air circulation. Another trick is to build a lean-to shape against a log that's on the ground, leaning the kindling against the larger log.

STEP 3: PREPARE YOUR TINDER

Tinder usually needs a bit of prep to work. Shred your dry bark. Make loose piles of dry grass and mosses. Fluff up the Vaseline-smeared cotton balls. Take whatever you have, and build it into a tinder bundle about the same size and general shape as a songbird nest. A good trick is to build this tinder nest on a flat piece of bark. It helps keep everything together and off the ground, and you can raise it up to blow air on the tinder as needed.

STEP 4: IGNITION

If you're using a magnesium striker, place the rod of the striker over your tinder and use the back of your knife to slowly shave a pile of material onto the tinder. With the rod tight against the tinder bundle, make your ignition sparks with the attached striker or your knife. Don't half-ass it— strike hard and fast so that you send a thick shower of hot sparks raining down into the tinder. Gently blow on the tinder, turning sparks into a glowing coal that bursts into flame.

To ignite your tinder with waterproof matches, take them out of their waterproof case, peel off any coating if needed, and light against the striker pad or a nearby rock. Long waterproof matches allow you to reach tinder deep inside the kindling. Keep the lit match in place until it burns the tip of your finger. If you're using a lighter, use your body to block the wind as you ignite the tinder and any areas of small kindling that'll catch from a small flame. Keep a close eye on your fire just after ignition; this is when fires will often fail to get going and slowly flame out.

STEP 5: FEED, MAINTAIN, AND PRESERVE

As the tinder catches, begin to feed in your kindling. Watch the fire closely at this point. Patiently feed the fire more small kindling as it begins to burn steadily—don't pile on too much too quickly, or you'll just suffocate the flame. Fan the flame and feed it steadily as it grows, gradually adding larger pieces of fuel. As the fire gets hot, place slightly wet logs you've collected just outside the fire to dry out a bit before they get added to the flames. As the fire develops a bed of coals, larger fuel should continue to burn steadily.

You want a fire that is compact but burning strong and hot, with a deep bed of coals. If you have a long log that you can't cut, lay it across the fire so that it eventually burns through into a log that can be broken in half. Or just stick the end of a long log into the fire. As that end burns down, you slide more of the log in.

To bank a fire for the night, let it burn down until it's just coals and a few small charcoal-like pieces of burned wood. Using a shovel or fire stick, push the coals against one side of the fire pit or ring.

Lightly cover the pile of coals with ash and dirt. The coals will continue to smolder slowly, and in the morning you can stir them up and quickly ignite more tinder and kindling to get the fire back and ripping. You can maintain a fire for days this way as long as it doesn't get doused.

ALTERNATE FIRE STRUCTURES

With a couple of small tweaks, you can design a fire that's optimized for cooking or keeping you warm. There are a few different variations out there, but here are a few of the fires we've found most useful.

Log cabin fire. Similar in function and purpose to the teepee fire, the log cabin fire is built by crisscrossing logs in the fashion of a child's Lincoln Log toy set. Place the kindling inside the structure before lighting. This method allows maximum air flow and can be left unattended for a while after it is lit, since the primary fuel will already be in place.

Parallel log fire. We've seen this fire type put to use by indigenous peoples in the Philippines, Guyana, and Bolivia. It is great for large

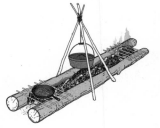

groups in need of cooking surfaces and warmth. Select two large logs anywhere from four feet to eight feet in length, depending on the size of your group. Diameters can range from eight inches to sixteen inches. Arrange the logs parallel to each other and spaced around eighteen inches to twenty-four inches apart. Light a fire between the logs, and then allow it to spread throughout the gap between the logs by piling in sticks and other fuel. Cooking racks and large pots can be suspended over the fire by placing them across the logs.

Reflector wall. If your primary purpose for making a fire is to keep yourself warm, you can direct more of the heat toward you by building a reflector wall. This can be as simple as leaning a large, flat rock on its edge on the far side of your fire ring to reflect heat your way, or piling several

smaller rocks on that side to make a wall. If you're going to be camping in one spot for a while, you could even build a small wall out of logs for the same purpose. A V-shaped wall that opens in your direction is even better.

Keyhole fire. Instead of building the standard circular fire ring used for cooking, it's helpful to add a narrow slot coming off one end so that

the whole thing looks from above like a keyhole. This construction allows you to build a big, warm fire in the main ring while pushing coals into the slot where you'll do your cooking. Arrange the coals to properly balance a grate, skillet, or Dutch oven, and keep them smoldering but not aflame so you maintain a consistent cooking temperature.

For fires meant to attract the attention of potential rescuers, see page 285.

A FINAL SAFETY NOTE ON FIRES

Natural wildfires are part of the normal cycle of renewal, but human-caused forest fires cause untold amounts of suffering and billions of dollars in property damage each year. Don't add to that by letting your campfire turn into an uncontrolled inferno.

- Use an existing fire ring when in an established campsite, or use stones to create one if possible.
- Never build a fire during high winds.
- Scrape away all dry grasses, leaves, and other organic matter from the spot where you intend to build a fire. Get down to bare soil, and extend the prepped area well beyond the edges of the flames.
- Keep water and a pile of dirt nearby to douse creeping flames. Extinguish the fire completely before leaving by dousing with water, breaking up any smoldering material, and stirring the coals. The surface of the fire pit should be cold to the touch.
- In the backcountry, dismantle the fire site according to leave-no-trace principles: scatter the ashes and debris, fill your pit back up with dirt, and return the rocks to where you found them.

SKILL: FELLING A TREE

There are situations in the outdoors when you may be confronted with the need to cut down a tree. Collecting a whole bunch of firewood is the most obvious reason, but it's also possible that you might need to build a makeshift bridge across a swollen stream. Whatever the purpose, technique is important, as tree felling done the wrong way could kill you. Felling a tree safely with a chainsaw requires three basic cuts and some work with an axe or sledgehammer. But before you whip out your tools, you'll need to run through the following series of safety checks.

First, visually evaluate the tree. Take note of visible cracks, damage, rot, hanging limbs, or any neighboring trees that might be leaning against the tree you selected. If there are any visible hazards, move on.

Next, assess the tree's lean. When possible, you want to fell a tree so that it falls in the direction of its natural lean. Visualize the path the tree would take to the ground, taking note of any structures or neighboring trees you need to avoid.

Finally, devise an escape plan. Evaluate the opposite side of the tree, visualizing two pathways jutting out at 45° angles to each side. These are your escape routes. Make sure they are clear of debris so that you can quickly and safely exit away from the tree as it falls.

FELLING A TREE WITH A CHAINSAW

Once you've run through your safety checks, you can move on to making your cuts.

Make your face cuts. Your first two cuts will remove a wedge-shaped piece of wood and shift the tree's center of gravity. Standing next to the tree, make cut A level and

perpendicular to the direction you want the tree to fall. Cut approximately one-third of the way into the tree, remove the chainsaw bar, and line up for cut B. Make cut B at a 45° downward angle, meeting up with the end of cut A. Remove the wood wedge and ensure that your two cuts meet perfectly; if not, adjust accordingly.

Make your back cut. Move your attention to the back side of the tree for cut C, which releases tension and allows the tree to fall. Cut C should be level with cut A, but an inch higher up the tree. The uncut wood between the angle created by cuts A and B and the endpoint of cut C—the all-important "hinge"— should retain a thickness measuring about 10 percent of the tree's diameter; you never

want to completely cut the tree off the stump while it is standing. As you cut, keep the bottom of the chainsaw bar perpendicular to the direction you want the tree to fall. This will ensure an even section of hinge wood to guide the tree to the ground in the intended direction and keep the tree from jumping back off the stump. For larger trees, place a plastic felling wedge into the saw kerf (the space created by the back cut you've just made) as soon as possible before continuing with the cut. Trees smaller than 8 inches in diameter usually do not need this step. As you work, always keep an eye on the tree's canopy for movement and falling limbs from adjacent trees.

Strike the felling wedge (if using). Once your hinge is at the desired width, stop cutting and begin to strike the felling wedge with an axe or sledgehammer. This should create the final lift needed to tip the tree. If the size of the tree does not warrant a felling wedge, the tree should fall on its own as you make your C cut.

Safely exit away from the tree. Once the tree commits to its fall, quickly use your escape route to exit. The tree should fall completely to the ground. Give the tree a moment to settle and keep an eye out above for branches that may have come loose from nearby trees. You can now move on to bucking that tree into pieces of whatever lengths you'll need.

FELLING A TREE WITH AN AXE

If you are felling a tree without a chainsaw, using only an axe, your cuts will need to fall differently.

Make your face cuts. Using a series of axe swings, begin to make cut A—it should fall at a 45° upward angle instead of level (see diagram). After your first strike, proceed to cut B, which should fall at a 45° downward angle. Switching between the two cuts with each alternating strike, chip out a large trapezoid-shaped piece of wood. Repeat, alternating chops between cut A and cut B, until you have created a wedge that cuts approximately halfway into the tree. Start both cuts far enough apart that your two cutting angles do not meet before the de- sired halfway point, or you'll have a hard time achieving the required depth. Once you have completed your face cuts, move around the tree for your back cuts.

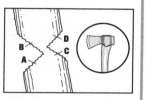

Make your back cuts. You want to make cuts C and D at the same angles as A and B, and with alternating chops; however, you want them to meet approximately a half-inch above where cuts A and B meet. Once you are approaching the ideal size for the hinge, stop al- ternating between cuts C and D and continue only with cut D. Direct, powerful chops will sever the last bit of wood as you set your hinge. Again, you don't want to completely cut the tree off the stump; in- stead, your goal is to have the tree commit to its fall, allowing the re- maining hinge wood to guide the tree to the ground. Axe-felling is a less precise practice than saw-felling; however, it is a great skill to master.

> —By Richard Hutton, a hunter and angler with a background in forest
> management who is currently the operations manager for FHF Gear

CHAPTER 6

※※※✕※※※

Navigation and Wilderness Travel

I MOVED FROM MY HOME state of Michigan to western Montana shortly after finishing college. During my first summer there, I took a long hiking trip in the Bitterroot Mountains with a friend of mine from Kansas. There we were, two born-and-raised flatlanders trying to navigate a landscape of interwoven ridgelines and alpine lakes that all looked remarkably similar. On our third day out, we started to notice that our map was making less and less sense. What looked to be east-west ridges on paper were actually running north-south, and lakes that were supposed to be present were mysteriously missing. Things got so bad that when we spied a lake far below us, we hiked down to it in hopes of finding some campers or fishermen who might be able to set us straight. We didn't find any of those, but we did locate a small wooden sign identifying the body of water as Meadow Lake. All we needed to do was find the name of the lake on our map and we'd know exactly where we were and how to get out of there. But no matter how hard we scoured our map, we couldn't find a Meadow Lake in any part of western Montana. Perplexed, I kept looking farther and farther away from where I reckoned we were until I finally managed to stumble across a body of water called Meadow Lake. You might imagine that I was relieved by the discovery, but quite the opposite was true. My map showed the lake being in Idaho. Not only were we hiking the wrong ridgeline, we were hiking in the wrong state.

Of all the times I've been turned around or lost, that was probably the most embarrassing. But it can get a hell of a lot worse. Consider the famous line from the explorer and hunter Daniel Boone, who once acknowledged, "I have never been lost, but I will admit to being confused for several weeks." Granted, things were a lot different back in Boone's day, before you could walk around with a continent's worth of digitized and searchable satellite imagery on a palm-sized device in your back pocket. Considering the ease of use and capabilities of modern technology, it seems like it ought to be impossible to get lost nowadays. Yet it still happens to many people every year, including to folks with impressive backcountry résumés. And unfortunately, sometimes getting lost can have fatal consequences.

Keeping you and your companions safe from disaster or from the simple inconvenience of being lost for a few hours requires a cocktail of preparation, education, and diligence. Preparation comes down to pre-trip planning and the accumulation of the maps and electronic tools that will assist you on your journey. Education amounts to learning how to actually use that stuff, as well as how to get by in its absence. Diligence refers to updating and monitoring your navigation tools while in the field, as well as maintaining the necessary level of spatial awareness amid fatigue, discomfort, and distractions such as scenery and chitchat.

There's obviously a lot more to wilderness travel than simply not getting lost. You also need to know how to travel efficiently and safely, and with the necessary confidence to behave in a bold and sometimes aggressive fashion in order to accomplish your goals. The diversity of landscapes that an adventurous traveler might encounter in his or her lifetime is staggering. The methods of travel are just as staggering, from skiff to canoe to snowmobile to boot leather. Just because you enjoy an intimate knowledge of one environment and its typical mode of transport—say, canoe travel in the Boundary Waters, or packrafting in the Wyoming high country—doesn't mean you're gonna enjoy that same expert status everywhere you go. After my "confusion," as Boone calls it, along the Idaho-Montana border, I did manage to develop a high degree of proficiency at mountain navigation in the northern Rockies. Soon after, though, I remember the feelings of inept vulnerability that washed over me the first time I stepped foot on the Arctic tundra. I did three or four trips up there before I finally started to feel slightly at home. My next challenge was equatorial jungle. After a few visits down there, I'd like to tell you that I now have that dialed in as well, but that'd be a lie.

What I've learned from going through this cycle of ignorance to knowledge is that it's just that—a cycle. Gaining familiarity with this cycle makes the experience of going through it that much easier. In other words, uneasiness with a landscape is a lot more tolerable when you can imagine how and when that uneasiness will go away. The information in this chapter will greatly shorten the length of that cycle as well, as it contains both basic and advanced techniques for navigation and wilderness travel that will come in handy—and maybe even save your life—the next time you step into the wild.

SPATIAL AWARENESS AND THE NAVIGATION MINDSET

If you're like most people, you do a better job of remembering how you got somewhere when you're driving than when you're a passenger. That's a simple function of awareness. As the driver, you have to pay attention. As a passenger, you're permitted to zone out. Whenever you're out in the wild, you need to put yourself in the driver's seat, so to speak, and pay attention to all of the twists, turns, and landmarks.

Maintaining a strong sense of spatial awareness begins before you head into the wild. The first step is to develop a general, high-level understanding of the area where you're going to be spending time. You need to know how it fits into the landscape on a grand scale. In much of the Lower 48, it's difficult to find spots that are more than 2 or 3 miles from a road. In places like Canada and Alaska, you can be hundreds of miles from a road. If you traveled westward from the Trans-Alaska Pipeline, you'd hike and swim a long ways before hitting a road in northern Asia. Obviously, that's the kind of information you want at your disposal. Below are the sorts of questions that you *should* ask yourself as you prepare for an outing. Not only will this information be directly helpful, but the simple act of accumulating it will prepare your mind to gather a much more detailed layer of understanding once you hit the ground.

- What are the nearest roads and highways? What direction do the roads run? Where are those roads and highways relative to where you'll be traveling?
- What are the most prominent landforms and features in the area? Peaks, ridgelines, buttes, lakes, rivers? How large are the features— what's the length of the lake and the elevation of the peak?
- What are the nearest towns or places of permanent habitation?
- Generally, what direction do the ridgelines run?

- What are the elevation variances in the area? Is it generally flat, or is the country steep? When traveling up a streamside trail, how many feet of elevation do you gain per mile?
- How does water move through the area? What streams and rivers drain it? What direction, in general, do those streams and rivers run? In turn, what do those streams and rivers flow into?
- How much annual precipitation does the area get? Are the streams and rivers always full, or are they ephemeral?
- Who owns or administers the land? Is it federal, state, provincial, or private? What agencies are responsible for the land? What, if any, travel restrictions exist in the area? Are motor vehicles allowed? Watercraft? Aircraft?

Once you've established a good understanding of a given area from afar, you'll have the necessary context to understand what you're seeing and experiencing on the ground. You'll find yourself saying, "Oh, this creek I'm crossing must be draining off from such-and-such peak and flowing west into such-and-such river. And everything on the far side of that distant ridge probably flows east into such-and-such lake." When you get to that level of detailed understanding, navigation and travel become fun. What's more, getting lost becomes hard to imagine.

There will still be surprises. No matter how much you prepare for an expedition by studying maps and satellite imagery, everything is theoretical until you actually set your feet on the ground. You might find that a ridge you thought would yield a daylong hunt is easily traversed in a few hours; conversely, that ridge you thought would occupy a few hours might take a day to climb. A topo map doesn't show you every single cliff or rocky outcrop, or the blowdown that happened two years ago when an avalanche moved a bunch of trees and rocks into the path you thought you were going to take. Even in terrain you're familiar with, a path that looked smooth last spring might be in totally different shape the following year. Contingencies like these are a big part of the reason you need enough food and gear to get you through an expedition that takes longer than planned; they also reinforce the need for the spatial awareness and flexibility that will enable you to map a new course if needed.

When traveling through unfamiliar terrain, make a point to acknowledge and discuss features and landmarks along the way. If you have a companion, discuss them openly and out loud. If you're alone, remark on them to yourself: "Here's a large tree that was struck by lightning; I'm at a fork in the creek, and I'm taking the right fork; look at this big avalanche scar that I'm crossing; I can see a small cattail marsh through the trees there." This strategy might feel a little hokey, but it's actually pretty important. Communicating about landmarks, rather than just silently noting them and filing them away, increases the chances that you'll remember that lightning-struck tree on your way back, as well as the odds that everyone in the group will have taken notice. That way, should a member of the group become separated, there is a better chance that they'll be able to sort themselves out and determine whether they're on the right track or wrong track.

NAVIGATION TOOLS: MODERN TECHNOLOGY AND OLD-SCHOOL WOODSMANSHIP

Some folks feel that carrying any form of electronic technology into the wilderness cheapens the outdoor experience. That notion makes for a lively debate around the campfire among friends. There's no escaping the romance and mythology surrounding explorers who navigated uncharted territory using only the stars and sun as their guides. There's also some real value to be found in woodsmanship skills like compass and map reading. From a practical standpoint, however, there's no question that modern technologies like cellphones and GPS units save lives in the outdoors. They also enhance our understanding of our surroundings by providing place names, land ownership details, and a broader sense of how our precise location fits into the large-scale natural system around us. But don't let them become a crutch. Use technology, for sure, but also develop the skills to navigate without the aid of electronics.

HANDHELD GPS UNITS

GPS (global positioning system) units are devices that communicate with satellites to determine their user's location and direction of travel. Today, the technology is familiar, and voice-command navigation systems come standard in many vehicles. But early versions of GPS navigation were developed by the Defense Department for military use, with testing beginning as far back as the early 1960s. It wasn't until 1983 that the federal government approved GPS for public use, and the first handheld GPS unit (made by the company Magellan) appeared on the market six years later. It took a little while for the device to catch on, but eventually millions of hunters, anglers, mountain climbers, and hikers would come to rely on handheld GPS units for navigating safely in the outdoors. Most of us began carrying GPS units long before smartphone mapping technology existed. Early models were very simple and slow. The screens were tiny, with a low-resolution grayscale display of your position in relation to the basic contours of the surrounding topography. Still, they offered real-time information that paper maps couldn't provide.

As GPS technology improved, it became possible to gather a much more thorough understanding of the landscape. Navigating electronically through the woods and on the water grew easier with the addition of memory cards loaded with area-specific mapping information, and the tools have become extremely customizable. Handheld GPS units now provide users with the ability to overlay their position on highly detailed topo maps that show place names, water sources, trails, roads, land ownership, and minute elevation contours. GPS units can be loaded with marine charts that show buoys, channel markers, depth soundings, bottom contours, and boating hazards. Last but not least, their waypoint function (see sidebar on page 272) can be used as a record of your movements and means of annotating your maps.

Several companies make good GPS devices, but Garmin is a leader in producing top-notch handheld units. We highly recommend their Montana 610; we've been using this model for years to navigate everywhere from rural checkerboard sections of public and private land to remote, mountainous terrain to the open ocean. It's waterproof, has a large color touchscreen, accepts external mapping chips, and is preloaded with features like a built-in base map, wireless waypoint sharing, and point-to-point navigation. You can also use the sight-and-go tool to create waypoints at specified distances from your position. This is an especially useful tool for hunters, who might down a game animal at a known distance of 300 or 400 yards. With sight-and-go, you can mark a waypoint at the animal's location and then follow the GPS to that point even through thick brush or disorienting terrain. The breadcrumb setting allows you to leave a visible record of your route in case you need to backtrack. Other valuable features include weather updates, sunrise and sunset times, and an alarm clock that can be used at night without burning through any battery power.

Keep in mind that a standard GPS uses micro SD cards. These need to be updated manually, by connecting to a computer. If you enjoy wilderness travel in multiple states, you'll need multiple cards.

GPS AND THE WAYPOINT ADVANTAGE

The ability to use GPS to mark waypoints in advance of or during a trip has made our travel routes through the woods and on the water significantly more efficient and safer. You can drop thousands of waypoints into a single device, from forks on a trail to your ultimate destination. Be sure to create waypoints for the spot where your vehicle is parked at the trailhead as well as the location of your campsite. Doing so could prevent you from getting lost if you're forced to hike back to your rig or tent at night.

The ability to drop waypoints allows you to do more than just get home safely—we're constantly adding waypoints for interesting terrain features, productive fishing holes, active game trails, hilltops that provide a good view, and even stuff like berry bushes and mushroom patches. All those little details add up when you're mapping out a larger landscape on the GPS screen and in your head.

CELLPHONES

It's easy to forget most of us weren't carrying any type of cellphone at all twenty years ago, or that smartphones only came into widespread use in the last decade. Back then, the safety net cellphones provide simply didn't exist for the average outdoorsman or woman. But these days, it would be considered foolish by most people, and negligent by some, if you didn't bring your phone into the woods with you. As long as you're in an area with adequate coverage, you can maintain contact with your friends and family; consult a plethora of apps on subjects from birding to plant identification to constellations; and access any number of books, magazines, or games that might help you pass the time when you're stuck in your tent on a rainy day. Cellphones can even be used by search and rescue crews as a means of locating your position should you become lost or injured. But smartphones are more than just a link to the outside world (with a handy built-in camera). They're also a valuable navigation tool. In fact, they've largely replaced handheld GPS units for many people.

All smartphones have a built-in compass—just remember to calibrate it before using it in the field. Google Earth can be used to obtain bird's-eye and ground-level views of the landscape in advance of trips, or even during trips as long as there's a cell signal. And because smartphones have a built-in GPS capability that can function independently of a cellular signal, you can also use your phone just like you would a handheld GPS unit, provided you've downloaded a mapping app.

We prefer the onX app, because it enables you to download maps of specific areas for use in remote wilderness where there is no hope of finding coverage, no matter how high you climb searching for a signal. Despite claims to the contrary by wireless providers, there are massive gaps in reliable coverage throughout the country in rural areas outside of major population centers. No matter where you are, onX can be used to display the direction in which you are traveling and your exact location down to a few feet. Trails, roads, elevation demarcations, topography, terrain features, water sources, and even vegetation cover are clearly visible. It's also possible to get real-time weather updates, track your progress, and estimate the distance to important landmarks. Sharing waypoints with other onX users directly from the app via text or email is another nice feature that lets you show someone at home your exact itinerary in advance of a trip, or arrange to meet someone at a particular time and place during a trip. All the data saved to the app, such as waypoints and tracks, is also backed up on the company's servers. If you lose your phone, you'll have access to all that information on your new device. Yearly subscriptions are reasonably priced and can be purchased for individual states, or for all fifty states.

Properly equipped, a phone can fulfill many of the functions we once needed specialized devices for. But as handy as smartphones are, they can't do it all, and there are still arguments to be made for carrying other devices: redundancy (as backup in case your phone gets lost or is damaged), durability (some handheld GPS devices are specifically designed to withstand tough environments), and battery life (lithium AAs outperform cellphone batteries).

PERSONAL LOCATOR BEACONS AND SATELLITE MESSENGERS

Dialing 911 to call for emergency medical help or a search and rescue crew isn't an option in areas where reliable cell service doesn't exist. In these locations, the safest bet is to carry a personal locator beacon (PLB) or satellite messenger device. Both systems can communicate emergency distress calls that transmit the user's location via satellite signals. And as long as you have a relatively clear view of the sky, these signals can be acquired pretty much everywhere on the face of the planet. Unless you happen to be trapped in an underground cave system, PLBs and satellite messenger devices offer a fail-safe way to quickly call in the cavalry, no matter where you are or what you're doing. If you spend a lot of time in areas with poor or nonexistent cell coverage, we strongly recommend investing in either a PLB or a satellite messenger. A search and rescue professional recently told us that he thought these devices should be considered mandatory equipment on all trips into the backcountry.

However, there are significant differences between PLBs and satellite messenger devices that you'll want to consider before choosing one over the other. PLB devices are based on the emergency position-indicating radio beacons (EPIRB) used on seagoing vessels in the event of a maritime disaster. Like EPIRBs, personal locator beacons use radio frequencies to send an emergency distress signal and the location from which that signal was sent via global satellite systems. Worldwide, the International Cospas-Sarsat Programme relays emergency notifications to search and rescue operations; in the United States, NOAA is in charge of monitoring PLB signals. By law, you must register PLB devices with NOAA, providing personal contact information and, optionally, pertinent medical information. The process is free, but registrations must be updated every two years.

Personal locator beacons are roughly the size of handheld GPS units. They're durable and waterproof, and their batteries last for five years, with the capability of repeatedly transmitting a distress signal for at least twenty-four hours. When you're navigating through remote areas or hazardous terrain, you can carry a PLB knowing it's going to work if you need to be rescued. Remember, though, that PLBs are single-use devices—once turned on, a PLB signal cannot be shut off or canceled, and search and rescue crews will be rallying to your position. If you decide to activate a PLB, it had better be for a good reason. You should only flip the switch in the event of a life-threatening emergency, serious immobilizing injuries, or when you've become so hopelessly lost that there is no possibility of self-rescue. False alerts can result in fines and other penalties.

Satellite messenger devices have the same ability to send emergency distress signals as personal locator beacons, along with some added features that make them more versatile and user-friendly. All satellite messengers allow you to text-message friends and family to keep them updated on your status when you're in remote terrain. Some have a small selection of preloaded messages like "I'm OK"; others can send and receive personalized texts. This is a handy feature during non-life-threatening situations, whether you twist an ankle or kill a bull elk and need help packing it out. Many satellite messenger devices can also be used to navigate, with similar capabilities as handheld GPS units. And if you absolutely must post your backcountry adventures to your social media accounts in real time, some satellite messenger devices have that option, too. Be prepared to pay more for those added features, and remember that in addition to the purchase price, satellite messengers require activation and subscription fees. Usually you'll need to sign up for a plan with a yearlong commitment. Both SPOT and Garmin make excellent devices that are waterproof and impact-resistant. If you're looking for a simple satellite messenger with the ability to send a few preloaded messages and a distress signal, go with the SPOT Gen3. Garmin's inReach Explorer+ is a more advanced device that can send and receive personalized messages, does double duty as a GPS navigation unit, and pairs with your smartphone. The unit is smaller than a pack of cigarettes.

SATELLITE PHONE

Despite the increasing popularity of satellite messenger devices, satellite phones also provide a dependable line of communication in very remote locations. Although sat phones don't have navigation features like GPS units or smartphones, they're worth mentioning here because they allow you to talk directly with another person in places where you could walk for days without any hope of finding a cellphone signal. We cherish the fact there are still places like that left in the world, but we'll be the first to admit that it's damn nice to be able to talk to your loved ones when you haven't seen them for a while. Almost every year, we'll spend a couple weeks hunting moose or caribou in the Alaska wilderness. On those trips, a satellite phone gets passed around every couple of days or so just to check in with family. We also use our satellite phone to get updates from bush pilots on pickup times, which can get bumped by a few hours or even a few days due to weather. And in the event of an emergency that might require a complicated rescue operation, you can only communicate so much information via texts made with a satellite messenger. Keep in mind, though, that sat phones are expensive to own and operate. A handset will set you back well over a thousand bucks, and service plans start around $50 per month for just ten minutes of talk time. Unlimited plans run hundreds of dollars per month. Renting a satellite phone is a better option for those who will only need the device for a week or two at a time. Globalstar and Iridium both offer satellite phone purchase and rental options.

TWO-WAY RADIOS

Handheld two-way radios, or walkie-talkies, are another electronic voice communication option in the outdoors. Walkie-talkies rely strictly on preset radio frequencies, so they're not as reliable as satellite messengers or satellite phones, but they do work in places that lack wireless coverage. Walkies are often used by groups of people that separate from each other now and then, such as mountaineers who want to communicate with base camp or backcountry hunters who split up and hike into different areas each day. Two-way radios can be used to communicate throughout the day with members of your own party on preselected radio channels. Should an emergency arise, a two-way radio will also enable you to get in touch with anyone else in the general area who is using a radio. This might be other hunters or hikers, or the law enforcement officers and game wardens who frequently monitor these channels. The latter category brings up the point that conversations among your group might be heard by anyone using the same channel and subchannel you're using. Keep this in mind if you're discussing sensitive information.

Still, anyone who has used walkie-talkies knows they don't offer a failsafe line of communication. Their range can reach up to 20 miles or more in flat, open terrain; but in broken, mountainous topography or thick woods, communication between users can be limited to a mile or two. Cloud cover, precipitation, and lightning can also interfere with two-way radio signals. For safety's sake, they should only be considered short-range communication devices. We recommend investing in devices that combine walkie-talkie features with GPS navigation units, like the Garmin Rino 700 series.

CELLPHONE AND MAPPING APP TIPS

No matter what type of additional devices you might be carrying with you, your cellphone can offer a lot of bang for the buck when you're in the outdoors. Here are a few ways to make sure you're getting the most out of your device.

- Invest in a quality phone case even if your phone is rated to withstand submersion in water. The best cases protect against not only water but also impact and dust. We like OtterBox and LifeProof phone cases. Also put a screen protector on your phone for added insurance.

- Set your phone to airplane mode and low-power mode unless you need to use it to communicate. On these settings, a full charge can last several days and even longer if you turn your phone off when it's not needed.
- Pay up for the full version of any GPS app you're using in order to download maps for offline use. (And don't forget to actually download the maps while you still have reliable service.)
- Check your orientation. You can orient your GPS mapping app to its default setting, true north, with the top of the screen reflecting north in the orientation typical to paper maps, or to your own changing position, so that the top of the screen reflects the direction you're facing. Many folks find it easier to navigate by orienting the screen with the second method.
- Use the app's tracking function to create an electronic breadcrumb trail when traveling through unfamiliar terrain. Tracking mode will eat up more battery, but it can be extremely useful if you get turned around. The tracking function is especially helpful when you need to retrace your route in the dark. Without really thinking about it, you are constantly dodging to the left and right of obstacles when you're traveling in the daylight. Even when walking in a "straight" line, you go around steep ledges and steer clear of briar patches. When returning in the dark along the same course, you're likely to stumble into these obstacles due to the lack of visibility. The track function helps you follow the more nuanced course that you chose while enjoying the luxury of long-range visibility.
- If you're not using the tracking function, use the app to mark waypoints for campsites, forks in the trail, and landmarks big and small. Make a habit of dropping waypoints—you can always delete them later if you don't need them.
- Always be sure to start the trip by marking a waypoint for your car as well as your destination.
- Use your phone for self-rescue. In the event that you are lost or injured without cell service or a PLB, turn off your phone when you're not using it in order to preserve battery—but occasionally turn it on and off again. Search and rescue may be able to triangulate your position if your phone successfully pings a nearby tower or two.
- Charge all devices fully prior to leaving your vehicle or home,

and carry external chargers and/or backup batteries for all electronic devices.

NAVIGATING WITHOUT ELECTRONICS

As should be clear by now, we don't set out on outdoor adventures of any length without prepping and charging a few essential pieces of tech. But there are lots of reasons we also pack paper maps and traditional compasses—from doubling up in case of loss to the additional functionality these tools provide.

Paper map. There's nothing wrong with relying primarily on paper maps; they worked for hundreds of years and still work today. What we recommend, however, is an approach to navigation that takes advantage of both electronic and traditional navigation methods. Used in conjunction with electronics, paper maps can prevent you from getting boxed in by the confines of a small screen on your phone or GPS unit. They open your area up for full view and can provide an illuminating perspective on your surroundings. By far, quadrangles are the best maps for on-the-ground use in the United States. Commonly known as "quads," they come in varying scales and are named after physiographic features—so you might buy a quad for Burnt Fork Lake in Montana. A map scale of 1:24,000 with 40-foot contour interval lines provides a high level of detail in an easily digestible way; such a map covers between 48 and 70 square miles, with a mile of ground being represented by 3 inches of map space.

The best paper maps are not, in fact, made of paper—they're printed on Tyvek and other waterproof, tearproof, and durable materials. Ordering them online should give you access to the best quality maps, along with the added benefit of customization. A backcountry trip of any length is almost certain to cover an area that expands beyond a single quadrangle. While it's common practice to carry a stack of quads folded up in a gallon-size zip-lock bag, you often find that you're carrying a lot of extra paper and only using a small corner of some of your maps. Instead, you can order a single custom map from a printer such as MyTopo .com and specify the size, scale, and area of coverage. It's a great tool, especially for areas where you'll be spending significant amounts of time.

Compass. When your phone or GPS device fails, runs out of juice, gets misplaced, or dies a watery death, you'll want a traditional compass.

Buy a good one. Nothing reduces your faith in a compass quite like watching it stagger and stop as it tries to orient itself toward magnetic north. Be suspicious of any compass that is built into something else. A $2 compass glued to a Rambo knife or a deer call might not prove to be your

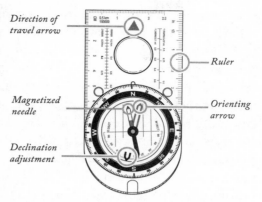

Direction of travel arrow

Ruler

Magnetized needle

Orienting arrow

Declination adjustment

best friend in a time of true need. But you don't need to max out your credit card to get a valuable tool. You can get a Suunto A-30 or Silva Explorer for around thirty bucks. They are durable, reliable, and easily packable.

A compass is essential for applying that broader sense of spatial awareness that we advocated above. If you're in a boat that gets caught in a fog bank, and you know that a commercial shipping channel lies to the north, open ocean lies to the west, and the beach lies to the south, you're gonna want to know which way you're drifting. Compasses are also a great companion to paper maps. They allow you to orient your map toward the north, so you know which way you're facing and which way your map is facing. Without this information, your ability to use a map is seriously limited because you can't effectively place yourself in the map's context. With an oriented map, you're able to identify surrounding landmarks and correlate them to your own position. You can easily put a name and location to distant peaks, lakes, ridgelines, and other features that are in your view.

For precise compass use, it's necessary to set the declination. In most locations around the world, magnetic north—which is where your compass will point—is not the same as true north. Most maps will give you the necessary declination, or correction, for the area you're in, so that you can adjust your compass. For instance, the quad for Burnt Fork Lake, Montana, calls for an 18.5° east correction. In that case, magnetic north

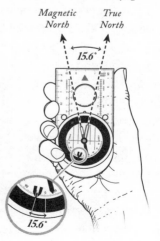

Magnetic North

True North

15.6°

15.6°

is skewed eastward of true north. Using an uncorrected compass, you could be off course by over 600 yards after only 1 mile of walking.

A compass allows you to take a bearing, which is just a precise way of describing a direction. Knowing that your truck is to "the north" is helpful, but that limited amount of information is hardly gonna land you at the exact spot. Once you've adjusted your compass for the declination, true north is at 0°. Due east would be 90°. Due south is 180°. West, 270°. Bearings can become very fine-tuned, down to fractions of a degree, but for general on-the-ground navigation you seldom need to operate with more specificity than a single degree. Knowing that your truck is at a bearing of 341° is going to land you pretty damn close if you can stay on course. A good method for orienteering when using bearings is to identify landmarks (prominent trees, rocky outcrops, cellphone towers, etc.) that are on the line of travel you need to assume. Then you travel to the landmark. From there, take a new compass bearing and pick off your next target. That saves you the hassle of trying to walk or paddle or run an engine with your compass in your hand, and it lends itself to much greater accuracy.

Triangulation

A compass can also help you pinpoint your exact location on a map through the use of triangulation. To pull this off, you must have a map, and you must be able to see multiple physical landmarks (such as fire towers, peaks, or lakes) that are represented on the map.

Step 1: Set the declination on your compass, and then use the compass to get your map oriented to true north.

Step 2: Take a bearing on a physical landmark that you can see in the distance. On your map, draw a line that begins at the landmark and crosses the map along the course of the bearing. If you're somewhere on a trail but you don't know where, the intersection of

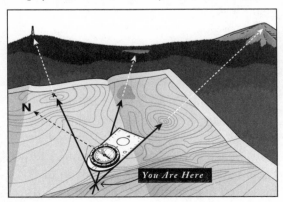

You Are Here

this bearing line and the trail on the map will give you a good idea of where you're standing.

Step 3: If you still can't locate yourself (you can't tell if you're 5 miles from the peak or 2 miles), you need to repeat the process with another landmark—ideally one that's at least 60° or so away from the first landmark. When you draw that line on the map, you'll pinpoint yourself in the vicinity of where the two lines cross.

Step 4: Repeat with additional landmarks, if possible, to fine-tune your positioning.

TOOL-FREE NAVIGATION TECHNIQUES

A map and compass might seem quaint in this day and age, but those things are cutting-edge technologies compared to such ancient navigation tools as the sun, stars, wind, and clouds. These tools might not be as user friendly and precise as modern instruments, but you don't have to pay for them, and they never run out of batteries. Even if you never wind up using these techniques, it's nice to know that with a little knowledge and woodsmanship, you could be empty-handed and still get yourself out of a jam in an unfamiliar place. The movement of air and the travel patterns of animals can also be useful directional clues. Light pollution emitted by nearby cities is a less romantic but equally useful source of information.

The Sun

Folks of a certain age will recall the old American Airlines ditty, "From the sunrise in the east to the sunset in the west, we're American Airlines, doing what we do best." It's an infectious and handy way to remember an important detail about our most basic celestial navigation aid. But don't get too cocky when it comes to navigating through use of the sun's position, because it only rises *exactly* due east and sets *exactly* due west two days a year—on the spring and fall equinoxes. Every other day of the year, the sun sets and rises either slightly to the north or south of those positions. The sun reaches the apex of its northerly travels on the summer solstice, and reaches the southern point of its winter travels on the winter solstice.

There are a handful of ways to derive a more precise sense of direction from the sun, regardless of the season. The most basic and easy to remember approach is the stick-and-shadow method, which requires fairly clear skies. Find a stick about a yard long and poke it into the ground in the center of a small clearing during the midday period. Mark the end of the stick's shadow with a pebble or other small object. Then wait fifteen or so minutes and mark the end of the stick's shadow. A line drawn between the two pebbles will be an approximate east-west line. The second pebble sits to the east of the first. Intersect this line perpendicularly and you'll have an approximate north-south line.

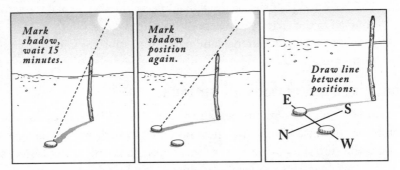

Use the stick-and-shadow method to set your bearings.

The Stars

Like the sun, all of the stars and planets (including the moon) rise in an easterly direction and set in a westerly direction. And, like the sun, they are an imprecise means of gauging direction. A more accurate approach is to find the celestial poles by using the Big Dipper in the Northern Hemisphere and the Southern Cross in the Southern Hemisphere.

In the Northern Hemisphere, the North Star is the most accurate natural navigation aid. Commonly known as Polaris, it appears to remain fixed in the night sky. From the perspective of an earthling, the rest of the stars and constellations spin around this fixed northern point like a wheel around a hub. The convenient thing about Polaris is that it can be

located through the aid of the Big Dipper, which is one of the most easily identified constellations. Using the distance between the outer two stars in the Big Dipper's cup as a unit of measurement, go six spaces away from the cup. That bright shining star where you've landed is the North Star.

Celestial south is not marked by a star; rather, mariners refer to that portion of the night sky as the "southern pit," as it's noticeably void of stars. However, the constellation known as Crux, or the Southern Cross, can effectively point you to the south. Using the distance between the "head" and "foot" of the Southern Cross

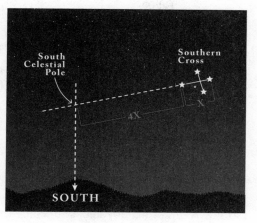

as a unit of measurement, you'll find the celestial south pole located four units down from the foot of the cross.

Light Pollution

Although it can put a damper on your stargazing, come nightfall, light pollution can be put to use as a navigation aid. You could be dozens of miles away from even a small community and still see the stain of its light on the horizon at night. Since the pollution will penetrate skyward for quite a ways, it's still possible to see human settlements even when they're hidden deep down in canyons, behind ranges of mountains or hills, or over the roll of the horizon when you're far out at sea. Large development sites such as airports and refineries throw enough light pollution to be seen from great distances as well.

Wind

Knowing the dominant wind direction in an area where you're traveling is another helpful piece of information. However, dominant wind directions can change seasonally as well as in accordance with shifting weather patterns. In areas with topographical relief, thermal-driven movements of air can also affect wind patterns. Still, the movement of air can be a helpful navigation aid when you combine that piece of knowledge with an array of other natural navigation aids.

Birds

The movements of animals and evidence of their passing can be helpful navigation aids. (See page 60 for information about using wildlife to find drinking water.) In the Northern Hemisphere, large, high-flying

V-shaped flights of migratory waterfowl (ducks and geese) will generally be headed north in the spring and south in the summer, vice versa in the Southern Hemisphere. On the ocean, the presence of birds can signify nearby landmasses. Pelagic birds such as frigate birds, albatrosses, and boobies can be found hundreds of miles from land, though ocean-dwelling birds that roost out of the water (pelicans, cormorants) seldom stray too far. Birds that are incapable of landing on water—finches, sparrows, warblers, etc.—are either very close to land or very lost.

GETTING LOST

No government agency keeps official records of how many people get lost in the woods or on the waters of the United States every year. However, a number of private estimates suggest dozens of people get lost every day. The Coast Guard, National Park Service, Forest Service, county sheriffs, state police, local agencies, and volunteers embark on tens of thousands of search and rescue missions every year. Many, if not most, of the people they're looking for are outdoor enthusiasts, and no users group is immune to getting lost. You might think that people who spend more time far back in remote areas are more likely to get lost, but in fact, day hikers are one of the most likely groups of people to get lost. One study found that 41 percent of folks lost in the woods had simply wandered off the trail. In general, more search and rescue operations are conducted in mountainous areas than any other environment, but plenty of people get lost hiking trails in small county parks and suburban open spaces, too. Additionally, more young and middle-aged men get lost than any other demographic; men are more likely to overestimate their ability to navigate without maps, and push forward when they should be turning around.

No two stories about getting lost are ever the same, but there are recurring themes. Situational awareness, preparedness, knowledge of an area, simple common sense, and a fair bit of grit seem to be shared among those who get found, while the one unifying characteristic of people who get lost or die out of doors is that they were unprepared for the environment and unfamiliar with the landscape.

SIGNALING FOR HELP

Let's assume that, despite following the advice we've laid out, you're lost. Some survival guidebooks of generations past spilled a lot of ink on getting rescued by building a signal fire to send messages through various patterns of smoke. We're not going to follow suit. Sure, smoke generated by a fire of your own making might help identify your location to people who are looking for you. A search and rescue crew on foot could potentially spot a campfire smoke column from miles away and a helicopter might fly directly to your location. But while smoke can attract rescuers' attention under the right conditions, making a particular pattern with smoke isn't going to make a damn bit of difference. All you really need to do is build a big fire and cover it with green leaves, rubber tires, or anything else that will generate a lot of smoke. Remember, though, you'll need to keep the fire burning and the smoke rising long enough to get noticed. That will take a lot of wood and time. And if conditions are windy enough to obliterate your smoke signal or prevent you from getting a fire started, you'd better have a backup signaling plan.

That said, there are many ways to signal for help, and the choice of which to use will largely be dictated by your position, your situation, and the resources at your disposal. The most reliable method under any conditions is to use a Garmin InReach, SPOT locator, EPIRB, or other emergency satellite beacon. You may also be able to communicate a distress signal using a cellphone, walkie-talkie, or VHF radio. But, lacking such electronic devices, you can use sight or sound. Visual and audio signals can help search and rescue crews home in on your location and alert folks who aren't even looking for you that you're in trouble. Make sure you're carrying emergency signaling items like whistles, mirrors, and flashlights.

- Shouting for help is a good place to start if you're separated from your group or think there may be other people in the area.
- The international emergency audio distress signal, or mayday signal, is three of any sound you can make. That's based on the Morse code for SOS ("save our souls"), which is three short taps or blasts, then three long taps, then three short taps, spelling S-O-S. Sounding off three blasts on a car horn, air horn, or whistle can be used as a distress signal, as can firing three gunshots. Keep in mind, though, that gunshots may be ignored in heavily hunted areas.
- Building three fires or repeatedly flashing a mirror three times are good visual SOS signals.
- Most boats (page 337) and airplanes are required to have signal flares on board in case of emergency. Remember, flare gun kits only have a

few cartridges. They may attract the attention of passing planes or boats, but they'll be most useful if you have a good reason to believe they'll be seen by search and rescue teams.

- Lost hikers and hunters have saved their skins by piling rocks or branches to spell "HELP" or "SOS" in giant letters on snowy mountaintops and open fields. Passing planes at relatively high altitude might see a message if you write it big enough.
- Colorful or reflective flagging that contrasts with the surrounding area is an effective visual distress signal. Fluorescent orange hunting vests, Mylar space blankets, and brightly colored clothing, sleeping bags, or tents will attract notice.
- Roadside flares, car headlights, boat running lights, fires, glowsticks, headlamps, and flashlights can all be seen from long distances at night.

SHOULD YOU STAY OR SHOULD YOU GO?

If you're truly lost without any form of communication or navigation tools, stay calm, stop moving, and don't panic. Take the time to think before you act. The smartest, safest plan is to wait for rescuers to find you. Across the board, search and rescue professionals recommend staying put when you're lost. It's almost always easier to locate people who remain in one spot than to locate a moving target. Despite that advice, a study of lost hikers in the Smoky Mountains found that two out of three people kept moving rather than staying in place, but only a quarter of the lost hikers who tried to find their way out actually managed to do so. The rest were found by search and rescue teams.

But how long should you wait for search and rescue? And what happens if nobody knows you're lost? Or maybe someone knows you should have returned home from a trip but they have no idea where you might be. What if days pass, you're out of food or water, and all your attempts at signaling for help go unnoticed? There are some circumstances when it makes more sense to try finding your way to safety on your own rather than wait to be found.

Let's say you're hunting an unfamiliar patch of thick, swampy midwestern woods and you get hopelessly turned around just as the sun is setting. But you know the area is a cookie-cutter pattern of 1-square-mile pieces of land that are surrounded by a grid of dirt roads on all sides. Unless you're injured and immobilized, all you really have to do is pick a direction and start walking. Before too long, you'll run into a road. From there, head one way or the other and pretty soon you'll find a farmhouse or a passing vehicle.

Now imagine you're on an early fall overnight through-hike in a remote wilderness area. You were planning on camping along the trail, but somewhere along the way you veered off it by mistake. You try to find your way back to the trail without any luck, and when darkness falls, you pitch your tent. During the night a foot of snow falls, and when you wake up, you have no clue where you are. But your ride is expecting to pick you up that afternoon at a trailhead. Your best bet is to locate an open area where rescuers can find you, build a fire, and hunker down.

Not every situation will be as clear-cut as those examples. Your decision to stay or go when you're lost should be based on a number of factors. If someone knows your plan, stay put. It's also smart to remain near a trail or with a stuck or broken-down vehicle. But if you're sure no one knows where you are and there is no one looking for you, your only choice may be to move. Never wander aimlessly, though. Develop a plan. For instance, it's never a good idea to keep moving at night, unless you're very confident you're headed in the right direction. Wait until morning to move—you may be able to determine compass directions, identify landmarks, or follow a stream to a trail or road. Pick a heading that will keep you moving in as straight a line as possible and stick to it. Stay calm, remain positive, and set achievable goals for yourself. Rushing will only make matters worse. You'll end up getting injured or panicked enough to make irrational decisions that will only worsen your situation. Move methodically and safely across the landscape and you've got a good chance of saving yourself.

NAVIGATING THROUGH DIFFERENT ENVIRONMENTS

There are certain absolutes when it comes to navigation and orienteering: compasses point north, the sun rises more or less in the east and sets more or less in the west, rivers flow downhill. But a lot also hinges on the type of landscape you'll be traveling through. From the Arctic tundra to the high desert to rainforest jungles, we've spent time in just about every type of large-scale environment on the planet. Over and over, we've learned the important lesson that each environment comes with its own set of navigational challenges. Paddling a canoe down a coastal river in Oregon will be much different from paddling down a river in Iowa's farm country. Moreover, you'll often find different navigational challenges within the same environment. In Colorado's Holy Cross Wilderness, crossing a 2-mile section of lodgepole pine that was leveled like scattered toothpicks by a windstorm could take the better part of a day. On the other hand, you could traverse the open alpine park a hundred yards uphill from that tangled patch of lodgepole pine in just thirty minutes. The lesson here is that unless you've spent a bunch of time learning the nuances of a particular landscape, you're probably going to run into unexpected obstacles. And even when you do have a good idea of how to navigate a certain type of environment, you shouldn't let your experience lead to overconfidence. Mother Nature has a way of throwing you curveballs: fog banks can reduce visibility to near zero; heavy rainfall that happens 20 miles away can turn a small creek you were planning to wade across into a torrent of whitewater; what appeared to be a navigable slope on a map might end in a sheer cliff face that forces you to backtrack to search for a better route. It's wise to have a solid plan for getting from point A to point B—but be prepared to adjust that plan in order to get back home safely. Finally, bear in mind that the various environments and ecosystems described in the following pages often border or overlap one another. You might hike through a desert to reach the mountains, or cross a swamp to reach the coast. It's wise to prepare for every environmental challenge you might have to deal with.

MOUNTAINS

It's often been said, "The mountain doesn't care about you." While that sentiment can be applied to just about every environment from the desert to the ocean, the mountains are where many of us first developed a clear understanding that the landscape itself can kill you, if you fail to pay it the proper amount of respect. Out of all the different types of landscapes in North America, we've collectively spent more time in mountain environments than anywhere else. The midwestern woodlots, farm fields, lakes, and streams where I hunted and fished as a kid were a good training ground for many of the skills discussed in this book, but the Rocky Mountains were where I learned how to navigate large, roadless tracts of land. Because I grew up as a flatlander, it took me a while to get used to the scope of the landscapes that straddle the Continental Divide. In the Intermountain West, the peaks top out several thousand feet above the valley floor. And many of those craggy peaks are covered in snow and ice all year. Unlike the rest of the country, where you can walk a mile or two in any direction and run into a well-traveled paved road, you might have to cross an entire mountain range just to find a two-track dirt road that rarely sees any traffic at all. Then there are the places where roads don't exist. The large majority of federally designated roadless wilderness areas, where motorized travel of any form is illegal, are found in the Rockies. And even where federal law doesn't prohibit motorized travel, there is still a lot of big, wild country left there.

There's plenty of it left in other mountain ranges, too. Alaska is crisscrossed with ranges that are far more remote than any in the Lower 48. The mountains of the Coastal, Cascade, and Olympic ranges in the Pacific Northwest are just as big and bad as the Rockies, but with thick vegetation and near-constant rainfall and fog. Arizona's isolated "sky island" mountains are surrounded by the arid deserts. Back east, the mountains may not rise as high as the Rockies, but in places they're just as rugged and dangerous. In New York's Adirondack Mountains, there are peaks that rise into areas of treeless alpine tundra. At the northern end of the Appalachian Mountains, New Hampshire's Mount Washington is one of the country's most dangerous peaks. It's known for some of the most extreme weather conditions in the entire country—winds there have been recorded at over 200 miles an hour. Over 160 people have died from exposure, falling, and other backcountry mishaps on Mount Washington's slopes.

The first step toward avoiding that fate is to get in what we call "mountain shape." Physical exertion at high altitudes takes a toll on the human body even when you're in decent condition, so you can't expect to be able to take on a multi-day hiking adventure in the mountains if you're in poor physical shape. Doing so will lead to injuries like torn muscles, sprained ankles, or worse. The same goes for traveling from sea level to high altitudes. One of the biggest safety precautions you should take for a trip into the mountains is to exercise regularly and acclimate yourself to high-altitude environments before hitting the trail. Being in good shape minimizes the risk of altitude sickness (covered on page 363) and allows you to truly enjoy yourself in the mountains.

It is also important to understand that when you're in the mountains, you'll have to contend with more than just rapid rises in elevation. A single mountain range can often support a wide range of micro-environments, geology, vegetation, and terrain. Experienced elk hunters know the animals prefer to feed on open, grassy, south-facing sides of ridges before bedding down on the timbered north side. That's the kind of knowledge that can make a big difference when you're choosing a route through the mountains. Extended hiking trips could take you through multiple landscapes, including lush river bottoms, high desert scrublands, brush-choked hillsides, thick timber, rocky avalanche chutes, and treeless alpine basins. In some mountains, you might also run into swampy beaver ponds, loose scree slopes, narrow cliff bands, and other navigational impediments. In other words, sometimes just getting around can be a pain in the ass, but it will be a little easier if you know what to expect.

Mountains present inherent challenges other than steep slopes, thin air, and constantly changing landscapes. Notably, they create their own weather, and they can create it with little advance notice. From hurricane-force winds in the winter to violent summer thunderstorms to early fall blizzards, severe mountain weather events can happen at any time. The unpredictability stems from the warm air that rises from surrounding valleys and drops in temperature at higher elevations, collecting moisture along the way. Another contributing factor is the uneven, upthrusting topography of the mountains, which alters predominant wind patterns unpredictably. This volatile mix of air currents adds up to a recipe for isolated storms that can drop large quantities of rain or snow in a short period of time. Many times, we've watched blizzards and thunderstorms pound a mountain just a couple miles from our location on a warm, sunny slope. And just as often, we've had storms build up right on top of us in a matter of minutes. These storms tend to pass pretty quickly, but it's not unusual to get socked in by weather systems that get hung up in the mountains. We've huddled in our tents for days riding out mountain storms that brought continuous bands of fog, rain, and snow, broken up by occasional periods of clear, sunny skies called "sucker holes." These sucker holes can fool you into thinking the worst has passed, but it's best to wait a while to confirm that it's safe to start moving again.

DOS AND DON'TS OF MOUNTAIN NAVIGATION

- Do check the map for streams. Man-made trails and game trails that offer easy travel routes often parallel streams. If a stream happens to run in a direction that's convenient to your destination, using the stream's riparian corridor to travel will usually provide a pathway that is less thickly forested and flatter.
- Do head downhill to escape high winds and precipitation. Generally, conditions are worse uphill than downhill.
- Do hike on switchbacks. Instead of going straight up the side of the

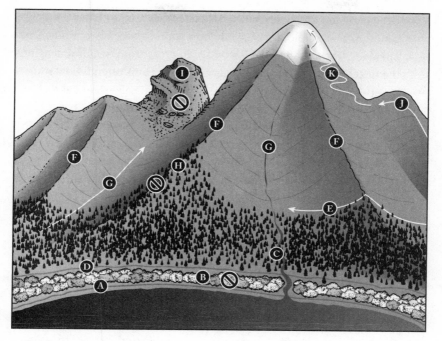

A: Game trails

B: Thick brush

C: Streams

D: Trails between timber and brush

E: Sidehilling

F: Ridges

G: Drainage bottoms

H: Heavily timbered steep slopes

I: Loose, overhanging rock

J: Saddles

K: Switchbacking

mountain and burning the hell out of your quads, conserve your energy by taking trails that zigzag up the face of a mountain. You can do this even where man-made trails don't exist by following natural contours. You'll be adding some mileage, but it's easier, both mentally and physically, to hike manageable travel routes than to struggle up steep slopes. In the end, you'll save time without wearing yourself out.

- Do sidehill. If a steep ridge or mountain stands between you and your destination and it's possible to skirt the obstacle entirely, you may be able to conserve massive amounts of energy and time. You'll often find game trails that sidehill around a steep terrain feature rather than going straight over it.

- Do hike along ridges. The spine, or top, of a ridge is an ideal travel route that provides ready-made, flat trails, saving you all kinds of trouble. Use smaller finger ridges to connect to larger main ridges.

- Do use mountain passes and saddles. Saddles are just what they sound like—a shallow U-shaped depression between two mountains or ridges. They're often the best place to cross from one drainage into the next. Established hiking trails and game trails often follow routes to saddles and passes. Mountain passes are typically found at the head of drainages. To travel between large mountains when a pathway isn't obvious, find an alpine basin by following creeks upstream. These basins are large-scale versions of saddles at the upper terminus of a water system.

- If you get completely turned around in the mountains, heading downhill is a solid plan. In general, you're more likely to find help in a valley than on top of a mountain. But before you start moving, you may want to climb to a good vantage point to see if you can spot any roads or human settlements that you can hike toward.

- Don't get cliffed out. Getting cliffed out is a scary, dangerous situation. It usually happens in the middle of a climb up a steep face when you discover that you can't safely climb any higher or get back down without falling. Essentially, you're stuck on the side of a cliff. Study your topo maps before you choose a path; the closer together the contour lines are stacked, the steeper the climb. But remember, even a detailed topo map might not tell you there is a 20-foot cliff band on the side of a ridge that is going to be impassable. Go where the contour lines are spaced wider apart if you can.

- Don't be a gambler. One mistake we've made a bunch of times in the mountains is to take a chance on a shortcut. It's tempting to look for shortcuts when you're faced with a 5-mile nighttime hike back to your camp, but unless the way in was truly treacherous, it's usually better to stick with the path you know—even if it sucks. What might appear to be the fastest, easiest path could end up being the most difficult, dangerous route.

- Don't assume you can walk in a straight line. You can get so focused on your phone or GPS that you make the mistake of forging ahead in a straight line to your destination when it doesn't make sense. Your GPS can't account for things like timber blowdowns, thick brush, scree fields, boulder fields, and other natural impediments to traveling quickly and safely. Sometimes it makes more sense to take a roundabout route to your destination.

- Don't lose elevation. When climbing steep slopes, avoid losing elevation in order to dodge obstructions or search for easier routes.

Even if the uphill path is brutally steep and slow and the downhill path seems clearer and faster, you'll often waste time and energy by dropping down and then climbing back up again.

- Do recognize that there's a difference between hiking and mountaineering. Hikers should resist the temptation to access areas that can't be reached using your hands, legs, and a set of trekking poles. Equipment such as harnesses, ascending cams, belay devices, and quick-draws are highly technical. To use them, you need hands-on experience under the guidance of expert instructors.

SNOW AND ICE

In much of the world, snow and ice are regarded as a novel aesthetic treat if and when they occur at all. They can make for some temporarily hazardous driving conditions, sure, but they come and go within a few days and don't change the course of your life all that much. In other places, snow and ice are very real obstacles (or assets, depending on your viewpoint) that can define the landscape for months on end—or even the majority of the year. In these regions, learning how to deal with snow and ice is hardly optional. If you want to maximize your opportunities in the wild, you need to get comfortable traveling through frozen landscapes.

SNOW TRAVEL

Shallow snow—say, up to 12 inches—is fairly benign. It can soak your boots and make for slippery conditions, but these annoyances are easily solved with proper footwear, gaiters, and traction devices or ice grippers that can be strapped to your boots. It's common to see people out snowshoeing in ankle-deep snow as a form of recreation, but from a practical standpoint snowshoes are pointless if you're looking to cover ground in snow at this depth. The added weight and klutziness of the snowshoes make them a hindrance rather than a help until the snow accumulates to the depth of your upper shins or knees.

Deep snow is exhausting to walk through and completely changes your normal patterns of muscle use and fatigue. While a typical dryland hike of 5 miles might make your hamstrings a little sore, a mile of walking through deep snow could bring agony to every muscle from your calves to your lower back. When trudging through snow with companions, put your most powerful hiker in the lead to break trail. It might feel awkward to those who are following, but they should place their footsteps in the leader's boot tracks in order to minimize drag from the snow. If possible, switch leaders on a regular basis in order to maximize the collective longevity of the group.

"Post-holing" is a term for walking through snow that's deep enough to inhibit your normal stride. Instead of taking a step as you normally would, you punch your foot straight down through the snow and draw it straight up before thrusting it forward. It's not easy or enjoyable, and it's especially bad when a crust forms on the snow and you have to apply pressure just to bust through. In such cases, traveling at night or early in the morning can be beneficial, as the colder temperatures will freeze or stiffen the crust and you might be able to cruise along the surface without breaking through. However, hard-crusted snow that supports your weight can also become a hazard on steep slopes. If you slip and start to slide, stopping can be extremely difficult. On a 30° slope, your body can hit nearly the same speed as it would during a free fall. When there's a heightened risk of falling, take the time to kick in foot placements before you take a step. An ice axe, a sharpened stick, or even a knife can be used to carve out especially hardened snow.

Snowshoes will increase the surface area of your foot and prevent you from sinking in. Designs have come a long way since the traditional wooden frames wrapped in a webbing of rawhide. The most versatile and durable snowshoes have a tubular metal frame fitted with synthetic decking materials and hinged, easy-to-use bindings that accommodate a variety of boot styles. Most come equipped with toothed metal plates positioned beneath the ball of the foot to act as crampons that grip ice and crusted snow. Models that feature serrated metal plates on the heel and along the sides can provide additional traction. A pair of ski poles or trekking poles is helpful when snowshoeing, especially on slopes, in rocky terrain, or while balancing a heavy backpack.

Of course, in the right context, skis will enable you to travel long distances much more efficiently than snowshoes. The best skis for off-trail travel through mixed terrain are called Nordic touring skis. They are usually shorter, fatter, and stiffer than classic cross-country skis, which are best used on groomed trails. Nordic touring skis almost always come with metal edges, which are a must for turning in snow depths ranging from just a few inches of consolidated snow to several feet of accumulated powder. They come in a range of widths and lengths, suitable for everything from flatlands to steep downhill slopes. As the terrain becomes steeper, you'll want to go with increasingly longer, wider, and heavier skis that are closer to traditional downhill skis. The same principle applies to boots and bindings. The burlier the ski, the burlier the binding and boot need to be to control and turn the skis while going downhill at a higher rate of speed. This increased downhill performance does come at the cost of increased weight. Lighter setups sacrifice control going downhill, but they do make going uphill easier.

To ascend slopes on skis, you'll either need skis with a fish-scale finish on the bottom or a set of skins to attach to your skis. Skins were originally made from seal hides that native peoples of the Arctic strapped onto skis to travel more efficiently across snowy landscapes. Today, skins are made of nylon and mohair fabric, attached by a reusable glue that keeps them stuck to the base of the ski. The glue comes off easily without leaving a residue. The hairs in the fabric are all positioned in a rearward direction. As you slide your skis uphill, the hairs lie flat against the base of the ski; as you pause to apply weight to the ski to kick forward again, the hairs are pushed down into the snow. Fish scales are a raised, overlapping pattern stamped or molded into the base of the ski below where your boot attaches to the binding on the top of the ski. They work the same way as skins, providing uphill traction while preventing rearward slip. Both systems work well, but some folks feel scaled skis are more convenient since there's no need to pack skins, strap them on your skis, and then take them off when they're not needed.

ICE TRAVEL

For some, walking on a frozen body of water engenders an almost primal fear. No doubt, the thought of being trapped in a bath of death-inducing ice water is unpleasant. It can be especially bad when you have to pioneer a route onto new ice without the encouragement of seeing others who've ventured before you. In our view, however, while ice certainly deserves respect, it needn't be feared. Common sense and a healthy dose of caution should keep you on the surface of the ice and not beneath it.

The two primary considerations when considering ice safety are thickness and quality. Both can be assessed by chopping a hole in the ice with an axe, spud, or auger. For thickness, there are some generally accepted rules of thumb—*generally* being the keyword, as there is considerable debate about what constitutes safety when traveling on the ice.

Any measurement guidelines assume that you're dealing with quality ice. The best stuff is dark but clear. White ice is caused by bubbles and frozen snow; it is not as strong as dark ice. Ice that is more than a few weeks old often has a stratified appearance that comes from freeze/thaw cycles and the addition of snow. The ice will show distinct layers when viewed from the side as a cutaway. The top layer might appear soft and

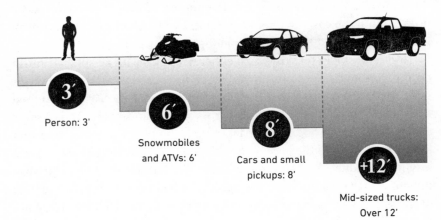

Person: 3'

Snowmobiles
and ATVs: 6'

Cars and small
pickups: 8'

Mid-sized trucks:
Over 12'

shitty in warm weather, while the bottom layers remain hard. If the top layer is really bad, subtract its depth from your measurement and just take the good stuff into account. Ice travel can be annoying (and terribly wet) when an accumulation of snow falls on the ice and then melts, creating a layer of slush or even open water that sits on top of the ice. The weight of the snow can also press down on the ice, causing water to come up from beneath and flood the ice through holes and open edges. Sometimes the surface of this water will then freeze, creating additional layers of ice with water sandwiched between them. Again, when assessing ice safety, disregard these upper layers of ice and rely only on the lower layers of good, uninterrupted ice.

Ice is seldom uniform over an entire body of water. Current can have dramatic impacts on thickness. In a river, for instance, it's possible to have ice that's safe enough to drive on along the shore while the fast-moving center channel remains completely unfrozen. What makes traveling on frozen rivers and creeks particularly dangerous, beyond just the variabilities of ice thickness, is that the current can carry you away from your hole if you bust through. You have little chance of breaking an exit hole through the ice from underwater. If you get swept away from the hole you went through, you're likely dead. Even the frequent passage of muskrats and beavers swimming beneath the ice can have major impacts on ice thickness. Near their dens and lodges, these aquatic rodents can create narrow leads of open water or thin ice. An unsuspecting ice fisherman might step on 10 inches of ice with one foot and then plunge through a semi-frozen beaver run with the next step. Subsurface springs, tributaries, decaying aquatic vegetation, and pressure cracks from high wind that actually move the ice can all create unsafe conditions on bodies of water that are otherwise safe. You need to constantly monitor the condition of ice between your feet or vehicle. Do this by testing the ice often with your axe or spud, and by watching for color changes in the ice. Often, abrupt changes in color will betray ice of varying vintages. Check it out before proceeding. And keep your ears open. Ice can make a lot of noise, and not all of it is bad. Echoing booms and cracks that seem to travel across the body of water often signify thickening and expanding ice. Sharp cracks that come from directly beneath your feet are often a bad sign.

Ice is buoyant. Its strength relies on the fact that it floats and is supported from beneath by the water. Falling water levels, especially in rivers, can create hazardous conditions where ice is hanging over open air. This ice will give out with very little pressure and land you in open water beneath that has yet to refreeze. Occasionally, water levels in rivers will drop drastically and then refreeze, creating open-air caverns between the two layers of ice. On rare occasions, people have been trapped by falling into these caverns.

Wind presents another risk when you're traveling on ice, particularly on the frozen bays and inlets of larger bodies of water that otherwise remain open. Strong winds can actually blow rafts of ice out to sea, carrying along ice fishermen or other adventurers who then have no way to reach dry ground. In the Great Lakes region, it's a common occurrence to hear of helicopter and hovercraft rescues in these situations.

Keep your distance from others when traveling on thin ice. Stay 10 feet or more apart and walk in single file, so that the second person in line is traveling over ice that the first person has already tested. This way, you can help each other out if the lead individual goes through. At minimum, carry ice safety picks when walking on ice. If you fall through a hole, it can be exceedingly difficult to pull yourself up once you're in the water; an ice pick will allow you to get a grip on the slippery wet ice. The fishing gear company Frabill makes retractable models that can be worn around your neck. Punch them on the ice and the sharpened point bites in for a solid grip. Another trick is to carry a long pole—8 to 10 feet— when walking on thin ice. If you go through, the ends of the pole will catch on the edges of the hole, and you can use it as a handhold to help get yourself out.

If you end up in a sketchy situation on really thin ice, distribute your weight as much as possible. An extreme version is to get down on your belly and slither along on the ice. You can cross some extremely thin ice in this fashion. The downside is that you're going to get awfully wet if you do punch through.

Take precautions to extremes when traveling on ice in snowmobiles, ATVs, or cars and trucks. At minimum, keep cars and trucks 20 yards apart and move them every few hours when parked on the ice. Where possible, follow established routes that have been driven by other vehicles. Keep windows open, doors unlocked, and safety belts off. If it's too cold to keep windows open and you have passengers in the backseat, make sure to enable the rear window controls.

Self-rescue after falling through ice. If you can't quickly pull yourself out using an ice pick, the most immediate risks will be cold shock, swim failure, and drowning—more so than hypothermia, which might take a couple of hours to kill you. To prevent drowning, get your breathing under control and get calm as quickly as possible. Before exhaustion sets in, remove backpacks, ski boots, or any other item that's cumbersome and inhibits movement. Focus your energy on exiting the water from the same place where you fell in; at least you know the ice was solid enough there to get you to this point. In the absence of an ice pick, try to think of anything that could be stabbed into the ice to give you some grip: a pocketknife, a belt buckle, the carbide tip of a trekking pole. If it's well below freezing, get your arms up on the ice so that your jacket freezes to the surface; this might give you enough purchase to pull yourself out. Your instinct will be to pull and kick yourself up out of the water in order to get your chest on the ice, just like a seal, and that's exactly what you should do. Then try to get one leg up and roll away from the hole. Slide or crawl away, distributing your weight as much as possible, until you reach safe ice. Get moving to build body heat before hypothermia kicks in.

Rescuing others who have fallen through ice. Rescuing others on ice presents obvious danger to the rescuer, who is exposing themselves to the same degree of peril as the victim. Ideally, the rescuer can simply advise the victim from a distance on how to get out of the water by using the information in the self-rescue section. Failing that, try to reach the victim with an object that can be thrown or extended to them: rope, clothing, a tree limb, a ladder, anything long enough and strong enough to pull them out. If this can't be achieved and there are no other options, crawl or slither forward to do the rescue by hand. Preferably you'll have a flotation device of some sort and the assistance of another rescuer who's in a safe position and tethered to you by rope, or can reach you with a pole.

GLACIERS

In general, glaciers are far riskier than frozen lakes and rivers. Traveling on glaciers requires special skills and equipment. Casual hikers should avoid glaciers, though mountaineers and alpine hunters often take advantage of them because their smooth surfaces allow for swift travel through terrain that would be difficult to navigate otherwise. Sometimes, however, it's simply necessary to cross a glacier in order to get to your destination.

No matter the situation, glaciers should be taken very seriously. If you are not familiar with them, avoid them at all costs unless you're accompanied by an experienced travelmate.

Glaciers constantly change. In mountainous terrain, a glacier might "flow" downhill between 50 and 500 yards per year. Some are much slower, some are much faster. All are living, dynamic things. Crevasses, or cracks, are the primary hazards of glacier travel. These can be just inches wide and easily hopped over, or they can be many feet wide and concealed by snow bridges that can break away beneath your boots.

The movement of a glacier creates many unstable surfaces, including on the abraded rock walls of canyons as well as in places where ice and rock get jumbled into towers by the moving sheets. As much as possible, steer clear of potential icefall and rockfall by avoiding overhead debris that appears loose or tenuous, especially in warm conditions when things are melting and getting loosened up. Moats are another real hazard. These form where the walls of a glacier melt away from rock faces that radiate the sun's heat. Moats can be deep enough—and slippery enough—to swallow you whole, and make recovery impossible. They can be especially challenging in places where your line of travel requires you to move between a rock face and the glacier. Scout for a safe place to make the jump, and don't take any stupid risks. Meltwater presents another serious challenge, as it can form swift channels of water flowing over ice. To say that it can be exceedingly slippery is an understatement. What's more, meltwater can tunnel or cut into the glacier and form subsurface rivers. Never attempt to cross flowing meltwater if there's any question whatsoever about your ability to cross safely.

DOS AND DON'TS FOR TRAVEL ON SNOW AND ICE

- Don't make the mistake of thinking that sunglasses and sunscreen are meant only for warm environments. In addition to general discomfort, sun glare from snow and ice can cause temporary and painful blindness. You can also get a wicked sunburn on exposed skin, no matter the temperature. It's especially bad at high elevations.
- When traveling on frozen lakes or rivers, do strap a pair of ice traction cleats to your boots. This is especially important when on smooth, snowless ice and in places where high wind is a possibility. We've seen people get literally blown away across the ice in high winds because they couldn't get a grip.
- Do consider crampons for climbing on snow and glaciers, but don't let having crampons get you into trouble. Outside of use by trained experts, crampons should be regarded as a way to walk away from dicey situations rather than walking toward them.
- If you must travel on a glacier, do so in the cool of the morning. During the warm part of the day, meltwater, icefall, and rockfall will all increase as the ice melts. Ditto with glacier-fed streams and rivers. They will reach their highest flow levels in the late afternoon and their lowest flow levels at dawn.
- Do treat leather boots with Sno-Seal or another waterproofing boot wax when you'll be out in snowy conditions, especially when the snow is wet or slushy. Your boots can get soaked through from wet snow almost as quickly as if you were standing in water.
- Don't put unwavering faith in your ability to retrace your route simply by following your own boot tracks back through the snow. In good conditions, a set of boot tracks can last for days or even weeks. In poor conditions, such as a sudden melt or snowstorm, they can vanish in a hurry.
- Do consider the sun's exposure when planning your travel routes. South- and east-facing exposures will tend to have less snow, as they get the bulk of the winter's sun. North- and west-facing exposures will tend to have more. Wind can make a big difference as well. Snow that is blown free from the windward side of a mountain can accumulate in deep drifts on the leeward side.

SKILL: AVOIDING AND SURVIVING AVALANCHES

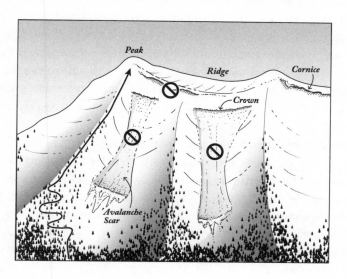

Avalanches occur when a large quantity of snow is released from a mountain side and slides down that mountain in a swift, violent cascade. According to the National Weather Service, six people die on average in some of the thousands of avalanches that happen in Colorado each year, and there are twenty-five to thirty avalanche-related fatalities annually throughout the United States.

Snowmobilers traveling through backcountry terrain are the most highly represented group on the fatality lists, followed by snow bikers, skiers, and snowboarders.

For those caught in avalanches, the two biggest risks for fatalities are massive blunt force trauma when the energy of the avalanche slams victims into rocks or trees or pushes them off cliffs, or asphyxiation due to being buried under the snow. So anyone purposely heading into mountainous backcountry during the winter should be carrying basic avalanche survival equipment in their backpack, including a beacon, a shovel, and a probe pole. But carrying them isn't enough—you also need to be proficient in their use and take at least a level 1 avalanche safety class that uses the curriculum offered by the American Institute for Avalanche Research and Education.

If you haven't taken an avalanche safety course and find yourself in the mountains in the winter, there are some important things to keep in mind. As snow falls and accumulates over the course of a winter, it creates layers. Depending on the type of snow and temperatures, these layers may bond well, creating a strong snowpack, or they may have weak bonds, creating an unstable snowpack. If you were to closely examine a hunk of snow, you'd be able to see the difference—a strong snowpack looks like snowflakes holding hands, and a weak snowpack looks more like ball bearings laying on top of each other.

Avalanches can happen wherever the right combination of deep snow and steep slopes is found. On rare occasions, they occur in high peaks of the northern Appalachian Mountains. In places like California's Sierra Range and Washington's Olympic Mountains, avalanches are more common, but mild, maritime climates with consistent temperatures and wetter snow generally create more stable snowpacks than the Rocky Mountains, where extreme temperature fluctuations and drier weather produce less stable, more dangerous snowpacks. During the winter in Colorado or Montana, it's not uncommon to have nighttime lows plunge below zero and daytime highs go above freezing. Come spring, daily temperature swings are even more severe, from well below freezing at night to over 60°F during the day. The freeze-thaw cycle brought on by warmer temperatures deteriorates the bond between individual snowflakes. Instead of snowflakes holding hands, they behave more like slippery ball bearings. This makes it more likely that the bond between separate layers of accumulated snow will fail and an avalanche will occur. Springtime avalanches can be huge and devastating because the entire snowpack can shear off the mountain in one big layer. If it goes, it goes big, oftentimes all the way to the bottom of the mountain, leaving nothing but bare rock and upended trees behind.

Traveling through terrain that is prone to avalanches requires special considerations. Before you set out into the backcountry in a high-risk area during avalanche season, check the avalanche forecasts online. You should also be aware of the following signs of potential snowpack instability:

- Avalanche risk is highest on slopes with a grade between 30° and 45°. On slopes with an incline of less than 30°, gravity simply doesn't pull as hard on the snowpack. On slopes steeper than 45°, the snow constantly falls away without building up layers.

- Keep an eye out for fracture lines in the snow and crowns from previous avalanches.
- If you're snowshoeing or skiing and the snow settles or drops underneath your feet with an audible "wumph," this is a sign of unstable layers collapsing. In flat terrain, that kind of collapse poses no risk, but that same unstable snowpack clinging precariously to a mountainside is prime for an avalanche.
- Whenever possible, stay off steep slopes covered in deep snow, including the "toe" of the slope. This is where the slope meets the flatter ground below. In extremely loaded snow conditions, your movements at the bottom of a slope could set off a chain reaction, triggering an avalanche that starts far above you. Imagine taking out one of the bottom cards from a house of cards and the whole house collapsing.
- Steer clear of old avalanche paths—wide, smooth channels through heavily treed slopes that look barren or are dotted with small, young trees. Avalanche paths may have mature trees in them as well; they've withstood the power of the avalanches that occur there, but there's a good chance that their lower branches have not. Trunks stripped bare of branches or branches growing only on the downhill side are an indicator of a slide path. If a slope has run in the past, there's a pretty good chance it's gonna run again. Walking or snowmobiling across such a path could cause it to release and slide again.
- Gullies or ravines can be death traps. These terrain features are often found well away from the giant peaks most often associated with avalanches, but a steep-sided gully that is only 20 feet deep can have the same conditions and consequences as a 1,000-foot avalanche chute.
- Stay off cornices and the slopes below cornices. A cornice is an overhanging mass of snow found on the leeward side of ridges. Snow is blown from the windward side of a ridge and deposited on the leeward side, building cornices as well as loading the slope below with additional snow. Walking on cornices can cause them to collapse, which could trigger an avalanche.

- Look for exposed rocks or windswept ridges, which signify shallow snow. These are often areas where mountain goats and sheep make it through the winter, and they're usually safe to travel through.
- In the spring, the snow on steep slopes is more stable in the morning, when temperatures are cold, and it becomes more prone to slides as the day warms. If you must travel across a steep snow-loaded slope during the spring, do it early in the morning.
- Tightly spaced trees indicate a safe travel zone. They act as anchors for the snow, and they're a good sign that an avalanche has never come through. Slopes that produce good conditions for an avalanche are likely to be repeat offenders.

If you get caught in an avalanche, try staying near the surface of snow by "swimming" or crawling sideways out of the slide's path. This will make it easier for you to dig your way out or be found by rescuers. If you do become buried, use your hands to make as much space around your face as possible; this could make the difference between asphyxiating and having enough oxygen to last until rescue arrives. If you're able to dig, determining direction may be difficult after you are buried. Spitting into the space beneath your hands and noting which way the spit runs will let you know which way is down. Dig in the opposite direction to get yourself to the surface.

FOREST

There's a pervasive legend out there that a tree squirrel could have traveled from the Atlantic Coast to the Mississippi River without touching the ground prior to the arrival of Europeans. It's certainly untrue, as wildfires and windstorms had contributed to localized deforestation at the time, and Native Americans were present on the landscape before there were dense, canopied forests in the eastern United States. At the time, during the late Pleistocene, it would have looked more like interior Alaska. But it's still fun to imagine that squirrel and its endless forest, whether the image is realistic or not. And it's weirdly sort of comforting. The majority of the people reading this book will be far more familiar with forested terrain than any of the other more extreme landscapes discussed in this chapter. While mountains, glaciers, and deserts might all seem severe and foreboding to some, forests are less intimidating. Forests have water. They provide shelter. They generally have an abundance of food. The climates tend to be mild. They are livable.

Regardless, there are unique challenges to traveling in forests. Primarily, the closed canopy and sometimes undifferentiated appearance of forested landscapes can make navigation very difficult. When everything looks the same and you can't see very far, it's hard to track your own progress. It's easy to veer off course, and you might even stand up after eating lunch and get confused about which way you were walking and where you came from. There are no proven secrets or tricks to solving this issue; instead, it comes down to maintaining that heightened sense of spatial awareness that we described at the top of this chapter, and not being lazy or flippant about the use of your compass or GPS as navigation aids.

Trails are hugely beneficial for travel in the forest. Game trails are good, but they seldom go very far before petering out. Take advantage of them when you can, but don't blindly follow game trails under the assumption that they're leading somewhere of significance to a human. They often connect bedding and feeding areas. Obviously, a deer's definition of good sleeping conditions and proper food is very different from yours. Human trails, on the other hand, are of high value. They often connect large sources of standing water with human infrastructure such as roads and trailheads. At a minimum, they provide smooth passage through what otherwise might be tough terrain. Trails can become obscured by low vegetation and downed timber; often, a lost trail that has petered out can be picked back up again by looping ahead in a half circle about 30 yards out from where the trail ended. Look also for old blazes on trees (these are marks cut into the bark of a tree by an axe) or pieces of ribbon. Saw-cut logs are another indicator that, at least once upon a time, there was a decent trail cutting through.

Thick brush, especially alders and briars, can be a major pain in the ass. It obscures your vision, grabs at your clothes and backpack, and generally makes forward progress a difficult thing to achieve. Avoid brush by sticking to trails and taking advantage of openings in the forest. These can often be identified from far away by a low-lying patch of light in the distance or a glimpse of sky or horizon. An opening will give you at least a few minutes of relief from the brush. Also avoid brush by heading toward the biggest, highest trees you can see. If the upper canopy of the forest is thick enough to block out light, the floor of the forest will be more open and easier to navigate. Another way to avoid brush, or to at least limit your exposure to brush, is to head uphill. Ridgetops are usually much less brushy than creek bottoms and low places that harbor moisture and good soils.

DOS AND DON'TS OF FOREST TRAVEL

- Don't camp beneath widow-makers. This term commonly applies to a partially fallen tree that has become entangled on another, but it can also refer to dead limbs or damaged trees that pose a risk should they break loose and fall. It is not uncommon to lie in your tent during a severe windstorm and hear two or three trees topple around you during the night. During high winds or under a load of wet snow, it is almost shocking how many limbs can come down.
- Do look for openings or meadows to make camp. You'll avoid falling trees, you can get a reading on where the sun is rising and setting, and if you're hunting, wildlife abounds on the edge habitats created around openings in the forest.
- Don't be careless with campfires (see page 262) in forested terrain. A buildup of leaf litter and pine needles on a forest floor can smolder out of sight for days after you supposedly put out the fire. A gust of wind is all it takes to kindle them into open flame.
- Do take advantage of fallen logs for smooth travel, especially through thick, brushy vegetation or to cross small creeks, but don't overestimate your ability to maintain your footing when walking on nature's balance beams. Wet, moss-covered logs can be extremely slippery, and if a fallen tree is more than a couple feet high off the forest floor, avoid it. Easy travel is nice, but not enough to risk a broken leg.
- Don't walk in circles. It's easy to get disoriented in dense forests, but you can maintain a straight line of travel by using distant trees as landmarks. Pick out a tree in the direction you want to go and walk to it. Find another tree that lies directly in your intended path and move to that one. Repeat until you get where you want to go.
- Do climb trees to get the lay of the land. Sometimes gaining just 10 or 20 feet of elevation will give you a long-range perspective that is impossible to attain from the forest floor.
- Do mark your trail in thick woods. Early explorers marked their path

for return trips or for those who followed by "trailblazing." They used hatchets to make highly visible scars, or "blazes," on trees by chipping the bark off the trunk. In the absence of trails, you can do a high-tech version of the same thing by periodically dropping waypoint breadcrumbs on your GPS as described on page 277. Or tie lengths of brightly colored surveyor's tape at eye level around tree trunks or branches at evenly spaced intervals. We've used this technique in the woods to mark paths to treestands so routes would be easy to follow by the light of a headlamp in the predawn darkness. Before you leave, always remove any tape or physical markers placed on the land. (Seriously, remove it!)

BULLSHIT ALERT: THE MOSS MYTH

One of the oldest adages in survival lore is that moss always grows on the north side of trees, and that its orientation can be used as a navigational aid. The truth is that moss doesn't give a damn about compass directions. Moss growth on a tree trunk, rock, or even an old log cabin is dependent on two things: moisture and shade. If you consistently find moss facing one direction on trees where all sides have similar conditions, then it's likely because that area is out of the sun at midday most of the time. In the Northern Hemisphere, the north side of trees tend to be shadier, but moss can grow wherever favorable conditions exist. If the base of a tree has a creek on one side and dry ground on the other, moss is more likely to thrive on the creek side. If there's a sodden overhanging branch that drips down to the trunk, moss is more likely to grow there. Also consider the angle of the tree trunk. If the tree leans toward a steep east-facing slope, then the well-shaded side of the trunk will probably have more moss. And in areas of thick overhead cover where full sunlight doesn't penetrate all the way to the ground, moss can be found growing just about anywhere. This is often the case in wet rainforest environments with thick canopies, like the Pacific Northwest. By all means, pay attention to where moss tends to grow more often when you're roaming around in the woods. It'll help you build a better understanding of that landscape. But don't count on it as a reliable navigation tool. The sun and the stars—or better yet, your compass—are way more reliable.

DESERT

Large-scale desert environments dominate the entire southwestern portion of the country, from the Chihuahuan Desert in western Texas and the Sonoran Desert in southern Arizona to California's Mojave Desert and the Great Basin, which covers parts of Oregon, Utah, and Idaho and much of Nevada. High desert sagebrush steppe environments are also found in parts of New Mexico, Colorado, and Wyoming. In total, there are well over 500,000 square miles of desert in the United States. Equally massive deserts can be found in Mexico.

Many people picture the sun beating down on an endless sea of sand when they envision a desert, but deserts are far more diverse environments than many folks realize. Sure, there's sand, but there are also mountains, canyonlands, shrubby vegetation and trees, and even snowstorms at times. Regardless of these differences, they all share the same underlying feature—a lack of permanent water sources. Officially, areas that receive an average of less than 10 inches of precipitation annually are considered deserts; semi-arid high desert steppes may see up to 20 inches. Although deserts do have extremely dry climates, this doesn't mean they're also uniformly hot climates, at least not all the time. Average nighttime temperatures can be 50°F lower than daytime highs. Seasonal differences can be even greater—summer temperatures in the Sonoran Desert regularly soar over 100°F, but during the winter it gets cold enough to freeze the water in your Nalgene. Meanwhile, farther north in Wyoming's Red Desert, high temperatures in the winter might not climb above zero for days on end. Just like in every other environment, navigating safely through deserts is largely dependent on being prepared for the weather conditions. (Obviously, the other major consideration is the lack of water. To account for that, see the strategy on page 62.)

As scarce as water can be in the desert, under certain conditions too much of it can become your worst nightmare. When rain does come to the desert, it often comes in a deluge. Dying of thirst takes time, but flash floods can kill you in seconds. Deserts lack absorbent soil that sucks up water during rainstorms. When a lot of rain falls in a short amount of time, that water tends to stay near the surface of the soil, flowing quickly into sandy washes that connect to gullies that lead to dry creek beds, gathering volume and speed as it goes. If you're caught in the path of a desert flash flood, you may not have time to get out of the way. Hiking through deserts in low-lying sandy washes and creek beds that cut through slot canyons is often faster and more efficient than scrambling over rough, broken terrain and through thorny vegetation. But you'd be wise to stick to higher ground while it's raining. Even on sunny days, your safety isn't guaranteed in canyon bottoms. Flash floods usually happen within a few hours of heavy rainfall, but they can flow for many miles from where they originated.

Ask most people to describe a desert and they'll likely mention cacti. These thorny plants do abound in desert environs, but they're hardly the only vegetation type that can shred your clothes and give you painful scratches. There's also agave, catclaw, mesquite, and a host of other culprits. It's nearly impossible to completely steer clear of thorns, and attempting to do so is a good way to get off track and potentially add miles to your journey. Thorns are especially hard to avoid during night hikes, a time when cooler temperatures might otherwise make for a more pleasurable hiking experience. Wear long sleeves and long pants at all times when hiking in the desert. Don't make the mistake of attempting to cover ground in sandals or open-toed shoes, a common cause of those "flip-flop rescues" we mentioned earlier. You want full foot protection. Not only does this give you thorn protection; it gives you sun and insect protection as well. For off-trail hikes, steer clear of extremely lightweight trail pants. They'll get shredded. Instead, go with pants that are as durable as you can tolerate without being too hot. First Lite's Sawbuck brush pant is a great option for desert travel because it lets you grease through the thorns while still being fairly cool and breathable.

Heroic feats of endurance can come at a high cost in the desert. There's a saying among desert travelers that captures this sentiment well: "Conserve sweat, not water." To put it yet another way, pay attention to your body and do not push yourself to extremes. Toughing it out to hike that extra 10 miles in the mountains is great, but in the heat and aridity of the desert it can cost you your life before you even realize there's a problem. Heat stroke is insidious; it often seems to come out of nowhere. This is especially true for people who are not acclimated to desert heat and who might not recognize the early signs of trouble. Take any feeling of nausea or dizziness seriously. Symptoms that you might write off as inconsequential under normal circumstances could be a serious warning about an impending disaster in the desert. Even going downhill can be taxing in extreme heat, so don't just assume that turning around and heading back down toward your vehicle will bring relief in time. Protect yourself from the sun. Seek out shade whenever possible. Drink lots of water. Move slowly on the uphill climbs. Pay attention to what your body is telling you.

DOS AND DON'TS OF DESERT NAVIGATION

- Do pick a good campsite. Pitch your tent on high, sandy ground in an area that's clear of cacti that can poke holes in your tent or sleeping pad. Avoid brushy and rocky areas where scorpions and snakes tend to congregate.
- Do wear protective clothing. Wide-brimmed hats, buffs, long-sleeved shirts, and pants will protect you from sunburn. Keep clothing on no matter how hot it gets. You'll become dehydrated much faster if your skin is exposed to the sun.
- Don't forget to pack a warm jacket and sleeping bag. It's just as possible to die from hypothermia as from heat stroke in the desert.
- Do identify water sources before your trip, or pack extra water into the area in advance.
- Do travel at night if you become lost in an extremely hot desert environment. You'll conserve energy and water by traveling when it's cooler.
- Don't stick your hands into cracks or crevices in the rocks. During the day, rattlesnakes and other venomous critters like to hole up in these dark hiding spots.
- Don't hike in slot canyons. From flash floods to falling rock, these narrow canyons are full of danger. Navigating a route through them without getting lost is also extremely difficult. They twist and turn and split into different branches.
- Don't lie down to rest on ground exposed to the sun. The ground temperature can be 30°F hotter than the air temperature, while a shaded patch of ground might be as much as 30°F cooler than the air temperature.
- Do take a lesson from other mammals in the desert. You'll notice that creatures from coyotes to rabbits carry out most of their activities in the cool temperatures of the morning and evening. When nothing else is moving, consider doing the same.

SWAMPS AND MARSHES

Paddling through a swamp or marsh in a canoe is pure heaven; the sights and sounds created by the explosion of life in these environs are thrilling. But if you're planning to hike through a swamp or marsh, prepare for something that can approach hell if it's not handled properly.

Walk slowly in wetlands, always moving your feet out in a tentative fashion without putting your full weight down until you test the depth and the firmness of the ground. Better yet, prod the path ahead with a walking stick or staff as you check for submerged obstacles or deep holes. But don't take the advice of moving slowly too literally. One of the primary risks in swamp travel is getting your feet or legs stuck in the mud. This happens most often when you stand in one place for too long. If your foot gets stuck, take the weight off and try to draw your leg straight out. Do not wiggle your foot around and then put your weight back on it, as you'll probably just sink deeper down. If both of your feet are stuck, use your upper body to grab on to any sturdy object you can find—a downed tree trunk, cattail stalks, a canoe gunwale—in order to lift some of the body weight from your legs. As a last-ditch effort, if you really can't get your feet out, try to pull your foot free from your footwear. There's a chance you'll lose your boot forever, but at least you'll have your legs.

Unless you have a need or want that requires you to enter a wetland, the best advice for travel is to avoid them altogether. When you're assessing how to get around or through a marsh, vegetation is the number one thing to consider. Unless the landscape is in flood stage, the presence of trees, particularly mature hardwoods and conifers, will reveal the firmest and driest ground in the area. Picking your way from tree patch to tree patch is the best way to avoid boot-sucking muck or impassable terrain. When crossing a marsh, look for peninsulas of timber that jut into the marsh and try to head from one to the next in order to minimize time spent in the water. In the absence of trees, look for the lush growths of woody-stemmed shrubs and bushes. Not only do they signify the presence of dry ground, their root structures often create firm surfaces to walk on even when the land is inundated with water.

Cattails can be hit or miss. They often signify shorelines or borders between water and land, particularly when they grow in thin strips. But cattails can also grow across entire marshes where no shallows or dry ground can be found. When you're lucky, the interwoven root structures of cattails form dense mats that can support your weight and prevent you from sinking into crotch-deep muck. At other times, cattails can leave you wading through chest-deep water as your feet punch through the root mats. Typically, the firmest ground will be found among the densest growth.

Beware of lily pads. Water lilies can grow on firm, shallow bottoms, but they tend to be thinly distributed in such situations. Dense growths of lily pads usually mean fairly deep water, and their stems and roots can be seriously cumbersome to swim through. Dense mats of lily pad roots will create something that we call "floating land." It feels like a solid bottom, but you'll notice that it has a slight bounce when you walk on it. This stuff is very dangerous, as your feet can punch through the false bottom and become stuck. If you punch both feet through the root mat, getting out can be a serious hassle. There are plenty of other vegetation types that create similar bog mats. Watch out for them.

Generally, open water means either that it's too deep for marsh vegetation (excluding, of course, aquatic vegetation that does not need open-air exposure) or that the swamp bottom is too sandy or gravelly to support vegetation. The first scenario is more typical. If muck and vegetation prevent passage, the only way to get through a swamp or marsh may be to swim. In these instances, stick to the open water so that you're not exhausting yourself in a battle with weeds and vegetation. The worst situation is to get bogged down in muck in a place where the bottom will not support your weight.

DOS AND DON'TS OF WETLANDS TRAVEL

- Do look for muskrat huts and beaver lodges when traveling in marshes and swamps, as these might be the only dry places where you can get up out of the water. It's common for muskrat trappers to rest and eat on top of muskrat huts; on a warm day you can even pull off your boots and dry them out.
- Do not enter a marsh or swamp in flip-flops, and think twice before entering in strap-on sandals such as Tevas or Chacos. The flip-flops will get stripped off your feet in a hurry. With strap-on sandals, sticks and debris are all but guaranteed to get between your feet and the straps, or wedged between your feet and the soles. This will drive you crazy. Lightweight closed-toe shoes, neoprene wading boots, or even hip or chest waders are the way to go.
- As underwater vegetation decomposes, it produces heat that impedes freezing. If you're traveling on ice through a marsh or swamp, step

gingerly. Ice over deep, open water is generally much thicker and safer than ice that covers shallow, weedy areas.

- Do get to know the flora and fauna of any wetlands that you need to spend time in, and be especially aware of the dangerous kinds. Things tend to happen quickly in wetlands, and in tight quarters. Know the risks and how to respond.
- If you're wearing chest waders in a marsh—or anytime, really—do cinch a belt tightly around your waist on the outside of your waders to prevent the intrusion of water if you take a spill. Trying to swim or get your footing when your boots are full of water is challenging.

WATER NAVIGATION

From small creeks and beaver ponds to major rivers and the open ocean, waterways are as varied as land-based environments. Much of our childhoods were spent in and around water: fishing and swimming on lakes, hunting in marshes, running rivers, and trapping along streams. We still enjoy doing all of the above, and we've added free-diving, spearfishing, and saltwater angling to our repertoire of water-based activities. We also have a lifetime's worth of experience paddling canoes, rowing whitewater rafts, and running motorized boats. What we've learned in all our time in and around the different types of watery environments is that water can be both a benefit and a hindrance to navigation. While you shouldn't shy away from outdoor activities that revolve around water, you should always be cognizant of the unique difficulties and dangers that rivers, lakes, and oceans present. That starts with developing a good understanding of how to get around in these environments safely in order to avoid becoming one of the many bodies that the U.S. Coast Guard, law enforcement agencies, fish and game wardens, and other search and rescue personnel drag out of the water on a yearly basis. (See sidebar on page 328.)

RIVERS

There are over 3.5 million miles of rivers, streams, and small creeks that flow year-round in the United States. Additionally, there are untold numbers of seasonal streams that flow intermittently during periods of heavy precipitation. The sheer volume of water that moves across the landscape via flowing streams really hits home when you take a look at a hydrology map of the entire country, or even a particular river drainage. Follow massive river systems like the Mississippi or Columbia upstream from their mouth at the ocean and what you'll see is an ever-expanding web of large tributary rivers that are fed by smaller rivers that are fed by even more streams that are fed by countless tiny creeks.

Each of these different branches of flowing water has a unique character shaped by many factors. Some plunge rapidly through mountain gorges and others wind lazily through open plains. Some carve a single narrow channel and others split into a confusing network of intertwined braids. Some are over a mile wide and others can be hopped across. But it's important to remember that while any stream might display a certain set of general characteristics and behave a certain way most of the time, rivers are constantly changing environments. Typically, their behavior mutates as they flow downstream through different terrain and geology. A river may accrue a long series of whitewater rapids as it flows through a rapidly descending rocky canyon, only to turn into a series of slow-moving, meandering bends and oxbows as it passes through a flat valley. Rivers are also influenced by other forces, both natural and man-made. A small spring creek that bubbles out of the ground in the Texas hill country might average a trickle of 20 cubic feet of water per second, but a severe tropical storm could send flows skyrocketing to over 200,000 cubic feet per second, which is why it's important to learn how to read stream flows remotely (see sidebar, page 324). In northern tier states, most rivers are at their highest flows of the year during spring runoff due to snowmelt. Periods of unseasonably hot weather can trigger massive spring flooding caused by melted snow; conversely, the normally high flows of spring runoff can be curtailed by storage diversions into man-made impoundments. Lastly, man-made hydraulic architecture may play a part. A dam-controlled river like the Colorado River at Lee's Ferry in Glen Canyon might be flowing high and fast in the morning for maximum electricity production, but at night, when electricity needs are diminished, flows are restricted to a fraction of the daytime output. The reality is that because rivers are often unpredictable, traveling in and around them can also be unpredictable. There are, however, certain absolutes in terms of what you can do to keep yourself safe.

DOS AND DON'TS OF CROSSING A RIVER

With cold water, swift currents, deep holes, slick rocks, and deposits of waist-deep mud, river crossings invite risks you'll never encounter on dry land. Approach a river with careful planning, a calm head, and caution.

- Do wear a wading belt. If you're wearing chest waders, cinch your belt up tight before you cross. If you slip and fall or step into a hole deeper than your waders, they won't turn into water-filled anchors that drag you under. Wading belts trap air in your waders and make you more buoyant. If you fall in, water will come in eventually, but the belt buys you some time to get to shore. Hip boots lack this safety feature—tread carefully when crossing a river in them.

- Do keep your gear dry. Before you cross, make sure anything you don't want to get wet is stored inside your backpack. Buckle your pack's belt, cinch down your straps tightly, and close all zippered compartments. If you know your outing will include wading across rivers, it's a good idea to store your gear in a dry bag inside your backpack. Anything that won't fit inside the pack should be strapped securely to the outside. If the crossing is particularly treacherous and going down is a serious risk, consider leaving your waist belt unclipped so that you can ditch the pack in a hurry. Keep in mind, though, chances of recovering your pack are slim.

- Do find safe spots to cross. Take the time to look for the shallowest areas with the slowest current, and cross there. This might require walking a ways upstream or downstream. Typically, you'll find the best crossings at the very end, or "tailout," of long, slow pools just upstream from the faster riffles that will precede the next pool.

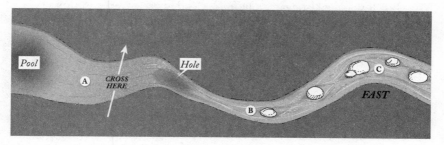

A. Look for wide, shallow crossing points with low current velocity.
B. Fast, narrow water can be treacherous even when only knee-deep.
C. Avoid the temptation to rock hop on slick, widely spaced rocks.

- Do cross at the right time. On glacial streams and during spring runoff on streams fed by snowmelt, flows increase as temperatures rise throughout the day and fall as temperatures drop at night. Flows are usually at their lowest point during the early morning hours. Heavy rainstorms can also raise river levels, forcing you to wait days for flows to recede to the point where you're able to cross a river safely.

- Don't wade in deep water. Avoid crossing in water deeper than your knees. Any deeper and you risk losing your balance or stepping into a deep hole. Once you are in waist-deep water, your high center of gravity combined with the increased force of the river greatly increases your chance of losing your balance and getting swept away by the current.

- Don't wade in whitewater. If you're forced to cross a stream where the current is fast, avoid areas of whitewater, which often runs fast enough to knock you down in depths not much higher than your knees.

- Do hesitate before descending into stream channels in steep, mountainous country. Following mountain streams might give you a clear, quick path to lower elevations, or it might leave you trapped between the walls of a narrow gorge. Often, mountain streams are best followed from above by coursing down the parallel ridgelines.

- Don't cross at river bends. If at all possible, avoid crossing at bends in a river. The water at the inside of bends is usually shallow and slow, but on the outside of bends, the currents run faster, the water will be much deeper, and the banks are steeper.

- Don't step on rocks. You'll lower your chances of slipping if you wade around and between, rather than on top of, rocks larger than a bowling ball. Also watch out for rocks that are covered in slippery green algae, or "rock snot," as it's often called.

- Do or don't take your boots off. You'll have to decide if you should keep your hiking boots on or take them off when you're crossing a river. Hiking boots have hard soles that don't grip wet, slippery, algae-covered rocks well, but they do protect your feet from getting punctured by sharp sticks and banged up on rocks while you're crossing. Removing your boots and crossing wearing just socks has the obvious advantage of keeping your boots dry, and socks grip slick rocks very well. (Remember: wet socks grip rocks.) If it's too cold to hike in wet boots and you don't have an extra pair of dry socks, crossing barefoot is also an option, although it's safest if the river or stream has a gravel or sandy bottom.

- Do keep your pants dry. In cold weather, either remove or roll up your pants before crossing. Having your pants on isn't going to add much warmth during the crossing, but having a dry set of britches on the other side will.

- Do use a wading staff. Wading staffs allow you to always maintain at least two points of contact with the river bottom when you're moving, which makes keeping your balance in a fast current much easier. They also allow you to probe the bottom to check for deep spots and big rocks you may have to go around. If you're not carrying trekking poles or a commercially designed wading staff, use a sturdy stick. Ideally, you'll find a stick a couple inches in diameter that reaches at least up to your belly button but doesn't go much higher than your sternum. Brittle dead wood that might break under pressure is not a good choice, nor is green limber wood that gives way under pressure.

- Don't turn your back to the river. When crossing a river, never face downstream. In faster streams, the force of the current can be enough to buckle your knees and knock you over. Your knees should face toward the opposite bank with your wading staff on your upstream side. This position puts the least amount of surface area into the current.

- Do pick your exit spot before getting into the water. Make sure it's not a steep bank next to fast, deep water. In case you do fall and get pushed downstream, give yourself some wiggle room by making sure there is nothing dangerous like a big rapid or a logjam just downstream from the exit point.

- Do move slowly and carefully. Take short steps and move only one foot at a time. Get a solid foothold before taking another step. If you start doing the "oh shit" river dance, freeze and regain your balance before taking another step. If the current pushes one or both feet off the bottom momentarily, don't panic and begin thrashing and flailing around for footing. Let your feet come back down and slide with the current into a solid foothold.

- Do use a partner. Crossing a river with a partner is generally safer than going solo. Wade side by side, with an arm wrapped around each other's shoulders. One of you should have a wading staff on the upstream side, and the other on the downstream side. Proceed slowly and coordinate your movements.

- Do use a safety line. Set up a safety line for crossing streams if you are traveling in a group and you have the right equipment. First, anchor a length of rope long enough to reach the other side to a sturdy tree or large rock. Next send the strongest wader across the river with the rope. On the other side, stretch the rope as tightly as possible before securely anchoring it. The rest of the group can then use the rope as a handhold while crossing.

- Do know the risks of swimming. Swimming across rivers is a last resort; it should only be intentionally attempted under ideal conditions, including mild air and water temperatures, slow current, and no visible hazards like partially submerged trees. Even under ideal conditions, you should never attempt swimming long distances across wide rivers. You might get lucky and reach the other side after drifting downstream. Or you might drown when you become exhausted, bang your head on a rock, get pushed under a logjam, or are sucked into a whirlpool.

WHITEWATER BOATING SAFETY TIPS

Before you embark on any river float trip, you have to make an honest assessment of your skills and whether you're capable of handling the section of river you'll be floating. This is easier to do if you understand river hazards and how whitewater rapids are classified. Whether you bought a new canoe for paddling down the local river or you're undertaking an eighteen-day, 300-mile rafting expedition down the Grand Canyon, you'll need all the basic maneuvering skills, plus the special techniques and added safety precautions that navigating moving water requires. Don't make the mistake of biting off more than you can chew, and heed the following safety tips:

- Current speed is the first hazard to consider for canoers, kayakers, and rafters. Fast water is more dangerous than slow water. Slowing the boat down is more work and you'll have less time to maneuver away from hazards.

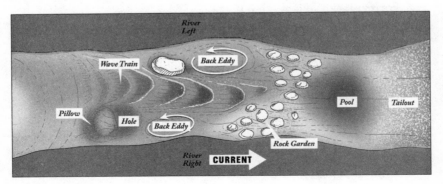

- When navigating a river with a partner or group, it may be necessary to call out lines of travel or hazards. In river runner parlance, "river right" and "river left" are immutable positions based on where right and left fall when you're facing downstream. If you were to turn upstream, "river right" would be on your left side.

- When a river splits into multiple channels, or braids, go with the biggest one. Small braids can be blocked by trees or become too shallow to paddle or row.

- Rapids (see page 320) are caused by fast currents flowing over submerged or partially submerged obstacles like rocks. The faster a river drops in elevation (gradient), the more rapids it will have.

- Large waves and wave trains (a series of continuous waves) can flip a boat and eject paddlers and rowers. Avoid tall standing waves, breaking waves, and reflector waves that bounce off cliff walls or boulders at angles counter to the main flow of the river.

- Hitting a rock can punch holes in boats and eject passengers, so do your best to avoid them; some crafty whitewater guides will occasionally intentionally bump their raft into rocks to help steer the boat, but that's another story. Rocks above and below the surface can also flip and snag boats. If your boat gets hung up on a rock, perform the high side maneuver: lean or move toward the high side of the boat (usually the downstream side), in order to allow the current to flow under the boat and lift it off the rock.

- River hydraulics can include a number of potentially dangerous recirculating currents. Among them are reverse eddies off a main river channel (they flow contrary to the main flow of the river) and suck holes (whose vertically flowing reverse currents mimic the action of a washing machine). Suck holes are usually found on the downstream side of large rocks.

- Pillows are smooth uplifted currents that form above and on top of partially submerged hazards like rocks and logs, called sleepers. Sleepers are hard to see, and there are often hidden suck holes below them.

- Sweepers, branches or entire trees that hang over the river, can dislodge a boater. Fortunately, they're easy to see.

- Strainers are partially submerged trees that flip or snag boats and trap swimmers.

- Waterfalls occur where the entire river plunges over rocks or cliffs, but even minor drops where only a small portion of the river falls just a few feet can be dangerous to boaters.
- Bends and sharp turns in the river can sometimes be hazardous. Slower, safer flows are found on the inside of bends. Currents run deeper and faster on the outside of bends, often against steep banks or cliff walls.
- Confluences are found where tributary streams dump into a river. These areas often have fast, conflicting currents and hydraulics.
- Man-made wing dams directing a portion of river flows into diversions such as irrigation ditches can be another hazard to kayakers or canoers. They're usually cement structures but are sometimes made out of piles of river rock.
- Cement drop dams and spillways spanning the entire river present man-made hazards that should be avoided at all costs. These often create powerful hydraulics that can trap or sweep up boats and swimmers.
- Of all man-made and naturally occurring hazards, bridges are among the worst. It's not uncommon to see a canoe, drift boat, or raft literally wrapped around a bridge piling as a result of the dangerous hydraulics that form around them. Bridges also collect large piles of debris, like tree trunks and root wads, that present hazards above and below the surface.

RAPID CLASSIFICATION AND THE IMPORTANCE OF SCOUTING RAPIDS

If you're going anywhere near whitewater, it's helpful to familiarize yourself with the International Scale of River Difficulty and its five categories of rapids. Be aware that accidents can and do still happen in the lower classes of rapids. Whenever you're in a boat, always wear a life jacket, no matter how calm the water is. Cold water kills quickly, whether it's moving or not. River conditions can change rapidly—heavy rains can increase flows enough to turn Class I water into Class III water. Trees can fall into any river, creating dangerous hazards.

- **Class I** water has a very low gradient, with slow current. Unskilled rowers and paddlers can maneuver rafts, kayaks, and canoes safely in Class I water. This is the kind of water you'll see tubers floating down while they're drinking beer.
- **Class II** water has some fast current, small waves, and short drops that require basic paddling and rowing skills. Inexperienced canoers can run into trouble on Class II water.
- **Class III** water has faster currents, some whitewater, and medium-sized waves and drops. Submerged and partially submerged rocks may present the occasional hazard. Class III rapids require some advanced maneuvering skills. Class III water might be extremely dangerous for novices but a piece of cake for experts.
- **Class IV** rapids have extremely fast current, churning recirculators and eddies, continuous whitewater, big waves, drops, rocks, and other hazards. Only boaters with advanced paddling or rowing skills should attempt to run Class IV rapids. Wearing a dry suit and helmet is recommended in Class IV and above water. Canoers should not paddle Class IV rapids; this type of water should be reserved for highly maneuverable whitewater kayaks and buoyant whitewater rafts.
- **Class V** water has long, continuous whitewater, dangerous rapids, enormous waves, steep drops and waterfalls, large rocks, powerful suck holes, whirlpools, and other boating hazards that demand the highest level of paddling or rowing expertise. Missing an oar stroke or losing a paddle in a Class V rapid will almost certainly result in a flipped boat. The water is so rough that life jackets may not prevent drowning. (Note that while the scale technically ends here, some river rats also use a Class VI rating to describe giant, unrunnable rapids and waterfalls that are almost certain to kill anyone attempting to navigate them.)

Whenever possible, rapids and their associated hazards should always be scouted before you commit to running them. Some scouting can be done well in advance of your trip. Study a river map or check in with a local guide or outfitter that can tell you exactly where you'll encounter rapids or other known hazards, then mark them on your GPS or smartphone mapping app. Later, when you're on the water, you can pull over, secure your boat upstream of the rapids, and scout them on foot.

What you're looking for is the safest line through the rapid. At the top of the rapid, start by looking for the tongue, a V-shaped section of relatively calm water that points downstream. This is where you want to enter a rapid. Next, identify where and when you'll need to make any moves, such as slowing down, speeding up, turning, or ferrying across the current in order to avoid hazards and take the safest line through the rapid. Walk downstream along the bank as far as is necessary to scout the entire rapid. Run it only if you're able to chart a safe course. If your group consists of multiple boats, only one vessel should run the rapid at a time. The most experienced boater should proceed first and each boat should wait at the end of the rapid, ready to provide rescue assistance, until everyone is safely through.

PORTAGING THROUGH IMPASSABLE STRETCHES OF WATER

The term "portage" has its origins among French fur trappers who traveled the waterways of the New World in large, heavy canoes. It was often necessary to carry these canoes across a piece of dry land between two waterways or around dangerous rapids and other river hazards. The sections of water that were known to require hauling canoes around or over obstacles became known as portages. The term is still used today in places like Minnesota's Boundary Waters Canoe Area Wilderness. There, portage distances are estimated in rod length. A rod is 16.5 feet long, or about the length of a canoe, and some portages in the Boundary Waters are several hundred rods, or a couple miles, in length. Fur trappers and frontier explorers were known to make much longer portages. The Lewis and Clark expedition was forced to make an 18-mile portage around the Great Falls of the Missouri River, which took thirty-one days to complete.

That's a long way to carry boats loaded down with hundreds of pounds of gear and pelts, but those early explorers knew better than to risk their lives and livelihood by capsizing a boat in the wilderness. In that respect, nothing has changed in the last few hundred years. If you take the chance of running a dangerous rapid, you risk losing your boat and all your gear and possibly drowning in the process.

Portaging your boat and gear will wear you out and slow you down, but it's better than the alternative. Sometimes, with the use of ropes, boats can be guided through a rapid from shore, but first make sure all your gear is tied down in case the boat gets swamped as you are working your way downstream. This is often the fastest, easiest method of portaging, but it's not always feasible. The current may be too fast and strong or the river may drop into a canyon with vertical walls. In cases like these, you'll need to get the boat out of the water and carry it. The most efficient way to carry kayaks and canoes is by flipping them over and balancing them on your shoulders. Kayaks and small, light canoes can be carried solo this way, but you'll need a partner for larger canoes. Portaging rafts is more work: you'll need at least a couple people to carry one, and it might be necessary to take off the frame and carry that separately. And remember, you may need to shuttle things like oars and paddles, coolers, and camping gear. You'll need to account for how long portaging will take—and it's always longer than you think. If it's late in the day, set up camp and wait until the next morning.

WHITEWATER SELF-RESCUE

Accidents can still happen even if you're an expert rower or paddler who takes all the necessary safety precautions. Just as moving water and river hazards make maneuvering a vessel more difficult, swimming to safety in rivers is more complicated than in still water. If you end up getting thrown into the river, you need to know how to save yourself. The following recommendations are a good starting point.

- Assume the whitewater position if you go overboard. Get into a face-up sitting position in the water, with your feet pointed downstream. Slow yourself down and steer away from obstacles by backstroking. This protects  your head and allows you to use your feet to kick away from and off of rocks and other hazards. Backstroke toward an area of calm current near shore until your butt hits the bottom, then exit the river.
- There is some debate on whether you should stay with a capsized boat in whitewater, but the safest plan is to get away from the boat. If you choose to hang on to your boat, it can pin you against rocks, bridge pilings, and other dangerous hazards. Boats can also drag you into even bigger downstream rapids.

- If you end up under a flipped boat, use your hands to "walk" yourself in one direction out from underneath it.
- If strong currents are carrying you toward a strainer (downed tree, logjam, root wad), exit the sitting whitewater position and swim aggressively toward the strainer. Your goal is to stay on the surface of the water until you can climb out and up onto the strainer. Otherwise, you risk getting tangled up and trapped in branches under the surface.
- If you get stuck in a recirculating hydraulic, don't fight against the current. Swim aggressively *with* the current and use it to propel you out of the hydraulic.

THE VALUE OF READING STREAMFLOWS REMOTELY

In the old days, river guides wouldn't know what conditions they'd be facing until they showed up at the boat ramp with their clients. Today, it's possible to access websites and smartphone apps that provide real-time flow charts for the majority of streams in the Lower 48. The United States Geological Survey maintains a network of over 10,000 solar-powered streamgages. The USGS also conducts supplemental manual flow readings. The information recorded by streamgages and field personnel is then posted to the USGS Water Resources website.

Streamflow data is typically updated hourly and displayed on an easy-to-read graph. You can also access historical average, high, and low flow statistics for specific streams on specific dates. Many state agencies also maintain streamflow data websites, and smartphone apps like RiverCast and RiverApp that supply USGS data are also available.

These websites and smartphone apps provide river level information in a couple of different ways. The first is gage height and the second is CFS, or cubic feet per second. Gage height measures the level of the river's surface above or below the average high-water mark at a certain spot, and CFS measures the volume and speed of water flowing through a particular location on a stream. Each system works well. Kayakers and whitewater guides often prefer checking gage height, but I feel the CFS system is more precise and easier to translate into a mental picture of the river's level.

Regardless, what you really want to look at is the graph, which will look the same no matter what data system you're using. It pays to check the graph right before you head out for a trip. If it shows a relatively level line spiking upward over a short period of time, you'll know to expect an increase in flows. It's also smart to make a habit of following the flow charts over a long period of time to build up a bank of general knowledge about certain rivers, many of which have multiple streamgages along their course. Knowing how a certain river behaves at different flows is valuable information.

From studying USGS flow charts for many years, I know the section of river where I usually guided fly fishermen is easy to wade across at 200 CFS and perfect for fishing from a raft at 1,000 CFS. At or above 2,500 CFS, there is not adequate clearance beneath a defunct railroad that spanned the river. I also know a section of another river I liked to fish will go from clear to muddy in a matter of minutes if the gage just below an upstream dam shows an increase in water being released from the reservoir above the dam. I learned I could stay well ahead of the mud by floating a section 30 miles downstream of the dam. Over time, the knowledge you'll gain from following streamflow data will also make it possible to predict how things like reservoir levels, downstream irrigation demands, droughts, rainstorms, and periods of hot or cold air temperatures will impact flows on any given river. And even if you're not a river guide, streamflow data can be used for more than determining how good or bad the fishing is going to be or how easy or tough a rapid will be to run in your raft or kayak: hikers can determine in advance whether it will be possible to cross a mountain stream, campers might find out that it's a good idea to move their tents away from a riverside sandbar, and canoers could be prepared to drag their boat through a half-mile section of river that's too shallow to paddle.

—By Brody Henderson, senior editor at MeatEater and a former fly fishing guide who lives in Bozeman, Montana, with his wife and two sons

OPEN WATER: LAKES AND OCEANS

On November 11, 1940, an unexpected early winter blizzard swept across the upper Midwest region, bringing heavy snow, zero visibility, and 80-mph winds. The Armistice Day storm was so powerful, it sank a 420-foot freight ship on Lake Michigan and killed everyone on board. Such are the potential dangers of lakes. They range greatly in size, from prairie "potholes" in the Dakotas to vast man-made desert impoundments like Lake Powell to the giant, ocean-like bodies of the Great Lakes. Each has a different character, depending on its surrounding environment and geology. Oregon's Crater Lake is only a few miles long but, at nearly 2,000 feet deep, is one of the deepest lakes in the country. It's a cold body of water, too, with average temperatures in the 40s. In contrast, Florida's massive Lake Okeechobee has a surface area of 730 square miles of water that averages less than 10 feet deep and rarely dips below 75°F. When you're planning a trip to a new lake, it's a good idea to do a little advance research to learn of the particular hazards you might encounter and how to avoid them.

From a recreational and navigational perspective, it would obviously be a mistake to think of our oceans as nothing more than big lakes. They carry every danger that can be found in freshwater, plus a whole lot more. According to the National Oceanic and Atmospheric Administration, the United States alone has over 95,000 miles of coastal shoreline, ranging from brackish shallows to surf-pounded cliffs. Their environments change constantly, not only on a broad geographic scale but also on a minute local level. A sandbar near shore that once provided a great place to wade-fish might shift hundreds of yards into deeper water after a powerful storm. During low tide, you could run your boat aground in a channel that was navigable during high tide just a few hours earlier. Or what was dry land in the morning could be covered in 10 feet of water by lunchtime. Oceans require every bit of respect and care that you can muster. But there are some principles of open-water safety that can apply to both.

DOS AND DON'TS OF OPEN-WATER NAVIGATION AND SAFETY

- Do listen to NOAA's marine weather radio channels. NOAA provides marine forecasts that are updated hourly. These include weather conditions, wind speed and direction, red flag warnings, wave heights, and small craft advisories for specific areas.
- Do keep a tide chart for your specific area handy. Knowing the timing of high, low, and slack tides will prevent things like running into hazards that are exposed during low tide but submerged during high tide or sitting in a grounded boat for hours while you wait for water levels to rise.
- Do use marine bathymetric, or bottom, charts that show bottom contours and depth soundings. You can use paper charts as a backup,

but for regular use, we recommend marine charts that can be loaded onto your GPS unit. You can buy chips or download marine charts for specific areas.

- Do have a reliable way to signal and communicate.
- Don't push the limits of your vessel. It's all too easy to sink a small boat by overloading it or running it in high seas.
- Don't neglect engine care and maintenance. Keep your boat's engine in good running order to avoid becoming adrift and "dead in the water."
- Don't forget to watch for deadheads and other flotsam and jetsam. Deadheads are low-floating logs that can be very difficult to see. Running into one could punch a hole in your boat. Getting your propeller tangled in a crab trap line could disable your engine.
- Don't swim against a riptide, a strong current created by tidal flows. If you're swimming or fall from a boat and get caught in a riptide, go with the flow. Swim with the current until it diminishes enough to allow you to swim out of it by exiting off to the side.
- Do throw buoyant items overboard if your boat is sinking. Gas cans, hatch covers, bumpers, buoys, coolers, and more could help you stay afloat and partially out of the water as you swim to shore or wait for help.
- Do swim away from a sinking boat. You don't want to get pulled down with it.

BOATING SAFETY TIPS FROM A COAST GUARD RESCUE PILOT

Over the past two decades of performing search and rescue (SAR) operations with the U.S. Coast Guard, I have seen plenty of survivors go home to their families after enduring extremely arduous and terrifying situations. Unfortunately, many others were infinitely less fortunate. This list is the difference maker. Whether you're easing a canoe into the water for a predawn duck hunt or heading far offshore to catch some tuna and mahi, add the following items to your checklist before getting under way. They'll help prevent a dangerous situation, or help get you through one.

1. **A float plan.** A float plan is a simple itinerary detailing where you'll be going and when you'll be back. Float plans should be left with a responsible person on shore. Prearranged check-in times are also a good idea for longer trips. Many times, con-

cerned family members have initiated lifesaving search and rescue efforts based on float plan itineraries that weren't met. Search and rescue agencies appreciate them as well—a good float plan will enable an informed, specific, and often successful search. Make a float plan and stick to it.

2. **The right comms.** Cellphones are not the be-all and end-all of emergency lifelines. They often have limited capabilities for communication on the water. Take your cellphone with you, but also outfit your boat with a VHF radio and an EPIRB. On smaller watercraft like canoes or kayaks, keep a personal locator beacon or satellite messenger attached to your life jacket. These devices have significant battery life. They are waterproof, they'll float on the surface of the water, and they utilize a satellite network rather than cell towers. Most importantly, you can send an immediate alert and precise location to authorities, with the push of a button.

3. **Signaling devices.** Consider a worst-case scenario: you're in the water on a dark night and well offshore. Even if you managed to send a distress signal, your life expectancy clock is ticking. Now, imagine yourself as part of the helicopter search team. The aircraft will follow a search pattern to account for drift while maintaining a flight profile of 70 knots about 300 feet above the water. Add some wind, wave action, whitecaps, and rain or snow and the flying becomes demanding and a successful search is difficult at best. Fortunately, the helicopter crew would be operating an electro-optical infrared (EO/IR) sensor system that can identify body heat signatures, and the crew would be wearing night-vision goggles, which expand the spectrum of visible light by 10,000 times. That makes our job easier, but you can give rescuers a better chance of locating you by making yourself more noticeable. If a person in the water has something to signal with (page 285), their chances of being rescued obviously become much greater. Flare guns (page 336), flagging made out of brightly colored clothing, mirrors, flashlights, and even the sparking action from a water-soaked lighter have all resulted in rescues that I've been part of.

4. **A dry bag.** Sealable dry bags can be clipped to watercraft and yourself. They should contain your most important survival gear. They'll also float and can be used as a makeshift PFD. You al-

ways have to imagine a scenario in which your vessel rolls over or sinks and everything ends up in the water. What floats? What sinks? What is contained or secured and which gear will you never see again? Keep what you need to survive in a sealed dry bag.

5. **Strapped-on survival aids.** An otherwise pleasant day on the water can quite rapidly evolve into a survival situation. If you have survival gear (fire starter, signaling device, flotation, etc.) that is not secured to your person when things go bad, you may not have access to it again. On the flip side, wearing hip or chest waders on a boat is a bad idea, as I found out as a kid during Pennsylvania's trout opener. One morning I was fishing for trout from a log laid across a deep hole near a bend in the creek when I slipped and fell in. Before I knew it, I was fully submerged, getting dragged downstream by hip waders full of water. Luckily, I made it to shore. Many years later, on a guided float trip in British Columbia, our guide explained that his colleague had passed away the previous season when he fell out of his boat with chest waders on. In shallow water waders will keep your pants dry, but if you fall out of a boat into deep water, they can kill you.

6. **Your life jacket.** Easily the most valuable and least-heeded advice given on the water is to always wear a life jacket. Personally, I've seen too many people drown in 10 or 12 feet of water during beautiful weather. Often, a life jacket would have allowed the additional time needed for rescue. On Lake Ontario, I was involved in a search for three young kayakers who hadn't made it home on time. We searched for hours before two of the boys made it to shore without their boats, a dozen miles downwind from where their cars were parked. They were wearing life jackets. The third boy was located and recovered from the water, deceased. Without a life jacket, the boy's body might never have been recovered. It's a grim reality, but if nothing else, a life jacket will allow for a proper burial and closure for your loved ones.

7. **A positive mindset.** Regardless of how dire the situation appears, your attitude may be the single most significant factor in your survival. I spent a few weeks of temporary duty at the Coast Guard Small Boat Station in Fort Myers Beach, Florida, in 2010. Early one morning, a call came in for an overdue fisherman. We

got under way and searched all morning. Suddenly and unexpectedly, the case was closed and we were sent back to the station. As it turned out, the fisherman's vessel had overturned the previous evening, more than 10 miles offshore, but the lone fisherman decided it wasn't his time. He kept his eyes on the lights of the shoreline and swam through the night. At midmorning he crawled out of the surf and asked a beachgoer for their phone to call his wife . . . and, yes, he was wearing his life jacket.

—By Matthew Keiper, a hunter, angler, and active-duty U.S. Coast Guard search and rescue helicopter pilot with two decades of service in Alaska's Aleutian Islands, the Great Lakes region, and the Caribbean Sea

WATERCRAFT

Boats allow outdoorsmen and women to travel to areas on both land and water that they'd never be able to access otherwise. In that respect they're a boon to exploring the outdoors, but when it comes to boats, you need to pick the right tool for the job. Some boats are specifically designed for traveling on certain types of water, while others are more versatile. Most of us own at least a couple of the types of boats discussed in this section, though you'll notice the lack of specialty watercraft like sailboats, airboats, and large offshore fishing vessels. Operating those types of boats safely requires a fair bit of knowledge and experience that's outside the scope of this book, but most outdoorsmen and women will eventually find themselves sitting in one of the watercraft listed below.

Kayaks. There are two basic types of kayaks. Whitewater kayaks are short and highly maneuverable, designed for negotiating fast current, rapids, and waves that require some advanced paddling skills. They have very little storage capacity, so they're not a good choice for extended river trips. Touring kayaks are long and fairly stable, track better than whitewater kayaks, and are easy to paddle long distances. They're designed for use on calmer, open water. Touring kayaks have enough storage capacity and places to lash extra gear that they can be used for multi-day trips. They can also be outfitted with all kinds of extras, like fish finders, GPS units, anchor systems, rod holders, and steering rudders. Choose a kayak made out of roto-molded plastic with sealed storage chambers. Companies like Wilderness Systems and Dagger make some great touring kayaks. Wood and canvas kayaks and even fiberglass models lack the durability of plastic versions.

Canoes. Canoes are our favorite type of human-powered watercraft for traveling through marshes and swamps, down slow rivers, and across lakes and sheltered saltwater bays. They're available in a range of sizes, but for the best combination of agility, stability, and capacity, we prefer models between 16 and 17 feet long with a beam width of 36 inches. Canoes of this size can accommodate a couple of passengers along with enough gear for extended trips. We use them for fishing, trapping, and traveling to and from hunting areas. Experienced paddlers can quietly and efficiently cover a lot of miles in them. And in the right hands, a two-person canoe can safely handle small whitewater rapids. Canoes are made from a wide variety of materials, including wood, aluminum, plastic, and complex composites. Aluminum canoes are durable, but they're noisy and heavy, and hull damage is hard to repair. Wooden canoes are beautiful, but they require a lot of maintenance. They're also very difficult to repair, and they're even heavier than aluminum canoes. Plastic and composite canoes are easily the best choices for outdoor enthusiasts who are going to use a canoe on a regular basis. Canoes made of layered polyethylene, such as those produced by Old Town, are durable, affordable, and fairly light. Fixing hull damage on location is possible provided you're carrying the manufacturer-recommended materials in your survival gear.

SKILL: HOW TO RIGHT RAFTS AND CANOES

In the event that your raft flips in a rapid or your canoe gets flooded or capsized, you need to know the quickest, easiest ways to get them righted. If there are multiple adults in your party, it's a simple matter to manhandle a raft or canoe back into the proper position on shore or in slow, shallow water simply by lifting it and flipping it. But doing the same by yourself or with a partner in deep water is no easy task.

The weight of a flipped-over raft makes it hard to get it facing right side up, and the suction vacuum that's created in the pocket of air trapped between the raft and the water adds even more difficulty. The trick is to use leverage rather than brute strength. If you're by yourself, attach a rope to a D-ring, the frame, or the oar-locks on the opposite side of the raft. If you have a partner, attach one rope near the front of the opposite side of the raft and one near the back. Next, standing on the near side of the raft, pull on the rope to break suction with the water and lift the far side of the boat up until it flips back over in your direction.

There are a couple ways to right a canoe in deep water. If the canoe is capsized, you can swim under the boat and push up on the gunwale (side) or the floor of the boat to flip it back over, but be aware that using this method entails a lot of risk. First, you can't see what's going on outside the boat when you're underneath it. In moving water, the boat (and you) could be drifting toward any number of dangerous hazards. And while you're under the canoe, it could bash you on the head as it's getting pushed by the wind or being tossed around by waves.

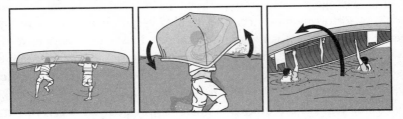

A second method is used when the canoe is full of water but facing right side up. If you're by yourself, position yourself in the water at the center of the canoe. If you're with a partner, space yourselves evenly in the middle third of the canoe. Pull the near side of the boat down toward the water with one arm while you reach toward the opposite side with your other arm. Grab hold of the gunwale on the opposite side and rock the canoe back and forth to get as much water out of the boat as possible.

To reenter the canoe, push the near gunwale down toward the water as you lift your torso up onto the boat. Then grab hold of the opposite gunwale and pull yourself into the boat. If you're with a

partner, one person should stabilize the boat from the water while the other gets back in. Then the second person can very carefully reenter the canoe, taking care not to flip the boat again.

Packrafts. Packrafts are inflatable mini-rafts that can be carried on your back. Most packrafters use lightweight, collapsible paddles that can be strapped to your pack. Packrafts are ideal for crossing rivers that are too deep to wade, but they can also be used on shorter float trips. Most are designed to hold only one person, and they're not the best choice for navigating heavy whitewater. Nor should they be loaded down with a bunch of heavy gear, although we have occasionally used packrafts to shuttle loads of meat downstream. It's hard to beat Alpacka's Scout or Caribou packrafts for a durable one-person boat that weighs only a few pounds.

Whitewater rafts. Inflatable self-bailing whitewater rafts are the safest choice for extended river journeys, especially for boaters with limited rowing experience. Despite their inflatable construction, quality models made by companies like AIRE and NRS are extremely durable. The basic rowing strokes used to maneuver rafts are pretty easy to learn. Their buoyancy makes them ideal for running big rapids, they'll float even if they flip. Any water that splashes into the boat will drain through the self-bailing floor instead of filling the raft and sinking it. And because the bodies of rafts are divided into multiple airtight chambers, they'll keep floating even if they get punctured. A standard 14-foot raft can easily hold three people and enough gear for long expeditions. We have used them on ten-day, 80-mile moose-hunting float trips down remote Alaskan rivers. You can paddle rafts, but we recommend outfitting them with oars and a sturdy aluminum rowing frame that can be customized with seats, casting braces, and even motor mounts. Frames also provide lashing points to securely attach dry bags and other gear to the boat.

Dories and drift boats. River dories and drift boats can be made out of aluminum, wood, fiberglass, or even plastic. Fiberglass is your best choice for all-around use, although heavy-duty aluminum models are sometimes preferred on large, fast-flowing rivers like the Kenai in Alaska, where drift boats are often outfitted with large outboard jet motors. Some companies are now making injection-molded drift boats with a thick plastic shell that surrounds a foam core. These boats are buoyant and unsinkable like rafts and are also very durable.

You'll hear some rowers claim that drift boats and dories are capable of handling whitewater as well as rafts. It's true that giant Class IV rapids in places like the Grand Canyon are occasionally run in dories, but these types of boats can sink if they flip, if they get swamped, or if the hull gets breached. This makes them a poor choice for rowing rivers with large, rock-strewn whitewater rapids. But on rivers with nothing more than the occasional Class III rapid, they're often preferred because they're roomy and more comfortable than rafts. You can fit three people and a load of camping gear in a drift boat with a standard length of around 17 feet. Drift boats and dories are designed for floating rivers, but they perform well on still water, especially with the addition of a small outboard engine. However, high winds can be a nightmare in a drift boat, as these lightweight boats are easily blown off course.

Skiffs and johnboats. Skiffs, which are sometimes referred to as johnboats, are a basic, utilitarian type of motorized watercraft. We use them as our primary source of transportation on the waters surrounding Prince of Wales Island in southeastern Alaska and on large western rivers like the Yellowstone and Missouri. Skiffs generally run from 12 to 20 feet in length, with boats in the 16-to-18-foot range being the most popular size. They can be constructed out of aluminum or fiberglass. Aluminum skiffs are lighter and sturdier, and they require less maintenance. Skiffs can be designed with a flat bottom for running shallow rivers and swamps or a V-shaped hull for running in deeper, open water. Depending on where you'll be using them, skiffs can be outfitted with outboard propeller motors, propless jet drive motors, or long-tail mud motors. They can also be set up with oarlocks for rowing.

WATER SAFETY EQUIPMENT

There are certain items you should always have in your boat, for your safety and the safety of your passengers. Depending on the size and type of your boat, some safety equipment, like navigation lights, may be required by law. Other items are mandatory for all types of watercraft. We've been boarded by the Coast Guard, and we can tell you those folks are all business during safety inspections. They won't hesitate to issue you a big ticket for any violations, and may even escort you back to shore. Each state also has its own set of boating regulations, so expect game wardens and park rangers to enforce these rules, too. On rafting trips in Colorado, we've been pulled over to make sure we're carrying a long list of required safety items, including a first-aid kit, an extra oar, at least 20 feet of stern line, and even a can of glue in our raft repair kit. Drowning ranks as the fifth-leading cause of accidental death in the United States, so government agencies take boating safety equipment very seriously. Make a habit of checking the regulations regarding what boating safety equipment you're required to carry.

Personal flotation devices. A life jacket, or personal flotation device (PFD), is the single most important piece of water safety equipment, and the number one rule of boating safety is to always wear one. Laws surrounding the use of life jackets vary widely and may even differ from one body of water to the next within the same state. In some places, everyone must wear a PFD at all times; in others, only kids twelve and under must wear them. Life jackets do you absolutely no good if they're stored where you can't get to them within a few seconds. And all too often, boaters make a habit of leaving PFDs lashed to raft frames, stashed under the seats of drift boats, or shoved into locked compartments on motorboats. While you could be excused for occasionally taking your PFD off in calm water, it should never be out of reach.

Personal flotation devices come in a variety of styles. There are the old-school orange foam lifeboat PFDs that wrap around your neck like a horse collar. They are bulky and uncomfortable as all hell, but they'll keep you floating. Zip-up kayaking and fishing life vests sold by companies like NRS and Stohlquist can run a couple hundred dollars, but for active pursuits on the water, they're worth the money. They come in a range of sizes that fit snugly and comfortably without impeding mobility.

Plus they have handy zip-up pockets, D-rings, and other attachment points for fishing and safety gear. These kinds of life jackets typically lack the headrests found on emergency PFDs, so they're not the best choice for kids or for those who can't swim. Small children should always wear a life jacket with head and neck support that keeps them floating with their face up and out of the water.

Float coats are thick zip-up jackets full of buoyant foam. They're popular among commercial fishermen and other professionals working at sea, but we wear them a lot in the cold, rainy weather in southeastern Alaska. They're bulky, but they keep you warm when you're out of the water and floating when you're in it.

PFDs that utilize a small CO_2 canister to inflate airtight bladders are another option, albeit not the most reliable choice. Most inflatable PFDs are worn like suspenders, but some are made to wrap around the hip like a belt. When you fall in the water, either you pull a cord to immediately inflate the device or the life jacket automatically inflates when a small chemical tablet becomes waterlogged and dissolves. The advantages of these PFDs include being compact, lightweight, and low profile. But failure is always a possibility with a mechanical apparatus, and unfortunately mechanical failure is a common complaint when it comes to inflatable PFDs.

Boat box or dry bag. Most of us keep any safety equipment that isn't attached to our bodies or our boats stored in a waterproof box or bag that lives in the boat. That way you won't accidentally forget it. Many of the items listed below must be in your boat, but there are many others discussed throughout this book that you should consider including as well. It's a good idea to keep a full set of survival gear and a first-aid kit in your dry bag. Extra clothes, fire starters, bandages, water purification devices, and compasses are just as relevant for water travel as they are on land. Also make sure you have other necessities like a basic tool kit for engine repairs and the correct socket or Allen wrench for tightening bolts on your raft frame.

Flares. Boats over 16 feet long or any that will be operating at night are required to carry pyrotechnic flares to signal distress to rescuers or other boaters. You must have three for day use and three for night use, or three combination flares. Make sure they are kept in their original packaging or in a watertight container until use, as some can be destroyed when they get wet. Also make sure to check the expiration date; the Coast Guard certainly will.

Sound-producing device. The Coast Guard recommends that any watercraft or boater carry some form of device to make a loud sound to signal to or get the attention of other boats. We think it's a great idea to always have a whistle (one that works when wet) attached to your life jacket. On a boat with a little storage space, an air horn is a damn good idea, too.

Marine charts. Charts, as maps are called on the water, are arguably even more important than on land. At night or in fog, you could easily run into an unseen hazard that could sink your boat. It's very easy to get disoriented on the water and accidentally head in the wrong direction. Classic nautical charts with depth soundings (often in fathoms, which are 6 feet) are useful, but bathymetric charts (showing underwater topography) are even better, especially for locating good spots to fish. Many depth sounders/fish finders now come equipped with GPS capability, but don't expect it to work right out of the box. You often have to download the actual chart, buy a chip, or activate a service. A handheld GPS can be loaded with the same data, and many smartphone apps offer great lake, river, and marine charts with real-time location.

Throw bag. In any situation that might include whitewater, it's mandatory to have a throw bag—usually 60 feet of rope packed in a mesh sack that unfurls in the air as you throw it to rescue someone in the water. To use one, open the drawstring on the bag and grasp the knot at the loose end of the rope in one hand. Call out to the swimmer to let them know it's coming. Then, with your other hand, throw the bag underhand to the swimmer while he or she is still upstream of your position in the boat or on the bank. Aim the bag well past the swimmer so it doesn't come up short, and slightly downstream of their location so they don't miss it. The swimmer should grab the rope (not the bag) and hold on tight. The rescuer also must brace hard against whatever solid object is available, to keep from getting pulled in when the line comes tight and the swimmer pendulum-swings into the bank. If you're unable to pull someone to safety with a throw bag, you may have to swim to save them. But remem-

ber, many people drown while swimming to save others, and drowning
victims are often panicked and confused enough to pull their rescuers
down with them. Use the technique
pictured here to pull another person
to safety without putting yourself at
risk.

Knife. Most whitewater guides are required to carry a safety knife on
their life vest, usually on the chest or shoulder strap. Most serious rafters
and kayakers carry them, too. These specialty knives are designed to be
pulled quickly from their sheath during emergencies. Most have blunt
tips to minimize the risk of accidentally stabbing someone, and they usually have a serrated blade designed for cutting through rope or life jacket
straps that get hung up on strainers. Even if you're not running big waves
or don't want to drop the dough on a specialty knife, it's still good practice to keep a pocketknife or hip knife handy whenever you're in a boat,
in case you fall in and need to untangle yourself from the bow line or
anchor rope.

Anchor. An anchor can be a valuable tool for self-arresting a boat, but it
can also be very dangerous if deployed incorrectly. If you're in a motor-
boat, drop the anchor off the bow facing into the wind and waves. When
anchoring rafts or drift boats in a river, the anchor should be dropped off
the stern since the back end of the boat takes the force of the current.
Anchoring using these techniques will minimize the back-and-forth
swaying that can be violent enough to flip a boat. Never, ever set an anchor off the side of a boat; such placement could easily capsize your vessel if the line comes under tension. Most canoes and kayaks can be
anchored on lakes in calm weather, but given how prone they are to flipping, it would be a bad idea to drop anchor in waves or current.

ADDITIONAL BOATING SAFETY ITEMS

- Waterproof marine flashlight
- Bailing device such as a bucket
- Extra paddle or oar (even on motorboats!)

- Extra gas
- Extra drain plugs
- Patch kit for rafts and fiberglass canoes
- Bow line/tow line
- Throwable floating seat cushions

CHAPTER 7

–»»»⟩⟩⟩⟨⟨⟨«–

Medical and Safety

I'VE HAD ENOUGH near misses and close calls out in the wilds that I'm honestly baffled by the fact that nothing catastrophic has happened to me or my friends. Grizzly charges, accidental firearm discharges, falling out of trees, falling down mountains, falling through the ice, capsized boats, truck crashes, ATV accidents, electric eel zaps, cooking fuel burns, snake run-ins, frostbite, snow slides, rock falls, moose charges, and hundreds of assorted cuts, scrapes, and bruises—it's a treacherous world out there. Which has a lot to do with why I love it. Things that are frightening in the moment tend to feel like a hell of a lot of fun just as soon as they're over—as long as everyone's okay.

Almost inevitably, though, there will be situations in the wild when things do not end well. The bear will actually bite, or the slippery mountain slope that's carrying someone away will end at a cliff rather than a shelf. At that point, when luck ends and an ambulance or medevac team is hours or even days away, whatever medical skills you carried with you into the wilderness must take over. It's an unfortunate truth that most people, including myself, are woefully inadequate in this respect. I've used firearms and archery equipment since I was a little kid, yet I didn't know how or when to properly apply a tourniquet until I was in my mid-forties. Until recently, I had no idea whether you were actually supposed to suck venom out of a snakebite. I was unfamiliar with how to irrigate a wound. I carried an EpiPen for severe allergic reactions to insect bites but couldn't have told you whether the recipient of a dose of epinephrine required follow-up medical care or not. I could go on, but you get the point. I've spent my life trying to master every aspect of outdoor knowledge, except perhaps the most important one: how to step in during an emergency and keep someone alive.

If I had to justify my ignorance about wilderness medicine, I might say that technology and infrastructure have reduced our collective need to understand first aid at all. Virtually everyone has a cellphone that can instantaneously connect them to emergency assistance, at least in the vast majority of the places where we spend our time. Within a minute, you could easily call 911 from your local park and then do a web search on "bee sting, swelling of throat" to determine the best course of action while waiting for the help that's already on its way. Given the mind-boggling array of medical emergencies that could potentially strike in the outdoors, the prospect of committing all that information to memory is daunting. What's more, best practices around first aid and medical care tend to evolve. Ideas about how to treat everything from bacterial infections to heart attacks change all of the time, which can leave you fearful that what you do know is outdated and might do more harm than good. Finally, the "wilderness" in wilderness medicine takes something that is already intimidating and makes it downright daunting. You might understand that you're not supposed to move someone with a neck injury, but what happens when that person is becoming hypothermic on a riverbank and help is hours away? The calculus changes.

None of these excuses matter. There are massive gaps in cell coverage across North America, including the vast majority of Alaska and Canada and huge chunks of the Lower 48. Even the best cellular networks leave between 25 and 75 percent of the United States uncovered. These areas without service overlay our least populated landscapes, which are the exact same places that attract folks who like to hike, paddle, hunt, ski, fish, dive, climb, boat, or explore. You simply cannot afford to think that you'll save the day just by placing a phone call.

With regard to uncertainty around current best practices, don't let such concerns lead you down the path of "bystander apathy." That's a social psychological term for when groups of people stand around watching a disaster unfold without doing anything because each of them has arrived at the decision that someone else is better equipped. It's far better to take action as a moderately informed person than to stand by in willful ignorance. Your life—and, more importantly, the lives of your friends—could depend on it.

HYGIENE FOR DIRTBAGS

Over the years, the term "dirtbag" has morphed into something of a badge of honor for folks who use it to lovingly describe a life lived in tune with nature, free from the confines and distractions of city life. As cool as it might be to fall into that category of grubby-looking outdoor badasses, you're asking for trouble if you allow yourself to become a literal dirtbag. By giving up something as simple and fundamental as washing your hands, you could be inviting all manner of troubles into your camp. Minor cuts on your fingers can turn into major infections, and viruses and foodborne pathogens can be readily passed from one person to the next just by sharing equipment or preparing food. Simply put, germs don't go on holiday when you're out in the sweet-smelling mountain air.

THE POOP PROBLEM

In our humble opinion, one of the lowest forms of life in the outdoor world is a surface shitter. That's a person who wanders away from the campsite or trail to take a shit and then just leaves it lying out there for all to see, with toilet paper blowing in the wind. Exposed fecal matter can lead to all kinds of problems, including the contamination of nearby sources of drinking water, especially if the issue is widespread. On any given day, there are millions of people enjoying America's outdoor spaces. We'd love to assume only a small fraction of them are surface shitters, but even if that's the case, there's still a hell of a lot of poop being deposited on the ground. In some areas, the potential for disease transmission is a significant concern. A National Park Service geologist recently estimated that as much as 215,000 pounds of feces has been tossed haphazardly into crevasses along the climbing route on Denali National Park's Kahiltna Glacier, where climbers melt snow for drinking water. It's often said that "shit flows downhill." And when you're shitting on the slopes of the continent's highest peak, it's a long way down.

There's no perfect solution, but the safest practice for shitting outside is to dig a "cat hole" that's at least 8 inches deep and then bury your waste in it. The best tool for that job is a small collapsible shovel known in the military as an entrenching tool, or E-tool. E-tools are built to have other uses, including chopping small chunks of firewood and clearing brush. They can also serve as an emergency boat anchor or paddle, so they're worth packing on trips where you're not forced to minimize your gear selection. But if packing a shovel adds too much weight to your kit, you can do your digging with rocks, sticks, or any other version of what we like to call "early man tools." In a pinch, you can also flip over partially buried basketball-sized rocks, or even a log, to expose a cat hole. Then you just roll the rock or log back to its original position to cover everything up.

Even when burying waste, it's very important to do your business well away from any streams or lakes. As a general guideline, 200 feet is considered the minimum safe distance to rule out contamination of water sources. And please be considerate of other outdoorsmen and women by crapping at least that far from campsites and hiking trails. All of these rules should also be applied to your canine companions.

If you're new to taking a dump anywhere but in a toilet, there are a few different ways to go about pooping in a hole in the ground. Depending on the type of terrain and surrounding vegetation, you can assume a simple squat position, lean your back against a tree or boulder, or grab hold of a small tree trunk or branch and lean back to maintain balance. However you get the job done, it's imperative to properly dispose of used toilet paper and to disinfect your hands with a generous dollop of hand sanitizer (don't forget the back of the hands and your fingernails, and let the stuff dry on its own) in order to prevent hand-to-mouth contamination. If you've ever pulled into a primitive campsite only to find the area littered with scattered piles of old toilet paper, you'll understand our emphasis on that first point—used TP is not only a disgusting eyesore but also a biohazard. You can either bury biodegradable toilet paper in your cat hole or burn it to ash. We often keep a lighter right in the same ziplock baggie as our toilet paper just for this purpose. Use the burning option only where and when it's safe to do so. If you're partial to using wipes instead of toilet paper, we recommend alcohol-free baby wipes. Just remember that you'll have to either burn them or pack them out since they don't decompose like toilet paper.

In the event that you run out (a path blazed by countless outdoorspeople through the ages), you can use the classic grass, leaves, or snow methods. Or sacrifice a sock or a T-shirt sleeve if you want to get fancy about it. Just be sure to bury organic matter and carry anything else out.

Finally, be aware that in some places, you might be legally required to pack out solid waste. Such rules exist in sensitive, pristine environments where the rate of natural decomposition can't keep pace with the amount of waste that's being deposited on the landscape. "Pack out your poop" rules apply to backcountry hikers in some wilderness areas and national parks, such as Denali National Park. This is also a common requirement for people on river float trips through places like the Grand Canyon, so be sure to check the regulations before you launch your boat. Single-use waste alleviation gelling bags, or "wag bags," are commercially designed for the purpose of storing and transporting solid waste. Regulations dictate that you bring enough of them to accommodate your entire party for the length of the trip. And where you're not legally obligated to use wag bags, you may be required to go 50 feet or more above high-water marks to defecate. Common sense dictates that one should do this anyway.

STAYING CLEAN

As we've already stressed, not having access to a modern bathroom is no excuse to forgo a strict regimen of washing your hands. There are other potential disease vectors besides fecal contamination to be worried about. Hunters get blood and intestinal fluids on their hands after gutting an animal, and a common illness like the flu could jump from one person to another until your entire camp is sick. At the very least, stay on the safe side by washing your hands with soap before every meal, before and after treating any open wounds, or after gutting fish and game animals. Highly concentrated camp soap is available in small containers for easy packability; you only need a little bit of this stuff combined with water to thoroughly disinfect your hands and face. It's also a good practice to keep your fingernails trimmed short to prevent germ-laden crud from building up underneath them.

For the sake of your own health and comfort, and for the sake of your travelmates, it's important that you bathe at least occasionally. You'll feel better, smell better, and avoid the potential for bacterial buildup and fungal growth in warm, moist places like your crotch, ass crack, the area between your toes, and armpits. Of course, whether you're at your family deer camp for a few days or hiking the Appalachian Trail for weeks on end, it's generally not practical, or even possible, to bathe on a daily basis. On extended wilderness hunts, we'll often go a week or more without a shower, but we do our level best to stay as clean as our situation allows.

You might need to get creative to pull off backcountry bathing, but we're not talking about a long soak in a tub full of warm suds. All you really need is a pot of water heated on your camp stove. Strip down, give yourself a good wipe with a soapy washcloth, and reserve enough water for a quick rinse. Dry off with a small, lightweight microfiber camp towel. If the weather is warm enough and you're willing to suffer a little bit of cold water, you can skip the heated water and give yourself a wash in a creek or pond. Just be sure to use biodegradable soap. You can even forgo the soap and water and use a few baby wipes or larger single-use wipes like those made by Shower Pouch.

No matter how clean you keep your body, however, your clothes are going to get dirty. In some cases, like when heavy rains turn trails into muddy trenches, or if you've gutted and field-butchered a large game animal like an elk, your clothes might get pretty soiled and rank. This isn't a big deal if you're only going to be outside for a day or two. But on longer trips, you may need to wash your clothes in the field. Moist, dirty clothes can become an ideal breeding ground for fungus and bacteria. And freshening them up isn't only necessary from a hygiene perspective—some technical apparel only functions well when it's relatively clean. For instance, breathable Gore-Tex rain gear doesn't breathe when it's gummed up with mud, and moisture-wicking merino socks fail to keep your feet warm and dry when they're so caked in dried-up sweat and trail dust that they come close to standing up on their own.

If you're wearing the same set of grimy duds for several days, it is worth taking the time to give them a good rinse, assuming the weather conditions allow for it. Synthetic and merino apparel dries out pretty quickly when it's hung on a tree branch or the outside of your backpack and exposed to the sun and breeze.

HYGIENE ESSENTIALS KIT

- Wet wipes
- Large "shower in a bag" wipes
- Toothpaste, toothbrush, and dental floss
- Biodegradable toilet paper
- Alcohol-based hand sanitizer
- Concentrated biodegradable soap like Campsuds or Dr. Bronner's
- Quick-dry microfiber camp towel
- Bandana/washcloth

FOOD AND WATER SAFETY

At home, most of us take it for granted that the food we eat and the water we drink is safe to consume. In the outdoors, there are no refrigerators or water sanitation plants. Perishable food can go bad in a hurry, pathogens are present even in water that looks as clean as the stuff that comes out of your faucet, and wild fish and game occasionally carry parasites or disease. Consequently, it is vitally important that you assiduously follow the food safety and water purification protocols we describe in the chapters on food (page 67) and water (page 40).

MEDICAL KITS

It's an obvious point, but one that still warrants mentioning: it's better to practice common sense and safety in the woods than it is to practice medicine. But even if you do everything by the book, it's still impossible to prevent all medical emergencies, which is why anyone who spends time in the outdoors needs a first-aid kit. When we're out on excursions, hardly a day goes by when someone isn't digging into a first-aid kit for ibuprofen, bandages, or a set of tweezers to pluck out a thorn. Minor stuff, for sure, but we've had enough close calls with real disasters that we'd feel extremely vulnerable if we forgot to bring our kits along.

Most of those cheap, preassembled kits you find at places like Walmart are not what you're looking for. They're filled with more Band-Aids than you'll ever need, and they're missing key components. Wilderness first-aid kits available from places like REI and the National Outdoor Leadership School (NOLS) are better suited for outdoor pursuits, but the best option is to build your own medical kit outfitted with all the necessities. You can then add and subtract from that kit in order to customize it for specific adventures.

Before each trip, tailor your medical kit contents to the type of activity, length of trip, number of people, and general environment encountered. For example, there is no sense in bringing fifty Band-Aids on an overnight solo camping trip. Waterproof labels for medications are essential; it's all too common to find tablets and ointments in your kit that you can't readily identify because the printing has become obscured or worn and you can't remember what it was. It's even worse for others who go to use your kit without understanding whatever system you might have employed when you put it together. Check expiration dates, too, and replace things often. Alcohol swabs dry out; antidiarrheal tablets turn to mushy powder; adhesive bandages lose their stickiness. Check and recheck supplies. The kit itself should be compact, organized, and housed in a durable waterproof bag or pouch. All adults should have their own basic first-aid kit that they keep on themselves, even when there's a larger expedition-grade first-aid kit that stays in camp. Redundancy equates to safety in the wilderness. And remember that it's smart to include multiple-use items that can be handy for first aid as well as for unrelated jobs, like waterproof medical tape and safety pins. Some items in that category, such as multi-tools and flashlights, might not be regarded as first-aid equipment but are actually integral to wilderness medicine.

Here are the items we always carry in our first-aid kits, regardless of the pursuit or location:

- **Prescription medication.** This one is a no-brainer and should be first on your list. Just make sure your medication is clearly labeled and stored in a sturdy waterproof container. Also notify your companions in advance of what meds you're taking and why. Make them aware of your dosage requirements in case you're incapacitated. Always pack along a buffer to account for any unplanned trip extensions. If you think you're going to be gone for a week, bring enough for at least ten days. If the medication is absolutely essential, pack a duplicate load somewhere else in your gear to hedge against loss or damage to your meds.
- **Tourniquet.** Bleeding injuries are common in the outdoors, and if they're severe, medical experts agree that a tourniquet is the only thing that's going to save your life when professional medical help isn't nearby. Improvised versions made with a backpack strap, belt, or bandana are better than nothing. A better choice is to carry a combat application tourniquet (CAT) or rapid application tourniquet (RAT). They're preferred by medical and military professionals and can be purchased online. We'll explain how to use them on page 378.
- **SAM splint.** Again, it's possible to improvise a splint in the field, but structural aluminum malleable (SAM) splints are light and handy—they can be cut and formed to brace sprains or broken bones on different parts of the body. They're reusable and can even be cut down to size for splinting broken fingers; see page 360 for more on how they're used.
- **General medication.** Carry an assortment of over-the-counter medications that can be used to treat a broad spectrum of common ailments. Buy tablets rather than liquid-gels whenever possible, and search for single-dose meds packaged for travel. Your general medication selection should include acetaminophen, ibuprofen, and aspirin for fever reduction and pain control (see page 349); ibuprofen

also reduces swelling. For diarrhea, carry an anti-diarrheal medication like loperamide (brand name Imodium). Diphenhydramine is an antihistamine that can be used to treat allergy and cold symptoms and seasickness. It is also an effective sleep aid. Include something like Dayquil tablets to treat cold and flu symptoms. For stomach acid, upset stomach, and nausea, use Pepto-Bismol tablets. For extended trips or overseas excursions, it is reasonable to request advance prescriptions from your doctor for antibiotics like Augmentin or Bactrim, which are used to treat pneumonia, severe diarrhea, skin infections, and urinary tract infections. It's worth noting that the generic versions of these medications are just as good and less expensive than the brand names.

- **Hemostatic wound pads.** These blood-clotting wound pads are used to treat severe bleeding injuries. Be aware that they must be packed deeply into wounds in order to effectively accelerate the clotting process (see page 376). QuikClot and Celox gauze are used by medical professionals and military personnel but can be purchased by civilians.
- **Irrigation syringe.** This tool is used to clean wounds with water. In a pinch you can fill a plastic bag with water, poke a tiny hole in it, and squeeze to irrigate a wound. (Plastic water bottles work well for this, too.) Just make sure you're using water that's been treated, filtered, or boiled.
- **Waterproof gel wound pads.** Waterproof, absorbent pads such as Elastogel keep open wounds and burns clean and reduce the chance of infection.

Here are some additional items that should round out the contents of your first-aid kit:

- **Antiseptic wipes.** Use alcohol-infused wipes for disinfecting minor cuts and scrapes.
- **Antibacterial ointment.** Prevents infections in small wounds.
- **Adhesive bandages.** Carry Band-Aids in various shapes and sizes.
- **Butterfly bandages.** Use to close smaller lacerations that are not significantly pulled apart or under tension.
- **Gauze pads.** Use to dress and protect a wound.
- **Waterproof medical tape.** Use as a bandage or to hold wound

dressings in place in wet conditions. Also good for small repair jobs and protecting rifle muzzles from intrusions of snow or mud.

- **Moleskin.** Adhesive padding for blisters.
- **Razor blade.** Use to cut wound dressings to size, or for simple, minor procedures like removing an ingrown toenail.
- **Tweezers.** Remove splinters and cactus needles from skin, and glass, dirt, or other debris in wounds.
- **Safety pins.** Hold wound dressing and slings in place.
- **Cloth triangular bandage.** Use to make slings and splints.
- **Ace bandage.** Elastic bandage for wrapping sprains or fractures.
- **Rolled gauze.** Use for wound dressing.
- **Superglue.** In addition to multiple gear repair applications, superglue can be used to close wounds or even cap a chipped tooth.
- **Needle and thread.** In an emergency, thin silk or nylon thread can be used to suture (stitch) wounds. Less irritating to skin than cotton thread, it's also handy for repairing ripped clothes, tents, backpacks, or sleeping bags.
- **Nitrile or latex gloves.** Wear when treating wounds to protect yourself and others from pathogens. (Nitrile gloves provide an alternative for those with latex allergies and tend to be more durable.)
- **Lubricating eye drops.** Small bottles of the stuff come in handy for treating dry or irritated eyes.

OVER-THE-COUNTER PAIN MANAGEMENT

If you're thinking about transferring those two-year-old Percocet tablets left over from your knee operation into your first-aid kit, don't do it. Prescription narcotic pain medications are powerful enough to dull your senses, potentially impairing your ability to make rational decisions in a moment of crisis. And they come with potentially dangerous and fatal side effects ranging from addiction to dizziness to respiratory arrest. Though they do have their place when administered by professionals in battlefield and emergency medicine applications, there are far better and safer choices for the average outdoorsman. Clinical studies of people suffering from chronic pain have shown that using plain old Advil (ibuprofen) and Tylenol (acetaminophen) in tandem to manage pain is as effective as using opioids. Ibuprofen treats pain and inflammation at the site of an injury. Acetaminophen blocks the release of chemical compounds that cause pain after an injury. You might have thought you needed only ibuprofen or acetaminophen in your first-aid kit, but you oughta be carrying both. Alternating doses of these two medications is a simple way to manage even severe pain for extended periods of time. Just don't exceed dosages recommended on the label.

EDUCATION, MINDSET, AND PREPARATION: ESSENTIAL TOOLS AND CONCEPTS

Keeping a well-stocked first-aid kit in your vehicle and pack is important, but its usefulness only goes as far as your knowledge and preparation. You can't be expected to be much help to yourself or anyone else during a medical emergency unless you know how to diagnose and treat illnesses and injuries. And you need to be able to make sound decisions and take appropriate action without endangering your own life or compounding the danger to those you're trying to help. To that end, heed the following guidelines for decision-making and general protocol.

- **Education.** Carry a first-aid manual with you in the field, and prepare by taking a certified first-aid/CPR course from the American Heart Association or Red Cross. Everyone who ventures into the outdoors needs to have at least a basic understanding of how to treat everything from dehydration and sprained ankles to massive bleeding trauma and cardiac arrest. First-aid techniques recommended by medical professionals are frequently changed or updated, so keep your certifications current. Classes are offered at college campuses, local community centers, and online. We recommend taking more advanced wilderness emergency medicine courses from places like NOLS or Advanced Wilderness Life Support.
- **Communication.** We bring our medical problems with us wherever we go. The risks those problems pose are multiplied in the backcountry, so it's important to avoid any surprises. Before every trip, all members of your party should exchange medical histories, including current and preexisting conditions. Whenever you're headed out on a solo trip, you need to be very honest with yourself about your fitness level and any other physical limitations you might have. Do your best to avoid getting into situations that you're likely to be unable to handle. Every year, dozens of out-of-shape hunters keel over and die from massive heart attacks because they stubbornly overexerted themselves climbing a mountain or dragging a deer out of the woods. The same goes for injuries. Countless search and rescue

operations are the result of people getting injured or dying because they were doing something they shouldn't have been doing (or going somewhere they never should have been) in the first place.

- **Curb your panic.** Medical emergencies are stressful. It's easy to panic, but in order to get through one you'll need to employ the kind of clinical detachment that doctors rely on. It's been proven over and over that, no matter how harrowing their plight, the people who are able to remain calm and focused are the ones who make it out of survival situations alive. So when something does go wrong, don't panic. Instead, abide by the emergency medicine maxim our friend Dr. Alan Lazzara told us about: "Don't just stand there. Do something." Staying calm and focusing on the actions you need to take during an emergency will allow you to make smart decisions and come up with a plan that will improve your situation. The vast majority of the time, it'll be something you can handle, as long as you keep a cool head and have a well-stocked first-aid kit.

- **Risk assessment.** Tragic stories of parents drowning while trying to save a child from the same fate are all too common, but it's easy to understand why someone would risk their own life for the sake of their child's. Putting emotion aside for a moment, though, statistics show that many people die during dangerous rescue attempts. Though your instincts may compel you to act like a firefighter rushing headlong into a burning house, it's best to make sure the scene is safe before you decide to take action. If the danger is too great, wait until it's safe to approach the area.

If we're being completely honest with ourselves, we've got to admit that if it came down to saving a close friend or family member, we'd be willing to accept a substantial amount of risk. But it would be irresponsible of us not to remind readers that you won't be able to help anyone if you wind up hurt or dead yourself.

A NOTE ON CHILDREN

Generally speaking, wilderness first-aid measures for children are the same as those for adults, though there may be different decision rules and treatment guidelines for children during an emergency. For instance, infant and child CPR and choking first-aid procedures are different from adult procedures. Kids should be a part of your outdoor adventures, but if they are, we strongly advise taking a first-aid course specifically designed for diagnosing and treating young children.

SOME USEFUL ACRONYMS FOR ASSESSMENT AND DIAGNOSIS

Once you've deemed it safe to help someone, you need to diagnose medical emergencies with a top-down approach. The most serious symptoms of any illness or injury must always be treated first. These acronyms will help you assess medical emergencies quickly:

- **The three P's.** Preserve life, Prevent further harm, and Promote recovery—the goals of any first-aid responder, professional or otherwise.
- **AMPLE.** If a victim is conscious, coherent, and able to communicate, the AMPLE acronym can provide valuable information—Allergies, Medication, Past medical history, Last meal, and Events leading to injury or illness. This information can be helpful later, during diagnosis and treatment.
- **ABC(D).** If the person isn't breathing or their heart has stopped, they're not going to be able to communicate any of the above information, and you'll need to take lifesaving measures right away. Anyone who has taken a basic first-aid course is probably familiar with the acronym ABC, which stands for Airway, Breathing, and Circulation. The abbreviation is useful in determining how to evaluate someone who may need CPR or other emergency first-aid measures. First make sure the airway is clear. Next, check for breathing, and lastly, check for a pulse. Many first responders add a D on to the ABC list for Disability, a neurological assessment of whether the victim can move all extremities equally and respond to questioning. In an outdoors setting, it's unlikely you'll have the option of applying an electrical defibrillation device to someone whose heart has stopped. However, portable automated external defibrillators (AEDs) are being made available in more and more areas where people congregate to play outside. Increasingly, you'll find them in state parks or at boat launches and ski areas. Their electronic voice commands make them easy to use, and they save lives—so it's worth taking note of their location.
- **MARCH.** The protocols outlined in the ABC acronym have been standard first-aid practice for years, and they're still valid. But first

responders have taken to using a slightly different approach to assessing trauma victims, one that emerged from modern combat care. Because a high percentage of soldiers who are wounded on the battlefield die before they're transported to a hospital, modern combat casualty care has been increasingly guided by the MARCH acronym—Massive hemorrhage, Airway, Respiratory, Circulation, and Head/hypothermia. Think of MARCH as a more complete version of the ABCs. The main idea is that the most dangerous symptoms need to be treated first. For example, a broken leg is bad news for sure, but if it's accompanied by arterial hemorrhage, the fracture isn't even close to your first priority. These first-aid measures are worth committing to memory, but for a couple bucks you can buy a MARCH card online. The quick reference chart includes a step-by-step guide for diagnosing and treating each portion of the acronym. It's definitely worth adding one to your first-aid kit.

A NOTE ON RED FLAGS

When emergency medicine doctors examine a patient, they keep an eye out for what they call red flags. Red flags are any worrisome symptoms described by the patient, observed by the doctor, or suspected upon evaluation of risk factors present in the patient's medical history. Some red flags are obvious. If someone who is experiencing chest pains is middle-aged or older and overweight, then there's a high likelihood that person is having a heart attack. Other red flags aren't so easily identified. If a skier takes a tumble one day and the next day experiences abdominal pain, that could be a sign of internal bleeding. Red flags are just as important in the outdoors as they are in the emergency room. Where appropriate, we'll make note of things to watch out for that may indicate a bigger problem, but keep in mind this isn't a medical textbook, nor are we trained physicians. In the event of a serious injury or illness, always seek out professional medical care as soon as possible.

MAKING DECISIONS IN THE FIELD

During any emergency, survival often hinges on the skills and expertise of medical professionals. However, there are situations in the outdoors where access to such professionals is greatly limited. Hospitals and urgent care facilities might be far away, and victims might be immobilized to the extent that they can't be moved. In such situations, you might be forced to make a choice between trying to find help and waiting for help to find you.

For instance, let's say your hiking partner slipped and fell at the bottom of a steep gully, suffering a broken leg. You let someone know where you were going, but there's no cell service and it's a 3-mile hike back to the car followed by a thirty-minute drive to a spot where you can get a signal. You've worked through basic first-aid measures and there is no massive hemorrhaging or other life-threatening trauma. You've done everything you can for your partner, but they can't climb out of the gully on their own and there's no way you can carry them out. You both have a survival kit, rain gear, warm clothes, some snacks, and a full water bottle. It's still early in the day and the forecast called for pleasant weather. In a case like this, the best move is probably to get your partner comfortable, give them some ibuprofen, and hike out for help—provided you know exactly where you are and can direct or guide rescuers back to the area.

Now let's say the same thing happened at dusk during a raging snowstorm with plummeting temperatures. In this case, it makes sense to stay with your partner through the night in order to monitor their condition and help keep them warm. Your best bet is to build a fire and a makeshift shelter, and stay put. Help will be on the way, and if necessary, you can hike out for help once daylight returns and the weather clears.

Not every situation will be as straightforward as those examples. Clearly, you'll need to stay with anyone who might die unless you continue to provide lifesaving first-aid measures. If you determine that the best chance someone has for survival is for you to leave them, make sure they're stable and as comfortable as possible, then take action without further delay.

INJURIES AND AILMENTS BY THE NUMBERS: A FIELD INCIDENT DATABASE

In preparing for potential medical emergencies in the wild, it's useful to focus on the ailments most likely to afflict us. To that end, we dipped into a field incident database maintained by the National Outdoor Leadership School. The NOLS database catalogs 14,000 field incidents incurred over 4 million person-days in the outdoors.

In order to be included, incidents must meet one of the following criteria: an injury or illness that requires more than just a simple, one-time first-aid treatment; that involves follow-up care or prescription medicines; that interferes with participation in activities for more than twelve hours; or that requires evacuation. The chart pictured here represents incidents that made the cut over the period between 2002 and 2005.

NOLS Field Incident Stats

996 Total Incidents	**518** Traumatic Injuries			**478** Medical Illnesses	

Traumatic Injuries Requiring Intervention	55% Muscle, ligament, or tendon strains or sprains	17% Wounds, bruises, or lacerations	5.2% Dental injuries	4% Skin infections	3.7% Burns
Cause of Traumatic Injury	47.7% Hiking	13.5% Campground activities	9.8% Water-related activities	9.7% Mountaineering	
Most Common Medical Ailments Requiring Intervention	23.6% Nausea/ vomiting, diarrhea	15.7% Viral or bacterial infections	9.2% Flu and cold symptoms	8.2% Allergic reactions	6.9% Abdominal pain

DIAGNOSIS AND TREATMENT OF COMMON AILMENTS

The ideal trip into the outdoors is one that ends with nothing more than good memories, but you're going to run up against some medical challenges now and then. The good news and bad news is that they probably won't be the kind you're worrying about. We all seem to focus on the worst imaginable scenarios: contracting exotic fatal diseases, getting mauled by mountain lions, falling off cliffs, dying of thirst, freezing to death . . . Sure, those things do occasionally happen, but the most common wilderness-related traumatic injuries are sprains, muscle strains, and other minor soft tissue injuries like cuts, scrapes, and bruises. Meanwhile, run-of-the-mill nausea, vomiting, diarrhea, flu, and colds top the list of the most prevalent wilderness illnesses. Additionally, there's often a direct correlation between activity and ailment: backpackers get blisters and sprained ankles, kayakers hurt their shoulders, and mountain climbers experience altitude sickness. As for us, we rarely come out of the woods without getting a little dinged up. We've all suffered from the flu or nicked ourselves with a hunting knife in the field.

Most folks are capable of handling these types of minor ailments, but you should never go into the woods without the knowledge and materials needed to deal with the stuff that can kill if you don't act fast. It's perfectly acceptable to improvise treatments during emergencies: superglue can be used in lieu of butterfly strips, slings can be crafted out of backpack straps, and maxi pads can be used to pack bleeding wounds. Just make sure you're following the standardized first-aid practices recommended by the medical community. From tipping your head back to stop a bloody nose to giving booze to hypothermia victims, there are plenty of outdated, stupid, or flat-out dangerous treatments that can do more harm than good.

GENERAL ACHES AND PAINS

No matter the outdoor activity, you're probably not doing things right if you aren't a little sore when you hit the sack at the end of the day. The thing is, over the course of a few days, general aches and pains can build up to the point where you're more apt to suffer an actual injury. Staying in shape goes a long way toward minimizing general aches and pains, as does drinking plenty of water, eating right, and getting enough sleep. Taking some time during a hike to stop and stretch your muscles and joints is also a big help. Some members of the MeatEater crew are convinced that a couple yoga sessions per week keeps them more limber and less sore. But no matter how well you prepare, you're still going to get achy now and then. If you need some pain relief, pop a couple ibuprofen tablets (see page 349 for more information). And keep in mind, if any part of your body is constantly in pain, that could be a red flag for a latent injury.

MUSCLE CRAMPS

These involuntary muscle contractions and spasms may be temporary in nature, but they can be extremely debilitating. You can't predict when they're going to happen, either. It sucks when you cramp up with a stitch in your stomach halfway through a tough climb, but it's even worse when your calf twists up into a painful ball of agony in the middle of the night. Cramps can happen in any muscle group, but they most commonly occur in the calf, thigh, abdomen, and neck. Lasting anywhere from a few seconds to several minutes, cramps are most closely associated with prolonged physical exertion. Other causes include pinched nerves, strained muscles, poor blood flow, low electrolyte levels, and dehydration. Cramps should be treated with rest, stretching, massage, heat, and fluids.

MUSCLE CONTUSIONS

Muscle contusions, or bruises, are caused by impact trauma that causes minor bleeding within the muscle. This bleeding results in visible discoloration of the skin that ranges between shades of red, purple, blue, black, yellow, and green. Contusions are usually accompanied by swelling, stiffness, and pain that correlates directly with the severity of the injury.

An even more minor, surface-level contusion could affect the tissue overlying muscles. It's also possible to bruise a bone, although no skin discoloration will be visible. Symptoms are more severe, and bone contusions can take weeks to heal.

Treat contusions by resting and elevating the area above the heart, if possible. Cold compresses will alleviate symptoms and speed healing, as will gentle compression with an elastic bandage. Use over-the-counter pain medication as necessary.

MUSCLE STRAINS

Muscle strains are often called "pulled" or "torn" muscles. They occur when muscles or tendon fibers are overstretched or torn. Strains are diagnosed according to severity. First-degree strains cause mild pain and generally don't limit mobility. Second-degree strains are more painful, produce swelling, and inhibit mobility. Movement may be impossible with third-degree strains. Treatment is covered by the acronym RICE—rest, periodic ice treatments, compression, and elevation.

LIGAMENT SPRAINS

Sprains happen when a ligament that attaches two bones together at a joint is overstretched or torn. Like muscle strains, ligament sprains are classified by degree. Pain, swelling, and mobility impairment depend on severity, although some severe sprains may involve more swelling and mobility impairment than pain. First-aid treatment is the same as for muscle strains, though sprains often require splinting (see page 360) to immobilize and support the joint. Severe sprains commonly take weeks to heal properly and may need to be surgically repaired. Ankle sprains are far and away the most common injury for hikers. And while it's impossible to completely avoid twisted ankles, wearing the kind of sturdy, supportive hiking boots described on page 23 is a step in the right direction.

DISLOCATED BONES

Dislocations are injuries to joints that force bones out of their normal position. In Hollywood action movies, it is standard practice for the hero to bash a dislocated shoulder against the wall to pop it back into place (the medical term is "reduction"). Properly fixing a dislocation isn't that simple or crude, especially in the case of major joints like shoulders and hips. Even with a finger, you risk permanent damage to nerves, blood vessels, and ligaments if you do things the wrong way. The best course of action is to wait and have the professionals take care of it; in fact, the only absolute indication for reducing a dislocation in the field is compromised blood flow to the distal extremity (e.g., knee dislocation with lack of blood flow to the foot). But if you absolutely have to address the problem, you can try to pop the dislocated bone back into place. To do so, it's helpful to have a partner who can slowly rotate the dislocated limb or finger back into the joint by applying gentle and persistent traction in line with the joint. For a dislocated shoulder, you may be able to try it yourself by forming a circle with your arms and pushing your knee against your interlocked fingers to put gentle self-traction on your shoulder. Attempts to adjust are usually more painful than the initial injury. Don't force it— sling the shoulder and arm in a comfortable position if reduction attempts are not working. There may be an additional underlying fracture in or near the joint (elbows are notorious for this), and multiple attempts at reduction can put bone edges precariously close to nerve and blood vessels, doing more harm than good. In either case, you'll want to be examined by a doctor as soon as possible.

BROKEN BONES

We've already made the case for enrolling in a wilderness medicine course, but we'll do it again here. From a first-aid perspective, broken bones can't be boiled down into a single category of injuries with simple treatment protocols that cover every situation. Bone fractures can occur over a wide spectrum of locations and severity. From broken fingers and cracked ribs to a broken back or a compound fracture (aka open fracture) of the femur, how you handle bone injuries varies greatly. In some cases, you'll be able to tough it out and delay professional medical care, but others might demand a medevac trip out in a helicopter.

You may have seen the famous and horrific footage of NFL quarterback Joe Theisman's leg getting snapped in half like a broken pencil. As hard as that is to watch, not all fractures will be easily identified by appendages twisted into obviously distorted angles. In some cases—if the bone is merely cracked and not completely broken, for instance—the injury may only be visible through imaging. Generally speaking, broken bones are accompanied by sharp pain when the victim tries to move. But the opposite might happen as well—sometimes a broken bone causes a loss of feeling in the injured area. Movement, stability, and weight bearing can be restricted or made altogether impossible. There may also be redness and swelling around the fracture.

Fractures can be complicated injuries to diagnose and treat, but there are some standard protocols to follow when dealing with them. If the injury is an open fracture where broken bone has sliced through flesh and skin, the priority is to stop any bleeding. This may require locating arterial pressure points (see page 377) above the fracture. Do not apply pressure directly or try to "set" the fracture by moving the bone back into place (for information on how to handle fractures, see page 360).

Head, neck (cervical), or spinal fractures may be accompanied by pain, tingling in the arms and legs, or lack of feeling or movement in the arms and legs. If this type of injury is suspected, do not move an immobile victim unless it's absolutely necessary in order to get them to a safer place. If that's the case, stabilize the victim's cervical spine by grasping their trapezius muscles and the base of their neck, using your forearms to prevent head movement. Avoid bending the spine. Remember, though, that spinal cord injuries are more likely to result from the actual inciting injury than if, or how, the patient was immobilized. Once the victim is safely lying down, place clothing or sleeping bags around them to support them and keep them from moving; pad the sides of their neck to prevent them from accidentally whipping their head around. Monitor breathing, check for signs of shock (see page 381), and get medical help immediately.

Fractured ribs are extremely painful and can impair breathing. Do not bind or wrap fractured ribs all the way around, as this can lead to worsened breathing and eventual pneumonia. Instead, create a splinting effect by using athletic tape or duct tape to brace the fractured rib. The victim should be placed in as comfortable a position as possible, focusing on using only their abdominal muscles to breathe if breathing is causing pain. Broken ribs can cause lung bruising, hemorrhage, or collapse; if breathing becomes seriously impaired, immediate evacuation may be necessary.

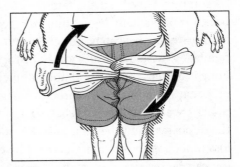

Pelvic fractures can also be very serious medical emergencies, as they're often accompanied by internal bleeding. You'll need to stabilize and support the victim to prevent movement and further injury. Ambulance crews and emergency rooms have pelvic binders designed

Place the makeshift pelvic sling low on the hip area over the greater trochanter.

specifically for this purpose, but you'll probably have to improvise by snugly wrapping a makeshift sling around the hip area using clothing or a sleeping bag.

Splinting is more easily accomplished when you're dealing with broken fingers, arms, or legs. Ideally, the splint will immobilize the injured area by extending past the joints above and below the fracture.

Finger splint   Forearm splint

We recommend carrying SAM splints in your first-aid kit (see page 347), but you can improvise splints in the field with magazines, sticks, tent poles, collapsible trekking poles, or anything else that can be used to secure the area of the injury to prevent further damage. Splints can be firmly attached with tape, zip ties, backpack straps, or belts, but don't tie them on so tightly that blood flow will be impeded. Slings should be applied to broken arms after they're splinted. You can use cloth triangular bandages or clothing for this purpose.

For a broken arm, you can turn the shirt you're wearing into a splint by flipping up the bottom edge and nesting the injured arm inside it, as pictured below.

Once the fracture has been stabilized with a splint, elevate

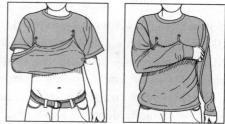

Improvised arm splint, two ways

the injury if possible. At no point should you try to set the broken bone; doing so can put bone edges precariously close to nerve and blood vessels. Ibuprofen and acetaminophen can be given for pain and swelling. As with dislocations, the only absolute indication for reducing a fracture in the field is if there is compromised blood flow to the distal extremity (e.g., knee dislocation with lack of blood flow to the foot); reduction restores blood flow by returning the bones and arteries to their anatomically correct position.

DIARRHEA

A bad case of the runs is by far the most common illness you're likely to suffer in the outdoors. Diarrhea can be caused by any number of factors, from your buddy's five-alarm chili recipe to the flu virus. Outdoorsy types often experience what's called "traveler's diarrhea," which is generally caused by ingesting food or water contaminated by human or animal feces that harbor any number of harmful bacteria, viruses, or protozoa. A case of traveler's diarrhea leaves victims dehydrated and weak. It might pass within a few hours, but it could last for months if left untreated. While most of us tend to think of diarrhea as a temporary annoyance that can ruin a trip, the truth is that it can prove deadly. Dysentery killed hundreds of thousands of soldiers during World War I, and today, diarrhea still kills millions of people every year in developing countries. If you or a travelmate experiences acute diarrhea accompanied by severe abdominal pain, vomiting, fever, or bloody stools, seek medical help immediately.

Out in the field, it may not be possible to cure whatever is causing diarrhea, but fortunately you can at least treat the symptoms by carrying a couple of over-the-counter medications. Pepto-Bismol helps to settle the stomach and relieve diarrhea symptoms by reducing gut secretions; note that it'll turn your tongue and fecal matter dark or black, which is totally normal. Imodium (loperamide) is an effective anti-diarrheal, bowel-slowing drug. Doctors can also provide advance prescriptions for Lomotil, which is both an anti-diarrheal and an anti-cholinergic (medication that reduces muscle spasms). It's common practice for us to secure such prescriptions before traveling overseas or embarking on long trips through remote country where medical help is difficult to reach. Remember, though, diarrhea is your body's way of ridding itself of the infection; these drugs should be used sparingly in the case of diarrhea caused by bacteria or viruses. If diarrhea is accompanied by persistent high fever or blood in the stool, these medications should not be used.

Note: Diarrhea depletes your body of both water and electrolytes, sometimes faster than you can replace them. Severe dehydration is a dangerous side effect of acute diarrhea. See below for more information on treating dehydration.

DEHYDRATION

Humans are made up of about 70 percent water, so it might seem like you've got plenty of H_2O to spare. You don't. Your body's various systems will not function properly without the proper ratio of weight to water. Dehydration sets in as soon as your body starts to lose more water than it's taking in. Even mild dehydration will impact your physical performance and leave you feeling horrible. More significant health problems can occur when the amount of liquid in your body begins to drop more than a couple percentage points below normal. Brain damage, organ failure, and death can occur in the most severe cases, particularly in young children, pregnant women, and those with preexisting health problems such as diabetes. Dehydration can be caused by a number of factors, including altitude, some medications, alcohol consumption, fever, diarrhea, vomiting, excessive sweating, physical exertion, sunburn, and heat exposure. But don't assume you're only at risk of becoming dehydrated if you're sick or exposed to a blistering hot sun. It's all too easy to ignore your body's need for water when it's cold and wet outside, which is why many hypothermia victims also suffer from dehydration.

Fortunately, the symptoms of dehydration are usually pretty easy to identify. Thirst is a signal that you're probably already in the early stages of dehydration. The color of your urine is a good visual indicator that dehydration is further along. Clearish, lemonade-colored urine means your liquid levels are good. Lack of urine or dark brownish yellow piss signifies advanced dehydration. Headaches, cottonmouth, dry skin, and lethargy are also common side effects. More severe symptoms may include dizziness, inability to produce sweat, and increased heart rate.

Once you've recognized these signs, the process of reversing the effects of dehydration with fluid replacement therapy is pretty simple. Provided you have ample access to clean drinking water, preventing dehydration in the first place is also easy; see page 42 for recommendations. If you're already dehydrated, the most effective way to rehydrate is to drink small amounts at regular intervals rather than chugging a whole Nalgene in one shot.

Remember, too, that your body loses more than just liquid when you become dehydrated. Part of your dehydration prevention and treatment regimen should include replacing vital sugars, salts, and other electrolyte minerals like potassium, which are lost through sweat, urine, and other bodily processes. We use powdered rehydration sports drinks from Gatorade and MTN OPS that come in small single-serving packets. One or two of these packets added to your drinking water each day will replace lost electrolytes and help your body absorb more water. You can also toss a healthy pinch of salt and a palmful of sugar in a quart of water and eat a couple of crackers while you're drinking to get the same basic effect; the crackers provide bicarbonate via their baking soda, plentiful in saltines but present in many brands.

ALTITUDE SICKNESS AND NASTY HANGOVERS

My guiding career spanned almost twenty years in Colorado's high country. During that time, I took a lot of flatlanders fly fishing at altitudes between 7,000 and 8,000 feet, and sometimes over 10,000 feet. Even at those altitudes, guided fly fishing isn't exactly a strenuous activity—most of my clients spent their days floating down a river in my raft, although some walk-and-wade trips required short hikes. Despite the lack of hard-core physical exertion, a fair number of my clients complained about headaches, fatigue, shortness of breath, dehydration, sleeplessness, and generally feeling like shit. What they were experiencing was a mild form of "mountain sickness."

Luckily, it's pretty easy to avoid the worst of those symptoms, even if you're traveling from sea level to the Rockies. Flatlanders need to give their bodies some time to acclimate to mountain elevations before jumping into any outdoor activities. The higher you go, the less oxygen there is in the atmosphere, but over the course of a couple days, your body will naturally adjust to lower oxygen levels—provided you're physically fit. If you're headed out west on your first elk hunt, to hike the Continental Divide Trail, or for any other physically demanding high country adventure, the very best thing you can do to avoid feeling like crap the entire time is to get in shape beforehand. You'll adjust to higher altitudes much easier and faster if you're working with strong muscles and an efficient cardiovascular system. Finally, I can't tell you how many times my clients complained about altitude sickness when what they really had was an unexpected hangover after having had only a couple of drinks. Be warned—the nasty side effects of alcohol consumption only increase with altitude. At higher elevations, it's wise to drink more water and less alcohol.

Mild altitude sickness leaves you feeling horrible, but it is true that more acute versions can kill you. High-altitude pulmonary edema (HAPE) and high-altitude cerebral edema (HACE) happen when the rate of oxygen depletion is faster than the rate at which red blood cells are able to replenish oxygen, resulting in dangerous amounts of fluid buildup in the lungs or brain. Cerebral edema can be reversed if descent is initiated promptly but can quickly become life-threatening. HAPE and HACE are more likely to happen when climbers ascend to extreme altitudes quickly, rather than gradually. Both conditions can result in coma and death. The only definitive emergency first-aid measure is safely transporting victims to lower elevations or simulating a descent through hyperbaric treatment, although medications designed to reduce fluid buildup may be given as well. Fortunately, HAPE and HACE are very rare occurrences. Severe cases of altitude sickness are typically associated with technically advanced mountaineering expeditions on the world's highest peaks.

Still, take precautions if you're planning on being above 10,000 feet in elevation for extended periods of time by heeding the following guidelines:

- Acclimate yourself to high altitudes before physical exertion.
- Avoid climbing more than 1,000 feet in elevation per day.
- If you do gain more than 1,000 feet during the day, follow the mountaineering mantra "Climb high, sleep low." Drop down in elevation to sleep for the night.

- Add a day of rest for every 3,000 feet of elevation gain above 10,000 feet.
- Eat high-energy carbohydrates and drink at least 3 quarts of water per day.
- If any symptoms of altitude sickness (headache, nausea, and fatigue at the milder end of the spectrum and difficulty walking at the more severe end) appear, descend immediately to lower elevation.

—By Brody Henderson, senior editor at MeatEater and a former fly-fishing guide who lives in Bozeman, Montana, with his wife and two sons

COLD, FLU, AND PNEUMONIA

It's bad enough to have to suffer through a bad head cold or a case of the stomach flu at home. It's much worse when it's cold, your clothes are wet, and you're sleeping in a tent far from all the comforts of home. We wish we had some hot tips that apply strictly to dealing with colds or the flu in the outdoors, but other than doing everything possible to stay warm and dry, all you can do is drink plenty of fluids. And although colds and flus can't be cured by taking a pill, over-the-counter medications will help alleviate the symptoms while the virus runs its course.

Bear in mind that viral pneumonia almost always gets its start as a cold or flu. Initially, symptoms of pneumonia often mimic those of a cold or flu, but they quickly become much worse as the victim's condition deteriorates. Some red flags to watch out for are exhaustion, sharp pain while coughing and breathing, high fever, severe chills and shivering, and shortness of breath. If you suspect a cold or case of the flu has progressed to pneumonia, seek medical attention immediately, as the disease can be fatal if left untreated.

FEVER

Fevers range from low-grade versions that are mild and annoying to severe cases that raise your body temperature enough to kill you. They can be caused by heat exhaustion, toxins, and adverse reactions to some medications. More often, though, they're a reaction to some form of infection, whether from a wound or from an illness. Fever is your body's way of fighting infection by temporarily creating an environment that makes it harder for bacteria and viruses to flourish. Increased body temperature (hyperthermia) is also thought to help immunity cells respond to infections more effectively.

With adults, fevers related to infections aren't usually considered all that dangerous unless they hover at or above 104°F for a prolonged period. In infants and young children, a persistent low-grade fever could be a red flag signaling a serious infection. While fevers do serve a beneficial role, they can indicate larger underlying problems. Get to a doctor as soon as possible if a fever approaches 106°F (for children, the number is lower, and the benchmarks vary depending on age) or is accompanied by seizures, persistent vomiting, rashes, confusion, labored breathing, or severe abdominal pain.

Anyone with a fever should consume plenty of liquids to avoid dehydration. Antibiotics may be necessary to effectively treat bacterial infections that cause fevers, though they won't help with viral infections. Ibuprofen, acetaminophen, or aspirin (the last for adults only) will lower body temperature and reduce fever symptoms associated with infections, but if the fever is the result of heat exhaustion or heat stroke, the victim will need to be physically cooled down (see below).

HEAT INJURY

Heat exhaustion, aka hyperthermia, occurs when the body's water and/or salt reserves are depleted to dangerously low levels through excessive sweating. As the loss of moisture progresses, the ability to sweat is compromised, the body cannot cool itself, and its core temperature begins to rise. This can result in thirst, headaches, dizziness, nausea, vomiting, and fevers approaching 104°F. Heat exhaustion victims should be given liquids containing electrolytes, such as Gatorade or a host of other sports drinks. "Passive cooling" is also a necessary treatment step. Get the victim into the shade, loosen all tight clothing, and apply ice packs or cool, moist towels. Without proper treatment, heat exhaustion can progress to heat stroke, which is an even more dangerous condition.

Heat stroke completely shuts down the body's ability to cool itself by sweating, causing a life-threatening medical emergency. The condition is defined by hot, dry, red skin (although occasionally sweating can still take place) and a core body temperature over 104°F. When these symptoms are joined by symptoms of neurological compromise such as altered mental status, the situation has become dire. Victims of heat stroke may experience disorientation, nausea, and seizures. Patients will be tachycardic (experiencing a fast heart rate), tachypneic (fast breathing), and may pass out. Extreme cases can result in coma, organ failure, brain damage, and death. Heat stroke victims need immediate medical attention, starting with the ice bath immersions they would receive in a medical setting. It's unlikely you'll have that option in the outdoors, but a cold creek or pond might be nearby. Lacking that possibility, a shaded place is better than a sunny one. If possible, call 911, remove clothing, and begin passive cooling procedures such as the placement of ice packs over the neck, armpits, and groin. Begin fluid replacement therapy immediately if the victim is conscious and able to drink.

It's important to note that it's possible to avoid, if not completely prevent, heat exhaustion and heat stroke by forgoing physical exertion during periods of extreme heat. Additionally, people who aren't used to exercising in hot climates are more prone to suffering heat injuries. If you're planning a trip to a warmer climate, it's a good idea to acclimate yourself to those conditions before embarking on a big, grueling adventure like hiking to the bottom of the Grand Canyon and back out in the middle of the summer. Prior to your trip, spend at least a week exercising for an hour or so in hot conditions—your body will learn to sweat properly and you'll learn what it feels like to exert yourself in the heat.

Anyone suffering from preexisting medical conditions affecting the cardiovascular system and/or the lungs, such as diabetes, heart problems, or asthma, needs to be particularly wary of overexertion in hot environments. With resting heart rate elevated in the heat, underlying issues can come to a head.

COLD INJURY

Unlike the many members of the animal kingdom armed with thick fur coats, waterproof down feathers, or heavy layers of insulating blubber, humans are unequipped for prolonged exposure to the cold. Without warm, waterproof clothing and footwear to protect us from frigid air or water temperatures, the onset of cold-related injuries is inevitable. And it isn't relegated to northern latitudes or subzero winter conditions. Pleasant summer days can rapidly turn cool and rainy. Many lakes and rivers remain cold during the warmer months. No matter the season, getting wet and staying wet can be just as hazardous to your health as extreme cold. Stay on top of your gear and clothing in order to avoid the following conditions, and learn the treatment protocols for what to do if they arise.

Trench foot. Your feet are particularly vulnerable to cold, wet environments. During World War I, infantry soldiers spent weeks on end in wet, muddy trenches dug as defensive positions. Many of them suffered from "trench foot," or immersion foot, as it is known in medical circles. Trench foot is what's considered a "non-freezing" cold injury that happens when feet are immersed in water by virtue of being encased in cold, wet socks and shoes for just a few days. Trench foot brings numbness, swelling, pain, and sensitivity. If the condition persists long enough, severe blistering and infections will develop. A century ago, British soldiers applied whale oil to their feet to stave off the symptoms of trench foot, but the condition is best treated by elevating the feet and then thoroughly warming and drying them—and prevention starts with the right socks and footwear (see page 21).

Frostnip and frostbite. The result of exposure to frigid air temperatures, these cold-weather injuries typically occur when bare skin is exposed to subzero conditions, although in extreme conditions even fingers and toes insulated by heavy gloves and boots can become frostbitten. Depending on air temperatures, wind speed, and duration of exposure, it may take anywhere from a few minutes to several days to develop symptoms.

Frostnip is a non-freezing injury on the surface of the skin, which remains flexible but becomes pale and numb. Victims may also experience a burning sensation known as paresthesia. Exposed noses, ears, and cheeks are particularly vulnerable body parts. Warming the area will quickly reverse the symptoms of frostnip. While easily treated, frostnip should be considered a red flag for impending frostbite, which is a much more dangerous condition.

Frostbite occurs when tissue—skin, muscle, even bone in very extreme cases—becomes frozen. Superficial (first- and second-degree) frostbite freezes only the surface layer of skin, which becomes rigid, turns white or yellow, and may exhibit blisters filled with clear or cloudy fluid. Deep (third- and fourth-degree) frostbite extends into subdermal tissue. Symptoms include blood-filled blisters, gray or bluish skin, swelling, pain, burning sensation, joint stiffness, and immobility. The most severe cases result in necrosis (dead tissue), black skin, and complete numbness, and in the extreme could lead to amputation. (To give you a sense of just how bad it can get, there's a story from the Greeley Arctic Expedition about a man whose foot fell off without him even knowing it.)

All frostbite requires emergency first-aid measures, but there's only so much one can do in the field beyond taking over-the-counter pain medication and wrapping the area loosely to protect damaged tissue. Mild cases of frostbite can be slowly and gently rewarmed with skin-to-skin contact or warm water immersion. Avoid friction and dry heat. For severe frostbite, professional medical attention is necessary and treatments may include antibiotics, tissue debriding (removal), or amputation. Permanent nerve damage may occur and long-term physical therapy is often needed to restore strength and mobility.

Prevention of frostbite boils down to limiting exposure and dressing properly. Humans aren't designed to survive for very long in high winds and −50°F temperatures without the right gear. But with the proper protection, it's possible to be relatively comfortable and safe when the mercury plunges below zero. Make sure no skin is exposed: cover your ears, face, and head with a hat, a hood, ski goggles, and a balaclava. Insulate your core with moisture-wicking base layers, lofty insulation, and wind- and waterproof outer layers. Take special care with hands and feet— amputations typically involve fingers and toes. Thick mittens retain more heat than gloves. Pac boots with heavy wool liners and "Mickey Mouse" boots designed by the military are the best choices for keeping your feet warm. See Chapter 1, "What to Pack and Wear," especially page 26, and Chapter 5, "Shelter and Warmth," especially page 239, for more information on surviving during cold weather.

Hypothermia. Unlike frostbite, hypothermia should be considered immediately life-threatening. The condition begins to set in when your core body temperature (typically 98.6°F) drops just a few degrees to 95°F. Incessant and intense shivering is a red flag that you're well on your way to becoming hypothermic. Other symptoms may include drowsiness, confusion, and skin that is cold and red. As body temperature drops to 90°F, shivering stops, skin color may change to pale gray or blue, the pulse weakens, breathing slows, and victims may lose consciousness. Death results from eventual respiratory, cardiovascular, and nervous system failures. Because hypothermia often sets in gradually and degrades mental faculties, victims may be unaware of what is happening to them. Hypothermia victims will often do something called "paradoxical undressing," the result of a false signal arising from the condition. When your body gets really cold, the blood vessels near the skin contract to limit the flow of blood to the surface—this keeps more blood near the body's core and its essential organs, where it can stay warm. But energy is required to keep these surface level blood vessels contracted; eventually, as the body continues to weaken, the vessels open up and allow warm blood to rush to the skin's surface. Victims get the sensation of intense heat and begin casting off clothing. Sometimes they even take off their jewelry.

Hypothermia can occur at much higher temperatures than you might expect. People without warm clothing can experience hypothermia after a couple days of exposure to air temperatures in the fifties. Add water to the equation and the timeline becomes much shorter. A wet human body loses heat as much as twenty-five times faster than a dry one. If you're caught out in cool weather during a downpour without proper rainwear, you may become hypothermic within a few hours. Complete immersion in water can cause hypothermia even faster. In water below 60°F, loss of dexterity occurs within minutes, loss of consciousness inside of a couple hours, and death shortly thereafter. Obviously, the colder the air or water, the greater the risk for hypothermia—if you end up submerged in water colder than 40°F, you'll be dead in a few minutes without a marine survival suit. The takeaway here is to do everything in your power to stay not only warm but dry.

Take steps to warm up anyone as soon as they begin shivering persistently. Mild hypothermia can be reversed in the field, provided victims can change into dry, warm clothing or be stripped of any wet clothing and bundled into sleeping bags. Chemical hand and body warming packets, heated water bottles, skin-to-skin contact (hopping into your friend's sleeping bag with them to warm them with your body heat), and warm liquids are additional options for warming the body's core. External heat sources such as campfires can be used for additional warmth and to dry out wet clothing. Victims of severe hypothermia should be evacuated as soon as possible. They'll need professional medical attention and special warming techniques.

DROWNING

Exposure to cold water increases the odds for hypothermia, but the majority of drownings happen during the summer in water that's warm enough for skinny-dipping. No matter the season, outdoorsmen and women should always exercise caution when it comes to water-related activities. From duck hunters and fly fishermen to beachgoers and boaters, water is rarely given the respect that it merits, even though drowning is one of the most common causes of accidental deaths, especially for children. Death can happen in under two minutes for adults and as little as thirty seconds in young children. From a first-aid perspective, the chances of reviving drowning victims are slim, though not impossible, as drowning kills by asphyxiation when the respiratory system is flooded with water and the oxygen supply to the brain and heart is cut off. You need to act fast—drowning victims are rarely able to call for help or self-rescue. If they are rescued before they expire, CPR may restore breathing. There is no indication for the Heimlich maneuver or pumping the legs against the body; these moves just delay resuscitation. Clear the airway of obvious water or debris (vomit, weeds) by turning the victim on their side and doing a finger sweep. The first five to ten minutes in a drowning resuscitation are the most important in reversing oxygen deprivation before brain damage occurs. Begin CPR with ventilation (mouth-to-mouth, bag-valve-mask) and administer oxygen if available. Victims breathing under their own power may be confused or unconscious, have a weak pulse, or have other complications. Monitor their condition closely and get medical help immediately.

ABDOMINAL PAIN

There are myriad potential causes for abdominal pain. A stomachache could be the result of a harmless bout of bad gas, or it could be a red flag for something as dangerous as appendicitis. Treatments also vary widely. Victims of internal bleeding might need an immediate medevac, while those merely suffering from an upset stomach may find relief by simply popping a couple of antacid tablets.

You should be most concerned about sharp, persistent, localized abdominal pain. Other red flags that indicate a medical emergency include abdominal pain accompanied by persistent fever, vomiting, or diarrhea. Also look out for bloody or black vomit or stools. Abdominal trauma with severe pain or bruising on the abdominal wall is symptomatic of internal bleeding. In women, lower abdominal pain could be indicative of dangerous complications associated with pregnancy. See the diagram on page 372 for detailed information on determining the causes of abdominal pain by quadrant.

POISONING

Poisoning can result from being exposed to a variety of harmful substances in a variety of ways. Various chemicals, gases, and drugs can be harmful or fatal if swallowed, inhaled, or touched. Although these types of medical emergencies aren't commonly associated with outdoor recre-

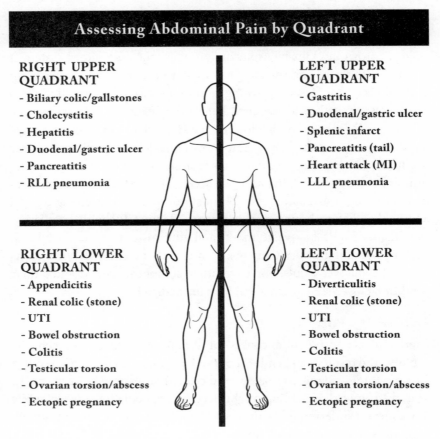

Assessing Abdominal Pain by Quadrant

RIGHT UPPER QUADRANT
- Biliary colic/gallstones
- Cholecystitis
- Hepatitis
- Duodenal/gastric ulcer
- Pancreatitis
- RLL pneumonia

LEFT UPPER QUADRANT
- Gastritis
- Duodenal/gastric ulcer
- Splenic infarct
- Pancreatitis (tail)
- Heart attack (MI)
- LLL pneumonia

RIGHT LOWER QUADRANT
- Appendicitis
- Renal colic (stone)
- UTI
- Bowel obstruction
- Colitis
- Testicular torsion
- Ovarian torsion/abscess
- Ectopic pregnancy

LEFT LOWER QUADRANT
- Diverticulitis
- Renal colic (stone)
- UTI
- Bowel obstruction
- Colitis
- Testicular torsion
- Ovarian torsion/abscess
- Ectopic pregnancy

ation, some types of poisoning are more likely when engaging in certain activities. For example, the likelihood of accidental carbon monoxide poisoning skyrockets when propane heaters or lanterns are used in enclosed spaces like campers that aren't adequately ventilated, and hikers risk exposure to toxic plants such as poison ivy. Additionally, hunters, anglers, and foragers should be aware of the dangers of toxic berries, poisonous mushrooms, and tainted meat or fish. (See Chapter 3, "Food," for more information on these types of risks.)

Seizures, vomiting, labored breathing, drowsiness, and confusion are all possible signs of poisoning. If someone has swallowed something poisonous, do not induce vomiting—medical experts no longer advocate this dated first-aid practice. Instead, have them drink a small amount of water. Move anyone who has inhaled poisonous fumes into fresh air, and use soap and water to wash any skin that has been exposed to toxic plants. In all such cases, call 911 or a poison control center immediately.

BURNS

There are several different types of burns, including friction, cold, chemical, electrical, thermal, and radiation burns. Friction burns in the outdoors generally have to do with poor choices in gear and footwear. Cold burns (frostnip and frostbite) were covered on page 368. Chemical and electrical burns are rare in outdoor settings. But every time we step outside, we face the risk of burns resulting from exposure to the elements.

Sunburn can be very painful, but unless it's extremely severe, it can be treated with over-the-counter medications, cool compresses, and aloe vera or moisturizing lotions. The real danger is the ultraviolet radiation that causes the burn, and it's a cumulative risk—your odds of contracting skin cancer rise with each new case of sunburn. In fact, the Skin Cancer Foundation warns that your chances of developing a deadly melanoma doubles with a history of just five sunburns. Peeling and blistering sunburns increase the risk even more, especially for children and young adults. Most people have woken up to the dangers of sunburn, but it's still worth mentioning that periodically taking a couple minutes to apply sunscreen with a rating of SPF 30 greatly reduces the risk of melanomas and other types of skin cancer, as does wearing wide-brimmed hats, neck gaiters or buffs, long sleeved-shirts, and pants. We prefer sport sunscreens that are resistant to sweat and water. Remember to apply sunscreen on cloudy days, too—as much as 80 percent of UV radiation penetrates cloud cover.

Just like sunburns, thermal burns are usually the result of lazy or negligent behavior. Unavoidable accidents do happen, but fire tends to get treated as a tool (or even a form of entertainment) that we have complete control over. The truth is, you can never use enough caution around campfires and cooking stoves—burns caused by hot pots and cooking utensils, scalding liquids, and open flames are some of the most common injuries in the outdoors.

Thermal burns are classified by degree of severity. First-degree burns only do minor damage to the upper layer of skin, which may be red and painful. Second-degree burns extend down into the lower dermal layer. The skin becomes bright red, swollen, blistered, painful, and shiny. Some second-degree burns may leave permanent scarring. Third-degree or full-thickness burns completely destroy both layers of skin, which will appear black, brown, white, or yellow; the burn area will quickly stiffen, acquiring an unnaturally wooden texture. Third-degree burns are very severe injuries, but since they also destroy nerve endings, victims may feel no pain. Full-thickness burns can extend into flesh, connective tissue, and bone. Third-degree burn victims require immediate medical attention; they are extremely vulnerable to life-threatening cases of shock in the short term and deadly infections in the long term.

First aid for all burns:

- Smother flames or eliminate contact with cause of burn.
- Remove burning material or clothing if possible—leave if it sticks to the burned area, and cut away surrounding clothing.
- Remove jewelry from both hands; in addition to swelling in the area of the burn, general extremity swelling can impact both sides of the body, making rings and bracelets difficult to remove.

First aid for first-degree burns:

- Submerge in cool water or cover with cold compress.
- Cover with sterile bandage or cloth.
- Apply petroleum jelly, aloe vera, or moisturizing lotion once per day.

First aid for second-degree burns:

- Submerge in cool water or cover with cool compress for fifteen minutes—do not apply ice, which can cause further damage.
- Do not puncture blisters without using proper sterilization procedures. Wash the blistered area with soap and sterilize your needle by holding a lighter's flame to it until the tip glows red. Let cool before using.
- Apply antibacterial ointment and cover with loose gauze or cloth.
- Get medical attention ASAP.

First aid for third-degree burns:

- Call 911 or send someone for help.
- Prevent shock: lay the victim down with feet and the burn area elevated above the heart. Cover with a blanket or clothing.
- Monitor vitals.

BLEEDING WOUNDS

There are a million ways to get cut when you're hunting, fishing, or camping. Those of us who spend a lot of time outside expect to accumulate a new collection of minor cuts and scrapes on every trip. Usually it's only necessary to clean small cuts, apply a dab of antibiotic ointment, slap a Band-Aid over it, and go on about your business. Once in a while, you might need to apply pressure to a cut for a minute or two to stop any bleeding before you close things up with a butterfly bandage or some superglue. These are first-aid practices anyone should be able to handle. After all, we aren't talking about trip-ending injuries. Even with flesh wounds that might need a few stitches, you don't need to rush to the emergency room if the bleeding has stopped.

It's the wounds that won't stop bleeding that can kill you. Severe, uncontrolled bleeding is most often the result of lacerations or puncture wounds that penetrate deeply into the flesh, major arteries, or vital organs, but hemorrhage can also be caused by massive blunt force trauma or crushing injuries. Red flags for potentially deadly bleeding include wounds with steadily flowing, pooling, or spurting blood. Additionally, trauma that causes bloody vomit, abdominal swelling, and chest pain could indicate severe internal bleeding.

Although our blood is equipped with clotting agents that stop bleeding in small wounds relatively fast, massive hemorrhage overwhelms the human body's natural clotting abilities. The average adult has about 5 quarts of blood in their body. The loss of a single quart of blood greatly impairs the delivery of oxygen to tissues as well the removal of carbon dioxide and can induce hemorrhagic shock—think of it like an engine seizing up due to low oil pressure. Losing more than a third of the blood supply can be fatal. In the United States, it's estimated that roughly 60,000 people die annually from massive hemorrhage caused by traumatic injuries. Not only do deaths caused by such severe blood loss happen frequently, they happen fast. More than half of the deaths that result from blood loss happen within several minutes of the initial injury. Depending on the location and nature of the injury, a person can bleed out in less than a minute.

If a severe bleeding injury occurs, call 911. If no cell service is available, send someone for help. If neither of those options are a possibility, stay with the victim and continue to provide medical assistance as long as necessary. You must also be prepared to perform these lifesaving measures on yourself if no one else is around to help.

In order to control severe bleeding, aggressive first-aid practices must be employed quickly. The first step in stopping bleeding is to identify the source. This might seem straightforward, but sometimes wounds can be obscured by thick clothing. Also be sure to look for less obvious trauma that's hidden by the blood of more visible wounds; there could be multiple injuries such as an entry and exit wound. If the injury was caused by a foreign object that is still lodged in the wound, leave it in place to avoid doing further damage.

Once you've identified the source of the bleeding, pack the wound tightly with gauze or a T-shirt if there is a cavity, and immediately begin applying direct pressure to the injury using two fingers, the heel of your hand, or even a knee. Push down hard—you're trying to entirely close off severed blood vessels. Don't let up until the bleeding stops or someone relieves you. Elevate the injured area above the heart if possible. If direct pressure on arm or leg wounds fails to stanch bleeding, maintain pressure on the wound while firmly pressing down on arterial pressure points above the injury (see illustration opposite).

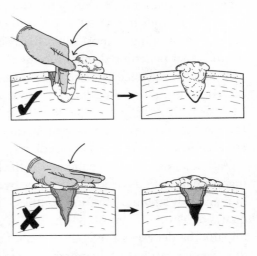

Hemostatic wound pads must be packed down into wounds for effective use.

If bleeding continues unabated despite direct pressure, it is necessary to use additional tools such as pressure bandages, hemostatic gauze, or tourniquets to prevent fatal blood loss. Commercially designed pressure bandages or lengths of absorbent dressing wrapped tightly around wounds will slow bleeding. Hemostatic wound pads utilize chemical compounds that accelerate the clotting process, but simply dressing bleeding injuries with a hemostatic pad isn't enough. They only work well if they're packed as far as possible into wounds (see illustration above), particularly in the case of deep punctures or penetrating wounds.

Hemostatic wound pads used in conjunction with pressure bandages

Arterial Pressure Guide
How to stop bleeding in an emergency

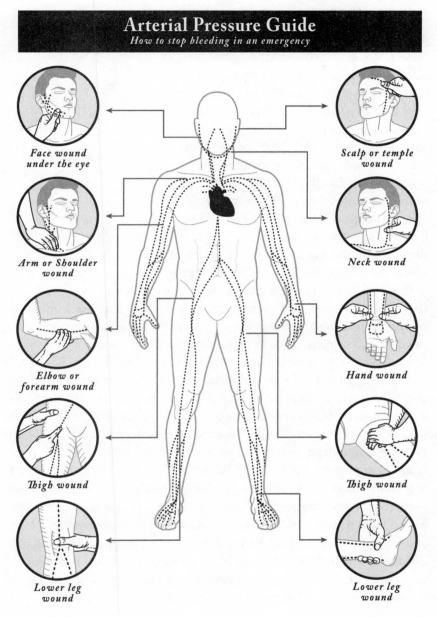

Face wound under the eye

Scalp or temple wound

Arm or Shoulder wound

Neck wound

Elbow or forearm wound

Hand wound

Thigh wound

Thigh wound

Lower leg wound

Lower leg wound

are a good choice for bleeding injuries to the torso or other areas of the body (neck, armpit, groin) where applying a tourniquet is not possible.

When injuries such as severed limbs or damage to major blood vessels like the femoral artery are spurting blood or releasing a large volume of blood at a rapid pace, apply direct pressure with the heel of your hand or your knee (so you can operate hands-free) and apply a tourniquet immediately. The MeatEater crew never bothered carrying tourniquets in our first-aid kits until an emergency medicine doctor set us straight on why we should always have one close at hand. Tourniquets are estimated to have saved the lives of over 3,000 American soldiers since 2006, when they became standard-issue military equipment. In the immediate aftermath of the 2013 Boston Marathon bombing, nearly 300 people were left gravely wounded, many with life-threatening bleeding injuries. Although three people died, the quick thinking of bystanders and the widespread use of makeshift tourniquets is credited with saving many lives that day. As for makeshift tourniquets, they're great if you're adaptable and quick-thinking enough to put one to use. But you can't beat having a real tourniquet located in a convenient place in your backpack. In the time it takes you to unlace your boot and tie the lace into a knot, your buddy could be dead.

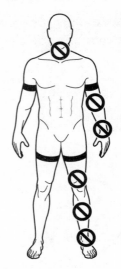

Safe tourniquet locations

However, in order for tourniquets to work, they need to be applied correctly. Tourniquets must be placed well above bleeding injuries to effectively seal off blood vessels. It's also crucial that they be cranked down very tightly. A properly applied tourniquet should be tightened enough to cause a significant amount of pain; anything short of that will allow blood to continue seeping out of the wound. It's also important to note that tourniquets can be left in place for up to about six hours without permanent tissue damage. This buys you the time you need when medical help isn't nearby. Once it's been applied, leave the tourniquet in place, and don't loosen it to check to see if the bleeding stopped. This will just dislodge formed clots and cause bleeding to begin. Know how tourniquets work, and practice using them before an emergency occurs. Go to www.BleedingControl.org for more information.

INFECTED WOUNDS

For the most part, uncontrolled bleeding is a much more immediate threat than infection. If you keep wounds clean and disinfected, there's a good chance that you'll be able to avoid the second fate altogether. Even if an infection does develop, generally speaking, it takes some time for that infection to become dangerously septic. So infections probably won't be your first concern in a survival situation—but they *can* become serious medical emergencies if help isn't readily available.

If an infected wound festers long enough without treatment, the dangerous condition known as sepsis may set in. As bacterial loads increase and spread from the wound throughout the body, chemicals are released to fight the infection. This leads to inflammation and septic shock, causing impaired blood flow, organ failure, and eventual death. Early signs of serious infection are red, swollen skin that's painful and warm to the touch. Yellow or green discharge of pus and red streaks on the skin running outward from the wound are symptoms that an infection has begun to fester and spread. Victims of sepsis experience confusion, fevers, nausea, and rapid pulses and breathing.

Again, dangerous infections generally take time to develop, but not all of them move slowly. Necrotizing fasciitis (flesh-eating disease) is largely sensationalized in the media, but it can be fatal in less than twenty-four hours. The bacteria that cause the flesh-eating disease are sometimes present in stagnant lakes or ponds, and can also be found in the ocean. The pathogens typically enter the body through open wounds, and this sort of infection is typified by pain out of proportion to the type and size of wound. If you have an unhealed cut or burn, avoid swimming or wading in warm bodies of water, especially if they're dirty or polluted.

Tetanus is another very dangerous infection caused by bacteria found more often in the outdoors. Commonly known as lockjaw, it's caused by a strain of bacteria found in dirt and manure. As kids, we believed that rusty metal was the source of lockjaw, and that if you skipped a tetanus shot and wound up stepping on a rusty nail, you'd die. The truth is more complicated. The bacteria that causes tetanus often clings to dirty, rusted metal. It's also an organism that thrives in oxygen-deprived environments like the puncture wounds caused by stepping on a nail. Tetanus infections release toxins that cause agonizing, paralytic muscle spasms that usually begin in the jaw and progress throughout the body, and the infection has a high mortality rate. Fortunately, tetanus infections are very rare and completely avoidable. As long as you stay current on your tetanus vaccinations (every ten years, or sooner if you experience a heavily contaminated wound), you've got nothing to worry about.

The danger of contracting tetanus is low, but you will need to take some precautions to avoid other, more common infections. Clean open wounds with sterile water and iodine solution or alcohol swabs and treat them with periodic applications of antibiotic ointment. Keep them covered and dry. By taking these simple steps, healthy individuals are usually able to fight off minor infections without further medical treatments. More serious infections that become septic require admission to a hospital for a course of antibiotic treatments, along with other medications and interventions.

AN EMERGENCY MEDICINE DOCTOR'S GUIDE TO WOUND CARE

Once an open wound has stopped bleeding, your next concern should be preventing infection. Wound irrigation will be your first line of defense—as we say, "The solution to pollution is dilution." Use lots of water, at least 50 ml per centimeter of cut. Ideally, the water should be sterile, but if not, it should at least appear clean. Don't use stagnant pond water. Do use an irrigation syringe or a sealable, gallon-size plastic bag filled with water. Bunch up the excess plastic as if you were using a cake frosting bag, poke a small hole in the bottom corner, and you'll have a nice pressurized stream that should be able to dislodge large contaminants and microscopic bacteria.

After a thorough cleaning, the next step is closing the wound by covering it with clean bandages—leave the stitching to the professionals. In the emergency department, lacerations are sutured as a means of restoring normal anatomy and reducing the risk of infection and scarring, a task that would be complicated by less-than-hygienic surroundings. On a hunting or camping trip in the woods, suturing a wound with homemade stitches isn't a good idea, although if you have clean equipment (a boiled needle and silk or nylon thread) and societal collapse is imminent, then sewing the wound shut is conceivable. For small, deep cuts without significant gapping, you can use superglue to close wounds—it's the same stuff we use in the hospital, just not as strong. Pinch the skin edges together, apply a thin layer on the top of the closed edges (not inside the wound), and hold for two to three minutes, until dry. If you get sloppy and need to do some cleanup, Vaseline or antibiotic ointment can help remove superglue from the skin or eyes.

Not all wounds can be closed with superglue, and sometimes wounds should be left open. Generally, if a wound is more than eight hours old, doctors don't sew it up, as there is an increased likelihood of infection due to prolonged exposure to bacteria in the environment. The laceration will heal as the edges grow inward, though it may leave a significant scar. The eight-hour rule is broken only when there is a laceration on sensitive tissue or on the face, since scarring there is generally unacceptable.

If you can't get to an emergency department quickly and your wound requires professional care, use regular soap and water to wash the wound, and change the dressing twice daily if you can; if neither step is possible, just keep the wound covered until you can get help. In the case of a deep puncture, you can be sure there are microscopic particles and foreign bodies down in there that will be hard to remove. Infection will be likely. Wounds over the knuckles of the hand and punctures to hands or the sole of the foot are particularly prone to deeper infections. You'll want to have these types of injuries examined by a doctor as soon as you can.

—By Dr. Alan Lazzara, an emergency medicine physician, hunter, wilderness medicine instructor, and devoted husband and father of three based in Ann Arbor, Michigan

SHOCK

Shock is a dangerous condition that can lead to organ failure, brain damage, and death. Often brought on by severe infections and massive hemorrhage, it can also be set in motion by a number of conditions including poisoning, burns, and allergic reactions. During trauma, blood flow is typically diverted away from the extremities and toward vital organs, inducing the dangerously low blood pressure that is a hallmark of shock. Your body responds with an influx of adrenaline, which causes the peripheral blood vessels to clamp down and makes your heart pump faster and faster. Symptoms include cool and pale or bluish skin, sweating, rapid breathing and pulse, weakness, dizziness, nausea and vomiting, and enlarged pupils. Some victims may become unconscious. Begin first aid immediately if you suspect someone is experiencing shock.

- Loosen tight clothing.
- Lay the person in a comfortable position with feet elevated.
- Wrap them in a warm blanket or sleeping bag.
- Don't give them anything to eat or drink.
- Call 911.
- Monitor vital signs and perform CPR if necessary.

HEAD AND NECK INJURIES

Although traumatic injuries to the head, neck, and spine sometimes occur in tandem with one another, they have separate diagnosis and treatment protocols depending on the site and on the specifics of the injury. Head injuries can present as open wounds with bleeding, as visible skull fractures, or as closed wounds that don't exhibit any obvious signs of trauma. Closed wounds can be just as dangerous as open wounds. The force of a blow to the head can smash the brain against the inside of the skull, resulting in concussion, intracranial hemorrhage, and swelling that can compress the brain. Aside from bleeding wounds, signs of possible cranial or brain trauma include skull deformities, bruising around the eyes or ears, dilated pupils or vision problems, clear fluid draining from the nose or ears, confusion, drowsiness, and loss of consciousness. Vomiting is another red flag for serious head injuries, especially in children.

Initial first-aid treatments for head wounds should immobilize the victim and control bleeding—scalp wounds bleed profusely. Monitor vitals and perform CPR if necessary. Be aware that head wounds are often accompanied by cervical (neck) fractures or damage to the spinal cord that may cause cold, clammy skin, tingling, numbness, or paralysis. Unless it's absolutely necessary in order to prevent further injury or death, do not move anyone who you suspect may have an injured neck—this can do further damage to the spinal cord and the nervous system. Support the head and neck with rolled-up clothing to prevent movement. Injuries to the head or neck can do lasting physical or neurological damage and be fatal. Do whatever is necessary to get professional medical help, and do it quickly.

BREATHING DIFFICULTIES

Described by the medical term "dyspnea," a sudden bout of shortness of breath and labored breathing can be caused by such a wide range of factors that identifying the culprit isn't always a straightforward process. Just a few possible causes for acute dyspnea include asthma attacks, altitude sickness, panic attacks, allergies, or even heart attacks. Any chronic breathing problems need to be diagnosed by a medical professional, and sudden acute shortness of breath should be investigated promptly.

But labored breathing might be the result of something as simple as pushing yourself too hard. We've got a simple fitness mantra around the

MeatEater office: "Legs and lungs." Basically, it's a way of reminding our-selves to stay in good shape. Do the same and you'll avoid prolonged breathing difficulties associated with physical exertion.

If you're unable to catch your breath after resting for a few minutes, at best you're probably grossly out of shape; at worst, you could be looking at a serious medical emergency and a trip to the hospital.

ALLERGIES

An uptick in allergy symptoms due to increased exposure to tree, grass, and weed pollens can be an unsurprising side effect of spending time outdoors. Most of the time, the symptoms are fairly manageable. We pack over-the-counter antihistamines and eye drops and use them to ease sneezing attacks, stuffy noses, and itchy eyes as needed. But those with severe allergies to specific plants, animals, or foods need to take extra precautions, especially when traveling beyond the immediate reach of emergency services.

Inform your companions of any serious allergies, including any medi-cines you are allergic to; if you wind up needing care and are unable to speak, passing along this information could save your life (though ide-ally you would also be wearing a medical ID bracelet). If you carry an EpiPen or an inhaler, let everybody know where you keep it.

Know the symptoms of a severe allergy attack. Asthma, a condition characterized by a swelling and narrowing of the airways, can be set off by both allergens and exercise; symptoms can range from mild to poten-tially lethal. Shortness of breath, coughing, and wheezing or whistling exhalations indicate a severe attack. If symptoms do not improve with the use of an inhaler and/or continue to worsen, seek immediate medical care.

Although they can have several causes, skin symptoms like rashes and hives are often telltale signs of an allergic reaction—whether they are the result of insect bites, contact dermatitis from exposure to plants such as poison oak (see page 164), or exposure due to inhalation or ingestion. Hives that involve swelling of the tongue or throat are always cause for concern, as they may inhibit breathing. Hives that are combined with vomiting require the administration of an EpiPen and a visit to the ER. But if hives symptoms are mild, do not impede breathing, are limited to the skin, and subside with the administration of antihistamines, further intervention may not be needed.

Unfortunately, hives can be the opening salvo in a series of escalating symptoms. Whether they ride along with hives or appear on their own, symptoms such as shortness of breath, constriction of the airways, anxiety and confusion, heart palpitations, dizziness and/or fainting, and diminished blood pressure marked by pallor or blue skin are signs of a potentially lethal condition called anaphylactic shock. An inflammation response during which the body overreacts in an attempt to fight an allergen, anaphylaxis can be deadly. The only treatment for anaphylactic shock is an injection of epinephrine (from an EpiPen) followed by a trip to the nearest emergency room. If the condition is serious enough to require that emergency services come to you, have the victim lie flat with their feet elevated, and cover them with a blanket or sleeping bag. The most common causes of severe allergic reactions are medications, peanuts and tree nuts, fish and shellfish, dairy, stings from bees and wasps, and bites from fire ants.

If you have known food allergies, it goes without saying that you need to be extra mindful about reading labels when purchasing food supplies; if multiple allergies make it challenging for you to find safe options in the camping foods aisle, consider making your own snacks and/or freeze-dried meals (see pages 76 and 73). Signs of allergic reactions to food include skin rash or hives, nausea, diarrhea, vomiting, and abdominal pain; serious food allergies may progress to anaphylactic shock. If a known serious allergen has been accidentally ingested, an EpiPen may be deployed as a preventive measure.

SEIZURES

Seizures are sudden electrical disturbances in the brain that can strike at any moment, and they're more common than you might think. While they're no more or less likely to occur in the outdoors than they are in everyday life, they can be exponentially more difficult to manage when help is hours or days away.

There are several types of seizures—from petit mal or absence seizures that might amount to a few moments of staring into space to grand mal seizures that involve muscle jerks and loss of consciousness. And there are countless potential causes—genetic seizure disorders such as epilepsy, low blood sugar or sodium levels, brain injury, infection, adverse reaction to medications, stroke (covered here on page 387), fever (page 365), and poisoning (page 371) among them. Diagnosis of seizures without a clear inciting event such as trauma or missed medications is extremely complex.

Not all seizures are cause for serious concern. Even in cases when an individual with epilepsy loses consciousness, if the seizure is shorter than five minutes and occurs as an isolated event, the CDC maintains that you don't need to call 911.

No matter the length, a call to emergency services *is* recommended for anyone suffering a seizure for the first time. Time the seizure if you can. Don't put a spoon or finger in the seizing person's mouth—that whole "swallow the tongue" thing is another one of those medical myths. Don't attempt to restrain the person if they are having jerky movements. Do carefully roll them onto their side to help them breathe, and loosen any item of clothing that might be restricting air flow. If low blood sugar in a diabetic is a suspected cause for a seizure, administer glucose gel or tabs (diabetics should carry some in their survival kits), rub honey on their gums, or have them drink some juice or eat a candy bar or energy bar.

Early warning signs of a seizure may include confusion, a gaze that goes vacant, and a mounting sense of anxiety. Sleep deprivation and stress are known triggers for those who suffer from epilepsy. As with any other medical conditions, those who suffer from epilepsy or other seizure disorders should alert their companions and travel with a medication buffer.

HEART ATTACKS

The result of a blockage in a coronary artery cutting off the flow of oxygen to the heart, a heart attack (myocardial infarction) falls into the category of ailments that are usually the result of an underlying condition. Coronary artery disease, high cholesterol, hypertension, poor diet, and lack of exercise are all indicators for potential heart troubles, but there are other possible causes, including congenital heart problems and blood-clotting disorders. Heart disease is the number one cause of premature death within the United States—a statistic that hammers home the importance of learning CPR.

Prevention boils down to the familiar edicts about regular exercise, eating a healthful diet, maintaining an appropriate weight, not smoking, and managing stress. For those over forty without a prior track record of regular exercise and/or with other common risk factors, a checkup is recommended before engaging in rigorous exercise. Anyone with significant risk factors should be particularly cautious about exerting themselves in hot environments—heat means that the resting heart rate will already be elevated.

Many heart attacks strike without warning, but some will be presaged by one or more of the following symptoms: recurring chest tightness and pain that can radiate into the arms or neck, weakness and light-headedness, fainting or near fainting, indigestion and/or vomiting, back and/or jaw pain, and shortness of breath. Not all heart attacks result in chest pain or dramatic falls to the ground—heart attacks that manifest with subtler symptoms can wind up being just as deadly.

Any suspected heart attack is cause for a trip to the ER. On the way there or while awaiting rescue, victims should chew a single dose of aspirin (325 mg), then swallow it with water. Sometimes prescribed in low doses as a daily regimen for heart attack prevention, aspirin has blood-thinning properties that can be a lifesaver in the case of heart attacks. (That same quality is the reason you should never give it to a person who is wounded and experiencing significant blood loss.)

If the victim is unconscious, run through the ABCs on page 352; if no pulse is found, cardiac arrest is likely. Begin performing CPR and continue to do so until emergency services arrive. If you have access to one of the portable automated external defibrillators increasingly being made available in heavily trafficked areas of national parks, apply the AED as you continue giving CPR; rangers are also increasingly being equipped with the devices and may be able to get to you in time, depending on your location.

Cardiac arrest is the cessation of the heart muscle pumping blood. This can occur during a heart attack, when abnormal heart rhythms stop the effective squeezing of the heart, but it can also be the result of other underlying cardiac issues. Cardiac arrest is a dire circumstance that can be permanently fatal if CPR is not administered or appropriate shocks from an AED are not delivered immediately. If blood flow is not restored, the brain will suffer irreparable damage, and death will occur in minutes.

STROKES

The fifth-leading cause of death in the United States, strokes are the brain equivalent of heart attacks. They occur when blood flow to the brain is suddenly halted or compromised, causing brain tissue that is cut off from oxygen and nutrients to begin to die.

There are two kinds of strokes: the more common ischemic strokes resulting from blocked arteries (clots), and the less common hemorrhagic strokes that occur when a blood vessel leaks or bursts. Emergency room treatment will differ depending on the type of stroke and the location of the clot or bleeding, but your own protocol should remain the same—getting to that emergency room as quickly as possible.

Know the classic signs of stroke:

- Slurring words, trouble speaking
- Paralysis or numbness on face, arm, or leg, often affecting only one side of the body
- Blurred or blackened vision, seeing double
- Sudden, severe headache, sometimes accompanied by vomiting and dizziness
- Dizziness and trouble walking
- Drooping of the face, often affecting only one side when smiling

If you or any of your companions experience any of these symptoms, immediately call 911. The quicker you can access treatment, the better the odds of preventing long-term loss of function. If blood flow to the brain is compromised only temporarily and resolves on its own, the stroke (in this case called a transient ischemic attack) may not cause lasting symptoms, but should be considered a warning sign for a more serious episode.

The best treatment for strokes is prevention. The same lifestyle factors that lead to increased risk of heart attacks are at play—poor diet, lack of exercise, excess weight, high blood pressure and cholesterol levels, smoking, or overindulging in alcohol. Stay on the straight and narrow to avoid becoming a statistic.

EYE INJURIES

It's all too easy to overlook how vulnerable our eyes are during outdoor pursuits. But unfortunately, there are a multitude of ways you could end up with an irritated, infected, or injured eye.

Exposure to dust, smoke, or pollen particles can make your eyes itchy, dry, and painful. Regularly flushing the eye with sterile water or saline solution will help to get rid of accumulations of tiny irritants. We carry small bottles of lubricating eye drops in our first-aid kits for this purpose. Larger debris that gets lodged in the eye can scratch the cornea and lead to keratitis, a painful inflammation that causes light sensitivity and blurry vision; keratitis can also be caused by contact lenses or water contaminated with bacteria.

Know that you can infect your eyes with dirty fingers just as easily as you can contaminate your food, so take a look back at the hygiene section of this chapter if you need to. Most cases of conjunctivitis, more commonly known as pinkeye, are viral in origin, but some are linked to bacterial infections. The pain, itching, and swelling associated with pinkeye are bad enough on their own, but the condition can lead to further infections in the ear, nose, and throat. To treat, use warm washcloth compresses five to six times per day, wiping the closed eyelid clean of any discharge. Avoid wiping the eyeball itself, and get follow-up care if the condition does not subside within a week. Some cases may require prescription topical or oral antibiotics.

Infections aside, the soft, sensitive tissue that makes up your eyeball is susceptible to all sorts of traumatic injuries. We've also witnessed folks getting their eyeballs burned by splattered cooking oil and fire embers, scratched by flying insects, and caught by fishing hooks. In the case of injuries like these, gently flush the injured eye with sterile water or saline. Next, cover the eye and do your best to keep it immobilized; blinking and moving the injured eye around to look at things can cause further damage. Cover the eye with soft gauze, then tape over the gauze to hold it in place until you get to a doctor. Ideally, you'd cover both eyes since they move in tandem; if you only cover the injured eye, it will still move when the uncovered eye does. Granted, this may not be practical if you need to navigate your way out of the woods or drive yourself to an emergency room.

It's worth emphasizing that most traumatic eye injuries can be avoided simply by wearing sunglasses. A couple years back, one of our camera operators, Dirt Myth, had his eyeball punctured by a pine needle during a backcountry bear hunt. Dirt is tough as nails, but his pain was so great he was forced to walk several miles back to the vehicle for an emergency visit to the nearest eye doctor. Had he been wearing sunglasses, he could have avoided the surgery that ensued. Close-fitting, wraparound-style sunglasses with shatterproof lenses are the best choice for eye protection. They keep out dust and debris and deflect branches and fishhooks. Of course, sunglasses are also handy for blocking out harmful UV rays, but we'll wear them even on cloudy days if we're busting through thick brush. If you don't have shooting glasses or safety goggles, wear sunglasses when you're using a firearm or a chainsaw. They should be considered mandatory outdoor safety equipment for everyone, so make sure your kids are wearing them, too.

PRESCRIPTION EYEWEAR AND BACKCOUNTRY LIVING

For active pursuits like hiking, hunting, skiing, and biking in the back-country, many of us prefer contact lenses over glasses. Unlike glasses, contacts won't constantly shift around or fall off (although on rare occasions they do pop out). Contact lenses are also a lot less likely to get scratched or broken. Whatever you choose to wear, how-ever, you need to put some effort into taking care of your eyes and eyewear in the outdoors. If you lose the ability to see properly, you could end up in a tough spot.

Glasses used in the backcountry should have sturdy frames and be secured on a lanyard or retainer. Bring a case for safe storage as well as a lens cloth and cleaning solution to keep things clean and clear. If you wear glasses daily, it's a good idea to pack prescription shades as well. If you're a contact lens wearer, you might consider bringing a pair of glasses as backup—although that's a personal de-cision based on the duration of the trip and just how screwed you'd be if you lost your contacts.

The best choice for backcountry contacts is daily-wear lenses rather than the extended-wear kind. Daily-wear lenses provide you with fresh, clean contacts every day with no washing or rinsing. One drawback is the small amount of plastic waste they create on a daily basis, but it amounts to less than an ounce over the course of a week, so the inconvenience of carrying out your used lenses is negligible. Daily-wear lenses are more expensive than extended-wear lenses, but the latter require more handling, along with a bottle of cleaning solution. Extended-wear lens cases can get grimy, and since it's very difficult to properly clean contacts in outdoor environments, the risk for infection or irritation of your eyes increases. Lenses stored in solution overnight are also at risk of freezing, which will ruin them. Be sure to keep them inside your sleeping bag with you on cold nights.

Sleeping with your contacts in is not recommended by optome-trists, but everyone forgets and does it at times. In fact, on a limited basis, it's not a bad idea in the backcountry. Sleeping in your contacts for a night keeps dirty fingers out of your eyes longer, and getting two days of wear from your contacts before replacement might be a worthwhile trade-off. Just remember to apply rewetting drops be-fore bed, in the morning, and throughout the day as needed. A dry contact lens could get stuck to your eyeball and cause a corneal abrasion.

No matter which lenses you decide on, you'll need to bring along some basic items for dealing with contacts.

1. A small mirror for inserting and extracting contacts. Your phone won't work well for this task, as its camera isn't directly in line with the screen. (The mirror can also be used for signaling.)

2. Soap for washing hands prior to handling contact lenses, in order to decrease risk of infection and irritation. Germs, grit, bug spray, sunscreen, and oils from your own skin can all cause irritation. Dr. Bronner's soap is super concentrated; a 1-ounce container could get you through a whole week of hand and face washing. Cleaning your hands with wipes also works, but if you use alcohol wipes, allow your hands to dry thoroughly before touching your eye with your finger—the alcohol will sting and irritate your eyes otherwise. Grimy contact lens cases are the source of many eye infections; treat the case with a brief weekly boil.

3. Rewetting drops to combat backcountry conditions like dust, wind, dry air, and high elevations, all of which can dry out eyes and contact lenses faster than normal conditions.

4. In addition to your daily supply of lenses, stash a couple of pairs of emergency backup lenses in your first-aid kit.

EAR INJURIES

Ear injuries aren't very common, but they should still be on your radar. It's not unheard of for people to get a tiny piece of woody debris, sand, or even a mosquito wedged inside their ear. We've heard horror stories of ticks burrowing into the ear canal to feed, only to get stuck there. The chances of something like that happening are slim, but they are increased in the outdoors. Such situations can be extremely annoying, painful, and potentially dangerous. Foreign objects that become lodged in the ear canal often need to be carefully removed by an ear, nose, and throat specialist. However, you may be able to flush the object out with sterile water if you have an irrigation syringe in your first-aid kit. If an insect becomes lodged in the ear canal, trying to dig it out will be futile (and could cause an eardrum perforation if you go too deep with a tool). However, you can quickly drown it by filling the ear canal with mineral oil or cooking oil in order to put a stop to its incessant buzzing. The insect can then later be removed by a physician with appropriate tools.

Ruptured eardrums caused by traumatic injuries or extremely loud noises (see the section on gunshots, below) should be examined by a doctor immediately. Dizziness, pain, nausea, vomiting, and ringing in the ear (tinnitus) are symptoms of a ruptured eardrum. Although these injuries usually heal on their own, ruptured eardrums may need to be surgically repaired and can lead to infections and loss of hearing without proper treatment.

DENTAL INJURIES

Painful tooth problems just plain suck, no matter where you are. But dealing with an exposed nerve on a chipped tooth or an infected, abscessed root while you're out in the wilderness is a truly horrible experience. The pain can be so distracting that your mental state deteriorates with each passing hour, making simple camp chores or hiking seem impossible. To make things worse, when you're miles from civilization, there is little you can do to permanently fix things. Short of practicing some old-fashioned frontier dentistry by yanking the problem tooth out of your jaw with multi-tool pliers, all you can do is temporarily reduce pain and discomfort.

We'd recommend staying away from the pliers unless you're deep in the backcountry, weeks from medical care, and have no other options. For short-term pain management, alternating between doses of ibuprofen and acetaminophen is an effective strategy. Using an injured or infected tooth to mash up an aspirin can have a numbing effect on the tooth, but don't overdo it—heavy doses of aspirin applied topically are caustic enough to cause sores inside the mouth. A more natural remedy calls for biting down on a tea bag. Black tea is a vasoconstrictor, helping to ease pain and inflammation by reducing blood flow to the injured tooth. In the case of a chipped tooth that throbs with every breath, it's possible to cap the tooth with a small amount of superglue; this prevents pain by eliminating air flow over the exposed nerve. Admittedly, this is a delicate process that requires a small and precisely placed application of glue. In order to avoid gluing your tongue to your teeth, it's best accomplished with the help of a partner who can see exactly what's going on.

Counterintuitively, an otherwise healthy tooth that gets completely knocked out, root and all, is a little easier to manage. Rinse the tooth with water to clean it, but do not scrub the root (it will damage the very necessary periodontal ligaments). Pay attention to the tooth orientation (front/back) and insert it gently back into the open socket. Time is of the essence—if the tooth is temporarily reimplanted in the socket within thirty minutes, it has 100 percent viability, potentially enabling a dentist to save it; if two hours have passed without reimplantation, the tooth is essentially dead. If you're not up to trying temporary reimplantation or if the tooth just won't go back in, you can store it between your cheek and gum, in a glass of milk, or even in a small amount of spit. A tooth preserved in this fashion has a much better chance of survival.

If it's a child's primary (baby) tooth that has been knocked out, it should never be reimplanted, as it may fuse with the underlying secondary tooth and ultimately cause a cosmetic deformity.

Remember, none of these are permanent solutions. Chipped teeth need to be fixed by a dentist, and oral surgery might be necessary for more serious injuries. Abscessed teeth require prescription antibiotics. Otherwise, they can quickly fester into dangerous, even deadly infections. In the event of any major dental problems, you need to pack up your gear, head for town, and get professional medical help pronto.

FOOT PROBLEMS

We've already mentioned that you can avoid all sorts of trouble with the right footwear, but it's inevitable that no matter what you've got on your feet, they're going to get dinged up now and then. If you want to avoid the kind of problems that can completely shut down an excursion, you need to put some serious effort into making sure your feet are in good working order.

Blisters. Watch out for blisters anytime you're hiking, but be especially vigilant over long distances in uneven terrain. Blisters develop when friction causes the outer layer of skin to separate from the lower layer of skin. This bubble of skin then fills with fluid. Blisters tend to occur most frequently on the heel, the toes, and the ball of the foot. In high-friction areas like these, blisters may burst and tear, or slough off completely. The resulting raw, extremely painful wound can severely hinder mobility. The best plan for dealing with blisters is prevention, which starts with quality hiking socks, footwear that fits properly, and keeping your feet dry. Next, watch out for hot spots on your feet. A patch of red, hot, itchy or painful skin is a precursor to a blister and shouldn't be ignored. At the first sign of a hot spot, take off your shoes and socks and let your feet air out. If your socks are damp, switch them out for a dry pair. That might be enough to get you back on the trail, but pay close attention to your feet. If things get worse and a blister starts to develop, you'll need to break out your first-aid kit right away.

As soon as a blister appears, you need to prevent the problem from worsening by creating a barrier between the surface of the blister and your sock (or the inside of your shoe if you're foolish enough to hike without socks). This can be done by covering the blister with bandages, medical tape, or even duct tape if that's all you have, but adhesive moleskin works even better. Moleskin comes in sheets or differently sized and shaped patches designed for certain spots on the foot; they can also be cut to size for a custom fit. The soft, fuzzy surface of moleskin creates a friction-free, protective cushion over the blister that should allow you to continue walking without too much pain. Some folks advocate lancing blisters with a needle in order to drain the liquid and speed healing. We haven't had much success with that technique. In fact, popping a blister only seems to make it more likely to turn into a raw, open sore that's at high risk of infection.

Ingrown toenails. Hikers can also be forced off their feet by an ingrown toenail—when the sharp edge of a nail digs painfully into the surrounding skin and flesh. They develop most often on the big toe and can cause swelling, infections, and abscesses if left untreated. Doctors often surgically remove the ingrown portion of the nail in order to alleviate pain and reduce inflammation. Normally, we wouldn't recommend performing surgery on yourself out in the field, but on long trips, your only option might be to carefully remove the offending edge of the toenail with a knife or razor blade if your toe becomes unbearably uncomfortable from getting jostled around inside your boot while hiking. First, be sure to sterilize your blade and multitool pliers with boiling water or alcohol swabs. Thoroughly wash the toe and your hands. Then cut the toenail as shown, being careful not to

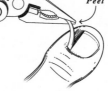

Cut the edge of the ingrown toenail straight down the nail bed as shown. Lift the cut edge away from the toe and grab it with your pliers, then pull it free.

slice into the flesh below the nail. Be sure to apply antibiotic ointment and bandage the toe when you're done. If the method is performed properly, relief and healing come quickly. In the meantime, take over-the-counter pain medication as necessary.

Jungle rot. Trench foot (see page 368) is associated with cold environments, but jungle rot happens in hot, humid climates. Like trench foot, it's a condition with a strong military connection. During the Vietnam War, soldiers wore leather combat boots that were designed for relatively dry environments. Because their feet stewed inside wet boots and socks in Vietnam's tropical jungles, soldiers experienced a variety of ulcerous fungal and bacterial infections on their feet; these collectively came to be known as jungle rot. If you're spending time in an environment where jungle rot thrives, you can steer clear of it by skipping the socks and wearing breathable shoes or closed-toe sandals that drain well and allow air to circulate around your feet. As an added precaution, take every available opportunity to remove your shoes and thoroughly dry out your feet.

Athlete's foot. While jungle rot is mostly limited to tropical environments, athlete's foot is a common contagious fungal infection that can strike anywhere. As the name suggests, people usually pick it up in warm, moist environments like pools, showers, and gym locker rooms. It can strike outdoors, too, if you regularly wear sweaty socks and shoes. Athlete's foot isn't as dangerous as trench foot or jungle rot, but it can cause itching, discomfort, and pain. Infected skin becomes red, dry, and flaky. Cracks, blisters, and sores may also develop, increasing the risk of infection. You can lower your chances of contracting athlete's foot by thoroughly washing your feet regularly in soapy water as well as changing socks and drying out your footwear on a daily basis. Topical ointments and powders used for treating athlete's foot are available over the counter, but prescription medications may be necessary to treat severe cases.

BITES, STINGS, AND MORE

We probably spend more time outdoors than we do in our own homes. In all that time, we've learned firsthand that there are all kinds of flora and fauna out there that can make you sick or hurt you. From a case of poison oak so bad it required hospitalization to contracting Lyme disease from a tick bite, the MeatEater crew is no stranger to getting laid low by Mother Nature's mean streak. For information on treating insect stings, snakebites, poisonous plant exposure, and more, see the chapter on the dangers of the plant and animal kingdom (page 161).

BULLSHIT ALERT:

WHAT HOLLYWOOD GETS WRONG

Just like a lot of things in real life that movies tend to get wildly wrong, Hollywood's version of lifesaving first-aid techniques is more fiction than fact. From countless old black-and-white westerns to big budget action films, Tinsel Town has proven over and over that movies shouldn't be your go-to source for good medical advice. Take snakebites, for instance.

The scene is a familiar one: Left for dead without a horse, our heroic protagonist wanders on foot through the desert. Sun beating down, he steps on a rattlesnake with a dusty cowboy boot. Somehow, the serpent manages to leap through the air and bite the hero on the forearm. He's in a tough spot, but not to worry. He wraps a bandana above the bite and uses an oversized Bowie knife to cut a deep X into the flesh across the fang marks. Then he sucks the venom from the wound and furiously spits the poison into the dirt. Our hero lives to see another day and strides off into the sunset to exact revenge on his enemies.

If you get bitten by a venomous snake and are tempted to try the method out, think again. As a real-world medical intervention, this bit of Hollywood magic wouldn't play out so smoothly. The venom-sucking method doesn't work and risks contaminating the wound with mouth bacteria. Venom spreads so quickly into the bloodstream that it would be hopeless to believe you could suck out enough to make any kind of a difference.

Cauterization is another cinematic self-rescue convention that doesn't pass muster, whether it's stopping the bleeding from a spurting stump with a red-hot knife or igniting a pile of loose gunpowder on top of a bullet wound. According to emergency medicine doctor Alan Lazzara, modern cautery is done with a very fine instrument that is pointedly directed at very small blood vessels. It's an almost microscopic process. Should you find yourself alone, injured, and shirtless, we don't recommend filling a wound with gunpowder and lighting it on fire with a flaming stick à la Rambo. "This is a terrible idea," Lazzara told us. "Large-scale cauterization may indeed stop some, but not all, of the bleeding. You'll still have hemorrhage along with the added cost of a third-degree burn. This would create more destruction to wide swaths of skin, blood vessels, and muscle, and vastly increase the likelihood of infection."

What about performing emergency surgery to remove a bullet or arrowhead from someone in order to save their life? Also bullshit, according to Lazzara. Without the proper surgical expertise and equipment, digging around in a hemorrhaging wound will only worsen the bleeding and send someone to the grave faster. In the event of a wound causing uncontrolled bleeding, applying a tourniquet is a far better course of action. And even if the bleeding has been brought under control, you risk introducing a deadly infection by further exposing the injury to bacteria. Prying a bloody bullet out of the hero's shoulder is an iconic part of the Hollywood action movie genre, but here in the real world, medical experts warn against removing foreign objects from wounds. Leave that to the professionals.

HUNTING AND ANGLING INJURIES

There's no escaping the reality that hunting and fishing come with hazards that other outdoor pastimes lack—more often than not, there's an unmistakable correlation between activity and injury. Falling out of a treestand simply isn't something that day hikers need to worry about, and we've never met anyone who sliced open their hand with a fillet knife while bird-watching.

Our aim in pointing this out isn't to disparage other outdoor hobbies as completely risk-free, especially given day hikers' propensity for twisting ankles or unexpectedly spending an unplanned night out in the woods. Rather, we're stressing the fact that the hook and bullet community regularly exposes itself to all kinds of things that could put them in harm's way. There's no need for hunters and anglers to become paranoid about getting hurt, but we should always be striving for a safe outdoors experience by maintaining constant vigilance. Many of the types of injuries that hunters and anglers are more likely to suffer are the result of laziness, inattention, or complacency. Don't assume these things won't happen to you—the minute you let your guard down is when bad things happen.

COMMON FISHING INJURIES

Norman Rockwell's bucolic images of youngsters and old codgers with cane poles at farm ponds didn't exactly paint fishing as a dangerous pastime. Usually it's not. But as counterintuitive as it might seem, we've witnessed far more injuries related to fishing than hunting. Although the vast majority weren't severe, some were trip-enders, and a few were bad enough to send people to the emergency room. A fly fishing guide we know broke her femur when a wind gust slammed an anchored drift boat into her leg, pinning her between the boat and the riverbank. A buddy of ours was standing on a coral head when he hooked into a shark. When the shark bit through the line, he lost his balance and fell onto a black urchin that impaled his hand. His fingers didn't work right for six months. In Alaska, we watched a guy get his hook snagged on a submerged log. He tightened down his drag and started walking backward up the riverbank in an effort to pull it free. When the line snapped under tremendous force, the guy's lead sinker came back at him and hit him right between the eyes, knocking him out cold. His buddies had to carry him out. Another acquaintance was setting a catfish trotline and fell out of the back of his boat; he drowned after receiving some serious prop gashes. Those are just a few examples; it's hard to list them all.

Water. The most obvious threat to anglers lies in the fact that fish are found in water and water is inherently dangerous. Drowning is a leading cause of accidental death for fishermen, and a study conducted by the Red Cross in Canada found that the rate of drowning deaths among anglers exceeded that of all swimmers, canoers, kayakers, and scuba divers combined. Of the hundreds of fishing-related deaths documented in the study, 90 percent of the victims weren't wearing life jackets and two-thirds were poor swimmers or non-swimmers. Many victims also engaged in careless behaviors such as overloading small fishing vessels, ignoring small craft advisories, and wading in deep, swift rivers. Finally, alcohol consumption was a factor in over half of fishing-related drownings. In citing these statistics, we're certainly not suggesting anyone avoid going fishing. On the contrary, we think fishing is pretty damn safe as long as you're using good judgment; for more information on water safety, see Chapter 6, "Navigation and Wilderness Travel" (page 266).

Hooks. Fishing equipment can also be dangerous, albeit not as life-threatening as getting drunk, losing your balance, and falling into cold water while you're taking a leak off the bow of a rocking boat. Over the years, we've seen dozens of gory images of fishing hooks buried in faces, hands, and even bare feet. All fishing hooks have sharp points, and most fishing hooks also have an equally sharp barb facing the opposite direction of the point. When the point of the hook penetrates into the mouth of a fish, the barb prevents the hook from sliding out.

That's good news for anglers who don't want to lose fish. It's also what makes removing hooks that are embedded in human flesh so difficult and painful. If you're planning on releasing fish, smash the barb down flat with a pair of pliers. That way, if you do get jabbed, the hook can be backed out easily without doing more damage. When a barbed hook gets stuck under your skin, removing it yourself won't be so simple. They are extremely difficult to extract from soft flesh, and in some cases they shouldn't be removed by anyone other than a doctor. If a barbed hook, especially a large one, gets stuck in your ear, cheek, neck, or any other soft spot, don't try pulling it out. Leave it there, cover it with tape, and head to the ER. The same goes for a hook that is deeply embedded in the hand; yanking it out could lead to lasting nerve damage. And in no case should you try to remove a hook that's anywhere near, or in, the eye—another great reason to wear sunglasses as protective gear. Remember, too, that fishing hook injuries may involve a tetanus risk, so stay current on your vaccinations.

SKILL: HOW TO SAFELY REMOVE A FISHHOOK

In areas of firm flesh away from large arteries, such as the tip of a finger or a forearm, it is possible to safely remove smaller barbed hooks that haven't penetrated deeply into the flesh. A few of our staff members were fishing guides in their former lives. The sheer number of hooks that flew through the air during an entire season of guiding meant being regularly forced to pluck hooks from their own flesh as well as from their clients'. Shutting down a trip to drive to the ER simply wasn't an option in the middle of long floats down remote stretches of river. Most of them used the DIY removal method pictured here. It's simple, effective, and relatively pain-free, and all you need is a short length of stout fishing line and a little faith. First, tie a couple feet of heavy line to the bend of the hook. Then, press downward on the eye of the hook and keep it depressed as you pull the barb out of the skin in a swift, smooth motion. Pull the barb in the opposite direction from the way the hook punctured the skin. We've never had this method fail us, but to stay on the safe side, don't use it with very large barbed hooks. Just remember, fishing hooks can be covered in all sorts of microscopic pathogens, and small puncture wounds are an ideal breeding ground for infections. After you get the hook out, you'll need to clean and treat the wound properly.

Fishing line. Fishing lines might not seem as dangerous as hooks to most anglers, but we've seen enough fingers get flayed open by line to know better. You can cut yourself with nylon monofilament and fluorocarbon lines, but most of the time, the worst injuries involve thin-diameter braided fishing line and fly line backing. These woven polyester lines act almost like tiny saw blades, and with just a little force, they can slice through flesh down to the bone as easily as a sharp knife. Typically, anglers cut themselves with braided line when they're pulling on it to tie a knot or to free a lure that's snagged on a rock or log. It can also happen when an angler lays a finger across the line during a battle with a large fish that is pulling line off the reel at a high rate of speed.

Fish. The fish themselves can do some serious damage, too, if you're not paying attention. Always take care when handling hooked fish. You're most likely to accidentally hook yourself while a fish is flopping around as you're trying to unhook it. Fabric or PVC-coated gloves make handling slippery fish easier and safer. Even just gripping fish with an old T-shirt or rag makes a huge difference in how well you can handle a fish. Needle-nose pliers and hemostats give you the leverage and distance to remove hooks without putting your fingers in the line of fire. If you're planning on eating your catch, it's a smart idea to dispatch it before unhooking it, especially when dealing with large, powerful fish like salmon. The easiest way to accomplish this quickly and humanely is through a sharp blow to the head with some sort of club. Bonking a fish on the head also eliminates the possibility of getting badly injured by the fish itself. Many species of popular game fish have razor-sharp teeth and gill rakers that can shred your hands. Really big fish like halibut and tuna have been known to break legs when they're thrashing around in the bottom of a boat. Even small fish like bullheads and bluegills have sharp spines to watch out for. You can let your guard down once your fish is in the frying pan.

COMMON HUNTING INJURIES

You'll hear hunters cite all kinds of statistics comparing the safety of hunting relative to other activities. There's an abundance of side-by-side risk comparisons showing that eating, driving a car, golfing, jogging, and playing baseball are all more dangerous than hunting. Unfortunately, these statistics can give hunters the illusion that, from a safety standpoint, they've got nothing to worry about. While we're not calling the veracity of the numbers into question, the comparisons have a bit of an apples-to-oranges quality. There are over 200 million more drivers in this country than hunters, and everyone needs to eat, most of us three times a day.

So yes, statistically, you stand a way better chance of getting injured in a car accident or choking on a hot dog than getting hurt or killed while you're hunting. But that's partly because you presumably eat and drive much more often than you hunt. Our aim isn't to overstress the dangers that hunting can entail, but to prevent hunters from mistakenly downplaying the risks involved or dismissing them altogether. Because when it comes to hunters acting unsafely, it only takes a few bad apples to spoil the whole bunch.

Firearms. Most forms of hunting involve firearms, and there is a widespread assumption that the use of guns is the most dangerous aspect of hunting. While it is true that accidental shootings involving hunters do happen on occasion, the risk of getting shot while you're hunting is actually extremely low. On average, an estimated 15 million hunting licenses are purchased every year in the United States. A study conducted by two American orthopedic surgeons concluded the rate of firearm injuries among hunters is 9 per 1 million hunting days. A separate study conducted by the International Hunters Education Association found that fewer than 1,000 accidental shootings involving hunters happen annually in the United States and Canada. Fewer than 100 of the incidents tied to hunting result in fatalities. When taken in context, those are astonishingly low numbers.

Still, we'd be remiss in failing to mention that bad things happen if guns are not handled properly and when standard hunting safety protocols are not strictly followed. A friend of ours blew off a couple of his toes when he was goose hunting out of a lay-down blind. As some geese approached the decoy spread, he disengaged the safety and accidentally pulled the trigger well before his gun cleared the blind and was safely pointed at a goose. A podcast listener related a story about his dad getting shot in the arm and chest on a pheasant hunt when his buddy fired his shotgun by mistake. Only the quick application of a tourniquet saved his life. Many hunters could share a similar story. The takeaway here is to always practice the safety protocols that were drilled into our heads in hunter safety courses: treat every firearm as if it were loaded; always point the firearm in a safe direction; be sure of your target and what is beyond; keep your finger off the trigger until you are ready to shoot.

It's also smart to keep your gun unloaded unless you're actively hunting. About half of all hunting-related firearm injuries are self-inflicted. Generally speaking, when we're big-game hunting with a rifle, we don't chamber a round until we're ready to shoot. That's because we do a lot of hunting in rough country where solid footing is never a guarantee. If an unexpected slip and fall took place, as they occasionally do, it's possible that your safety and trigger could get bumped and the gun could go off. The same thing could happen as you walk into your turkey or duck blind in the dark with a loaded shotgun. We've heard enough stories of loaded weapons going off from being bounced around in vehicles or getting stepped on by bird dogs to know that freak accidents happen. But they only happen with loaded guns. Make it a practice to check your firearm's safety incessantly, and to verify that your firearm is actually unloaded when you grab it in the morning or pull it out of your truck. If someone hands you their gun to hold while they're crossing a fence or taking a leak, don't take your hunting partner's word for it—check the gun yourself.

Archery equipment. Hunting accidents involving guns get all the attention, but archery hunters aren't immune to getting injured by their weapon of choice. Broadhead arrow tips used for hunting are made with multiple razor-blade-style cutting edges. They're designed to penetrate through thick animal hide, muscle, and bone. A well-aimed arrow tipped with a sharp broadhead will cause an elk weighing several hundred pounds to bleed out in under a minute. They can do the same to a human. Arrows can slip out of their rest or get knocked off the bowstring. Hunters can stumble and fall. When these things happen at the same time, the result can be deadly. We've spoken with several game wardens who'd had the experience of evacuating archery hunters after they'd impaled themselves on their own broadheads, and we know of other hunters who were skewered by one of their partner's arrows. It's perfectly safe to have an arrow ready to shoot if you're sitting stationary in a blind while you wait for an animal to show, but it's foolhardy to hike around with an arrow nocked on your bowstring. Another important safety measure is to regularly inspect carbon fiber arrows by flexing them to see if they hold up; cracks in the fibers can cause an arrow to splinter during a shot, impaling the archer's hand.

Knives. Broadheads aren't the only blades that should be handled with care. Both hunters and anglers handle knives a lot. Successful hunts always necessitate the use of knives for field dressing or breaking down your quarry into edible portions. Every step of the process—gutting, skinning, quartering, butchering—requires a knife. And some of these processes may take place at night, when visibility is limited. Even during the day, it's impossible to see exactly what's going on when you've got both hands shoved inside a deer's chest cavity. And even when you can see what's going on, knife blades may slip unexpectedly. The game wardens we spoke to had plenty of experience administering first aid to hunters who badly cut themselves while skinning deer and elk.

You might think that knives with the sharpest blades would be the most dangerous, but the opposite is actually true: the majority of accidental knife wounds can be attributed to dull blades. That's because sharp knives cut smoothly with little effort, allowing the handler to operate with more control. You need to put more effort into cutting with a dull blade. The harder you're working, the less control you have over the knife. Dull blades are also more prone to making jagged, erratic cuts. They tend to hang up, slip, and jump away from the area being cut and go into hands, arms, and legs. Fortunately, it's very easy to avoid these problems by carrying a sharpening tool in your backpack or tackle bag.

We like Work Sharp's Guided Field Sharpener for tuning up our knives before working on fish or game. We'll use the time when the fishing or hunting is slow or we're lounging in camp to give our knives a thorough sharpening. You should also remember to clean your knives with solvent after you work on fish or game. This will protect the blade from rust while removing any particles of flesh that might attract nasty bacteria— bacteria that could cause infections in the event that you cut yourself.

Treestands. Handling guns, arrows, and knives certainly adds an inescapable element of risk to hunting, but without question the most dangerous thing hunters do is climb into trees to kill deer. It's estimated that every year, more than 6,000 hunters are injured in falling accidents related to treestands. Three-quarters of those accidents happen when hunters are installing their stands or climbing up or down trees. One-fifth of the accidents are blamed on structural or equipment failure, and more than half of the hunters involved in treestand accidents were not wearing safety devices designed to arrest falls. Treestand accidents commonly result in severe fractures and spinal cord injuries. Fall victims who use safety harnesses and belts are at risk of suspension trauma if they're unable to get out of the harness and down to the ground safely and quickly. Treestand hunters would be wise to take every necessary precaution in order to avoid becoming a statistic; see the sidebar, below, for more information on treestand safety.

TEN POINTS OF TREESTAND SAFETY

Millions of deer hunters pursue their quarry from elevated platforms known as treestands. Unfortunately, every season the number of hunters who are injured or die due to treestand falls far outstrips the total number of firearms-related hunting incidents. Climbing up into a stand and spending time in an elevated position is statistically the most dangerous thing you can do as a hunter. However, most incidents involving treestands occur during setup or breakdown, or while hunters are getting into or out of the stand—and they're usually associated with technical issues or inattention. Given the data, here are a few pointers to help ensure a safe hunt and a timely return to your family and loved ones.

1. Choose only equipment that meets industry standards recognized by the Treestand Manufacturers Association (TMA). The use of homemade wooden stands nailed to trees is foolish and dangerous. Treestand equipment and safety equipment is not an area in which you want to cut corners or pinch pennies.
2. Before going to the woods, practice using all of your equipment at ground level with another responsible adult present. Follow all instructions for proper use of your product, and know your limitations. Some experienced hunters feel comfortable climbing to significant heights using ultralight climbing steps or sitting in tree saddles similar to those used by professional arborists. Less experienced hunters should start out with simple ladder stands and graduate to more advanced products as they gain additional experience.
3. Inspect your equipment before use.
   - Regularly check wear points, straps, and all related hardware. Replace as needed with parts produced by a reputable manufacturer that meet TMA industry standards.
   - Don't leave stands in the woods for extended periods of time. Treestand frames and parts can become compromised by prolonged exposure to sun, wind, water, ice, and even falling tree limbs.
4. Pick the right tree.
   - Only use a live, healthy tree that grows straight out of the ground.
   - Check the surrounding area to make sure that there are no dead trees or "widow-maker" limbs close to the chosen stand location.
   - If using a climbing treestand, select a species of tree that has bark favorable to the use of a climbing stand. Avoid trees with slick, hard bark that doesn't allow the teeth of your climber to dig in for a solid anchor. Likewise, stay away from trees with soft, crumbly bark that might give way under the weight of a human.

5. Stay connected. Given the many harness and rope systems on the market today, it is easier than ever to stay safe while installing and using treestands.

- Invest in a quality, properly fitting full-body safety harness, keep it in good condition, and always wear it in accordance with the manual.
- If you are using a hang-on treestand, use a lineman's climbing belt to attach your harness to the tree for the duration of the install and while climbing up into or out of the stand.
- Add treestand safety rope systems like the Hunters Safety System lifelines to both your ladder and hang-on stand set-ups for use after the initial install. These products are not very expensive and will allow you to easily stay connected to the tree while you are using the stand.
- If you are using a climbing treestand, use your tree tether and tree strap to keep you attached to the tree trunk from the time you leave the ground until you return. Remember to keep the two pieces (seat and standing platform) of the climber stand lashed together with a strap or piece of rope to prevent accidental separation.
- When in the stand, position your full body harness tree tether on the tree at least at eye level or higher while standing so there is little or no slack in the tether when you are seated. This will reduce the distance of a potential fall while also making it easier to recover.
- Practice suspension relief and recovery. Suspension trauma occurs when you've fallen from a tree and you're hanging from your harness safety line. Blood pooling in the lower extremities can be fatal if corrective actions aren't taken quickly. To prevent a major circulation problem, use your harness's suspension relief system (basically a stirrup) or cycle your legs until you can self-rescue or help arrives.

6. Don't take shortcuts.

- Have at least two adults on hand when installing a treestand.
- Avoid using a tree limb as a handhold—they have a nasty habit of breaking unexpectedly.
- When using a fixed-position stand, be sure to extend a climbing aid (fully assembled stick ladders or individual sec-

tions) above the stand so that you can use them as a hand-hold and step down into the center of the platform. The use of screw-in steps isn't recommended.

7. Never hurry.
   - Always use at least three points of contact while climbing: two hands and a foot, or two feet and a hand.
   - Slow and steady is the rule. Many accidents occur when hunters rush and take shortcuts.
8. Use a haul line to bring all equipment up into the stand.
   - Never climb with anything in your hands.
   - Never climb with guns or bows slung across your back.
9. Have your first-aid kit, signaling device, and/or cellphone within reach while you are strapped in.
   - If your full body harness hinders access, move your device so that it's within reach.
10. Plan your hunt and hunt your plan.
    - Let friends or family know where you will be and when you will return.
    - Don't change plans without notifying someone first.

—By Anthony Mann, a certified treestand safety instructor and boat accident investigator who has spent thirty years as a conservation officer in Indiana

A FINAL NOTE ON THE DANGER OF RECKLESS BEHAVIOR IN THE OUTDOORS

In biblical history, Nimrod was a legendary king and hunter who may have had a hand in bringing down the Lord's wrath upon humanity by attempting to build the Tower of Babel in order to reach the heavens. Fast-forward a few thousand years, and "nimrod" came to be used as an insulting slang term describing idiotic, bumbling hunters. It's believed the word was popularized in modern culture when Bugs Bunny began calling Elmer Fudd a nimrod almost a century ago.

Hunters have been plagued by the term ever since, and in some cases we deserve it. Hunting and fishing involve all sorts of activities that add a little more danger to our lives. We handle sharp knives more than the average person. We walk around in the woods when it's dark. We spend a lot of time in or on the water. We brave foul weather to do the things we love. Considering all the things that are just part of our daily routines, you'd think all the nimrods out there would avoid intentionally courting even more danger by acting foolish, but we all know someone who got injured doing something stupid while they were hunting or fishing. It's worth noting (again) that a sizable portion of the accidents and injuries that happen in the outdoors are completely avoidable. But it's hardly fair to even call it an accident if you're doing something that practically guarantees a bad outcome. Case in point: During an early winter waterfowl hunt, a high school buddy dared MeatEater editor Brody Henderson to cross a barely frozen beaver pond to retrieve a wood duck out of a small piece of open water. It shouldn't have come as a surprise when he fell through the ice into frigid water up to his neck. He managed to get out, but his clothes froze solid almost immediately. Luckily, he made the walk home before severe hypothermia set in. Had the walk been a little longer, he just as easily could have become a statistic. Any one of us could share equally dumb stories that might have concluded in our swift demise.

To really get a clear understanding of just how much some outdoorsmen take the safety of themselves and those closest to them for granted, we talked to a couple of game wardens in Colorado. Their first bit of advice wasn't exactly surprising: mixing alcohol with hunting and fishing is an extremely bad idea, especially when factors like ATVs and motorboats get thrown into the mix. Other categorically stupid things they've dealt with include quick-draw pistol competitions that have sent more than one hunter to the hospital with a bullet hole through the foot, third-degree burns from walking over hot coals barefoot, deep lacerations when axes bounced back during impromptu throwing contests, and even broken bones when a homemade zipline collapsed into a pile of logs.

These are just a few of the stories the game wardens told us, but they are more than enough to prove just how far some folks are willing to go to invite disaster into their lives. Like they say, it's all fun and games until someone gets hurt.

SOME PARTING THOUGHTS

→→→⟫⟫⟫ ⟪⟪⟪←←←

A T THIS POINT, I've been experiencing wild places and navigating the tricky circumstances that arise in those places for over four decades. In that time, I've had the good fortune to travel with some of the best and most accomplished outdoorsmen on the planet, as well as some of the worst. I learned a lot from the good ones, and cherished our time together. I also learned a lot from the bad ones.

Unfortunately, the sorts of lessons that I'm talking about—both the good and the bad—aren't things that can simply be passed along from one person to the next. They can't be memorized or rehearsed. Instead, they have to be experienced and contemplated in order to be fully understood. I used to be annoyed by people who use the term "practice" when it came to things such as yoga or religion. I thought it sounded pretentious. Eventually, though, I came to be comfortable with the word once I understood that it implies a sort of "living with," or a continuous journey. That is, a practice is not something that you master or simply do. It's something that you try to become. And that's how I view my relationship with the outdoors. It's a *practice*. Along the way, I've realized some things that I hope might eventually be helpful to you as you make your own journey. I'm fairly certain that you won't take my word for it all. You'll end up making the same mistakes that I did, and eventually you'll arrive at these same conclusions. So don't think of the below as a collection of things that you should learn right now. Instead, imagine it as my prediction of things that you'll come to realize once you've been at this as long as I have.

Don't waste your time in the outdoors with people of questionable character. Everything that you see and feel is more acute when you're out amid nature. The song of a bird in the wild is more beautiful than the song of that same bird at your bird feeder. Sunrises in the wild are felt, not just seen. Blood on the snow is art. That heightened intensity cuts both ways. You might brush off ignorance or selfishness or vanity in other people in your normal daily routines. But those traits are excruciating amid the heightened beauty and danger of wild places. Ugliness in people clashes with the beauty of the natural world. Stress from humans erodes your ability to handle and cherish the dangers of nature. If you question whether or not you like someone, answer that question at home. When you're hungry and cold and tired on the side of some mountain, it's no place to realize that you're sharing a tent with an asshole.

Likewise, prevent yourself from becoming an asshole. Be generous with others. One of the best reasons to be prepared is that you're ready to help the folks that you're with. I have watched people withhold dry layers of clothing from others who were soaking wet and cold simply because having a spare set of clothes in their backpack was more important to them than the comfort of others. This behavior will come around to get you in the end. Years ago, I hunted caribou on the Arctic slope with a small group of guys, and one of them had decided to bring all of his own meals and camp off to the side of everyone else, ostensibly to "keep things simple." He wanted the assistance and protection of the group if he needed it, but without any of the annoyance. Another time, after fishing salmon in south-central Alaska, this same guy walked away with his share of the fillets after the first few fish were ready and didn't stick around to help clean the rest of the fish. He said he had to be somewhere. The list of his infractions goes on and on. This behavior of his eroded the group cohesion that becomes essential when things get hard. By routinely looking out for himself, he eroded his own self-interest as well. Unless he was in a truly dire situation, I wouldn't cross the road (or a small creek, for that matter) to lend him a hand. I know a few other guys who feel the same way about him. Much better to go through life accumulating friends, earning respect, and developing a strong network of outdoor allies. If someone fails to properly tie up the canoe and it floats out into the lake, be the one who swims out to get it. If someone's headlamp goes dead while hiking at night, give her yours. If someone needs to go out in the wind and rain of a thunderstorm in order to add some guy lines to support the tent, do it. Believe me, that'll get you a lot further than being selfish ever will.

I have a friend, Rorke Denver, who ran the Navy SEAL BUD/S course for a number of years. The course serves as an elimination trial for volunteers looking to join one of the world's most elite fighting forces. Cadets going into the course are already among the best of the best. Through exposure to cold water and unfathomable amounts of physical torture, the course then peels away about 75 percent of those. As my friend describes it, what's left are the men who cannot quit. I think of this often. Who wants to be a quitter? I sure don't. But you need to realize that an inability to quit can also lead to disaster. You're hiking to a peak in midwinter and you realize that the avalanche risk is abnormally high today. Are you a quitter when you turn back? You were planning to fish halibut on a shallow bank that requires you to motor across a narrow strait. When you see that the strait is way too rough for safety, are you a quitter when you decide not to go for it? Admittedly, it sometimes feels like it. And it doesn't feel good.

I've learned to cope with my own concerns about being a quitter by cultivating something that I call flexible inflexibility. This has nothing to do with touching your toes. Instead, it has to do with setting goals that are rigid while maintaining an open, adaptive approach to achieving those goals. The objective is to maintain a strict, no-quitters lifestyle while still creating plenty of room for sanity. In many ways, success here comes down to how you define a goal. Rather than a goal of hiking up that avalanche-prone mountain, set a goal of total miles covered, with a preference for hitting that certain peak if it works out. And rather than a goal of fishing halibut in one particular spot no matter what, make a goal of putting in the right amount of hours in a variety of spots. With practice, you'll find that this approach to outdoor adventures actually makes you *less* of a quitter. I've known plenty of people who are routinely thwarted in their ambitious goals due to some obstacle, real or perceived. We've all heard the excuses: "I ditched my plans because the boat wouldn't start." "My flight was canceled." "We got to the spot and someone had beaten us to it." "The Forest Service closed the trail because of wildfire danger." "The river was flooded and we couldn't get across." Don't allow these situations to mean that it's time to head home. Instead, it's time to make your next move.

Here's another thing that I heard from a Navy SEAL: Slow is smooth and smooth is fast. There's another quote, often attributed to Napoleon, that says pretty much the same thing: Dress me slowly, I'm in a hurry. You get the point. Rushing leads to trouble and poor decision-making. One of the primary characteristics I've noticed among expert outdoorsmen and adventurers is that they are not easily excitable during moments of stress. I'm sure there's an element of natural temperament to this. Since calmness is essential to excelling in the outdoors, it makes sense that calm folks would rise above the rest. But I'm certain there's also a learned component to it. The more nerve-racking experiences you go through, the less excitable you become. When you feel your pulse quickening in a stressful moment, make a conscious decision to calm yourself down. It might seem impossible to calm yourself when the wind is ripping your tent apart or the ice on a lake has just opened up into a fissure between you and your buddy, but it can be done as long as you remember to do it. In time, the response may come naturally. Until then, force it.

Once you've mastered staying calm in the face of danger, the next step is learning how to enjoy it. This thought brings to mind an experience from a year ago when my wife's friend Savannah was visiting from out of town. We decided to throw our canoe in the river and do a short two-hour float. It was early June. I knew that water levels were high and that the river would be flowing strong, but I didn't realize how strong until we got there. It was ripping: flooded banks, dislodged trees in the current, tons of overhanging tree limbs reaching into the water. It was sketchy, but not too sketchy. I turned to my wife and Savannah and said, "If the three of us climb into that canoe, there's a 50/50 chance that we're gonna flip and take a swim."

We climbed in. I told my passengers not to look back or worry about the boat if we flip. "Face downstream," I said. "Butt down, chest up, your feet out in front of you as bumpers. Back paddle with your hands toward the bank when you see a safe landing place. And remember, don't look back." We then headed into the current and, sure enough, we were swimming within thirty minutes. We came barreling fast around a corner and the canoe was swept into the limbs of a tree that leaned out over an outside bend. The canoe rolled easily and fluidly, as if flipped by the hand of God. Just as I had instructed, my wife and Savannah didn't look back. As I struggled to hang on to the canoe and collect the paddles and gear, I watched them disappear in the rapids below me and then reappear as two small blobs among the waves before rounding the next bend and vanishing from sight.

Holy shit, I thought. There goes my wife! The mother of my three young children! What the hell was I thinking? I righted the canoe and cruised around the bend, paddling like some deranged lunatic. No wife. I hauled around the next bend. There, finally, stood my wife and Savannah. They were safe and sound on the riverbank. Not exactly happy, but not exactly unhappy, either. Instead, they just looked . . . *thrilled*. Thrilled for the wild ride. Thrilled to be alive. In turn, I was thrilled to see them. Over the next couple of hours, it was fun to watch that thrill morph into joy. By the time we were driving home, I don't think that any one of us would have swapped that experience for the safety of home. And that feeling of joy persisted. The other day, I drove along that stretch of river with my kids and pointed out the spot where Mommy took an unexpected swim in a flooded river. We all had a laugh. It reinforced a series of ideas that I want my family to know about ourselves: We are the kind of people who take risks. We learn what to do when those risks present themselves. We defeat fear. We laugh about it later. What doesn't kill us not only makes us stronger; it makes us funnier, too.

There's one last thing to add here, as the final thought of this book. It's gonna sound harsh, but I'll come out and say it. If you don't love Mother Nature, stay the hell away from her. There is no room left in the world for outdated "man versus wild" sentiments. For much of human history, we had wild places simply because we hadn't gotten around to destroying them yet. Back then, we celebrated those pioneers and explorers who sacrificed in the name of advancing the spread of civilization into wilderness. Those days have passed. We no longer need people who want to conquer nature or subdue it. Now, we need people who want to save it. It's time to accept the reality that wilderness and the dangers of wilderness exist only because we've made a conscious decision to preserve them. We have them simply because we have wished it to be so. The next time you step into the wild, remember this. Acknowledge your gratitude for every danger. Regard every risk as a blessing. Be thankful that there's something left to survive. That rustling noise outside your tent might be something that's coming to eat you. By all means, be prepared to punch it in the face. But when you throw the punch, throw it with love.

ACKNOWLEDGMENTS

MANY THANKS TO Brad Brooks, Remi Warren, Patrick Durkin, Samuel Thayer, Greg Fonts, Ronny Boehme, Rick Hutton, Matthew Keiper, and Anthony Mann for their contributions to this book.

A special dose of gratitude to Dr. Alan Lazzara, who generously lent his time to reviewing the medical information in this book.

Several of my colleagues here at *MeatEater* were of enormous help on this project, including Sam Lungren, Janis Putelis, Joe Ferronato, Spencer Neuharth, Katie Finch, and Anthony Licata.

At Random House, thanks to Ben Greenberg, Kaeli Subberwal, Nancy Delia, Greg Kubie, and Erin Richards.

Many thanks, as always, to my literary agent, Marc Gerald. (We've been at it for seventeen years, Marc.)

Pete Sucheski—thanks for jumping on another crazy project with us.

And finally, a special note of thanks to my friends and collaborators, Savannah Ashour and Brody Henderson.

INDEX

ABOUT THE AUTHOR

STEVEN RINELLA is an outdoorsman, writer, wild foods enthusiast, and television and podcast personality with an exceptional ability to communicate the hunting lifestyle to a wide variety of audiences. The host of the television show and podcast *MeatEater*, he is also the author of two volumes of *The Complete Guide to Hunting, Butchering, and Cooking Wild Game*; *Meat Eater: Adventures from the Life of an American Hunter*; *American Buffalo: In Search of a Lost Icon*; and *The Scavenger's Guide to Haute Cuisine*. His writing has appeared in many publications, including *Outside*, *Field & Stream*, *The New Yorker*, *Glamour*, the *New York Times*, *Men's Journal*, *Salon*, *O: The Oprah Magazine*, *Bowhunter*, and the anthologies *Best American Travel Writing* and *Best Food Writing*.

themeateater.com
Facebook.com/StevenRinellaMeatEater
Instagram: @stevenrinella and @meateater

ABOUT THE TYPE

This book was set in Minion, a 1990 Adobe Originals typeface by Robert Slimbach. Minion is inspired by classical, old-style typefaces of the late Renaissance, a period of elegant and beautiful type designs. Created primarily for text setting, Minion combines the aesthetic and functional qualities that make text type highly readable with the versatility of digital technology.